Illustrated Dictionary of
Building Design +
CONSTRUCTION

ERNEST BURDEN

McGraw-Hill
New York Chicago San Francisco Lisbon London Madrid Mexico City
Milan New Delhi San Juan Seoul Singapore Sydney Toronto

The McGraw·Hill Companies

Cataloging-in-Publication Data is on file with the Library of Congress

1 2 3 4 5 6 7 8 9 0   DOC/DOC   0 10 9 8 7 6 5 4

ISBN 0-07-144506-4

McGraw-Hill books are available at special quantity discounts to use as premiums and sales promotions, or for use in corporate training programs. For more information, please write to the Director of Special Sales, McGraw-Hill Professional, Two Penn Plaza, New York, NY 10121-2298. Or contact your local bookstore.

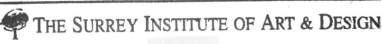

PREFACE

The process of building has been going on since the dawn of humankind, providing shelters for living and various structures for all kinds of human endeavors. Yet none were ever built in a vacuum. They all had a purpose, a site, a function, and a client, whether it was a patron, private benefactor, public entity, a gathering of worshippers. or an entire community.

As architecture evolved over the centuries, building techniques changed and evolved along with it. Architecture and construction were once integrated functions, and architects and builders were often one and the same person. Hence the term master builder was given to some architects. Today, that trend is re-emerging, only the individual has been replaced by a combined team of specialists.

Today the building industry is continuously growing and evolving. New building codes, new materials and products, and new techniques for construction have all impacted on a vocabulary that is unique to this industry. You will find all those terms included here in their current usage, including *design build, green design*, and *construction management*.

The construction process is also steeped in legal and contractual terms, including the relationship between the design and construction documents prepared by the architect. You will find all those contractual terms explained clearly here. This dictionary also builds the ties that link the design side of the equation with the construction side without using technical or archaic terminology.

Another aspect of the construction industry today is the growing number of restoration, renovation, and adaptive use projects. Terminology for these types of projects are included along with legal terms relating to property development, and construction contracts.

The result is a ready reference of authoritative information, of broad scope, and written with simplicity and clarity. It addresses the day-to-day working situations, while the illustrations depict on-the-job applications. This allows you to see the process at a glance, and gain a better understanding of the entire building design and construction process.

Acknowledgments

This book represents the combined talents of many who participated in its content and production. I want to thank Scott Grillo, publisher, for his support of the project, and Cary Sullivan, my editor, who guided it throughout the entire process.

On the production side I thank Tom Kowalczyk, who was always there when I needed an answer, Carol Levine, editing supervisor, and Margaret Webster-Shapiro, art director for the cover.

Thanks to my friend and colleague Fred Stitt, Director of the San Francisco Institute of Architecture, for the use of his working drawing details seen throughout the book.

A very special thanks to my wife, Joy, for her unending patience, encouragement, and understanding during the entire design and production process of this book.

INTRODUCTION

The typical function of a dictionary is to isolate and define individual elements, and to provide specialized information about them. This architectural dictionary carries that function to another level, by illustrating many of the definitions with photographs of the elements in their location within the structures.

The photographs in this book were selected from building sites around the world. Some examples are well known, while others are shown to provide a clear illustration of the definition. No attempt was made to identify the building type, location, date, architect, or contractor in any of the definitions.

The terms have all been selected to provide a broad-based reference of architectural and construction terms for architects, engineers, contractors, construction managers, real estate firms, students, and homeowners involved in construction or renovation projects.

Construction progress documentation is an extremely difficult process, not only from a personal safety angle, with insurance policies that prohibit on-site visits plus security issues against taking photographs of structures under construction, but it's also a quickly moving target. As buildings are put together, the skeleton is gradually covered up by layer after layer of materials, until the finished edifice stands ready for occupancy, and is no longer a construction site.

In this entire process, there are many conditions that are impossible to photograph, so you will find many architectural plans and details illustrating these items wherever possible. This combination of photographs and details will give you the best possible understanding of the definitions included in this book.

A

Abandonment
The failure of parties to abide by the terms of the contract; also, when a contractor stops work on a job and removes all personnel and equipment before it is completed.

Abatement
The reduction of a health risk from identified hazardous materials such as those containing lead or asbestos. Includes demolition and removal of the material as well as protection of the surrounding environment.

Abbreviations
A shortened form of words commonly used in architectural working drawings, relating to components and materials in the finished job.

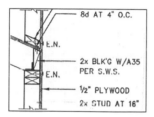

Abeyance
A lapse in the transfer of title to real property, where the title is not clearly established.

Above grade
Any part of the structure or foundation wall that is above the level of the surrounding ground.

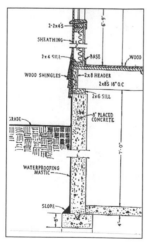

Abrasion
Wearing away of the surface of a material by the cutting action of solids or the use of abrasive materials.

Abrasion resistance
A material's ability to resist rubbing and scraping without wearing away.

Abrasion resistance index
An index that compares the abrasion resistance of a material to that of rubber.

Abrasion-finished surface
A surface that results from sanding with disks coated with abrasives.

Abrasive
A substance used for wearing away or polishing a surface by friction; usually a grinding material such as emery, sand, or diamond.

Abrasive cleaning
A method of cleaning façades or building elements by scraping or grinding; blasting a masonry surface with a dry or wet medium to remove dirt. The most common is blasting with sand from a pressure hose. Other substances include bicarbonate soda and water or fiberglass particles.

Abrasive paper
Cloth or paper covered on one side with a grinding material glued to the surface; used for sanding, smoothing, or polishing.

Abrasive resistance
The ability or capacity of a surface or material to resist deliberate abrasion or ordinary wear.

Abrasive surface
A surface that has been purposely roughened with a texture for safety.

Abrasive tool
An implement used for wearing down materials by friction or rubbing.

Absorption
The process whereby a liquid is drawn into the permeable pores of a solid.

Absorption bed
A large pit filled with gravel containing a distribution pipe system which allows absorption of septic tank effluent.

Absorption field
A plot of land engineered to receive effluent from a septic tank; consists of a series of drain tiles or perforated pipes set in trenches, which are often filled with gravel to help the effluent be absorbed into the soil.

Absorption rate
The amount of liquid absorbed into the permeable pores of a solid within a certain amount of time—for example, the amount of water absorbed by a brick in 1 minute.

Absorptive film
A film that prevents certain harmful wavelengths of sunlight from entering a building; usually applied to the interior side of the window glass.

Abstract of bids
A summary of prices based on bids received from contractors, prepared by the owner for a given job, to select the contractor to be awarded the job, and to inform all bidders of the results.

Abstract of title
A deed that outlines the history of ownership of a piece of real property and shows all current encumbrances.

Abut
To meet or touch with an end, as on a construction member meeting an adjoining one.

AC
The abbreviation for alternating current; the most commonly used in homes, which is delivered from the local utility company. It can be easily stepped up or down by transformers making it superior to direct current, which cannot.

AC generator
A generator producing alternating current.

Accelerated weathering
A means of determining the weather-resisting properties of materials by testing cycles that imitate natural weathering conditions as closely as possible.

Acceleration
The performance of construction at a faster rate than expected in the original schedule, and often used to recapture any delays in the project.

Accelerator
A substance added to gypsum, plaster, concrete, or mortar that speeds up the setting time; used when freezing is a danger. See also *Admixture*.

Acceptance
Agreement by both parties to the terms of the contract.

Acceptance inspection
An inspection that is required before acceptance of a project qualifies for payment from the owner.

Accepted bid
The proposed price that an owner uses when entering into a contract for construction on a project.

Access
Means of entry into a building or equipment room; also, an opening through which equipment may be inspected or repaired.

Access control system
Computerized building security control equipment for screening employees and visitors, such as badge readers, and package-scanning devices in government offices and facilities.

Access door
Any door that allows access to concealed equipment or parts of a building not often used, such as a door to concealed plumbing parts.

Access floor
A finished floor, generally elevated 12 to 18 inches above the concrete floor; used for electric cable, conduit, and ductwork. The floor system consists of 2-foot-square removable panels supported on pedestals on each corner that are adjustable for leveling the panels.

Access stair
A specific stair system to provide access to mechanical rooms or roofs, or to be used as an emergency exit.

Accessibility
The items and conditions specified in the Americans with Disabilities Act (ADA) that regulate and control access for physically handicapped people.

Accessibility audit
Evaluation as to the compliance of an existing building to the building code as it relates to handicapped accessibility.

Accessible
Anything that is easily accessed for repair, service, or removal without damaging the finish of the space enclosing it.

Accessory building
A secondary structure on a site, such as a detached garage, guest house, or shed.

Accordion door
A hinged door consisting of a system of panels hung from an overhead track, folding back like the bellows of an accordion. When open, the panels close flat; when closed, the panels interlock with each other.

Account number
A numeric identification for any work package; may be assigned to one or more activities.

Accountant
One who specializes in keeping financial records.

Accounts payable
Payment for goods and services owed to others.

Accounts receivable
Payments owed to the firm or company for services.

Accrual accounting
Recording income as accounts receivable when earned, and recording debts as accounts payable when they are incurred.

Acetone
A solvent that evaporates quickly; used in paint removers, thinners, and lacquers.

Acid cleaning
The process of washing concrete with a diluted solution of 10 to 15 percent muriatic acid, after the concrete has cured more than 2 weeks.

Acid etch
Using acid to remove the surface of concrete or to etch lines or designs into metal or glass, giving a lightly textured finish. Hydrochloric acid was used in the past, but this contributed to future erosion, and has been replaced with phosphoric acid.

Acid rain
Rain that contains sulfur dioxide from emissions released into the atmosphere, which combine with water and fall to the earth.

Acoustic construction
Any building method that reduces sound either entering, leaving, or transferring through a structure by means of landscaping, dense construction, double glazing, buffer elements, use of absorbent materials, or discontinuous construction. See also *Staggered studs*.

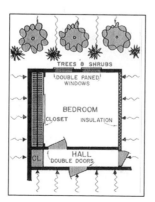

Acoustic glass
A special laminated glass designed for soundproofing.

Acoustic plaster
A plaster with a high degree of sound absorption.

Acoustical board
Any insulating material used in the control of sound.

Acoustical correction
Planning, shaping, and equipping a space to establish the best possible hearing conditions for faithful reproduction of sound within a space

Acoustical door
A door having a sound-deadening core, stops along the top and sides sealed by gaskets, and an automatic drop seal along the bottom; especially constructed to reduce noise transmission through it.

Acoustical material
Sound-absorbing material for covering walls and ceilings. This term is applied to special plasters, tile, or any material composed of mineral wool, wood, or cork used to deaden sound.

Acoustical reduction factor
The value of the reduction in sound as it passes through an absorptive material such as acoustical insulation board.

Acoustical tile
Any tile composed of materials having the property of absorbing or reducing the reflection and reverberation of sound waves.

Acoustics
The scientific study of sound upon the ear. The main factor influencing acoustical conditions are reverberation, extraneous noises, loudness of the original sound, and the shape of the space in which it is heard. Also called *sound control*.

Acre
A unit of measurement for large tracts of land. One acre is 43,860 square feet, and there are 640 acres in 1 square mile. A square acre is composed of land that is 208.71 feet on each side.

Acrylic
A plastic that in solid form is rigid, clear, and transparent.

Acrylic fiber
A synthetic polymer fiber.

Acrylic latex caulking
A compound that offers better adhesion, less shrinkage, and easier application than oil-based compounds, with a life span of 10 years.

Acrylic latex paint
A paint composed of acrylic resins suspended in a water base, as opposed to oil-based paint.

Acrylic plastic
A shatterproof material, available in transparent sheets for use in windows in high-breakage areas. Also called *Lucite* and *Plexiglas*.

Acrylic plastic glaze
A synthetic sheet material used on windows to produce a shatterproof glazing; used in high-breakage areas.

Acrylic resin
A thermoplastic resin that is stable, resistant to chemicals, and transparent; used as a binder; an air-curing adhesive, and as the main ingredient in some caulking compounds and sealants. Also in solid sheet form.

Act of God
An unforeseeable natural force, such as a flash flood, tornado, or lightning strike outside the control of any party, resulting in adversely affecting the performance of a contract. Insurance companies exclude most Acts of God from policy protection.

Actinic glass
Specially formulated glass or protective adhesive film on glass that screens out ultraviolet wavelengths of light that may be harmful to interior fabrics and finishes.

Active solar heater
A mechanical system for collecting solar energy. The water is heated in solar collectors, then stored in tanks for distribution within the building.

Activity
Any task, operation, or function on a project that is definable and consumes a specific amount of time.

Activity description
An explanation of the nature of the work to be performed which identifies any activity to recipients of the work schedule.

Activity duration
The length of time from the start of any activity to the finish of such activity, in working or calendar day units; may be estimated or actual time.

Activity splitting
Subdividing a big activity into smaller parts to allocate resources or technology more efficiently.

Actual size
The real size of a piece of material rather than its nominal dimension. Boards and framing members are one size when rough cut, and a smaller size after finishing. Brick and concrete block also have actual sizes that are smaller than the nominal dimensions. However, manufactured panels of most materials are the actual size specified.

AD plywood
A designation of quality of the surface layers of plywood; the "A" layer is the surface layer, and the "D" layer is the back side.

ADA Accessibility Guidelines
A document illustrating and describing barrier-free handicapped access as required by the Americans with Disabilities Act of 1990.

Adapter
An intermediary device that joins or matches the characteristics of one item with that of another, such as those used in the plumbing, electrical, and air-conditioning trades.

Adaptive abuse
Inappropriate conversion of a building to a new use that is detrimental to the structure's architectural character.

Adaptive reuse
Same as *Adaptive use.*

Adaptive use
The process of converting a building to a use other than that for which it was originally designed. This conversion is accomplished with varying alterations to the building, which may include removal of some or all of the interior building elements except the structure.

Addendum
An addition or revision to the drawings, specifications, or other contract document to clarify, correct, add to, or revise any part of the original document. Issued by the design professional only after the bidders have received the contract documents but before bids are received; therefore, it is not a change order, which only occurs once the contract is let. An addendum usually becomes part of the final contract documents.

Addition

Any construction or change in a building that increases its cubic contents by increasing its exterior dimensions. Also, designing one or more rooms joined to the main structure so as to create one architectural whole, with both parts constituting one and the same building in purpose and use, as distinct from alterations within an existing structure.

Additional services

Professional services approved by the owner and provided by the architect, beyond the basic services identified in the original agreement with the owner.

Additive

An admixture.

Additive alternate

An option for additional construction that results in an increase in the base bid.

Adhering cracks

Reestablishing the integrity of cracked stone blocks by injecting an adhesive through injection ports into the crack without removing the block.

Adhesion

The property of a material that allows it to bond to the surface to which it is applied.

Adhesive

A substance, such as glue, paste, mastic, or cement, that is capable of bonding materials together such that force is then required to separate the materials.

Adhesive caulking

A compound that acts both as a caulk for sealing joints and an adhesive for resetting ceramic tile or cracked porcelain. It is easy to work with and accepts paint.

Adhesive spreader

A trowel with a series of notches which spreads the adhesive in ridges. The adhesive spreads into the ridges when the material to be applied is pressed into it.

Adjust

To bring into a true position; to align exactly, as in the structural members of a building.

Adjustable bar hanger

A metal hanger that supports electrical outlet boxes, conduit, and other devices. It can be adjusted to the spacing of floor or ceiling joists.

Adjustable base cost

The total project cost after adjustments are made for additive or deductive alternates or addenda.

Adjustable clamp

A clamp with a screw thread or other type of adjustment, that moves the jaws against the work to be held, that allows the jaws to fit and firmly grasp materials in various sizes. Also, any clamp used to hold column forms while concrete is being poured.

Adjustable door frame

A door frame with a jamb that can be adapted to walls of different thickness.

Adjustable pipe hanger

In plumbing, a pipe hanger consisting of a beam clamp, an adjustable rod for length, and an adjustable ring for different diameter pipes.

Adjustable pliers

Pliers with a slot that allows the jaws to open wider to grip larger-sized objects.

Adjustable steel prop

A member with provisions for adjusting the length for leveling; used either as a vertical support for slab formwork or as an inclined member to hold vertical formwork plumb.

Adjustable triangle

A drafting triangle that can be adjusted by means of a moveable arm which pivots from the base arm through a series of angles; fastened with a locking nut.

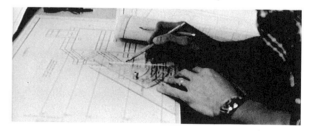

Adjustable wrench

A wrench with a pair of jaws; one fixed to the handle and the other is movable by means of a built-in adjusting screw to allow fitting different size fasteners.

Adjuster

A representative of an insurance company who negotiates with all parties involved in a claim in order to settle it equitably.

Adjusting nut
A button or nut that is used to lock on a screw on adjustable tools.

Adjusting plane
A carpenter's plane with adjustments to the cutting plane so it will cut shavings of any desired thickness.

Adjusting screw
A threaded device used to align parts, and often containing a locking nut to secure it in position.

Adjustment
In construction work, the process of placing and fixing of structural members in a related position.

Adjustments
In insurance, an examination made to determine the cause of a loss, whether it is covered by the policy, the amount of the loss, and the final amount due the claimant after allowances and deduction are made.

Admixture
A material other than water, aggregate, and cement used as an ingredient in concrete or mortar; may add coloring or control strength or decrease setting time.

Adobe
Large, roughly molded, sun-dried clay units consisting of varying sizes.

Adobe brick
Large, roughly molded, sun-dried clay brick of varying size and thickness.

Adobe structure
A structure built with sun-dried bricks of clay and straw. Adobe is one of the oldest building materials on earth, dating back to Neolithic times.

Adulteration
The substitution of inferior products or materials in place of those specified or shown on the contract documents.

Advertisement for bids
An announcement soliciting bids for a construction project that is published in a trade journal or local newspaper, and often referring to a Web site for details about the project. Such notices give a brief description of the project, name of the architect or engineer, and the time and date set for the bid opening. Such notices often conform to legal requirements for procuring public work.

Adze
A cutting tool resembling an ax with the thin arched blade set at a right angle to the handle; used for rough dressing timber.

Aerated concrete
A lightweight concrete made by infusing it with air; used for subfloors. Due to its cellular structure, it is a good retardant to sound transmission.

Aerator
A device that introduces air into a material such as soil, water, or sewage.

Aerial surveying
Photographs taken from airplanes, balloons, or satellites; used to provide visual data for large areas of land. By using known distances on the ground, other objects in the photograph can be scaled and plotted on a graphic rendition of the photograph, such as a map or outline of the area.

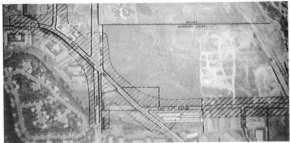

Aerosol caulking
A white foam applied from a pressurized can with a nozzle applicator. When hardened it is waterproof and can fill voids in wood or masonry.

Affidavit of noncollusion
A sworn statement by bidders that their prepared prices were determined without consultation with the other bidders, and were arrived at independently.

Agate
An ornamental translucent stone with multicolored bands.

Agent
One who has the authority to act on behalf of another.

Aggregate
Any of a variety of materials, such as sand and gravel, added to a cement mixture to make concrete. Also called *cement matrix*.

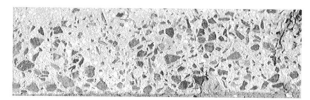

Aging
A process used by builders to make materials appear old or antique by artificial means. Also, the natural physical change in a material over time. Different materials age quite differently depending on exposure to weather and other environmental factors.

Aging of concrete
The final stage in the chemical reaction between cement and water, during which the concrete continues to slowly gain strength.

Agreement
A document that records a consensus on the obligations and performance of the parties, but may or may not fulfill all the essential elements of an enforceable contract, even though the two terms are used interchangeably.

Agreement form
A printed document describing the general provisions of a contract, with blank space provided for customizing the specific data to the project at hand.

Air balancing
Adjusting the flow of air in various spaces by using dampers, adjustable diffusers, and other means, so that the air-conditioning system maintains proper temperature in all areas in a system.

Air barrier
Plastic sheathing, building paper, or similar material used to cover the exterior walls to cut down on the passage of air into the structure.

Air brick
A hollow or perforated brick specially prepared for ventilating purposes.

Air chamber
A vertical pipe that is capped off and partially filled with air, fixed on the back side of a faucet or hose bibb to cushion the water flow when the fixture is turned off. Also called an *air cushion*.

Air change
The amount of air in a space being replaced by new air; the number of air changes per hour is a measure of ventilation.

Air changes
A method of expressing the amount of air supplied to or exhausted from a space in relation to the volume of the space.

Air changes per hour
A measurement of the amount of air filtration by determining the number of times that the entire volume of air within a building changes within 1 hour.

Air cleaner
A device that removes airborne impurities such as dust, gases, vapors, fumes, and smoke from an air-moving system. Types of cleaners include air filters, activated carbon, air washers, and electrostatic precipitators.

Air compressor
A device that forces air into a storage tank and releases it through a regulator into a base to power small tools.

Air conditioner
A specific air-treating combination, consisting of air circulation, air cleaning, and heat transfer, with means for controlling room temperature and humidity according to heating, ventilation, and air-conditioning (HVAC) engineering standards and practices.

Air duct
A duct, usually fabricated of metal, fiberglass, or cement, used to transfer air from a heating or cooling source to locations throughout a facility.

Air filter
A filtering device placed in an air stream, such as at the entrance to an air-conditioning equipment unit, to trap particles such as dust.

Air gun
A specially constructed gun used in the building trade in which the elastic force of condensed air projects atomized adhesive material onto the surface of a wall for insulating purposes.

Air-handling system
A complete system consisting of an air-handling unit for fresh and exhaust air, a damper at the building exterior, ductwork, supply air, diffusers, registers, and return air grills.

Air monitoring
A procedure to determine the content of hazardous material in the air over time; used in asbestos abatement work.

Air plenum
A duct or air space used to bring return air back to the air-handling unit.

Air right
A privilege or right, protected by law, to build in, occupy, or otherwise use a portion of airspace above real property at a stated elevation, in conjunction with specifically located spaces on the ground surface for the foundation and supporting columns.

Air shaft
A vertical space for the free passage of air; it may be small, such as an air duct, or air flue, or large enough to form a small space or courtyard between high buildings.

Air space
A cavity or space in walls or between various structural members.

Air system
A solar heating system in which air is forced through solar collectors by a fan to collect heat, and then circulated within the building or stored in a chamber before being returned to the collectors.

Air tool
Any attachment that uses compressed air for its power source to saw, spray, sand, drill, or nail.

Air trap
A U-shaped pipe filled with water and located beneath plumbing fixtures to form a seal against the passage of gas and odors.

Air washer
A component of an air-conditioning plant that removes suspended dirt by spraying or washing with water.

Air-conditioning
Artificial ventilation with cool air at a controlled temperature and humidity; often implies dehumidification.

Air-distributing ceiling
Air that comes through perforations in the ceiling tile in a suspended ceiling from a pressurized plenum above the ceiling.

Air-dried lumber
Sawn lumber that has been piled in yards or sheds to dry out for a specified period of time. Also called *Air seasoned lumber.*

Air-entrained concrete
Concrete containing the addition of an agent which causes millions of minute bubbles of air to be trapped within the concrete. It is resistant to a freeze-thaw cycle.

Air-handling unit
A single- or variable-speed fan that pushes air over hot or cold coils, for distribution through dampers and ducts, and into one or more rooms.

Air-seasoned lumber
Lumber seasoned by exposure to the atmosphere until there is no further loss in weight due to evaporation of moisture in the piece.

Airspace
A hollow space between the inner surfaces within a building or building component, such as between the panes of insulating glass, inner surfaces of masonry walls, between ceiling and floor in steel truss construction, and between an inner and outer dome.

Airtight drywall
A method of installing drywall using gasket or caulking between certain framing members to produce a continuous seal, allowing the drywall to act as a barrier against air infiltration.

Alabaster
A fine-grained, translucent variety of pure gypsum: delicately shaded, and used for ornamental work.

Align
To bring two or more pieces or objects into line with one another.

Alignment

The adjustment or formation of structural or construction elements in their relation to a predetermined line. Laying out bricks before installing them is an example.

Alkaline

Any of various soluble mineral salts found in natural water and soil; the opposite of an acid.

Alkaline resistance

The degree to which a paint resists reaction with alkaline materials such as lime cement or plaster; a necessary property for paints used in bathrooms, kitchens, and laundries.

Alkyd paint

A paint using alkyd resin as the vehicle for the pigment; available in exterior and fire-retardant types.

Alkyd plastics

A material used in paint and lacquers that is fast curing and dimensionally stable, has good insulation qualities, and is self-extinguishing.

Alkyd resin

One of a group of thermoplastic synthetic resins that are resistant to acids and oils and can withstand high temperatures. They are used for lacquers and enamel as a liquid.

Allen screw

A screw or butt with a depressed hexagonal socket in the head. Adjustable only with a hexagonal-shaped Allen wrench. See also *Allen wrench*.

Allen wrench

A hexagonal-shaped rod, with one part bent at a right angle to provide leverage, designed to fit a hex socket or Allen screw.

Alligator clip

A clip with a long nose and serrated jaws used to make temporary connections in an electrical current, or to hold small objects.

Alligatoring

A defect in a painted surface, appearing like alligator hide, from the application of a hard finishing coat over a soft primer coat, when the new coat cracks and slips over the old coat, exposing it to view.

Allowable load

The ultimate load on a member divided by the safety factor for that type of member.

Allowable soil pressure

A factor determined by the characteristics of soil, such as shear, compressibility, water content, and cohesion, that gives the allowable bearing capacity of the soil in pounds per square foot; used to determine the size of footings needed to support a structure. The higher the bearing value, the smaller the footing required.

Allowable stress

The maximum stress on members of a structure that is allowed by code, depending on the material and anticipated loading on the member.

Allowance

A stated sum in the contract to cover items or materials that cannot be fully determined or described on the contract documents. Also, the classification of connected parts or members of a structure based on their tightness or looseness once installed.

Alloy steel

Any steel containing a combination of one or more alloying elements other than carbon, such as chromium or nickel.

All-risk insurance

An insurance policy written to cover other risks of damage or loss from unexpected events beyond the normal protection from other insurance.

Alluvial soil

Soil and sand deposited by flowing water. Such soil is not stable enough to ensure a firm foundation for heavy structures.

Alteration

A term in the building code referring to any change in a structure that does not increase any of its exterior dimensions, or any modification in construction or grade of occupancy; also applies to any rearrangement in the structural parts or any extension on any side, or increase in height, or the moving of the structure from one location to another. Also, a construction project consisting of revisions within an existing structure, as distinct from additions to an existing structure.

Alternate
A clause in the contract documents that provides the owner with options to select alternative materials, products, or systems, or to add or delete portions of the work.

Alternate bid
A method of adjusting the base bid by adding or deducting an amount of money if certain changes are made in the contract documents.

Alternating current
Current in which the flow of electricity is reversed in direction at regular intervals as it passes through the circuit. Generally, a 60-cycle current is supplied to homes and industry.

Alternative dispute resolution
The provisions in a contract for the resolution of a dispute without litigation.

Aluminum
A lightweight metal that is malleable and nonmagnetic and has good conductivity; it is a good reflector of heat and light and is resistant to oxidation; it is often anodized for better corrosion resistance, color, and surface hardness.

Aluminum bronze
An alloy of aluminum and copper, used as an anodizing agent on door trim and window components.

Aluminum door
Used for storefront entrances, due to its high corrosion resistance.

Aluminum flashing
A sheet aluminum used to cover roof joints and other exterior conditions to make them waterproof.

Aluminum foil
A thin sheet of aluminum; commonly used for reflective insulation.

Aluminum nail
Lightweight, stainless, rustless, and sterilized nail made of aluminum.

Aluminum paint
A paint containing aluminum alloys, effective in preventing discoloration of painted surfaces in moist areas.

Aluminum roofing
Corrugated sheets used as a finished material; available in various colors and finishes.

Aluminum siding
Panels of aluminum, shaped liked siding, used to cover the exterior surface of a building.

Aluminum storefront
An exterior storefront composed of aluminum sections and glazing, with an entry and display area.

Aluminum window
A frame constructed of aluminum extruded shapes to hold glazing, and to fit into framed openings in an exterior wall.

Ambient sound
The noise level in a room from ventilation, motors, and outside sounds that penetrate through the windows.

Ambiguous
In a contract, any phrase or word that can have more than one meaning.

Amenity
A building or landscape feature that is more than purely utilitarian in that it makes an aesthetic contribution to the environment.

American Federation of Labor (AFL)
A labor organization formed in 1886. It provides an umbrella that represents the interests of workers in various trades related to manufacturing and construction.

American Federation of Labor and Committee for Industrial Organization (AFL-CIO)
A major union merger formed in 1955 that represents the workers in industry and construction for negotiating wages, benefits, and other interests of its members.

American Institute of Architects (AIA)
Founded in 1857 as a national professional society whose members are registered architects. The AIA sponsors the Committee on Historic Resources along with State Preservation Coordinators, and it is a signatory to the Historic American Buildings Survey (HABS). The organization also promotes public awareness of architectural and environmental issues and offers programs for continuing education; it also maintains a library at its headquarters in Washington, DC, and coordinates all state and local chapters.

American Institute of Timber Construction (AITC)
The national trade association of the structural glue-laminating industry.

American National Standards Institute (ANSI)
A private-sector organization of trade associations, technical societies, professional groups, and consumer organizations; publishes the American National Standards; approves standards and specifications for all areas of American building construction, safety, manufacturing, and engineering.

American Plywood Association (APA)
An association that represents the majority of American manufacturers of plywood and plywood construction panels. It determines minimum product standards, supervises quality control and testing, establishes installation procedures and applications, and engages in ongoing research and promotion of new panel products.

American Society for Testing and Materials (ASTM)
A nonprofit organization, established in 1898, that establishes standard tests and specifications for various construction materials and methods.

Americans with Disabilities Act (ADA) of 1990
A federal law that defines requirements for handicapped access to public facilities, as described in the ADA guidelines. It requires removal of existing barriers except any that would compromise the historic significance of a structure.

Amortization
The periodic repayment of a debt under a loan agreement; to write off expenditures by prorating them over a certain period of time.

Ampere
A basic unit of electricity; the amount of current that 1 volt of power can send through 1 ohm of resistance in the wires. Commonly called an amp; the electrical unit of measurement for the amount of current flowing in a wire.

Analysis
In renovation construction, the process of reducing a problem to its primary parts, as in the finding of forces in the various members of a loaded structure.

Anchor
A device used to give stability to one part of the structure by securing it to another part; includes concrete inserts, toggle bolts, expansion anchors, and lead shield anchors.

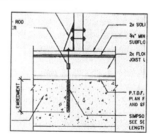

Anchor block
A block of wood built into a masonry wall to which partitions and fixtures may be secured later.

Anchor bolt
A bolt used to attach a structural member, such as by embedding it in the foundation to secure a sill to a foundation wall, and provide a nailing surface for the rest of the framing. Also called a *sill bolt*.

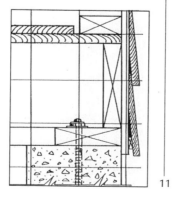

Anchor nailing
A method of driving nails at opposite angles through two or more boards.

Anchor plate
A metal plate on a masonry wall that holds the end of a tie rod; often of ornamental design.

Anchor rod
A metal rod attached to hangers to support pipe and ductwork.

Anchor tie
Any type of fastener used to secure the parts of a wall to some stable object, such as another wall.

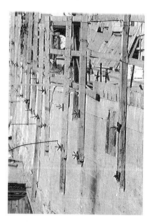

Anchored composite patches
Use of noncorrosive anchoring pins inserted into the original stone before patching is started. Stainless steel or threaded Teflon pins are commonly used.

Anchored dutchman
A large block of stone, anchored with cramps or dowels as well as adhesives.

Angle block
In woodwork, a small wooden block glued into right-angled joints, making them more rigid.

Angle bond
In masonry work, brick or metal ties used to bind the angles or corners of the walls.

Angle brace
A supporting member across the corner of a rectangular frame or structure.

Angle cleat
A small bracket formed of angle iron, which is used to locate or support a member of a structural framework.

Angle dozer
A piece of earthmoving equipment used to scrape soil off an excavation utilizing a blade mounted at an angle to the direction of travel. It is also used in moving earth and leveling a building site.

Angle iron
A steel section, either hot-rolled or cold-formed, consisting of two legs, almost always at a right angle.

Angle joist
A joist running diagonally from an internal girder to the corner intersection of two wall plates; used to support the feet of hip rafters.

Angle rafter
The rafter at the hip of a roof that receives the jack rafters. Also called a *hip rafter*.

Angle tie
A bar fixed across the inside of an angle in order to make a framework more rigid. Same as an *angle brace*.

Annealed wire
A pliable wire used for tying reinforcing bars and concrete forms.

Annual ring
The arrangement of the wood of a tree in concentric rings or layers each year, alternating between springwood, light and porous, and summerwood, dark and dense.

Anodizing
Coating aluminum parts with a hard surface film of aluminum oxide through an electrolytic process. The film acts as a protective coating and is an excellent paint base.

Anta
A pier or pilaster formed by a thickening at the end of a wall, most often used on the side of a doorway or beyond the face of an end wall.

Antefix
A decorated upright slab used in classical architecture and other derivatives to close or conceal the open end of a row of tiles that covers the joints of roof tiles.

Antiquing
A technique that combines a variety of materials and application methods to produce an appearance of age or weathering or wear on new wood.

Appendage
Any structure attached to the outer wall of a building, but not necessary to its stability.

Application for payment
A contractor's written request for payment for portions of the work completed and for materials for future work delivered and stored at the site or in a warehouse, if the contract so stipulates.

Applied molding
The arrangement of molding to give the appearance of paneling.

Appraisal
Professional evaluation of the market value of land, facilities, or property. Also, fixing a price or value on a property, through the process of making an estimate and valuation of the property.

Appraised value
The current market value of a piece of property or structure, as determined by professional appraisal methods, comparison with similar properties in the area, comparison with similar types, or estimating the replacement cost of a structure.

Apprentice
A young person who is legally bound to a craftsperson for a specified period of time in order to learn the skills of a particular trade.

Apprenticeship
Training for those occupations, skilled crafts, or trades that require a wide and diverse range of skills and knowledge, usually lasting 3 to 4 years. A worker is given thorough instruction and gains experience on and off the job in both theoretical and practical aspects of the job.

Approval
Materials, equipment, and workmanship that has been accepted by a building inspector; also, approval for payment, or approval for occupancy.

Approved
Meaning that a building inspector has found an installation to be in line with the building code.

Approved equal
Material, equipment, or method approved by the architect or engineer for use in the work as being acceptable as an equivalent to those originally specified in the contract documents.

Apron
A flat piece of trim below the interior sill of a window, limited to the width of the window.

Arbitration
A process by which parties agree to submit disputes to a third party rather than going to court, which saves time and money for all parties. The parties can agree to binding arbitration in advance, or at the time of the dispute.

Arc welding

An electrical welding process in which intense heat is obtained by the arcing between the welding rod and the metal to be welded. The molten metal from the tip of the electrode is then deposited in the joint and solidifies to form a strong uniform connection.

Arch
A basic architectural structure built over an opening, made up of wedge-shaped blocks, supported from the sides only. The downward pressure is transformed into a lateral thrust, keeping the blocks in position, and transferring the vertical pressure of the superimposed load laterally to the adjoining abutments.

Arched
Shapes formed by the curved, pointed, or rounded upper part of openings or supporting members.

Arched beam
A beam whose upper surface is slightly curved, similar to a camber beam.

Arched dormer
A dormer that has a semicylindrical shaped roof. The head of the window in the dormer may be either rounded or flat.

Arched truss
A truss with an arched upper chord and a straight bottom chord, with vertical hangers between the two chords.

Archeology
Studies by a professional with experience in research, excavation, and analysis of archeological sites and artifacts.

Architect
An individual who is engaged in the design of buildings and who often supervises the construction.

Architect of record
The name of the architect who is on the building permit for construction, issued by the department having authority over the project. If more than one permit is required, and work is performed by a different architect, there are additional architects of record.

Architect's approval
Permissions granted by the architect as agent for the owner, for decisions involving materials, equipment, installation, change orders, substitutions of materials, or payment for completed work.

Architect's scale
A ruler that uses a series of small measuring units, each representing 1 foot. This provides an accurate scaled-down version of the actual measurement on the job.

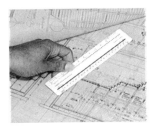

Architect-consultant agreement
A contract for professional services between an architect and another architect, engineer, or specialist.

Architect–engineer (AE)
An individual or firm that offers both architectural and engineering professional services. Also, the design team might include the architect and consulting engineers of various disciplines retained by the architect as subconsultants.

Architectural
Pertaining to architecture, its features, characteristics, or details. Also, pertaining to materials used to build or ornament a structure such as mosaic, bronze, wood, and the like.

Architectural conservation
The process of maintaining and/or repairing the materials of a building or structure to reduce or reverse the physical deterioration. It includes cleaning, repointing of masonry joints, and reattaching any loose elements.

Architectural design
A process that includes the analysis of a program that results in the restoration, renovation, rehabilitation, or adaptive reuse of a building.

Architectural drawings
Plans, elevations, and details of the building to be constructed; consists of foundation plan, floor plans, roof framing plan; electrical and plumbing and heating, ventilation, and air-conditioning (HVAC) diagrams; exterior and interior elevations, details of door and window installations, and structural connections.

Architectural element
A portion of a building or its ornamentation.

Architectural engineering
The art and science of engineering functions that relate to buildings or structures.

Architectural fee
The amount charged for architectural services, usually based on a percentage of the total contract amount with the owner, and it varies with the size and complexity of the project.

Architectural Graphic Standards
A publication that provides authoritative practice aids with illustrative examples, construction details, tables of data, and other explanations.

Architectural historian

A specialist in the history of the built environment, with special expertise in architecture, restoration, and rehabilitation.

Architectural review board

A local body that reviews proposed new construction, restoration, and alterations to existing buildings for conformance to their own established design guidelines and/or good design practice.

Architectural style

A classification that identifies the overall appearance of the architecture of a building, including its construction, form, arrangement of design components, use of materials, and ornamentation. The style may be a unique individual expression or part of a broad cultural pattern related to a particular time period, geographical region, or country of origin.

Architectural woodwork

Finish carpentry for casework, cabinets, or ornamental carvings.

Architecture

The art and science of designing and building or restoring structures or groups of structures, in keeping with aesthetic and functional criteria.

Area

The surface measurement of a defined space or shape expressed in square units such as square feet.

Area drain

A receptacle designed to collect surface or rainwater from an open area so that the water can be funneled to a drainage system.

Area method

An estimating system using square foot costs multiplied by the adjusted gross floor area of a building.

Areaway

An open subsurface space adjacent to a means of access to a basement window, door, or crawlspace under the structure.

Areaway grating

A cast-iron grating covering an areaway at ground level.

Areaway wall
Any wall built to hold back earth around an areaway; usually built of concrete, concrete blocks, brick, or stone.

Armored cable
Rubber-insulated wires that are spiral wrapped with a flexible steel covering; called BX cable. The addition of a separate ground wire as required by codes in recent times has replaced the earlier BX cable. Also called *conduit, metal tubing.*

Articulation
In architectural design, an arrangement of parts which is clearly distinguishable by joints or combination of materials. In structural engineering, the process of constructing movable joints using joint pins.

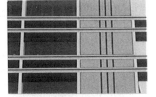

Artificial light
Light produced by an electrical process or the burning of fuel.

Artificial sky
A hemisphere or ceiling painted and illuminated to imitate the natural sky. Lighting effects can be used to simulate any time of day or night.

Artificial stone
A mixture of stone chips or fragments, usually embedded in a matrix of mortar, cement, or plaster; the surfaces may be ground, polished, molded, or otherwise treated to simulate natural stone.

Artificial wood
Any of the various mixtures that are molded to simulate wood. Often sawdust, paper, or other wood fiber is used as a major ingredient mixed with glue.

Artisan
An outdated term for a craftsperson or tradesperson.

Asbestos
A noncombustible, flexible fiber that is able to withstand high temperatures. It is fabricated into many forms, either alone or mixed with other ingredients.

Asbestos abatement
Removal of material that contains asbestos, which is considered a potential health hazard, in a way that minimizes risk to the abatement workers and the public.

Asbestos encapsulation
An airtight enclosure of asbestos fibers, with sealants or film that prevent the fibers from escaping.

Asbestos felt
A product made by saturating felted asbestos with asphalt or other binder, such as a synthetic elastomeric substance.

Asbestos removal
The removal of ceiling tile, fireproofing, and pipe insulation containing asbestos, as it has been identified as a hazardous material.

Asbestos shingle
A fireproof roofing shingle that is composed of cement reinforced with asbestos fibers and manufactured in various shapes and sizes.

Asbestos tile
An inexpensive flooring tile that is impregnated with asbestos.

Asbestos-cement board
A dense, noncombustible, rigid board containing a high percentage of asbestos fiber bonded with cement.

Asbestos-cement pipe
A pipe composed of portland cement reinforced with asbestos fibers, used for drainage or venting in a plumbing system.

As-built drawing
Drawings prepared by a contractor or architect after a job has been completed. These after-the-fact drawings indicate variations from the original design drawings, particularly in regard to concealed locations of mechanical and electrical work, to permit maintenance thereof and to preclude damage from future alterations.

As-built schedule
The final project timeline that depicts the actual start and completion dates, duration, costs, and consumed resources for each activity.

Ashlar masonry
Squared stones used on foundations and for facing certain types of masonry walls.

Aspect ratio
The ratio of the width to the depth of an object, as applied to ducts in an air-conditioning system.

Asphalt
A mixture of bitumens obtained from native deposits or as a petroleum by-product used for paving, waterproofing, and roofing applications.

Asphalt felt
A roofing material manufactured by saturating a dry felt with asphalt, then coating the saturated felt with a fine material or glass fiber; usually available in rolls.

Asphalt mastic
A thick adhesive, consisting of asphalt, bitumen or pitch, and a filler, such as sand; used for bedding woodblock floors, pointing window frames, and for laying and repairing flat roofs.

Asphalt roofing
A roofing material manufactured by saturating a dry felt sheet with asphalt and then coating the saturated felt with a harder asphalt coating, usually in roll form.

Asphalt shingle
A shingle manufactured from saturated roofing felt that is coated with asphalt, with mineral granules on the side that is exposed to the weather.

Asphalt tile
Resilient floor tile that is composed of asbestos fibers with asphalt binders; set in mastic and installed over wood or concrete floors.

Assembly drawing
A drawing in which all of an object's parts are shown in an exploded type of view, often to indicate the order in which the object is to be assembled, and the relationship of the parts to each other. Generally not part of an architectural drawing, but may be part of a shop drawing.

Assessment
A charge levied against a property owner for improvements which benefit the property, such as roads, sewers, flood control, or other similar improvements.

Assigned subcontractor
A subcontractor who is assigned to the prime contractor to function thereafter as a subcontractor; selected by the owner as a result of negotiation or competitive bidding.

Assignment
A transfer of rights and conditions of a contract from one party to another.

Associate
Closely connected as in function or office, but having secondary or subordinate status.

Associated architect
An architect who has a temporary joint venture or employment agreement or partnership with another architect in collaboration for the performance of services for a specific project, or series of projects.

ASTM
Abbreviation for American Society for Testing and Materials.

Astragal
A member or combination of members, fixed to one of a pair of doors or casement windows to cover the joint between the meeting stiles and to close the gap in order to prevent drafts and the passage of light, air, or noise.

Astragal weatherstripping
Strips of rubber, fabric, or plastic attached to the molding that is part of the astragal molding covering the joint between the two stiles of a door or casement window.

Atelier
A place where artwork or handicrafts are produced by skilled workers. Also, a studio where the fine arts, including architecture, are taught.

Atrium
The forecourt of an early Christian basilica, with colonnades on all four sides and usually containing a fountain in the center. Derived from the entrance court of a Roman dwelling, roofed to have a large opening to admit light. Rain was received in a cistern below.

Atrium

The modern version of an atrium in office or hotel complexes is a tall, open space within a structure that is clear of floor areas from the base to a ceiling skylight. The existing structural frame may be retained within the open area in renovated spaces.

Attached house

A house joined by a common wall with an adjacent house, including row houses and semidetached houses.

Attic

The space above the top floor ceiling and below a sloped roof. Also called *half story, loft, garret.*

Attic floor

The flooring of an attic, including the joists which support the floor.

Attic insulation

Loose insulation to weatherproof a facility that is blown into attic spaces, or fiberglass rolls that are installed between the ceiling joists.

Attic order

Small pillars or pilasters decorating the exterior of an attic story. In design and size they are subordinate, but related to the main order.

Attic ventilator

A mechanical fan in the attic of a house, which removes hot air from the roof space and discharges it to the outside.

Auger

A tool for drilling holes either in wood or soil. The handle of the auger is attached at a right angle to the stem. Handheld augers are sufficient for extracting small samples of soil. Larger, deeper holes or samples must be made with a powered drill.

Auger bit

An auger to be used in a brace; has a square shank made to fit a standard socket, which is also known as a brace and bit.

Autoclaved expanded concrete

A lightweight insulating cladding material that can be used in lieu of masonry on the exterior.

Automatic closing device

A mechanism that closes a door slowly after it has been opened. Also, a door that is closed automatically by a fuse that releases and closes a fire door, damper, or shutter in the event of a fire.

Automatic door

A power-operated door that opens and closes automatically at the approach of a person or vehicle.

Automatic fire alarm system

A system that detects smoke or fire and automatically initiates a signal at the site or on a remote monitor.

Automatic fire sprinkling system

A network of overhead pipes with outlets or "heads" which open at a predetermined temperature to discharge water onto a fire area. There are four types of systems: (1) a wet pipe system where the pipes are always full of water; (2) a dry pipe system, filled with pressurized air which allows water to enter when a head is opened; (3) a preaction system which is similar to a dry pipe system, but activated by an independent heat detector; and (4) the deluge system, where the heads are open at all times, and the pipes are without water until a separate heat detection system discharges a maximum amount of water to all heads. The latter is used in areas with a high degree of hazard.

Automatic level

A transit which automatically adjusts to a level position once it has been set, by using a suspended compensator device.

Auxillary view

A supplementary drawing on a set of plans, shown in relation to a smaller-scale drawing; used to provide greater detail of a portion of the principal view.

Award

A written resolution to a dispute, signed by an arbitrator, and given to the winning party.

Award of contract

The action by the owner that verifies to the contractor that the bid or proposal for construction has been accepted, and that a contract will be forthcoming.

Awl

A small, sharp-pointed instrument used by a carpenter for making small holes for nails or screws. Also used to score lines where pencil marks may not be as visible or may become erased.

Awning

A roof-like cover of canvas or other lightweight material, extending in front of a doorway or window, or over a deck, providing protection from the sun or rain.

Awning window

A window consisting of a number of top-hinged horizontal sashes one above the other, the bottom edges of which swing outward; operated by one control device.

Axial load

Forces that act directly along the primary axis of a structural member, such as a beam or column.

Axis of symmetry

A line, imaginary or real, about which a geometrical figure or drawing is developed equally on both sides of the line.

Azimuth

A compass reading in degrees and minutes from true North reading clockwise from 0 to 360°.

B

Back building

A detached or contiguous subsidiary structure behind the main building.

Back arch

An arch that supports an inner wall where the outer wall is supported in a different manner, such as a brick arch behind a stone lintel.

Back charge

A charge offsetting an invoice, made by an owner against a contractor, or a contractor against a subcontractor based on a claim for defective construction work; or for services rendered or materials furnished without prior approval; usually deducted from a progress or final payment owed to the subcontractor.

Back plastering

Applying a thick mortar coat on the back of the facing tier of masonry. Also called *parging*.

Back priming

A coat of paint applied to the backside and edges of woodwork or exterior siding to prevent excessive absorption of moisture.

Back vent

A pipe used for ventilating purposes that is attached to a waste pipe on the sewer side of its trap to prevent the siphoning of waste.

Backband molding

A piece of millwork used around a rectangular window or door casing to cover the gap between the casing and the wall, or used as a decorative feature.

Backfill

Crushed stone or coarse soil placed around the foundation walls to provide drainage for water collecting in the soil behind the wall. Also called *fill*.

Backflow

In plumbing, the flow of water or sewage opposite to its normal direction; the flow of water or other substances into the distribution pipes of a water drainage system, from an unintended source.

Backflow valve

In plumbing, a device inserted in the drain system of a building to prevent a reversal of the flow of sewage.

Backhoe loader

An excavating machine that has a loading bucket in front which is drawn toward the machine when it is used to gather material from the ground, and a scoop on the other end for gathering material and loading it onto a truck.

Backing
In masonry, rubble or broken stones used at the back of facing.

Backing brick
A relatively low-quality brick used behind the face brick or behind other masonry.

Backing tier
In masonry construction, the tier of rough brickwork which backs up the face tier, often by a cheaper grade of brick.

Backlog
The amount and dollar value of work contracted but not yet performed. It is reduced as work is completed and increased by the value of new projects signed up in a given period.

Backpriming
The application of paint or stain to the back side of wood siding to ensure stability of the wood by keeping moisture out of the piece as much as possible.

Backsaw
Any saw with a blade stiffened by an additional metal strip along its back; used in a miter box, or as a bench saw.

Back-to-back
Items that are placed in mirror image to one another, such as plumbing fixtures in adjacent bathrooms or kitchens that share a common wall.

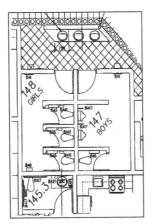

Backup heating system
A furnace, wood stove, or heater used to provide auxiliary heat to a solar heating system during periods when sunlight is not available.

Backup material
A material placed at the back of a curtain wall for fire or insulation purposes, or behind a finished face of masonry.

Baked enamel
A hard, glossy metal finish used in the early development of the spandrel panel used in curtain wall construction.

Balance
In building construction, the equilibrium between opposing forces, such as the stress and strain versus the resistance in various structural members.

Balanced circuit
In electrical work, a three-wire circuit with the same load on each side of the neutral wire.

Balanced earthwork
The process of cutting and filling earth in equal amounts at the same site.

Balanced sash
A sash in a double-hung window whose weight is counterbalanced with lead weights and pulleys, or with pretensioned springs.

Balcony beam
A horizontal beam or beams that supports a balcony, often anchored inside the structure, and cantilevers from the wall.

Bald cypress
A deciduous softwood tree resistant to decay and often used for parts of buildings that are in contact with the soil and for exposed elements such as wood shingles; also used for flooring and trim.

Ballast
Any material used as a nonstructural material to add dead weight.

Balloon framing
A system of framing a wooden building wherein all vertical studs in the exterior bearing walls and partitions extend the full height of the frame from sill to roof plate. The floor joists are supported by sills.

Balloon payment
A payment that is larger than the scheduled periodic payments, usually reserved for the final payment at the end of a loan, but can also be made anytime during the course of the loan.

Ball-peen hammer
A hammer used primarily for metal work, with one flat end and one hemispherical end on the hammer head.

Balsam fir
A softwood tree with coarse-grained wood, used for interior trim.

Balsam poplar
A large hardwood tree, with soft straight-grained wood used for painted millwork.

Baluster

One of a number of short vertical members used to support a stair or balcony railing; may be a turned wood spindle or a stone column, either square or with a varying round profile.

Balustrade

An entire railing system, as along the edge of a balcony, including a top rail, bottom rail, and balusters.

Band molding

A small broad, flat molding, projecting slightly, of rectangular or slightly convex profile, used to decorate a surface, either as a continuous strip or formed into various shapes.

Band saw

A saw with an endless serrated steel belt running on revolving pulleys; used for cutting millwork or curved lines and contours.

Banded door

A wood door with a thin molded band applied to the outside edge of the face of each stile and the top and bottom rail.

Banister

A slender pillar turned on a lathe, used to support the handrail of a stair.

Bar

A long, thin strip of material, especially iron, used for a variety of building purposes, particularly when inserted into an opening to prevent entry; often placed on the outside of a glazed window.

Bar chair

A manufactured device that holds the welded wire fabric at one-half the thickness of the concrete slab during the time of placing the concrete.

Bar chart

A graph used by builders for scheduling work. Each part of the job is represented by a bar, or line, with one end representing the start date and the other end the completion date. The progress of the job is represented visually against a set timeline.

Bar clamp

A clamping device used by carpenters, consisting of a long metal threaded bar with adjustable wooden clamping jaws.

Bar graph

A graphic representation of design or construction activities charted against a predetermined time frame. The various activities are arranged vertically, beginning with the first event, continuing down and across the chart with the remaining ones. The length of each bar represents the total time the event lasts. A calibrated base represents a specific time period; used to see how closely the actual activity came to the original goals.

Bar joist

An open web steel joist with the diagonal struts made of round or square steel bars. The top and bottom chords are made up of opposing pairs of steel angles, which enclose the diagonal struts.

Bar mat

An assembly of reinforcing made up of two or more layers of bars, placed at right angles to each other and tied together.

Bar molding

A rabbeted molding applied to the edge of a bar or counter to serve as a nosing.

Bar number

A number used to designate the size of reinforcing bar; approximately the bar diameter represented in eighths of an inch; thus, a number 5 bar is approximately 5/8 inch.

Bar placing subcontractor

A contractor or subcontractor who handles and places reinforcement and bar supports on a construction job.

Bar spacing
The distance between reinforcing bars in a beam or concrete slab; measured from center to center of the bars.

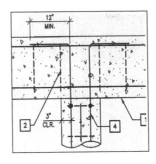

Bar support
A device, usually of formed wire, to support, hold, and space reinforcing bars. Also called *bar chair*.

Bare cost
The estimated cost of an item of work or material before the contractor's markup for overhead and profit.

Barge
A floating vessel or platform from which construction can be performed along waterfronts and rivers.

Barn door hangers
Consists of two pulleys at the top ends of a barn door that move along a horizontal track that hangs from a lintel, or projects slightly from it.

Barn door pull
Any large door pull suitable for extra-heavy doors, such as barn doors, garages, and warehouses.

Barn door roller
A device consisting of a sheave mounted in a frame fastened to the bottom of a barn door or any other extra-heavy door, which travels on a track or rail on the floor that carries the door.

Barn siding
Beveled or tongue-and-groove boards used for enclosing a barn or other farm building.

Barrel arch
An arch that is formed by a curved solid plate or slab, as contrasted with one formed with individual members or curved ribs.

Barrel bolt
A round tab made to slide into a cylindrical socket or barrel, for fastening a door or window sash.

Barrel vault
A masonry vault resting on two parallel walls having the form of a half cylinder; sometimes called a tunnel vault.

Barricade
An obstruction to prevent access or passage to an area, either temporary or permanent.

Basalt
A dense, dark gray volcanic rock, often full of small cavities; used as a building stone.

Base
The lowest and most visible part of a building, often treated with distinctive materials, such as rustication. Also, the lowest part of a column or pier that rests on a pedestal, plinth, or stylobate.

Base bid
Amount of money stated in a bid as the sum for which the bidder offers to perform the work required by the project documents. The base bid does not include the work for which alternate bids are submitted.

Base bid specifications
The specifications describing only those materials, equipment, and methods of construction upon which the base bid must be predicted, exclusive of any alternate bids.

Base cabinet
Kitchen cabinet that rests on the floor and supports the counter.

Base cap
A molding that covers the top of the baseboard junction with the wall.

Base coat
The first coat of a plaster finish, or the first layer of any coating applied in a liquid or plastic state, such as paint; also an initial coat applied to a wood surface before staining or otherwise finishing it.

Base course
The lowest course on a masonry wall or pier; may also be part of the footing.

Base drawing
A drawing made at the site, or drawings made for rectified photography or photogrammetry, that indicates the conditions of an existing structure.

Base flashing
The metal that goes under any roofing material and is turned up against a vertical surface, such as a parapet or wall. It is covered by counter flashing from above.

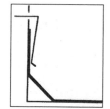

Base map
A map used in urban planning showing a graphic representation of a defined area, such as a particular site, neighborhood, town, region, or state; shows legal boundaries and physical features, such as streets, rivers, parks, railroads, and serves as a foundation for all subsequent mapping of new development.

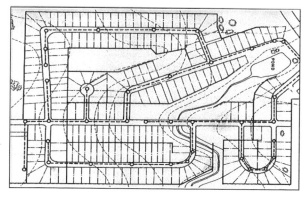

Base shoe
A quarter round molding strip used to cover the joint at the bottom of the baseboard and floor; generally required if the floor surface is uneven.

Baseboard
A flat projection from an interior wall or partition at the floor, covering the joint between the floor and wall; may be plain, beveled or molded. Also called *skirting*.

Baseboard heater
Heating elements, usually in long strips, placed at the junction of the wall and floor along the outside walls of a room.

Baseline
An established line in the construction from which measurements are taken when laying out building plans.

Basement window
Frames and sash of either wood or metal for use in basement openings. Usually such windows do not have more than two or three lights.

Baseplate
A steel plate for transmitting and distributing a column load to the supporting foundation.

Basketweave bond
A checkerboard pattern of bricks, laid either horizontally and vertically or on the diagonal.

Batching
Measuring the ingredients for a batch of concrete or mortar by weight or volume and introducing them in a mixer.

Batt insulation
An insulation which has been manufactured into a flexible blanketlike form, often with a vapor barrier on one side. It comes in widths that fit between standard stud or joist spacing in wood-framed structures.

Batten door
A door constructed of nailing boards together in a variety of ways. The solid batten door is composed of two layers of boards nailed at right angles to each other. Other types are constructed by securing vertical or diagonal members to each other by horizontal or diagonal ledger boards.

Batten plate
A spacer used to hold component parts of a member at the correct distance apart.

Batten siding
Vertical siding which has narrow vertical strips of wood covering the joints.

Batter board
A board nailed at exact elevations to posts located just outside the corners of a proposed building or addition. Strings are stretched across the boards to locate the outlines of the foundation.

Batter brace
An inclined brace at the end of a truss to give added strength and support.

Bay
A principal compartment or division in the architectural arrangement of a building, marked either by buttresses or pilasters in the wall, by the disposition of main arches and pillars, or by any repeated spatial units.

Bead molding
A narrow wood drip molded on one edge against which a door or window closes; a stop bead; a strip of metal or wood used around the periphery of a pane of glass to secure it in a window frame.

Beaded mortar joint
Recessed mortar joint in the form of a quirked bead: a joint with a raised bead in the center that projects past the surface of the brick or stone.

Beam
A rigid structural member whose prime function is to carry and transfer transverse loads across a span to the supports, such as a joist, girder, rafter, or purlin.

Beam ceiling
A ceiling formed by the underside of the floor, exposing the beams that support it; also applies to a false ceiling imitating exposed beams.

Beam fill
Masonry or concrete used to fill the spaces between joists, at the foundation wall and framework of the structure, to prevent fire which may start in the basement from spreading to the framework above.

Beam girder
Two or more beams fastened together by cover plates, bolts, or welds to form a single structural member.

Beam hanger
A strap, wire, or other hardware device that supports the framework from structural members.

Beam pocket
A space left open in a wall to receive a beam.

Beam schedule
A list in the working drawings that gives the number, size, and placement of steel beams used in a structure. See also *Column schedule*.

Bearing
That portion of a beam, truss, or other structural member that rests on the supports.

Bearing pile
A pile that carries a vertical load, as compared with a sheet pile, which resists earth pressure.

Bearing plate
A plate placed under a heavily loaded support of a beam or column, to distribute the load over a wider area. Also called *load plate*.

Bearing stratum
The soil or rock stratum on which a footing, pile, or caisson bears.

Bearing value
The load that a particular soil will sustain without substantial deformation.

Bearing wall
A wall that supports any vertical load in addition to its own weight.

Bed
In masonry and bricklaying, the side of a masonry which lies in the course of the wall; also, the layer of mortar on which a masonry unit is set.

Bed joint
The horizontal layer of mortar between two masonry courses on which the masonry is laid.

Bed puttying
Placing a thin layer of putty or bedding compound in the rabbet of a window sash and pressing the glass into the bed. Glazing points are then driven into the wood and the sash is face puttied.

Bedding
A filling of mortar, putty, or other substance in order to secure a firm bearing.

Bedplate
A plate, frame, or platform that supports a wall above.

Bedrock
Solid rock which underlies any superficial formation; hence, a firm foundation on which to erect a building.

Belcast eaves
A curve in the slope of a roof at the eaves; used not only because of its aesthetic appearance but because it protects the exterior walls from rainwater running off the roof.

Belcast gambrel roof
A type of gambrel roof with an upward slope in the eaves at the bottom of the roof.

Belgian block
A hard paving stone, typically granite, roughly cut to the shape of a truncated pyramid, where the top is slightly smaller than the base.

Bell and spigot joint
A common type of joint for cast-iron pipes in a plumbing system; each length having an enlarged bell on one end and a plain end on the other. The plain end is inserted into the bell and the joint is sealed with caulking.

Bell gable
A wall gable and parapet, with one or more openings that supports a bell; found mainly in Spanish Colonial architecture.

Bell-cast roof
A roof with a cross-section similar to that of a bell or a mansard-type roof in which the lower portion slopes downward in a straight line, then flares outward at the eaves.

Belt sander
A powered sander in which a continuous belt of abrasive material is driven over rollers at both ends across a faceplate.

Beltcourse
A projecting horizontal course of masonry, of the same or dissimilar material used to throw off water from the wall; usually coincides with the edge of an interior floor.

Bench
A seat with or without a back; most often constructed of wood.

Bench plane
A hand tool for planing that is used primarily on a workbench.

Benchmark
A permanent reference mark, fixed to a building or to the ground, whose height above a standard datum level has been accurately determined by survey.

Benchwork
Work which is done using small hand tools at a workbench; as distinct from work done throughout the structure.

Bending
A force which puts the top of the member in compression and the bottom of the member in tension.

Benefits
Personnel benefits fall under three classifications: (1) those required by law, such as social security, worker compensation, and disability insurance; (2) customary, such as leave, holidays, and vacation; and (3) optional with respect to each firm, such as life insurance, hospitalization programs, pension plans, and other retirement plans.

Bent
A framework that is transverse to the length of a framed structure, usually designed to carry both a lateral and a vertical load.

Bent bar
A reinforcing bar that is bent to a prescribed shape, such as a truss bar, hook bar, stirrup, or column tie.

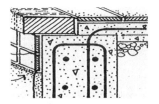

Bent wood
Wood formed into curves by steaming the wood and bending it to fit a form.

Benzene
A highly flammable hydrocarbon, used as a solvent and paint remover.

Beveled joint
Any joint in which the ends of the two abutting elements are cut at an angle, and not forming a right angle.

Beveled glass
A pane of glass with a beveled border; used at entrance doors and in other ornamental work.

Beveled molding
Milled molding with a slanted surface.

Beveled siding
Tapered boards used as siding, installed with the thinner part at the top.

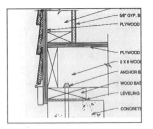

Bias
In carpentry, a line cut on the oblique or diagonal angle.

Bid
An offer or a proposal to supply a specific amount of materials, or labor, or both for a stated price. A base bid is where alternative prices for different scopes of work are included as additions or deletions from the base bid. A sub bid is when the contract would be with a prime contractor rather than directly with the owner.

Bid bond
A guarantee by a bonding company that a bidder will enter into a contract if awarded the job, and will supply performance and payment bonds.

Bid conditions
The conditions outlined in the instruction to bidders, the notice to bidders, or advertisement for bids, that prescribes the conditions under which bids are to be prepared, executed, submitted, received, and accepted.

Bid date
The date for the receipt of bids, usually established by the owner or architect.

Bid documents deposit
A monetary deposit required to obtain a set of construction documents and bidding requirements which are usually refunded on return of the documents in good condition within a specified time.

Bid form
A form prepared by the architect or owner on which each bidder fills in the amount of the bid and delivers it to the owner, usually in a sealed envelope, at the time of the bid opening.

Bid opening
The time, place, and date set by the owner for receiving and opening bids for a project. The opening may either be public or private. If public, each bid is opened and announced. If private, the winning contractor may or may not be informed of the other contractors' bid.

Bid package
A package consisting of all drawings, specifications, documents, estimates, bid forms, and bid bonds relevant to the construction of a project.

Bid price
The amount of money slated in the bid for which the bidder offers to perform the work.

Bid protest
A challenge to proceedings or outcome by an unsuccessful or dissatisfied bidder.

Bid security
A deposit submitted along with the bid which guarantees that the bidder, if awarded the job, will execute it in accordance with the contract documents. The deposit may be a certified check, money order, or bid bond.

Bid shopping
A contractor who is the low bidder in a project "shops" among subcontractors for a price lower than the one submitted by another subcontractor for the same work, thereby increasing the potential for profit.

Bid time
The date and hour established by the owner or the architect for the receipt of bids.

Bidder
A person who submits a bid for a prime contract with the owner; as opposed to a sub bidder who submits a bid to a prime bidder.

Bidding
The process where two or more contractors compete for a project by gathering all the sub bids from specialty subcontractors, adding overhead and profit for their portion of the work, and submitting a sealed bid at a specific time and place. The owner is usually not obligated to accept the lowest bid, or any bid.

Bidding period
The date between the time of issuance of bidding requirements and contract documents and the prescribed bid opening time.

Bifold door
A folding door that divides into two parts, the inner leaf of each part being hung from an overhead track, and the outer leaf hinged at the jamb.

Bill of materials
A list of materials needed to build the structure, giving quantities, description, and sizes.

Billable time
The actual time that is directly chargeable to the project and invoiced to the client. See also *Non-billable time*.

Binder
A material used to bind a mixture together, such as cement in concrete or mortar.

Biodeterioration
Agents that contribute to the deterioration of stone. Modes of disintegration are both physical and chemical, and are affected by bacteria, algae, lichen, fungi, mosses, and guano from birds and other mammals.

Birch
A moderately strong, high-density wood, yellowish to brown in color. Its uniform texture is well suited for veneer, flooring, and turned wood products.

Bird's mouth
A small V-shaped notch at the lower end of an inclined rafter, to provide a level bearing area on the top wall plate of a stud-framed wall. Also called *plate cut, rafter seat cut.*

Bit brace
A curved device used for holding boring or drilling tools, with a curved handle that can be rotated to drill.

Bit gage
An attachment to a bit which controls the drilling to a given depth.

Black mortar
Mortar to which ash has been added, either to blacken the color of the mortar for pointing or to reduce the cost.

Blank door
A recess in a wall, having the appearance of a door; usually used for symmetry of design. Also, any door that has been sealed off but is still visible on the surface.

Blank window
A recess in an exterior wall, having the external appearance of a window; a window that has been sealed off, but is still visible.

Blanket insulation
Thermal insulation in a rolled sheet form, with a flexible lightweight blanket of mineral wool or a similar material; often backed with a vapor barrier, such as felt-treated paper or vinyl sheeting.

Blast cleaning
Any cleaning method which uses air, liquid, or abrasive cleaners under pressure.

Bleaching
In wood finishing, the cleansing or whitening by the use of acid.

Bleeder tile
Tile placed in the foundation wall to allow surface water that is collected on the outside tile drains to connect to drain tile on the inside of the foundation wall.

Bleeding
In concrete work, excessive water rising to the surface of freshly placed concrete. This leaves behind a network of interconnected voids that reduces both the strength and the durability of the concrete.

Blemish
A minor defect in appearance that does not affect the durability or strength of wood, marble, or other material.

Blight
A deteriorating influence or condition that affects the value of a property or real estate. Any depleted tenement house district or any type of hazardous-use unit may be considered a blight on the neighboring real estate or property.

Blind arcade
An arcade without any actual openings; applied as decoration to a wall surface.

Blind arch
An arch within a wall containing a recessed flat wall rather than framing an opening. Used to enrich an unrelieved expanse of masonry, or to fill an existing arched opening.

Blind door
The representation of a door, inserted to complete a series of doors or to give the appearance of symmetry.

Blind dowel
A dowel that joins two pieces together, but cannot be seen once the connection is made as the dowel is inserted into holes that are not drilled completely through either piece.

Blind hinge
A cabinet or door hinge installed in a way that it is not visible when the door is closed.

Blind joint
A joint that is invisible.

Blind mortise
Any mortise that does not pass entirely through the material, but is cut only partway through.

Blind nailing
Driving nails in such a way that the holes are concealed, such as used in nailing tongue-and-groove flooring. Also called *secret nailing*.

Blind pocket
A pocket in the ceiling at a window head to accommodate a venetian blind when raised.

Blind story
A floor level without exterior windows.

Blistering
In painting, a defect arising on a painted surface due to being subjected to heat or moisture.

Block
A masonry unit, or a solid piece of wood or other material; a large piece of stone, taken from the quarry to the mill for sawing and further working. Also, a piece of wood used as a spacer.

Block and tackle
A device for gaining a mechanical advantage for lifting a heavy load; consists of two or more blocks with pulleys connected by rope. The mechanical advantage is equal to the number of ropes that support the load.

Blocked joint
A joint formed by holding two abutting members together through the use of a third member placed at the intersection of the two members.

Blocking
Pieces of wood used to secure, join, or reinforce framing members or to fill spaces between them.

Bloom
An efflorescence which appears on masonry walls; occurs most often within the first year after building.

Blower
A heavy-duty fan that forces air through ducts.

Blowtorch
A portable device which is used by plumbers, painters, and electricians to apply intense local heat. Consists of a tank that can be hand-pumped to create pressure and a nozzle that is opened and ignited, allowing the fuel within to be delivered with force.

Blue line print
A print of the architectural drawings reproduced on sensitized paper producing blue lines on a white background, the opposite of the archaic blueprint method. See also *Blueprint*.

Blueprint
An obsolete method of producing prints of original drawings, which were produced by exposing the drawing and paper to light and washing it out in water, where the lines turn out white on a blue background. Now refers to any reproduction method regardless of the color of the line. See also *Blue line print*.

Bluestone
A dense fine-grained sandstone that splits easily along bedding planes to form thin slabs.

Board
A long thin piece of lumber cut from a log; typically with a rectangular cross-section; can be hand-hewn, hand-sawn, or mill-sawn.

Board and batten
A form of sheathing for wood frame buildings consisting of wide boards, usually placed vertically, whose joints are covered by narrow strips of wood over the joints or cracks.

Board foot
A method of measuring lumber; 1 square foot, 1 inch thick, equals 1 board foot.

Board measure
A system of measurement for lumber. The unit of measure is one board foot; a piece of lumber 1 foot square and 1 inch thick.

Board sheathing
A waterproof, insulating, composition board which is made in large sheets of various dimensions.

Boards
Yard lumber 8 inches or more in width and less than 2 inches thick.

BOCA
Abbreviation for Building Officials and Code Administrators International, authors of the BOCA National Building Code.

Bolection molding
A molding projecting beyond the surface of the work that it decorates, such as between a panel and the surrounding stiles and rails; often used to conceal a joint when the joining surfaces are at different levels.

Bolster
A horizontal piece of timber that caps a column, pillar, or post to provide a greater bearing area to support a load from above; often has a carved profile.

Bolt
A metal connector, with a head on one end and a threaded section on the other where a nut can be installed. Most bolts have a hexagonal square head for tightening with a wrench; however, some smaller bolts have a round head with a slot for a screwdriver. Types include anchor bolt, carriage bolt, lag bolt, machine bolt, molly bolt, stove bolt, stud bolt, toggle bolt, and U-bolt.

Bolted connection
An assembly of structural members with plates and bolts, as opposed to a riveted or welded connection.

Bond
(1) A guarantee by a bonding company that an obligation described in a contract will be fulfilled regardless of any failure on the part of the contractor. Types include bid bond, completion bond, contract bond, payment bond, performance bond, and roofing bond.
(2) An arrangement of masonry units to provide strength, stability, and in some cases beauty by setting a pattern of overlapping units that may be connected with metal ties. Some units may extend into adjacent courses or extend through the wall, and vertical joints are not continuous. Adhesion exists between the mortar and the masonry units, or with the steel reinforcement.

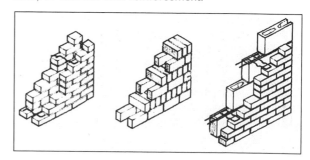

Bond beam
A reinforced concrete beam installed horizontally in a masonry wall to reduce the possibility of cracking.

Bond breaker
A material placed between other material to prevent bonding, such as a material coated on a concrete form before the concrete is poured so it will not stick to the forms.

Bond timber
Horizontal timbers once used as a bond for a brick wall.

Bonded roof
A roofing guarantee by a manufacturer covering materials and workmanship for a specified number of years, which may or may not be purchased by the owner.

Bonding capacity
The maximum total contract value that a bonding company will extend to a contractor in performance bonds, based on the contractor's credit standing and financial history.

Bonding company
A firm providing a surety bond for work to be performed by a contractor, or labor and materials furnished, payable to the owner in the event of default by the contractor.

Bonnet
A small, self-supporting protective hood or roof over an exterior doorway; may be constructed of any exterior material.

Bonus
A sum of money given in excess of a contractual amount for specific performance, such as finishing the project in less time than the contract calls for.

Bonus and penalty clause
A clause in the contract assigning a bonus payment to the contractor if the project is completed ahead of schedule. It also may contain a charge against the contractor for running past the completion date.

Book matched
Assembling wood veneer or sliced marble, alternating face up and face down so that the grain on pairs of pieces looks like a mirror image aligned at the center; also known as herringbone matched.

Boom
A cantilevered or projecting structural member, such as a beam or spar, that is used to support, hoist, or move a load.

Bootleg conversion
An illegal change in a structure that is against applicable zoning regulations, such as partitioning a single-family dwelling into additional units.

Bored pile
A pile formed by pouring concrete into a hole in the ground, usually containing some steel reinforcing, as opposed to a precast pile driven into the ground with a pile driver.

Borehole sample
A core sample obtained by boring or drilling for the purpose of determining the nature of the foundation material.

Borescope
A device for examining hidden areas in an existing structure, consisting of a flexible rod of fiber optics. One bundle of fibers carries light to the ends of the fibers; the other bundle is used for viewing or recording the image with a video camera.

Boring
The process of making holes in wood or metal for the insertion of bolts or other fasteners used in building construction.

Boring log
A description of the sequential layers of soil obtained from a soil boring, as to classification, moisture content, and color.

Bottom chord
The lower longitudinal member of a truss.

Bottom rail
The lowest horizontal member of a window sash or door.

Boundary
The outer limits of an area, such as a piece of property. A boundary may be defined by a series of markers, fence, or stone wall, or by some natural feature.

Boundary marker

A device located on a piece of land to indicate a boundary. May consist of a wooden stake, surveyor's marker, or monument located at a point where the perimeter changes directions, as indicated on a plot map.

Boundary survey

A perimeter survey made by a surveyor according to the distances and bearings contained in the land description. Permanent markers are usually set at all corners and changes of direction.

Bow

The distortion of a wooden board in which the face is either convex or concave along its length.

Bowstring truss

A truss with one curved member in the shape of a bow and a straight or cambered member, which ties together the two ends of the bow at the bearing points.

Box beam

One or more vertical plywood webs laminated to seasoned wood flanges. Vertical spacers separate the flanges at intervals along the length of the beam to distribute the loads and to provide stiffness.

Box bolt

A bolt similar to a barrel bolt except that it is square or flat in section.

Box column

A hollow, built-up column constructed of wood or metal, usually rectangular or square in section.

Box frame

The assembly of a sliding sash window where the sashes are counterbalanced by weights encased in a boxed wooden framework.

Box girder

A hollow beam with either a square, rectangular, or circular cross-section; sometimes vertical instead of horizontal, and attached firmly to the ground like a cantilever.

Box gutter

A gutter built into a roof, consisting of a horizontal trough of wood lined with galvanized iron, tin, or copper to make it water-tight.

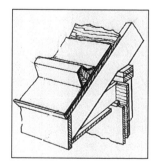

Box nail

Similar in appearance to a common nail, except thinner and only available from 2d (penny) to 40d (penny) in size. These nails are used for nailing wood that splits easily.

Box stair

An interior staircase constructed with a closed string on both sides, often enclosed by walls or partitions with door openings at various floor levels.

Box wrench

A wrench with a fixed end that is designed to fit a specific size nut; the portion of the wrench that grips the nut is a closed circle with a knurled inner surface for gripping the nut.

Boxed cornice

A cornice that is enclosed by boards and moldings so that the lower ends of the rafters are not visible. Also, a hollow cornice, built up of boards and moldings, resulting in a soffit under the eaves.

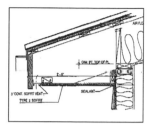

Boxed out

Rectangular or square framing around an opening or penetration, such as around a vertical pipe.

Box-head window

A double-hung window constructed so that the sashes can slide vertically into a recess at the head of the window, to provide a maximum opening for ventilation.

Brace

(1) A metal or wood member used to stiffen or support a structure, a strut that supports or fixes another member in position, or a tie used for the same purpose. (2) A hand-powered crank used with a drill bit to bore holes, or with a screwdriver to turn screws. Some are equipped with a ratchet, facilitating working in tight places. See also *Brace bit*.

Brace bit

A drill tool held in a brace for boring holes in wood.

Braced frame

The frame of a building in which resistance to lateral forces is provided by diagonal bracing, knee-bracing, or cross-bracing; sometimes uses girts that are mortised into solid posts, which are full frame height.

Braced framing

A framing system using heavy posts at the corners and at several intermediate points, connected by large horizontal members and a system of diagonal bracing to produce a rigid frame.

Bracing
The ties used for supporting and strengthening the various parts of a building, such as between studs or joists.

Bracket
A projection from a vertical surface providing structural or visual support under cornices, balconies, windows, or any other overhanging member.

Bracketed cornice
A deep cornice supported by ornamental brackets, sometimes in pairs; used in the Italianate and Prairie styles.

Bracketed hood
A projecting surface that is supported on brackets above a door or window; provides shelter or serves as ornamentation.

Brad
A very small, thin finish nail without a flat head.

Braided wire
A conductor composed of a number of small wires twisted together.

Branch circuit
In electrical wiring, a series of individual circuits that feed power to different parts of a house or structure. This reduces the size of wire needed for the branches, and allows portions of the electrical system to be shut off independently of the others.

Branch control center
An assembly of circuit breakers for the protection of branch circuits feeding from the control center.

Branch drain
A drainpipe that connects between a soil pipe, or sanitary fitting, and the main drainpipe.

Branch duct
A smaller duct in a heating, ventilation, and air-conditioning (HVAC) system that branches from the main duct. At each branch the cross-sectional area of the main duct is decreased.

Branch pipe
A length of pipe for a drain or vent that connects to a main drain or vent stack.

Branch vent
A vent connecting one or more individual vents to a vent stack.

Brass
Any copper alloy having zinc as the principal alloying element, but often with small quantities of other elements.

Brazing
Similar to welding, using a metal rod with a lower melting point than the metals to be joined. The rod melts to join the metals.

Breach of contract
A failure to carry out the terms of a legal contract.

Break ground
The first work performed when excavation is begun for a new structure.

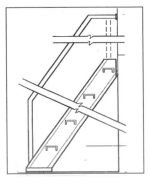

Break line
In drafting, a standard line and symbol used to indicate a missing part of the drawing. Used in pairs, it indicates that the object continues in the same configuration within the breaks.

Breakeven multiplier
A factor used to multiply all the relevant expenses to determine the amount billable to the client. It does not include profit.

Breaking of joints
Staggering joints to prevent a straight line of vertical joints, which weakens the bond.

Breakout schedule
A job-site schedule outlining all the day-to-day activities to all working levels on a project.

Breastsummer
Originally a long, heavy timber beam carrying the frontage of a building. Also, a very large lintel supporting a masonry or brick wall above an opening.

Brick
A solid or hollow masonry unit of clay mixed with sand, which is molded into a small rectangular shape while in a plastic state, then baked in a kiln or dried in the sun.

Brick bat
A broken or cut brick that has one complete end remaining and is less than half a full brick in length, used only where partial bricks are needed in wall construction.

Brick construction
A type of construction where the exterior walls are load-bearing walls, built of brick or a combination of brick and concrete block.

Brick facing
See *Brick veneer*.

Brick hammer
A tool used by bricklayers for dressing bricks, or for breaking them. It has a square flat head with sharp edges and a long curved blade with a chisel point on the other end. See also *Brickset*.

Brick molding
A wood molding used to cover the gap between a door or window frame and the masonry reveal into which the frame is set.

Brick nogging
Brickwork used to fill in the spaces between studs or timbers in a wood-framed wall.

Brick on edge
A coping or sill of headers laid on edge. Also called a *soldier course*.

Brick trowel
A flat triangular-shaped trowel used for picking up mortar and spreading it on the bedding plane.

Brick veneer
A type of building in which a wood frame or concrete block backing has an exterior surface of brick applied in one layer over the backing.

Brickset
A wide, chisel-like tool used to cut bricks when exact surfaces are required. A brick hammer is used to drive the brickset into the brick, splitting it into the desired size and shape.

Bridge
A structure spanning and providing passage over a waterway, railroad, roadway, or other obstacle.

Bridge crane
A hoisting device that traverses laterally across a bridge that traverses longitudinally along two overhead rails; usually a permanent setup.

Bridging
A series of braces placed between parallel framing members to prevent rotation about their vertical axes. Also called *bracing, cross supports*.

Bridle joint
In carpentry a joint in which a slotted end of one timber accepts the double-notched end of another timber; used to connect a rafter to a tie beam or two rafters at a ridge.

Brief
The detailed instructions given by a client to a design professional that outlines the client's program and requirements for a project.

British thermal unit (BTU)
The amount of heat required to raise the temperature of 1 pound of water 1 degree Farenheit.

Broken and dotted line
In an architectural drawing, a line that is made up of a dot and longer dash in consecutive order, for indicating projections above the plane of the drawing.

Broken joint
A joint in which the masonry pieces are installed so that they are not aligned with each other, but instead are alternating; used in flooring and brickwork.

Broken pediment
A pediment with its raking cornice split apart at the center; the gap is often filled with a cartouche, urn, or other ornament.

Bronze
An alloy of copper and tin, bronze in color, having a substantial admixture of copper to modify the properties of the principal element, as aluminum, bronze, and magnesium bronze. It is subject to corrosion caused by water, air, and salt compounds causing pitting of the surface.

Broom clean
The amount of cleanup to be done upon completion of the project; meaning sweeping, removing debris, and performing a light general cleaning of the structure, or portion of work.

Broom finish
A finish made by dragging a stiff broom across freshly placed concrete to provide a slip-resistant surface when hardened.

Brownstone
A dark brown or reddish-brown sandstone, used extensively for building in the United States during the middle and late nineteenth century.

Brownfield remediation
The following steps can be taken to clean up a brownfield area. Tanks, drums, and pipes that leak must be removed; soil may be removed and treated off-site with microorganisms; construction that has been contaminated can be demolished; lead paint can be removed by chemical peels; and hazardous materials can be encapsulated and bagged for removal.

Brushed surface
A texture obtained by brushing slightly hardened concrete with a stiff brush; to create a sandy texture that provides resistance to slipping when hardened.

Buck
The framing around an opening in a wall. A door buck encloses the opening in which a door is placed. Also called *doorframe*.

Buckle
A condition of bending under a compressive load. Very thin members may spring back if the load is removed. If the load continues and buckling continues above the yield point, the member will fail.

Budget
The planned allocation of money for all necessary resources on a project, such as professional fees, construction costs, or furnishings and fixtures. The planned cost of materials is usually subdivided into quantity and unit cost. The planned cost of labor is usually subdivided into estimated hours required multiplied by the prevailing wage rate.

Budgeting
The systematic planning of funds by the owner to cover specific anticipated costs, such as professional services, or cost of construction.

Buggy
A manual or powered vehicle used to transport fresh concrete from the mixer to the location where the concrete is to be placed.

Builder
A person who directs or performs the construction or renovation of a house or other structure. Also called *contractor.*

Builder's acid
A diluted solution of acid and water used to remove mortar stains from brick.

Builder's hardware
All hardware used in the construction of a building, such as joist hangers, brackets, structural shapes, door locks, and the like.

Builder's level
A telescope-like instrument, incorporating a bubble level that mounts on a tripod; used for laying out stakes and string lines.

Builder's risk insurance
A form of property insurance to cover work under construction.

Builder's tape
A measuring tape, either 25, 50, or 100 feet in length, made of steel and enclosed in a circular case with a retractable rewinding mechanism or a handle for rewinding.

Building
An enclosed and permanent structure for residential, commercial, industrial, or institutional use.

Building area
The total area of a site covered by buildings, as measured on a horizontal plane at ground level. Terraces and uncovered porches are usually not included in this total.

Building automation system
A network of integrated computer systems that automatically controls a range of building operations, such as heating, ventilation, and air-conditioning (HVAC), security, access control, lighting, energy management, maintenance, and fire safety control.

Building code
Local and national regulations that control design procedures and materials used in construction and renovation are based on public health and safety

standards. Codes are designed for new construction, but they are also applied to old buildings when substantial remodeling, renovation, or adaptive use is undertaken. They are a challenge to preservationists who want to maintain a property and still adhere to the requirements of the current safety codes. Three of the four national code organizations approved amendments in 1975 to deal with the special problems of historic buildings meeting the standards of public safety. Also called *building regulations.*

Building component
An element manufactured as an independent unit, which can be joined with other elements, including electrical, fire protection, mechanical, plumbing, structural, and all other systems affecting health and safety.

Building drain
The part of the plumbing system that receives discharge from soil, waste, and other stacks throughout a building.

Building envelope
The outer shape of a building. The maximum extent of the envelope of any building type may be defined by zoning laws.

Building environment
The combination of conditions that affect a person, piece of equipment, or system in a building, such as lighting, noise, temperature, and relative humidity.

Building grade
The ground elevation. Building grade is established by a regulating authority that determines the height of a building in a specific area.

Building height
The vertical distance measured from the grade level to a flat roof or to the average height of a pitched, gable, hip, or gambrel roof, not including bulkheads or penthouses.

Building industry
The general term used to include building, civil, mechanical, and electrical engineering.

Building inspector
A member of the building department who inspects construction to determine its conformity to the building code and the approved plans or who inspects occupied buildings for violations of the building code.

Building line
A line or lines established by law or agreement, usually parallel to the property lines, beyond which a structure may not extend; usually does not apply to uncovered entrance platforms or terraces. Also called *setback*.

Building material
Any material used in the construction or reconstruction of buildings, such as steel, concrete, brick, masonry, glass, and wood.

Building occupancy
The use or intended use of a building or structure, such as residential or commercial. The classification is used in building codes to outline the level of fire hazard for each use, and restrict the size and type of construction and means of egress permitted.

Building official
The person who administers enforcement of the applicable building code, or a duly authorized representative.

Building paper
A heavy, waterproof paper usually impregnated with tar and used over sheathing and subfloors to prevent the passage of moisture. Also called *felt, tar paper, sheathing, paper, roll roofing*.

Building permit
A written document that is granted by the municipal agency having jurisdiction, authorizing an applicant to proceed with construction of a specific project after the plans have been filed and reviewed.

Building program
The procedure proposed for solving the client's design problem. The building program explains the context, conditions, requirements, and objectives for the design and construction of the project.

Building restriction
Any of a number of restrictions imposed on the construction of a building or the use of land; may be included in a code or in other documents, such as a restrictive covenant.

Building services
The utilities and services supplied and distributed within a building, including heating, air-conditioning, lighting, water supply, drainage, gas and electric supply, fire protection, and security protection.

Building stone
Any stone that can be used in exterior construction, including granite, limestone, sandstone, brownstone, and marble.

Building subsystem
An assembly of components that performs a specific function in a building; for example, an air-conditioning system consisting of its components, such as ductwork, a fan, air diffusers, and controls.

Building survey
Detailed record of the present condition of a structure.

Building systems
Plans, specifications, and documentation for systems of building components, including structural, electrical, mechanical, plumbing, and fire protection systems.

Building trade
In building construction the classification of work, such as site work, masonry, ironwork, carpentry, millwork, roofing, plaster, drywall, painting, elevator, plumbing and sprinklers, mechanical, and electrical.

Building trades
All the various skilled and semi-skilled workers involved in the construction of a building, such as laborers, carpenters, plumbers, electricians, drywall experts, and the like.

Built environment
The physical surroundings created by humans as opposed to the natural environment.

Built up
Refers to a structural member made up of two or more parts fastened together so they act as a single unit.

Built-in
A builder's term for furniture that is fitted into a special position in a house.

Built-in cabinets
Any cabinet permanently fixed in position, by being built into the wall of the room.

Built-in furniture
Any item of furniture such as a cupboard, cabinet, bookcase, seating, or other item that is permanently built into the building. See also *Built-ins*.

Built-in nailing block
A wood block built into a masonry wall for use as a nailing block or anchor block.

Built-ins
Items included as an integral part of the structure such as bookcases, cabinets, bars, window seats, or other similar items.

Built-up beam
A beam composed of multiple parts, such as a box beam, compound beam, lattice beam, and angle girder.

Built-up column
A column composed of more than one piece.

Built-up member
A single component assembled from several other pieces fastened together with glue, bolts, nails, or screws.

Built-up roofing
A flat roof covered with multiple layers of roofing felt, secured with layers of hot tar, and topped with a layer of crushed stone.

Built-up steel lintel
A lintel fabricated by fastening two or more pieces of structural steel to act as one unit.

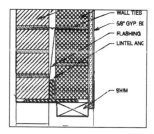

Built-up timber
Several pieces of timber fastened together with glue, nails, bolts, or other connectors that perform as a single member.

Bulkhead
A horizontal or inclined door over a stairway giving access to a cellar; a structure on the roof of a building covering a water tank, shaft, or service equipment.

Bulkhead door
A door, usually constructed of wood, that provides access to a roof or cellar bulkhead.

Bulkhead formwork
Temporary formwork that closes the end of a form at a planned construction joint.

Bulking
The increase in size of material due to the absorption of moisture.

Bull header
A brick made with one long corner rounded or angled, used for sills and corners.

Bulldozer
A tractor with caterpillar treads and a broad, blunt ram, which is used to push away debris for clearing an area or to demolish small buildings.

Bull-nosed step
A step, usually the lowest in a flight, having one or both ends rounded to a semicircle and projecting beyond the face of the stair string. The projection extends beyond and around the newel post.

Bundle
A grouping of items that are bound together, such as a quantity of shingles or shakes held together by wire for ease of handling.

Bundled bars
A group of parallel contiguous reinforcing bars tied together in a bundle.

Burden
The efforts required to carry the indirect expenses of the firm.

Burl
A decorative pattern in wood caused by adjacent knots.

Burlap
A coarse fabric used as a water-retaining covering while concrete is curing.

Burr
A ragged, sharp, projecting edge of particles of material produced by the use of a cutting tool.

Bus bar
A copper strip run on a switch and panel board from which all circuits are tapped. Also, a large copper bar to which the main feeders or circuits are connected.

Bus duct
A prefabricated unit consisting of a metal bar that provides a common connection for two or more circuits.

Bush-hammered finish
A stone or concrete surface dressed with a bush hammer; used decoratively, or to provide a roughened surface for treads, floors, and pavement requiring greater traction.

Bushing
A cylindrical lining for an opening, used to limit the size of the opening, to resist abrasion, or to act as a guide; a short threaded piece of pipe used to link other pipes in a plumbing system. They have male threads on one end and female threads on the other end, and are available in a variety of sizes.

Business plan
A devised plan that defines the strategies and tactics of the business and financial aspects of a firm or company.

Butt hinge
A hinge mortised into the edge of a door and the face of the jamb it meets when the door is closed. Only the knuckle of the hinge is visible when the door is closed.

Butt joint
A plain square joint between two members, when the contact surfaces are cut at right angles to the faces of the pieces. The two are filled squarely against each other rather than lapped.

Butt splice
A butt joint that is further secured by nailing a piece of wood to each side of it.

Butt weld
A welded joint connecting two pieces of metal in the same plane.

Buttering
Placing mortar on a masonry unit with a trowel.

Buttress
An exterior mass of masonry projecting from the wall to absorb the lateral thrusts from roof vaults; either unbroken in their height or broken into stages, with a successive reduction in their projection and width. Stages are generally sloped at a very acute angle and terminate at the top with a plain slope ending at the wall or with a triangular pediment. Also called *support*.

Butt-welded splice
A reinforcing bar splice, made by welding the butted ends of the bars; stronger than a lap splice, where the bars are overlapped a certain distance and tied with wires.

Butyl caulking
A rubber-based caulk with good weather resistance and elasticity. It works well between dissimilar materials and lasts up to 20 years. It is good where there is a lot of movement, but difficult to work once it has been installed.

BX cable
Insulated flexible electric wire that is spiral wrapped with steel. Same as armored cable. Not permitted after 1950, when it was replaced with wire carrying a ground. Also called *armored cable, conduit, metal casing*.

Bypass
A secondary pipe or duct providing an alternative route around an obstruction, usually controlled by a damper or valve, and connected back with the main passage.

C

Cabin
A small house that may have only one room.

Cabinet
A built-in or free-standing piece of furniture fitted with drawers and/or shelves, typically behind one or a pair of doors.

Cabinet door
A door used in cabinet construction.

Cabinet drawer
A drawer built into a cabinet, often with a decorative finished face on the front of the drawer.

Cabinetmaker
A craftsperson specializing in fine joinery, with the skills, materials, and tools necessary to make furniture and other pieces of woodwork.

Cabinetwork
Interior finish carpentry on all built-ins, including drawers, shelves, and cabinets.

Cable
Wires encased in an insulating sheath, used in an electrical system.

Cable box
A box which protects the connections or splices that join cables of one circuit to another.

Cable plan
A drawing prepared by the architect, or electrical system designer, for the electrician to use in wiring the building; it shows cable routing, electrical terminations, and the number of wires for each box. See also *Electrical diagram*.

Cable splice
A connection between two cables in an electrical circuit. Also, in construction, the joining of two wire rope cables by interweaving the wire strands.

Cable tray
A tray with a ladder-type bottom and side rails used to support electrical cables, where many are run side by side. The tray is supported or suspended from the framework and becomes a permanent part of the structure. See also *Cable tray support*.

Cable tray support
A structure or support to carry the load from cable trays.

CABO
Abbreviation for Council of American Building Officials.

CADD
Abbreviation for Computer Aided Design and Drafting.

Cage
A framework of reinforcing bars wired together, or an enclosure of slats and bars.

Caisson
A watertight box or circular tube used for surrounding foundation work on any structure that is below water.

Caisson

Also, a large diameter steel pipe used to buttress foundation sheet pilings until a slurry wall can be built.

Caisson pile
A cast-in-place concrete pile, made by driving a steel tube into the earth, excavating it, and filling it with concrete.

Calcium chloride
A salt granulate sometimes used with water in mixing concrete and mortar to speed up the setting time of concrete. See also *Accelerator*.

Calendar
A table showing the months, weeks, and days in at least one specific year. Used in scheduling the project activities by identifying working days, holidays, and the length of the working day in time units.

Caliper
A tool with two legs joined at one end, at least one of which is adjustable, and may be moved in relation to the other. The legs curve inward for measuring outside dimensions, and the legs curve outward for measuring inside dimensions.

Camber
A slight convex curvature intentionally built into a beam, girder, or truss to compensate for an anticipated deflection so that it will not sag under load. Also, any curved surface designed to facilitate the runoff of water.

Came
A slender rod of cast lead, used in casements and stained-glass windows to hold the panes of glass.

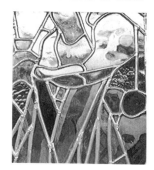

Canal

A channel or groove as in the recessed portions of the face of a triglyph.

Canopy

A decorative hood above a niche, pulpit, or stall; also a covered area that extends from the wall of a building, protecting an enclosure. *Also called awning, overhang.*

Cant molding

A square or rectangular molding having the outside face beveled.

Cant strip

A beveled piece of wood used under built-up roofing, providing a transition from a horizontal plane to a vertical parapet.

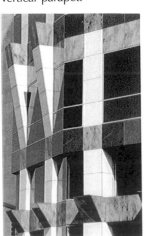

Cant wall

A wall canted in elevation from true vertical.

Cantilever

A form that has rigid structural members or surfaces that project significantly beyond their vertical support.

Cantilever joists

Short joists used to support a projecting balcony, bay window, or cornice where the overhang is parallel to the main framing joists.

Cantilever step

A step built into the wall at one end but supported at the other end only by the steps below.

Cap flashing

Flashing inserted into masonry joints and folded or crimped to produce a slanted vertical profile and used to cover the base flashing on a roof parapet. See also *Counterflashing.*

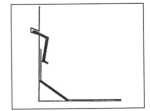

Cap molding

Trim at the top of a window or door, above the casing.

Capillary action

The movement of a liquid, such as water, into small spaces by molecular attraction.

Capital

The upper member of a column, pillar, pier, or pilaster, crowning the shaft; usually decorated. It may carry an architrave, arcade, or impost block.

Capital cost
The prime cost of construction, including acquisition of the land or existing structure, design, materials, equipment, and the actual erection or renovation.

Capital improvement
A significant improvement to real estate that extends the lifetime or increases the property's value; methods used include additions, renovations, replacement of mechanical equipment, or adaptive reuse through new construction, as opposed to maintenance work such as painting.

Capital value
The market value of a parcel of land or building, less the mortgage or other debts against it.

Capping brick
Bricks that are specially shaped for capping the exposed top of a wall. Same as *Coping brick*.

Capstan
A hoist consisting of a cable wound around a drum that is turned by a motor, which hoists a load.

Capstone
The stones that make up the coping on a wall or parapet.

Capturing space
Gaining additional space in a structure without adding on to it, such as reclaiming the attic or basement space. By adding space vertically, the cost of site work and additional foundations is saved.

Carbon arc welding
A carbon electrode is used to produce an electric arc that acts as a heat source that welds the metal with or without the addition of filler metal.

Carborundum
A trade name for a tough abrasive made of alumina, silicon carbide, and other material, used for abrasion.

Carborundum cloth
An abrasive cloth or paper made by covering the material with powdered carborundum held in place by an adhesive.

Carborundum stone
An abrasive stone, made of carborundum; used for sharpening tools such as plane bits and chisels.

Carpenter
A craftsperson who is skilled in the transformation of lumber into framing and enclosing a structure.

Carpenter's level
A bubble level, or levels, mounted in a long wooden or aluminum member; used to level horizontal surfaces and plumb vertical surfaces.

Carpenter's pencil
A flat wide pencil with a durable lead used by carpenters for marking measurements on the job.

Carpentry
Work which is performed in cutting, framing, and joining pieces of timber in the construction of buildings or other structures.

Carport
An open-sided garage attached to a building. A carport has a roof but only one or two side walls; it is generally found in milder climates.

Carriage
The framing members that support the treads of a staircase. Also called a *stringer*.

Carriage bolt
A round-headed bolt, which is usually square in section below the head to prevent the bolt from turning while it is being tightened or loosened with a nut. Also called a *Square bolt*.

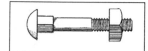

Carrying capacity
In electrical work, the amount of current or load that a wire can carry without becoming overheated.

Carver
A craftsperson who is skilled in the ornamental engraving and cutting of wood or stone, in various forms of relief.

Cased
Any structural member covered with a different material, usually of better quality.

Cased frame
The wood frame of a double-hung window, including hollow jambs which contain the sash pockets.

Cased opening
Any opening trimmed with casing but without a sash or door placed inside it.

Casein paint
A water-based paint, used in fresco painting on wet plaster.

Casement adjuster
A handle or rod for adjusting the sash of a casement window in an open position; a handle and cranking mechanism are also used on some wooden models.

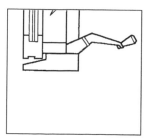

Casement frame
A frame of wood or metal enclosing part or all of the sash which may be opened by means of hinges attached to the outside vertical edges.

Casement window
A window ventilating sash, fixed at the sides of the opening into which it is fitted, which swings open on hinges along its entire length. Also called *hinged window*.

Casework
The assembled frame, shelves, doors, and drawers which make up a case or cabinet.

Cash accounting
Recording transactions as they occur, either money paid out or received.

Cash allowance
An amount of money outlined in the contract documents for inclusion in the contract sum to cover the cost of certain prescribed items not specified in detail.

Cash flow
The measure of liquidity of a business, by the rate of income.

Cash flow statement
A financial statement that shows the receipt and dispersal of cash during a given time period.

Casing
The exposed trim, flat or molded, molding, framing, or lining around a door or window; finished millwork, of uniform profile, that covers or encases a structural member such as a post or beam. Also called *window frame, door frame.*

Casing nail
A wire nail with a flared head; used for outside finishing and for nailing flooring.

Cast
An impression taken in wax, plaster of paris, or other plastic substance; used in renovation work in making replicas of missing components such as architectural moldings and ornamentation.

Cast iron
A hard, nonmalleable iron alloy containing carbon and silicon, which is poured into a sand mold and then machined to a desired architectural shape.

Cast stone
A mixture of fine stone chips and portland cement in a matrix. Once cast, it may be ground, polished, or otherwise treated to simulate natural stone.

Castellated nut
A nut whose top surface is notched, and can be locked into place by inserting a cotter pin through a hole in the shaft on which the nut is threaded, preventing the nut from turning.

Cast-in-place concrete
Concrete that is deposited in the place where it will harden as an integral part of the structure, as opposed to precast concrete.

Cast-iron lacework
A panel of ironwork employing an intricate ornamental design that is formed by a mass-produced casting process.

Cast-iron pipe
Pipes and fittings made of cast iron; used for drains and sewer pipes.

Caulk
Soft pliable materials used to seal gaps in framed openings. See *Adhesive caulking, Aerosol caulking, Butyl rubber caulking, Oil-based caulking,* and *Silicone caulking.*

Caulking
The process of making a joint watertight by using flexible sealants such as mastics, rubber, and silicone. Also called *sealer.*

Caulking compound
A soft material intended for sealing joints in buildings, preventing leakage, or providing a seal at expansion joints. Also called *grout.*

Caulking gun

A tool used to apply water-proofing material; consisting of a barrel with a small nozzle and a plunger operated by a ratcheted rod which pushes the caulking from an inserted tube out the nozzle in a controlled bead.

Caulking tool

A chisel-like offset tool used to drive tarred oakum into joints in cast-iron plumbing pipes.

Cavity wall

An exterior wall of masonry, consisting of an outer and inner course separated by a continuous airspace, connected together by wire or sheet-metal ties. The dead airspace provides improved thermal insulation, since moisture which collects inside can run out of weep holes instead of going through to the inside wall. Also called *hollow wall*.

C-clamp

A clamping device for securing wood or metal pieces in a fixed position. Consisting of jaws from 1 to 8 inches.

Cedar

A highly aromatic, moderately high-density, fine-textured wood of a distinctive red color with white streaks; widely used for fence posts, shingles, and closet linings.

Cedar shakes

A thick and rough shingle, hand cut from heartwood.

Cedar shingles

Shingles cut by machine from the heartwood of western red cedar and installed in courses as roofing and siding; fastened with hot-dipped galvanized nails. They are reddish-brown when installed and weather to a gray color.

Ceiling

The underside covering of a roof or floor; generally used to conceal the structural members from the room or roof above, or the underside surface of vaulting. It may have a flat or curved surface. It may be suspended from the structure above or placed in between exposed beams. It may also be left with all the elements exposed.

Ceiling diffuser

An air outlet from an air-conditioning duct, which diffuses the air over a large area to produce an even distribution and avoid drafts.

Ceiling grid

A system of metal supports for a suspended ceiling, typically for acoustical tile, including lighting fixtures or air diffusers.

Ceiling joist

Any joist that carries a ceiling; one of several small beams to which the ceiling of a room is attached. Ceiling joists are mortised into the sides of the main beams or suspended from them by strap hangers.

Ceiling plenum

A space below the floor and above a suspended ceiling that is part of the air distribution system, and accommodates mechanical and electrical equipment.

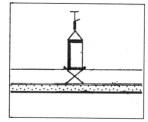

Ceiling suspension system

A grid work of metal rails and hangers erected for the support of a suspended ceiling, and ceiling-mounted items, such as air diffusers, lights, and fire detectors.

Cement

A material, or a mixture of materials without aggregate, which when in a plastic state, possesses adhesive and cohesive properties and hardens in place.

Cement board

A sheet formed from lightweight cement, designed to be used as a waterproof backing behind ceramic tile; usually ½ inch thick and measuring 3 × 4, 3 × 5, and 3 × 6 feet in length. It is installed similarly to drywall with screws and joint tape.

Cement finishing

The process of floating, troweling, and otherwise finishing a concrete surface; done by hand, or with a cement-finishing machine, consisting of a motorized device with rotating smooth steel blades.

Cement grout

A cementitious mixture of portland cement, sand, or other ingredients which produces a uniform paste used to fill joints in masonry units.

Cement gun

A mechanical device used for spraying fine concrete or cement mortar by means of pneumatic pressure.

Cement mason
A trade classification which includes cement finishers, plasterers, and related trades.

Cement mortar
A building material used for installing bricks, blocks, and terra-cotta units composed of portland cement, sand, and water.

Cement paint
A paint that is a mixture of cement and pigment. Also an alkali-resistant substance, such as casein, that is used over cement surfaces.

Cement plaster
A plaster made with portland cement as the binder; sand and lime are added on the job before installation.

Cement stucco dash brush
A stiff brush used to give a stucco effect to a plaster wall. The brush is dipped into the material and used to apply the material onto the surface using varying techniques, such as by swirling or stippling.

Cement tamper
A cement-finishing tool used on concrete slabs to tamp down the coarse aggregate, so that a smoother finish can be obtained.

Cement trowel
A flat, rectangular metal plate with a wooden handle; used to provide a smooth finish to concrete.

Cement-coated nails
Nails with a coating of plastic cement that drive easier and have increased holding power.

Center bit
A drill bit with a small sharp point extending from the cutting end, which is used to precisely locate the center of the hole to be drilled, eliminating the need for a center punch.

Centerline
A line on architectural drawings indicated by a dot and long dash, showing the center of an object, and providing a line from which to lay off measurements.

Center of gravity
The location of a point in a body or shape around which all the parts balance each other.

Center punch
A steel hand tool with a conical point, that makes a small dent in metal to give a starting point for a drilled hole.

Center stringer
The structural member of a stair system that supports the treads and risers at the midpoint of the treads.

Center to center
A linear measurement taken from the middle of one member to the middle of the next member.

Center-hung door
A door that is supported by and swings on a pivot that is recessed in the floor at a point located on the centerline of the door's thickness; may be either single-swing or double-acting.

Centigrade
A temperature scale where 0 degrees is the freezing point of water, and 100 degrees is the boiling point.

Centimeter
One-hundredth (0.001) of a meter in the metric system, and equal to 0.3937 inch.

Central air-conditioning
An air-conditioning system in which the air is treated by equipment at central locations and conveyed to and from these spaces by means of fans and pumps through ducts and pipes.

Central heating
A system in which heat is supplied to all areas of a building from a central plant through a network of ducts or pipes.

Central heating system
Consists of a heat-producing unit, such as an oil or gas burner; a heat exchanger or furnace; distributor, such as pipes for hot water, or ducts for warm air; and a control mechanism, such as a thermostat.

Central system
Utilizing a single source and distribution system for an area, such as central heating and/or air-conditioning system, central power system, and central water system.

Ceramic
Burnt clayware, consisting of a mixture of sand and clay which is shaped, dried, and finally fired in a kiln. Main types include terra-cotta, used mainly for unglazed air bricks, chimney pots, and floor tiles; fire clay, used for flue linings because it is fire resistant; and vitreous china, also used for plumbing fixtures.

Ceramic veneer
Architectural terra-cotta with either ceramic vitreous or glazed surfaces, characterized by large face dimensions and their sections; the back is either scored or ribbed.

Certificate for insurance
A document prepared by an insurance company that states the period of time for which the policy is in place, and the type and amount of coverage.

Certificate for payment
A written document prepared by the architect, engineer, or owner approving payment for work completed by the contractor.

Certificate of insurance
A memorandum stating the type, amount, and effective dates of insurance in force for an insured person, by an authorized representative of an insurance company.

Certificate of occupancy
A written statement signed by a building authority certifying that a structure meets all requirements set forth in the existing ordinances, or that a structure may be used lawfully for specified purposes.

Certificate of substantial completion
A written document, prepared by the architect, engineer, or owner indicating that the project is substantially complete. The document starts the time period for final payment to the contractor.

Certified historic structure
Any structure listed individually on the National Register of Historic Places, or located in a registered historic district, and subject to depreciation, or eligible for tax incentives as defined by the Internal Revenue Code.

Certified rehabilitation
Rehabilitation that the secretary of the interior has determined is consistent with the historic character of the certified property, or the district in which it is located.

Cesspool
A pit or cistern at the end of a drain for the storage of sewage. Also called *Seepage pit*. See also *Septic tank*.

CFM
Abbreviation for cubic feet per minute.

Chain
Interlocked metal links, assembled in various lengths, that can be used for fastening or lifting. See also *Chain hoist*.

Chain hoist
A hoist using a drum and chain mechanism for lifting loads.

Chain saw
A gasoline- or electric-powered saw used for rough sawing of openings. The teeth revolve around an elongated track.

Chain tongs
A device for turning pipe or conduit during installation, consisting of a heavy bar with sharp teeth near one end, which are held against the pipe by a chain wrapped around the pipe and tightened against the bar.

Chain wrench
A pipe wrench used in tight quarters; incorporates a chain with a ratchetlike action.

Chain-link fence
A fence made of heavy steel wire fabric, woven in a diamond pattern, held in place by metal posts.

Chair rail
A horizontal wood strip affixed to a plaster wall at a height that prevents the backs of chairs from damaging the wall surface.

Chalk line
A line made by coating a length of string with chalk, pulling it tight across a piece of material, and snapping it, thus producing a straight chalk line that serves as a guide for cutting the material.

Chalking
Disintegration of paint and other coatings, which produces loose powder at, or just beneath, the surface.

Chamfer stop
Any ornamentation that terminates a chamfer.

Change order
A written order to the contractor signed by the owner and architect or engineer, issued after the execution of a contract, authorizing a change in the work or an adjustment in the contract sum or contract time.

Changes in the work
Additions or revisions ordered by the owner that deviate from the general scope of the contract, and should be authorized by a change order if it involves adjustment to the contract sum or the contract time.

Channel
A rolled iron or steel or extruded aluminum structural member in the shape of a U, with a web and top and bottom flanges that project on the same side as the web; yjey are often installed in a vertical alignment with the web upright, and the shorter flanges in aligned in a horizontal position.

Channel beam
A structural member having a U-shaped cross-section, but installed with the web in the vertical position for greater strength.

Channel column
A steel column made up of a pair of channels attached with plates on the side, so that the channels are facing opposite each other, which creates a box-like column which has added strength.

Channeling
A decorative groove in carpentry or masonry: a series of grooves in an architectural member, such as the flutes in a column.

Chase
A covered recess in a wall that forms a vertical shaft, in which plumbing pipes or electrical wires are inserted.

45

Check
Checks or fissures in wood members; surface checks occur on the outside of a piece; end checks occur on the end of the piece; through checks extend from one surface through to the opposite side.

Check valve
A valve that automatically closes, preventing the backflow of water or other liquid from entering a plumbing system.

Checkerboard placement
The practice of planning a concrete job so that adjacent slabs of concrete can be placed at separate times. This placement method also creates a control joint at each section.

Checkerwork
In a wall or pavement, a pattern formed by laying masonry units so as to produce a checkerboard effect.

Checking
A defect in a coated surface characterized by the appearance of fine cracks in all directions. Also, the cracking of wood grain caused by improper drying.

Checklist
A detailed list of all the elements of a particular job; used to ensure that details are not overlooked in preparing an estimate or at other times during the course of a job.

Cheek
A narrow upright face, forming the end or side of an architectural or structural member, or one side of an opening.

Cheek cut
An oblique cut made in a rafter to permit a tight fit against a hip or valley rafter, or to square the lower end of a jack rafter.

Chemical anchor
A masonry anchor in which a high-strength adhesive is introduced into the hole to bond the bolt to the masonry.

Chemical cleaning
The use of detergent in combination with water to wash a building façade to remove heavy soiling from building stones. Acidic cleaners contain hydrochloric, hydrofluoric, phosphoric, and organic elements, such as acetic and citric acids. Alkaline cleaners based on sodium or potassium hydroxide are used to clean acid-sensitive materials such as limestone and marble.

Cherry
An even-textured, moderately high-density wood, rich red-brown in color; takes a high luster and is used for cabinetwork and paneling.

Cherry picker
Slang term for a relatively small crane mounted on a truck; used for installing items a short distance above the ground; includes a basket where workers can control the positioning of the crane from a working platform.

Chestnut
A light, coarse-grained, medium-hard wood, used for ornamental work and trim.

Chicken wire
A light-gage wire mesh with hexagonal-shaped openings; often used as light reinforcing in slabs to prevent cracking.

Chilled water system
A cooling system where water takes heat from the space to the evaporation section of the cooler, and water is also used to extract the heat from the condenser to the exterior of a building.

Chimney
A vertical noncombustible structure, containing one or more flues to carry smoke from the fireplaces to the outside, usually rising above the roof. Also called *smokestack*.

Chimney

Chimney breast
A projection into a room of the fireplace walls that form the front portion of the chimney stack.

Chimney cap
A cornice forming a crowning termination of a chimney.

Chimney cricket
A small false roof built over the main roof behind a chimney, used to provide protection against water leakage where the chimney penetrates the roof.

Chimney flashing
Any kind of metal or composition material placed around a chimney shaft to protect the roof against moisture from rainwater or snow.

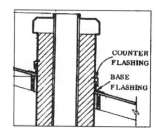

Chimney hood
A covering for a chimney to make it more ornamental, or to prevent rainwater from entering the flue, or to prevent downdrafts.

Chimney lining
Rectangular or round tiles placed within a chimney for protective purposes. The glazed surface of the tile provides resistance to the deteriorating effects of smoke and gas fumes.

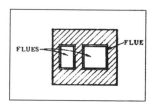

Chimney pot
A cylindrical pipe of brick, terra-cotta, or metal; placed atop a chimney to extend it and thereby increase the draft, often ornamental. Also called *flue cap*.

Chimney stack
That part of a chimney, or group of chimneys, that is carried above the roof of a building.

Chimney throat
That part of a chimney directly above the fireplace where the walls of the flue are brought close together as a means of increasing the draft.

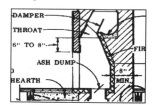

Chinking
Filling the voids between the logs of a log house with a substance, such as mortar or caulking.

Chip
A small piece of stone, wood, or other material cut off from a larger piece by a quick blow with a cutting tool, such as a chip axe.

Chipboard
A flat panel manufactured by bonding flakes of wood with a binder; used for sheathing, subflooring, and cabinetry.

Chipping
A process of cutting off small pieces of metal, wood, or stone with a cold chisel or hammer.

Chipping hammer
A lightweight hammer used by a mason to chip excess material from the back and edges of brick, concrete block, stone, or tile. See also *Mason's hammer*.

Chisel
A tool with a wide variety of uses for cutting. See also *Wood chisel*.

Chisel tooth saw blade
A cutting blade where the teeth and spaces between the teeth permit both crosscut and rip cuts. It is best suited for rough carpentry such as cutting framing members.

Chord
A principal member or pair of members of a truss extending from one end to the other, to resist bending.

Chute
A metal or fiber trough or tube used to transport debris from a scaffolding to a debris box below. Also a means of delivering concrete from the truck into the forms. Also called *trough*.

Cinder block
A building block whose principal materials are cement and cinders; used where appearance is not an issue, or when an insulating block is needed.

Cinder fill
A fill of cinders from 3 to 6 inches deep used under a basement floor as an aid in keeping the basement dry. Also used on the outside of a basement wall to a depth of 12 inches above the drain tile to facilitate drainage.

Cinders
The residue that remains after any material such as coal is burned. Also fragments of unburned lava from a volcano.

CIO
Abbreviation for Committee for Industrial Organizations, which was a labor union organized in 1935 to represent industrial workers. Created as a result of a dispute with the AFL. It was merged with the AFL in 1955. See also *American Federation of Labor*.

Circuit
The path taken by an electric current in flowing through a conductor from one terminal of the source supply to the other.

Circuit breaker
A device, such as the electromagnetic opening of a spring-loaded latch, or the heating of a metallic strip, that stops the flow of current by opening the circuit automatically when more electricity flows through the circuit than it is capable of carrying. Resetting can be automatic or manual.

Circular measure
Measurement in portions of a circle, such as radius, degrees, minutes, or seconds.

Circular saw
A hand held portable power saw with a circular toothed blade, a handle and trigger switch, and an adjustable platform to rest on top of the work to be cut. The circular saw provides a variety of cutting features, such as beveled cutting.

Circular stair
A stair having a cylindrical shape, with an opening in the center.

Circulation
In heating, the movement of air in the ducts, and in the heated spaces. In space planning, the passage from one space to another.

Circulation space
A space within a home or other facility that provides access between functional areas for people, goods, and services. Poor circulation is illustrated on the left below, and good circulation illustrated on the right.

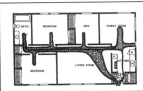
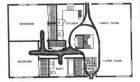

Circumscribe
To draw a line around a figure or object.

City planning
The control of growth or development in a city, town, or community, taking into account transportation, utilities, industry, and other environmental factors.

Civil engineering
A branch of engineering which specializes in the design of roadways, buildings, and bridges.

Civil Rights Act of 1964
A law that makes unlawful the practice of discrimination in matters of employment, education, and housing against any individual because of his or her race, color, religion, sex, or national origin; the Act applies to all construction jobs.

Clad
Covered with another material bonded to the base material; such as a rubber cladding on a metal pipe.

Cladding
The process or the resulting product produced by the bonding of one metal to another, to protect the inner metal from weathering.

Claim
A request by a contractor for additional money for extras for unknown conditions of the job, for anything that causes extra labor or materials, or for an extension of time pursuant to the terms of the contract.

Claims examiner
The supervisor who oversees the paperwork submitted by the field adjuster in an insurance claim.

Clamp
A mechanical device, such as screws and wedges, used to hold items together while other work is being performed.

Clamping time
The length of time that two members are held together with pressure applied by a clamp. The time is determined by the curing time of the adhesive.

Clapboard
A board used for siding, with a tapered cross-section, most commonly called *beveled siding*.

Clapboard siding
A wood siding commonly used as an exterior covering on a building of frame construction, applied horizontally and overlapped, with the grain running lengthwise, thicker along the lower edge than the upper.

Clarification drawings
An illustration provided by an architect or engineer to show more detail on a particular area, or as part of a job order modification.

Classical orders
A set of styles developed over the centuries based on Greek and Roman adaptations. The elements of each order consist of a base, column, and capital and an entablature with architrave, frieze, and cornice. The most common types are the Tuscan, Doric, Ionic, Corinthian, and Composite.

Classroom window
A wide window where the upper part is fixed, and the lower portion has an awning window which pivots inward.

Claw hammer
A carpenter's tool, with one end curved and split for use in pulling nails by providing leverage under the head.

Claw hatchet
A carpenter's hatchet with a notch on one side of the blade for use in pulling out nails.

Clay pipe
A pipe made of clay and glazed to eliminate porosity; used for drainage systems and sanitary sewers.

Clay tile flooring
Burnt clay tiles made in various sizes and thicknesses, usually laid on a concrete base. This type of flooring is most often used for kitchens and bathrooms, porches, vestibules, and fireplace hearths.

Clean room
A special room that is absent of dust, lint, or other particles. Filter systems are high efficiency, and the air change is a one-directional flow.

Cleanout
A unit with removable plate or plug allowing access into plumbing or other drainage pipes for cleaning out extraneous material.

Clear height
The unobstructed vertical distance between the lowest and highest point at any given spot in a structure.

Clear opening
The dimension between the two inside faces of an opening, or the distance between the surfaces of walls in a room.

Clear span
The horizontal distance between the inside faces of the supports on both sides.

Cleat
A small piece of timber or metal fixed to one member and used to reinforce and positively locate or support another member, a strip of wood, or other material applied to the wall, for the purpose of supporting another member fastened to it.

Clench nailing
Driving a nail so that it protrudes through the timber, then bending it over in the direction of the grain for a more secure fastening.

Clerestory
An upper story or row of windows rising above adjoining parts of the roof, designed to admit an increased amount of light into the inner space of the building.

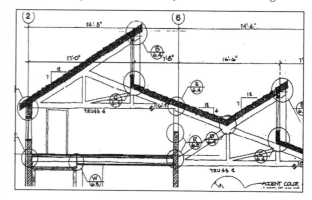

Clerk of the works
An outdated term used to denote the architect's or client's on-site representative for checking that the contractor carries out the work in accordance with the drawings and other contract documents. A person performing this job is now called the *owner's representative* or the *construction manager*.

Client
The person or organization having a need for a project. The client is responsible for the overall financing of the work and either directly or indirectly employs the entire design and building team.

Climbing crane
A type of crane that is supported on the building framework that is continually raised as the building is erected; used on the construction of tall buildings.

Climbing form
A vertical concrete framework, anchored to the concrete below, that is successively raised after each pour has hardened.

Clinker brick
A very hard burnt brick whose shape is distorted by nearly complete vitrification; used mainly for paving or as ornamental accents.

Clip angle
A short piece of angle iron attached to one piece of a column or beam with bolts, in preparation for attaching to another piece upon erection.

Clocktower
Any instrument for measuring or indicating time such as a mechanical device with a numbered dial and moving hands or pointers positioned in a single tower, or a tower-like portion of a structure.

Cloister
A square court surrounded by an open arcade, a covered walk around a courtyard, or the whole courtyard itself.

Close grain
Lumber that has narrow and inconspicuous annual rings, producing a fine-grained pattern.

Close tolerance
Deviations in dimensions smaller than would normally be allowed.

Close-up inspection
Viewing the structure from arm's length, either from the ground or on a pipe scaffold, or swing staging. Less conventional methods include using the zoom lens feature on a video camera, photographing with a telephoto lens, or viewing through binoculars. The use of digital photography is helpful in getting an immediate picture. See also *Visual inspection.*

Closed construction
Building components, assemblies, or systems that are manufactured in such a manner that all portions cannot be readily inspected at the installation site without disassembly. See *Open construction.*

Closed list of bidders
A list of contractors approved by the architect and owner as the only ones allowed to bid on the project.

Closed loop system
In a Building Automation System, the arrangement of heating, ventilation, and air-conditioning (HVAC) components so that the feedback from components affects and also controls the others.

Closed shop
A trade or skill that requires membership in a particular union to the exclusion of all others.

Closed specifications
Specifications that require certain tradename products or proprietary processes, and alternates will not be considered.

Closed-circuit television
A television circuit without broadcasting capabilities; used for security purposes in a building's automated system.

Closed-string stair
A staircase whose profile of treads and risers is covered at the side by a string, or sloping member that supports the balustrade.

Closer
The last stretcher brick that completes a course of brickwork. Types include a king closer and queen closer.

Closing costs
Legal fees, recording fees, title search, and insurance, associated with the sale or purchase of real estate, excluding the cost of the property itself.

Clustered housing
Homes that are grouped, collected, or gathered closely together and related by proximity to each other.

Coarse aggregate
Crushed stone or gravel used to reinforce concrete. Building codes regulate the size of the aggregate; stones that will not pass through a ¼-inch screen.

Coarse grain
Wood or lumber having wide and conspicuous annual rings in which there is considerable difference between the springwood and summerwood.

Coaxial cable
A cable with a tube of conducting material surrounding a central conductor; used to transmit telephone, television, and computer signals.

Cobble
Stone that is smaller than a boulder but larger than gravel.

Cobblestone
A rounded stone formed by natural erosion, used in paving, wall construction, and foundations.

Code
A standard that outlines minimum requirements for a design fabrication or construction that must be met if it is going to be considered as acceptable; the markings on the back of gypsum wallboard, plywood, or other material that identify the type, manufacturer, thickness, or quality.

Code compliance
Review of plans and specifications by a building official to ensure that all building code requirements are met.

Code enforcement
A principal tool used to ensure neighborhood upkeep, by enforcing local regulation of building practices, and safety and housing code provisions; includes on-site inspection by building officials and legal sanctions against owners of property that are in violation of the codes.

Code enforcement official
A representative of a governmental authority that inspects construction projects for compliance with all regulatory ordinances and requirements.

Code of practice
A publication by a trade or group of manufacturers of similar products that lists minimum quality standards for material, workmanship, or conduct that must be followed by its members.

Code regulations
Ordinances, or statutory requirements, of a governmental unit relating to building construction and occupancy. Such regulations are adopted and administered for the protection of the public health, safety, and welfare.

Codes
The legal requirements of local and other governing bodies concerning construction and occupancy. The enactment and enforcement of codes is intended to protect and safeguard public health, safety, and welfare.

Coefficient of friction
A measure of the resistance that occurs when one material slides on another. It is the ratio of the force required to move the material to the weight of the material being moved.

Coefficient of thermal expansion
Change in linear dimension per unit of length, or change in volume per unit volume per degree of temperature change.

Coffer
A recessed boxlike panel in a ceiling or vault, usually square or lozenge-shaped, sometimes dressed with simple moldings or elaborately ornamented.

Cogged joint
A carpentry joint formed by two crossed structural members, each of which is notched at the place where they cross.

Cohesion
The binding forces that cause soil particles to adhere to each other, caused by molecular attraction and the surface tension of the water in the spaces between the particles.

Cold chisel
A chisel that will stand up under the hardest usage, made of tool steel; used for cutting and chipping cold metal.

Cold-air return
The return air duct in a heating system that transports cold air back into the system to be reheated.

Collar
A flashing for a metal vent or chimney where it passes through a roof.

Collar beam
A horizontal member that ties together two opposite common rafters, usually at a point halfway up the length of the rafters below the ridge.

Collar beam roof
A roof in which the rafters are tied together and stiffened by collars.

Collar tie
In wood construction, a timber that prevents the roof framing from changing shape.

Collateral
Security of some form pledged by a borrower to protect the interest of the lender.

Collective bargaining
Union and employer representatives meet together to negotiate contracts.

Collector
Any of a wide variety of devices that collect and absorb radiation from the sun and convert it to heat in a solar heating system.

Collector aperture
The glazed area of a solar collector that absorbs sunlight.

Collector efficiency
The ratio of the amount of solar radiation absorbed by a solar collector, to the amount of solar radiation that strikes it.

Collusion
A secret agreement between two or more parties to take advantage of a party that they anticipate doing business with; such as setting and fixing prices for specific work. See also *Affidavit of noncollusion*.

Color and sample boards
Display boards prepared by the architect or interior designer that contain swatches of color, photos of furniture and samples of materials to be used in the construction and interior finish.

Color coding
Use of various colors for ease of sorting and to identify items of different values or applications.

Color retention
The ability of a paint to hold its color quality and intensity after exposure to the elements for long periods of time.

Colored cement
Portland cement blended with a pigment that does not react chemically with the component of the concrete.

Column
A vertical structural compression member or shaft supporting a load, which acts in the direction of its vertical axis. Also called *post, pillar*.

Column

Column clamp
A device used to encircle column forms and hold them together while pouring wet concrete. Also called *Column form clamp*.

Column form
A temporary assembly used to hold wet concrete in the form until the concrete has set.

Column reinforcement
Reinforcing steel added to a concrete column to prevent lateral expansion or buckling of the column under a compressive load.

Column schedule
A table on the working drawings giving the number, size, type, and placement of columns to be used in a structure.

Column ties
Bars bent into square, rectangular, circular, or U-shapes for holding the column's vertical bars laterally secure for the placement of concrete.

Columniation
A classification of column spacing on a Classical façade; diastyle (2), tetrastyle (4), pentastyle (5), hexastyle (6) heptastyle (7), octastyle (8), enneastyle (9), decastyle (10), and dodecastyle (12).

Comb grain
In quarter-sawn lumber, grain with narrow, nearly parallel stripes of plainly marked dark and light colors.

Combination fitting
A fitting for waste and soil pipe systems, resembling a Y-branch with a 45 degree bend on the side outlet.

Combination pliers
A tool with jaws adjustable to size of opening by means of a slip joint. The inner grip is notched for grasping round objects. The outer handle grip is scored.

Combination square
A carpenter's tool that is actually a combination of several tools including an inside square, an outside tri-square, meter square, plumb level, depth gauge, marking gauge, straightedge, bevel protractor, and a square head.

Combination window
Window having an inside removable section so the same frame serves in both summer and winter. In warm weather a screen may be inserted, and in winter a storm window can be installed in place of the screen.

Combined escutcheon plate
A metal plate for a door with both a knob socket and a keyhole.

Combustibility
A measure of the tendency of a material to support combustion and burn.

Combustible
The capacity of a material to burn; may or may not be flammable, that is, burn with a flame.

Comfort zone
The range of temperature and humidity in which the average person is comfortable.

Commission
A formal written assignment for a work of art or architecture, for which the artist or designer is paid.

Commissioning
The start-up testing and adjusting of a building's systems, such as heating, ventilation, and air-conditioning (HVAC), electrical, plumbing, and fire safety, to assure proper functioning and compliance to design criteria. It also includes the instruction of building managers and representatives in the proper use of the systems.

Common brick
A building brick that is not treated for texture or color.

Common brick bond
A brick bond in which every fifth or sixth course consists of headers; all the other courses consist of stretchers.

Common lumber
Boards with knots and other imperfections, commonly used where appearance is not the major factor.

Common nail
Available from 2d (penny) to 60d (penny) in length. Common nails are used most often where the appearance of the work is not important, such as in framing and building concrete formwork.

Common rafter
A sloped roof member that is smaller than the principal rafter, that spans from the top plate of the exterior wall to the roof ridge rafter.

Common services
A combination of systems for services designed to provide lighting, heating, plumbing, and air-conditioning for several families occupying the same building or several connected buildings.

Common wall
A wall jointly used by two parties. Also called *party wall*.

Compact
To increase the firmness or ability to support weight by the subgrade by pounding or compressing it with hand or power equipment.

Compaction test
A soil test to determine the compaction of filled soil, by extracting a sample, weighing it, and comparing its density to laboratory standard maximum density for that particular soil.

Compactor
A soil-compacting device with a motor, which vibrates a heavy flat plate that rests on the soil.

Compass
A drafting instrument with two legs joined at the top, used to draw circles and curves when laying out plans.

Compass brick
A wedge-shaped brick used in constructing arches or building curved walls. This type of brick has the two large faces inclined toward each other.

Compass roof
A convex-shaped roof formed with curved rafters.

Compass window
A rounded bay window that projects from the face of a wall. Also, a window having a rounded semicircular member at its head.

Compass-headed roof
A roof having curved rafters. Also, a form of timber roof in which the rafters, collar beams, and braces of each truss combine to form an arch.

Compatibility of materials
Conditions that exist between original materials on a structure and those considered for repair or replacement; considerations include matches for color, texture, weathering capability, permeability, reflectivity, coefficient of expansion, and chemical compatibility.

Compensation
Payment for services rendered or products or materials furnished or delivered. Also, payment in satisfaction of claims for damages suffered.

Compensatory damages
A sum of money devised to compensate a party for a calculated economic loss by the wrongful act of another.

Complementary colors
Those pairs of colors, such as red and green, that together embrace the entire spectrum. The complement of one of the three primary colors is a mixture of the other two.

Completion
The act of bringing a structure to the point of construction when it is physically ready for use and occupancy and is legally considered to be in a completed condition.

Completion bond
A bond posted by a contractor prior to beginning work on a project; intended to ensure the contractor's completion in accordance with the contract documents and terms and specifications of the contract, and to guarantee that the project will be completed free of liens against it.

Completion date
The date certified by the architect when the work, or a designated portion, is completed in accordance with the contract documents and the structure can be occupied by the owner.

Completion list
Often called a punch list; it contains all the items to be completed or corrected by the contractor before the job can be called complete, and request for final payment can be made.

Completion of contract accounting
A method of accounting whereby money is not counted as income until the contract has been totally completed.

Component construction
Structures made up of prefabricated modules that are assembled on the job site.

Components
The various structural framing or materials that go together to form the elements of a building.

Composite
Built up of different parts, prices, or materials.

Composite column
A column in which a metal structural member is completely encased in concrete containing special spiral reinforcement.

Composite door
A door with a wooden or metal covering over a light-weight foam core.

Composite patching
A process of duplicating messy or delaminated stone faces and projections. Key holes are first drilled into the stone to provide a base for the rough coat, followed by the application of a series of layers of mortar, and finished to match the appearance of surrounding stone.

Composite wall
A masonry wall made up of wythes of two or more different types of masonry units.

Composition board
A building board manufactured from wood fibers or other particles, and held together with a binder. Types include asbestos board, fiberboard, and particleboard.

Composition roofing
Roofing consisting of asbestos felt saturated with asphalt and assembled with asphalt cement.

Composition shingle
Any shingle made with a mixture of binder materials and fibers. Types include asbestos and asphalt shingles.

Compound beam
A timber beam built up from a number of pieces either nailed, glued, or bolted with connectors.

Compound pier
A pier that has several engaged shafts against its surface; used often in Romanesque and Gothic structures.

Compound vault
Any vault formed by the intersection of two or more vaults. Types include cloister vault, domical vault, groin vault, and segmental vault.

Compound wall
A wall constructed in two or more skins of different materials: for example, a timber-frame wall with brick veneer.

Comprehensive general liability
Insurance that covers all types of liability.

Comprehensive services
Professional services, such as project analysis, programming, land use studies, feasibility studies, historic preservation analysis, financing, construction management, and specialized consulting services performed by the architect, beyond the basic services that are generally offered.

Compression
Direct pushing force, in line with the axis of the member; the opposite of tension.

Compression bars
Steel used in concrete to resist compressive forces.

Compression failure
Deformation of the wood fibers resulting from excessive compression or in bending.

Compression fitting
A force that pushes connections on bends, elbows, tees, and unions together, and squeezes a metal or rubber gasket for a tight fit.

Compressive fracture test
A test of the strength of concrete, using a cylinder of cured cement and a specified compressive load applied to the cylinder, to assure that it can sustain the applied load without fracturing.

Compressive strength
The maximum compressive stress a material will bear without fracture, as expressed in pounds per square inch.

Compressive stress
The resistance of a material to an external pushing force.

Compressor
One of the main components of an air-conditioning system required in the cooling cycle.

Computer-aided design and drafting (CADD)
A sophisticated graphics program for use in computers, employing two- and three-dimensional drawings. In three-dimensional work, parts and components can be viewed from any angle outside or inside the assembly. Parts can be moved and animated as they would move during installation or maintenance procedures. The programs are used for designing and planning construction sequences and logistics for large and small building projects. The process can also be used for training and education.

Concave joint
A recessed masonry joint, formed in mortar by the use of a curved steel jointing tool. Because of its curved shape, it is very effective in resisting moisture.

Concealed ceiling grid
A framework of steel or aluminum provides the support for a suspended ceiling that is completely hidden by the ceiling tiles or panels that it supports.

Concealed gutter
A gutter that is constructed in such a manner that it cannot be seen. Also called a *hidden gutter*.

Concealed hinges
Hinges that are not visible when the door which they support is closed.

Concealed spaces
Any space that is generally not visible after construction is complete, such as furred spaces, pipe chases, duct shafts, and plenum spaces above ceilings, attics, and tunnels.

Concealed sprinkler
A sprinkler head that does not hang below the surface and that is installed flush with the ceiling.

Concealed wiring
Electrical wiring that is run inside the walls, floors, and ceilings, and is not visible.

Concentrated load
A load acting on a very small area of the structure's surface; the exact opposite of a distributed load.

Concentrating collector
A type of solar collector that uses a series of black painted pipes passing through a parabolic reflector which reflects the sun's rays onto the pipes; the reflectors are operated with machinery that pivots to follow the path of the sun.

Conceptual design
A preliminary study, with sufficient detail to define the basics of the scheme, that is the forerunner to schematic design.

Concrete
A composite artificial building material consisting of an aggregate of broken stone mixed with sand, water, and cement to bind the entire mass; fluid and plastic when wet and hard and strong when dry.

Concrete and masonry sealant
A sealant for repairing cracks or expansion joints in concrete and mortar.

Concrete bent construction
A system of construction in which precast concrete bent framing units are the load-bearing members. A concrete bent consists of a vertical and horizontal load-bearing member, that is cast in one piece and designed on the cantilever principle.

Concrete block
A hollow concrete masonry unit, rectangular in shape, made from portland cement and other aggregates.

Concrete block

Concrete column
A column composed of concrete with longitudinal bars placed inside to increase the load-carrying capacity. Lateral ties are placed around the bars to keep them from spreading under a compressive load.

Concrete cover
The clear distance from the face of the concrete to the reinforcing steel. Also called *concrete protection*.

Concrete cylinder test
Concrete cylinders are carefully made in metal containers, 6 inches in diameter and 12 inches high. They are sent to a laboratory and put into a hydraulic machine to measure the pressure needed to crush it. These tests are sometimes performed for each pour on a project that requires control of the strength of the concrete.

Concrete dowel
A pin embedded in concrete to strengthen two pieces where they are joined together or to create a place where other pieces of steel can be attached to it.

Concrete finishing
The final finishing operations of curing concrete, which may include a smooth trowel finish, a rough float finish, or a textured broom finish.

Concrete grille
An openwork barrier used to conceal, decorate, or protect an opening.

Concrete insert
A type of metal anchor used to secure structural wood parts to a concrete or masonry wall.

Concrete masonry
Construction consisting of concrete masonry units laid up in mortar or grout.

Concrete nail
A hardened-steel nail used for fastening wood to masonry work; consists of a short, thick nail with a sharp point and a scored shaft.

Concrete paint
A specially prepared thin paint, consisting of a mixture of cement and water, applied to the surface of a concrete wall to give it a uniform finish and to protect the joints against weathering.

Concrete pipe
A pipe manufactured under controlled conditions, which is used for drainage or sanitary sewers.

Concrete plank
A solid precast and prestressed hollow-core flat beam, used for roof or floor decking.

Concrete pump
A device which forces concrete through a pipeline or hose to the position of placement.

Concrete pumping
The placement of concrete to inaccessible areas by pumping it through a flexible hose to the point of discharge. The hoses range from 2 to 4 inches in diameter and are fed from a hopper which holds the concrete before it is pumped into the hose. See also *Slurry wall*.

Concrete reinforcement
Steel rods that are placed in the forms prior to pouring, that give additional strength to the wet concrete when hardened.

Concrete saw

A power saw used to cut sections of concrete to remove damaged sections of pavement, or to cut a groove in the surface to create a central joint, using a carborundum or diamond blade. The operation is often cooled with water. Other uses include cutting grooves in floors to place wires guiding robotic vehicles.

Concrete slab on the ground

A concrete structure such as a floor, patio, or driveway.

Condemn

The judicial exercise of the right of eminent domain; taking over of private property for public use, with just compensation to the owner.

Condemnation

A pronouncement by a legally constituted authority provided with police power, declaring a structure unfit for use or occupancy because of its threatened danger to persons or other property.

Condensation

The change of a substance from a vapor to a liquid state, caused by the temperature falling below the dew point; most likely to occur in cool weather when the temperature drops at night. Condensation will form when a cold surface comes in contact with warm moist air, and shows up on surfaces as a film, or as drops of water.

Condenser

The apparatus in a refrigeration cycle that discharges heat to the outside. Three types are commonly used: water-cooled, air-cooled, and evaporative. Condenser water is normally circulated through a cooling tower where heat is discharged to the atmosphere.

Condition

A state of readiness for use. Also, a requirement that is part of an agreement, such as conditions of the general contract for construction.

Condition assessment

The visual inspection of a structure to identify existing conditions prior to the design of a restoration, renovation, or adaptive reuse. This type of assessment may involve the testing or monitoring of structural elements to determine the safety of existing members.

Conditional payment clause

A clause in a subcontract making payment to the subcontractor for work performed a condition of payment by the owner to the prime contractor for such work.

Conditional use permit

A special permit granting the use of a structure or parcel of land that is not consistent with normal approved usage; typically regulated by the municipality having jurisdiction over that location.

Conditions of contract

A contract document that describes the rights and obligations of the client and contractor; may be original or adapted from a standard form of contract.

Condominium

An apartment house, office building, or other multiple-unit complex in which the units are individually owned and there is joint ownership of common elements such as hallways, elevators, and all mechanical systems.

Conduction

A mechanism of heat transfer through a material; the denser the material, the higher its rate of heat flow by conduction. Metals are excellent conductors and energy loss is at a minimum, so they are commonly used in electrical systems, copper being the most preferred.

Conductor

In electricity, a wire or path through which a current of electricity flows, such as aluminum or copper wire. Also, a rod used to carry lightning to the ground. In plumbing, a pipe for conveying rainwater from the roof gutter to the drain pipe. Also called *leader* or *downspout*.

Conduit

A natural or artificial channel for conveying liquids; also, a tube of metal or plastic that encloses electrical wires or cables. Also called *metal casing, BX, armored cable*.

Conduit bender

A tool with a curved head and a long straight handle that is used to form smooth curves in conduit and pipe; also called a *hickey*.

Conduit box

An iron or steel box located between the ends of a conduit where the wires are spliced, or where the wires are attached to a fixture or outlet. Also called an *outlet box* or *pull box*.

Conduit fittings

In electrical wiring, a term applied to all the auxiliary items, such as boxes and elbows, bushings, couplings, and connectors needed to construct the conduit system of wiring.

Conical roof

A roof shaped like an inverted cone on top of a cylindrical tower; used in the Chateau and Queen Anne styles; also called a *witch's hat*.

Conical vault
A vault having a cross-section in the form of a circular arch, which is larger at one end than the other.

Conifer
A tree belonging to the botanical group that bears cone. It includes all the softwoods used in building, particularly the pines and firs.

Connector
A device that joins two objects together, such as an electrical wire to another wire, or a piece of lumber to another member in a truss. Also called *splice*.

Consequential damage
The damage that results from the failure of one item and impacts or damages other related items.

Conserve
To preserve from loss; save.

Consistency
The workability of a building material, such as plaster, mortar, adhesive compounds, Also, the degree of firmness or stiffness of freshly mixed wet concrete, as measured by a slump test.

Consolidation
A treatment to arrest the deterioration or crumbling of stone with resins, acrylics, epoxies, polyesters, and other similar chemicals.

Construction
The fabrication and erection of a building by the process of assembly, or by combining building components or systems within an existing structure. Also, the on-site work done in building or altering structures, from land clearance through completion. It including excavation, erection, and the assembly and installation of components and equipment, all electrical and plumbing systems, interior and exterior finishes, flooring, trim, and landscaping, and all elements necessary to make the structure ready for occupancy.

Construction adhesive
A strong adhesive used to replace or supplant mechanical fasteners, such as nails. The adhesive gives an extra measure of bonding strength, ensuring that the material will stay in place, available in cartridges that fit into a caulking gun. See *Caulking gun*.

Construction administration
The special management services performed by the architect or others during the construction phase of the project under either a separate or special agreement with the owner.

Construction administrator
One who oversees the fulfillment of responsibilities of all parties to the contract, for the benefit of the owner.

Construction budget
The total amount of money established by the owner as available for construction of the project, including contingencies and changes during construction; also, the stipulated highest acceptable bid price for the project. In the case of multiple construction contracts, the stipulated aggregate total of all the highest acceptable bid prices. See also *Project budget*.

Construction change directive
A document that directs a change in the work and may be used in the absence of total agreement on the terms of the change order. It is prepared by the architect and signed by the owner and architect.

Construction classification
A method of classifying structures according to their fire resistance.

Construction cost
The cost of all of the construction portions of a project, generally based on the sum of the construction contracts, and other direct construction costs. Not included is compensation for professional services, land, rights-of-way, or other costs specified as the responsibility of the owner outlined in the contract.

Construction documents
The third phase of architectural basic services wherein drawings are prepared from the approved design development documents, consisting of working drawings and specifications and the necessary bidding information. The architect also assists the owner in the preparation of bid forms, conditions of the contract, and the form of agreement between owner and contractor.

Construction drawings
Includes architectural plans and details on how to construct the building. Drawings are to scale and include site plan, foundation plan, floor framing plans, floor plans, roof framing plan, exterior and interior elevations, sections through the structure, details of door and window placement, and door, window, and finish schedules.

Construction joint
A separation provided in a building that allows its component parts to move with respect to each other; a joint where two placements of concrete or other material meet.

Construction loads
The loads imposed on the building during construction due to the erection, assembly, and installation of building components and equipment.

Construction loan
An interim loan of money transacted at the beginning of construction or during construction and secured by a negotiable bond or mortgage or trust deed. The money obtained is intended to defray the cost of the building to be erected. Usually advanced in specified sums during the progress of construction. After completion, the loan is often converted into a long-term loan.

Construction management
A method of project delivery in which the prime contractor is responsible for obtaining and managing subcontractors who perform various tasks needed to complete the project; management services provided by a person or entity with the training and experience required by the owner. They may include advice on scheduling, cost control, purchasing of materials and long-lead items, and coordination of all construction activities.

Construction manager
An individual or firm that represents a property owner in taking bids from subcontractors and coordinating their activities, then administers all of the construction contracts, for a fee or guaranteed maximum price.

Construction observation
An on-site visit by the design architect or the engineer to determine if the construction materials and installations are in accordance with the construction documents and specifications, which includes review of testing reports.

Construction phase
The final phase of the architect's basic services, which includes the architect's general administration of the construction contract.

Construction process
The actual physical tasks and administrative processes of building.

Construction progress delays
Delays in construction caused by unforeseen events.

Construction representative
A government employee whose function is to inspect or supervise federal projects.

Construction Specification Institute (CSI)
An organization that has established a format for construction specifications, composed of four major groupings: bidding requirements, contract forms, general conditions, and specifications. Within the last grouping of specifications, 16 permanent divisions are listed.

Constructor
One who is in the business of managing and performing the construction process.

Consultant
A specialist who is consulted during building design, engineering, or construction; includes restoration and preservation specialists.

Consulting engineer
A person retained to give expert advice in regard to all engineering problems.

Contact cement
An adhesive applied to one surface that bonds instantly on contact with another surface, such as kitchen countertops and other cabinetwork.

Contaminate
To infect something with unsuitable, undesirable, or harmful material.

Contextual
Any doctrine emphasizing the importance of the context in establishing the meaning of terms, such as the setting into which a building is placed, its site, its natural environment, or its neighborhood.

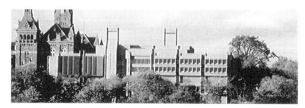

Contingency
A sum of money identified contractually to provide for unforeseen activities during the course of the contract.

Contingency agreement
An agreement that stipulates that the architect's fee is contingent upon events that may or may not happen, such as obtaining funding for the project, successful bond referendum, sale of bonds, securing other financing, or some other specially prescribed condition.

Contingency allowance
A sum designated to cover unpredictable or unforeseen items or circumstances in the work or changes subsequently required by the property owner.

Contingency planning
The process of anticipating and developing alternative actions that can be taken should a preferred course of action be disrupted or terminated.

Contingent liability
A liability that is dependent on the occurrence of an uncertain future event or uncertain specified condition.

Continuing education
Education pursued through accredited professional seminars, college curriculum, and other forms of organized study that promotes knowledge of the "state-of-the-art" of professional practice.

Continuous
A structural member having three or more supports, or extending over two or more panels, as a continuous beam, span, truss, or panel. See also *Continuous girder*.

Continuous beam
A beam that is continuous over intermediate supports and thus statically indeterminate; as opposed to a simply supported beam.

Continuous footing
A combined footing that acts like a continuous beam on the foundation.

Continuous girder
A girder or beam supported at more than three points and extending over the supports.

Continuous header
The top plate replaced by double 2 × 6's turned on edge and run around the entire house. This header is strong enough to act as a lintel over all wall openings, eliminating cutting studs and separate headers.

Continuous hinge
A long strip hinge used in furniture making. Also called a *piano hinge*.

Continuous underpinning
A form of underpinning an entire foundation that will remain in place. A series of pits are excavated under portions of the existing foundations, and new foundations and footings and foundation wall are built up to the underside of the existing one. New excavations are made adjacent to the new walls, and the process is repeated until the whole wall has been underpinned.

Contour
The outline of a figure, as the profile of a molding; also, a line joining points having the same elevation above or below some given level.

Contour gage
A tool for marking contours, consisting of a series of movable metal pins in a metal frame; when pressed against an object, the fingers conform to the object's contours, and can be used to copy that contour onto other shapes for fitting.

Contour interval
The amount of rise between lines on a contour map showing differences in elevation from a datum point, such as sea level.

Contour map
A topographic map that portrays relief by the use of contour lines that connect points of equal elevation; the closer the spacing of lines, the greater the relative slope in that area.

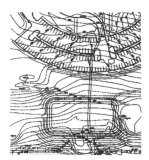

Contour plan
A plan view of a site showing finished grade elevations as indicated by contour lines. See also *Contour map*.

Contract administration
Architectural services and responsibilities of the architect during the construction phase, such as supervision, review of shop drawings and materials samples, and processing change orders and requests for payment from the contractor.

Contract conditions
The items in the contract that define the contract terminology, rights and responsibilities of the contracting parties, requirements for safety and compliance with laws and regulations, general procedures for the management of the work, payments to the contractor, and other provisions. They usually include general, supplementary, and other conditions.

Contract documents
Those documents that make up a contract including plans and/or drawings, specifications, all addenda, and modifications and changes, together with any other items stipulated as being specifically included.

Contract time
A stipulated period of time that covers the substantial completion of the work, including authorized revisions and extensions; the time frame established in the contract documents within which the work must be completed, and can only be adjusted by a change order.

Contract type
The specific format and pricing arrangement used for the performance of work under a contract; includes fixed-price, fixed-price incentive, cost plus fixed fee, cost plus incentive, and several others.

Contracting officer
A representative of a government agency with the authority to bind the government in contract matters.

Contraction joint
A control joint, such as a tooled groove made in the slab to allow for shrinkage in a concrete slab. See also *Control joint*.

Contractor

A person or company who has agreed to perform a defined scope of work in accordance with the contract documents and terms of the contract, and who contracts for a specific cost and schedule for completion of the work. A person may be a prime, contracting directly with the owner for the entire job, or a subcontractor who has contracted with the prime for part of the work. Also called *builder*.

Contractor's affidavit

A certified notarized statement by the contractor for evidence of protection for the owner, relating to such items as payments of debts and claims, or release of liens.

Contractor's bond

A bond required by the owner to ensure that the contractor fulfills all obligations.

Contractor's liability insurance

Insurance that protects the contractor from the specified claims that may result from the operations under the contract, whether made by the contractor, any subcontractor, or anyone employed by them.

Contractor's options

Provision of the contract documents under which the contractor may select certain specified materials, methods, or systems at his or her own option, without changes in the contract sum.

Contractor's qualification statement

A statement of the contractor's qualifications, experience, financial condition, business history, and staff composition and experience, plus selected references.

Contractor's quality control plan

A plan that outlines the procedure, instructions, reports, and personnel that the contractor intends to use in carrying out the quality control plan. It is prepared by the contractor and approved by the owner.

Contributory negligence

The legal responsibility attributed to one or more parties who contributed to loss or damage suffered by another party as the result of a specific occurrence.

Control date

The date within the control period that marks the end of restoration efforts on a historic property.

Control joint

In concrete block masonry, a continuous vertical joint without mortar, filled with rubber or plastic, which is sealed with caulking. Control joints are also used in long expanses of masonry where thermal expansion and contraction may cause cracking of the mortar joints. It creates a deliberately weakened section to induce cracking at the chosen location rather than at random.

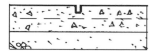 

Control period

The duration of restoration work on a historic structure.

Controlled photography

A method of photography that yields distortion-free scaled photographs with perspective parallax control, most easily done with large-format cameras, although there are perspective-control lenses for 35-mm cameras as well.

Controls

A mechanism that regulates the operation of a heating, ventilation, and air-conditioning (HVAC) system, or operation of a machine.

Convection

One method that heat transfers from one place to another; from a warmer area to a colder one, such as heat rising to an upper story of a house, or the ceiling of a room.

Convenience outlet

An electrical outlet in the wall that can be used for electrical devices. Also called a *receptacle*.

Conventions

A pictorial representation of items that cannot be shown by symbols on the plan views, such as fixtures, stairs, fireplaces, and the like.

Conversion

In adaptive reuse, change in the use of a property, such as from a railroad station to a commercial facility.

Conversion chart

A chart showing equivalent units of measurement from one standard to another.

Cooling tower

A structure usually located on the roof of a building, over which water is circulated to cool it by evaporation.

Cooperative apartment

A unit in a building owned and managed by a nonprofit corporation that sells shares in the building, entitling the shareholders to occupy apartments in the building.

Cooperative ownership

Ownership of property that is divided among several or many parties. See also *Condominium*.

Cope

To cut a shape out of a member or molding so it will fit closely against or into an adjoining member.

Coped

Cut to conform to the irregular outline of an abutting piece, such as two moldings meeting at an inside corner.

Coped joint

A joint cut with a coping saw used on baseboard junctions, door and window trim, and other junctions of moldings.

Coping

A protective covering over the top course of a wall or parapet, either flat or sloping on the upper surface to throw off water. If it extends beyond the wall, it may be cut with a drip to protect the wall surface below. Also called *cap*.

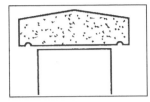

Coping saw

A saw used for cutting curves in moldings. It has a narrow blade which allows it to change directions more easily as it cuts.

Copper

A metal with good electrical conductivity, used for roofing, flashing, hardware, and plumbing applications. When exposed to air, copper oxidizes and develops a greenish patina that halts corrosion.

Copper flashing

Sheets of copper used on exterior open joints to prevent water from entering.

Copper pipe

Small hollow pipe connected using soldered joints; typically used for water supply due to its resistance to corrosion.

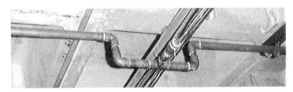

Copper wire

A metal wire that is used for electrical conduction.

Corbel

In masonry construction, a series of projections, each one stepped progressively outward from the vertical face of the wall as it rises up to support a cornice or overhanging member above.

Corbel

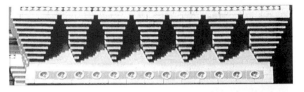

Corbel table

A raised band composed of small arches resting on corbels; a projecting course of masonry supported on corbels near the top of a wall, such as a parapet or cornice.

Corbeled chimney cap

The termination of a chimney using a series of successive courses of bricks that step out with the increasing height.

Corbeling

Masonry courses wherein each is extended out farther from the one below to form a rough arch-shaped lintel, vault, or dome.

Corbie gable
A gable finished roof line finished with corbiesteps.

Corbie stones
Stones used for covering the top of steps of a crowstepped gable wall.

Corbiestep gable
A gable that has a series of regular steps up each slope, following the roofline. See also *Corbie gable*.

Corbiesteps
A series of steplike projections along the slope of a gable wall; also called *crowsteps*.

Cordless screwdriver
A hand held device which uses a built-in rechargeable battery as its power source for driving screws, without the need for an external power supply.

Core
The interior structure of a hollow-core door; a cylindrical sample of concrete or rock; the center layers in a sheet of plywood; the vertical stack of service areas in a multistory building.

Core drill
A machine for drilling into rock or concrete yielding a continuous core as the drill bit sinks deeper. The cores are examined visually and tested physically by compressive tests.

Core drilling
A process used to obtain a cylindrical sample of rock, concrete, or soil; also used to install pipe of conduit through an existing concrete or masonry wall.

Core sample
A specimen of cylindrical material obtained from a core drill.

Coreboard
A 1-inch-thick gypsum board used between wallboard panels in a self-supporting gypsum wall. It is held in a metal channel at the top and bottom, and the finished wallboard is fastened to it using adhesives or screws.

Corinthian
Pertaining to the most ornate of the three Greek orders of architecture, characterized by the distinguishing feature of its bell-shaped capital adorned with rows of conventionalized acanthus leaves.

Cork
The outer bark of the cork oak tree; primarily used for floor tile and sound insulation board.

Cork tile
Tiles made from compressed cork. These tiles form a resilient floor covering with good insulating properties.

Corkboard
A board formed from compressed cork particles; provides a decorative and sound-deadening wall covering and offers good insulating qualities.

Corner angles
Metal fasteners used for either inside or outside corners, depending on which side of the angle is countersunk for the screw heads; ranging in size from 1 to 8 inches.

Corner bead
A vertical molding used to protect the external angle of two intersecting wall surfaces; a perforated metal strip used to strengthen and protect an external angle in plaster work or gypsum wallboard construction.

Corner blocks
Wood blocks positioned at the top corners of either window or door casings; often enhanced with design elements, such as concentric oval disks.

Corner board
A board that is used as trim on the external corner of a wood frame structure and against which the ends of the siding are fitted.

Corner brace
A diagonal brace at the corner of a frame wall to stiffen and strengthen the structure.

Corner clamp
A clamp that is designed to hold members in place that are joined at an angle.

Corner lot
A lot that abuts two or more streets at their point of intersection.

Corner posts
The two or three studs spiked together to form a corner in a frame structure.

Corner reinforcement
The reinforcement in the upper corners of a metal door frame. Also, the metal corner stops used at the corners of gypsum plaster or gypsum board insulation.

Cornerstone
A stone that is situated at a corner of a building uniting two intersecting walls, usually located near the base and often carrying information about the structure.

Cornice
The uppermost division of an entablature; a projecting shelf along the top of a wall supported by a series of brackets; the exterior trim at the meeting of a roof and wall, consisting of a soffit, fascia, and crown molding.

Cornice return
The continuation of a raked cornice in a horizontal direction, as at the gable end of a building.

Corporation
A group of persons who legally share powers, responsibilities, and liabilities as a group rather than as separate individuals.

Corrosion
A surface chemical reaction especially applied to metals that can be eaten away or corroded by the action of water, air, and chemicals.

Corrosion inhibitor
A protective layer of paint or other surface finish to prevent oxidation or chemical attack on the base material.

Corrugated glass
Molded glass that has been formed into a wavy shape to provide a greater diffusion of light and the image beyond.

Corrugated metal
Sheet metal that has been drawn or rolled into parallel ridges and furrows to provide additional mechanical strength. Aluminum and galvanized sheet metal are the most widely used.

Cosmetic improvements
Work that makes a property look better without additional structural elements.

Cost control
A technique used by architects and contractors to control the cost of a project by utilizing data on planned and actual expenditures by activity; reports on status of expenditures compared to those planned; a method of predicting ultimate cost compared with estimated cost that summarizes the data by accounting periods.

Cost estimate
A prediction of the total cost of a structure, determined by one of three methods: (1) by area and volume, such as a per square foot or cubic foot; (2) unit cost times the number of similar units; or (3) the in-place unit cost of each individual item.

Cost planning
A technique used to control the cost of a project within the budget during the design phase by reference to the historical costs of the elements.

Cost-benefit analysis
A process which studies the ability of a building to increase its revenue-producing potential by a percentage that reduces the overall first cost of the facility, a function now common in "green buildings." See also *Return on investment (ROI)*.

Cost-plus contract
A contract in which the actual prime cost of labor and materials is paid for at net cost to the contractor, plus a fee based on a percentage or fixed fee, to cover the contractor's overhead and profit.

Cost-plus-fee
A method of contracting where the contractor, subcontractor, or architect is reimbursed for all direct and indirect costs, and is paid a fee for services.

Cost-reimbursement contract
A contract which allows for repayment of allowable expenses incurred by the contractor while carrying out the work.

Council of American Building Officials (CABO)
An organization of building officials that standardize national construction codes and requirements.

Counter
A horizontal surface used for display in a store, or as a serving surface in a restaurant or on top of a kitchen cabinet.

Counterflashing
Flashing used on chimneys and parapet walls where one edge is embedded in the masonry joint and the other edge is turned downward and overlaps the roof flashing.

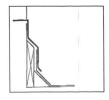

Counteroffer
A response to an offer which neither accepts nor rejects the offer but instead proposes modifications to the original offer.

Countersink
To make a depression in wood or metal for the reception of a plate of iron, head of a screw, or bolt, that will not protrude above the surface of the work.

Countersink bit
A drill or other tool for cutting a flared enlargement in the upper part of a hole where a screw is to be driven below the surface of the material.

Countersunk
Hardware installed in a recess that allows it to be flush with or below the surface on which it is installed.

Countersunk plug
A wooden plug inserted into a drilled hole in a wooden surface, such as flooring or cabinetwork.

Countertop
The top surface of a counter, installed above the cabinets; may be of wood, plastic laminate, or marble.

Couple roof
A pitched roof consisting of a pair of rafters fixed at the lower end to a wall plate and to the ridge at the upper end. Spans of this type are limited as they do not contain a tie beam at the bottom, and the thrust can force the walls outward.

Course
A layer of masonry units running horizontally in a wall or over an arch that is bonded with mortar. The horizontal joints run the entire length; the vertical joints are broken so that no two form a continuous line.

Coursed cobblestone
Small round stones of similar size laid up in courses with a rough beaded joint between the horizontal courses only.

Coursed masonry
Masonry construction in which the stones are laid in regular courses, not irregularly as in rough or random stonework.

Cove molding
A concave or canted interior corner molding, especially at the transition from the wall to a ceiling or floor.

Coved base
A trim piece at the base of a wall forming a concave rounded intersection with the floor.

Coved ceiling
A ceiling having a cove at the wall line or elsewhere.

Coved eaves
Eaves of a building covered with a curved surface, so the projecting rafters are not exposed.

Covenant
An agreement stating that the parties to a contract will abide by certain specified restrictions or regulations within the agreement.

Covenants and restrictions
Items contained in a deed that regulate how a property can be used once developed, such as design guidelines and color restrictions.

Cover
In reinforced concrete, the thickness of concrete overlying the steel bars nearest the surface. An adequate layer is needed to protect the reinforcement from rusting and from fire.

Cover molding
Any plain or molded wood strip covering a joint, as between sections of paneling, or covering a butt joint.

Coverage
The amount of surface or area that may be covered by a unit, gallon, bundle, square, or ton of building material.

Cowl
A metal cover fitted with louvers, often capable of rotating; fixed on a roof ventilator or chimney to improve the natural ventilation or draft.

Cracking
A common form of deterioration of masonry joints and concrete construction, often caused by uneven settlement or water seepage.

Craft
A manual skill, trade, or occupation; a skill in the execution of manual work, or special skill in an art or handwork.

Cramp
An iron or steel rod, with the ends bent at right angles to its length used to hold stone blocks together.

Crane
An overhead machine designed to lift and move material horizontally on a construction site using cables and a boom. The hoisting mechanism is an integral part of the boom. Types include bridge crane, climbing crane, crawler crane, jib crane, tower crane, and truck crane. See also *Derrick*.

Crane

Crane jib
An extension on the top of the crane that gives additional capabilities, such as a saddle jib, a horizontal extension at right angles to the tower, with a hook that moves on a trolley along the jib. A luffing jib pivots at the top of the tower.

Crawler
A piece of construction equipment that uses a continuous tracklike belt of interlocking steel treads, instead of tires, for better traction.

Crawler crane
Similar to a truck crane, but using crawler-type power; used when greater traction and maneuverability are needed, or in soil too soft to support a truck crane.

Crawl-hole vent
A screened sheet-metal frame, with a lift-out door, installed in a foundation wall, allowing for both ventilation and crawl space access.

Crawling
In painting, a defect that appears during the painting process, where the film breaks, separates, or raises as a result of applying the paint over a slick or glossy surface.

Crawlspace
A shallow space beneath the first floor of a house without a basement; used for access to pipes and ducts.

Crazing
In painting, a minute random cracking of a finish coat of paint due to uneven shrinking of the paint. In masonry, the appearance of very fine cracks while the surface is drying due to uneven contraction.

Credit report
An evaluation of the credit history and worthiness of an individual or business; also, a listing of their current financial condition, based on assets and liabilities and the ability to pay credit debts on schedule.

Creep
Deformation of a built-up roof system caused by thermal stresses; the tendency of hardened concrete to bend more and more under load over time.

Creosote
A distillate of coal tar, used as a wood preservative.

Creosoting
The process of injecting creosote into timber as a means of increasing its durability when it is to be exposed to wetting and drying.

Crib
A crate-like framing, used as a support for a structure above; any of various frameworks, as of logs and timbers used in construction.

Cribbing
Wooden beams placed under a structure to provide temporary support, either for jacking to repair foundations or to move a structure.

Cricket
A small tent-like construction built up on the back side of a chimney that protrudes through a sloping roof, to assist in shedding water away from the flat surface of the chimney. Also called *saddle*.

Crimp
A slight bend formed into a sheet metal section for fastening purposes, or to make the material less flexible; to offset the end of an angle or metal strip so it can overlap another piece. Also, to indent the ends of pipes, tubing, and flanges.

Crimping tool
A plierlike tool used in sheet metal work to make corrugations in the end of a duct.

Cripple
Any member shorter than most of the others in a structure, such as a stud beneath a window.

Cripple jack rafter
A jack rafter that is cut in between a hip and valley rafter.

Cripple rafter
A short rafter which runs from the ridge to the valley. Same as a *jack rafter*.

Cripple timbers
In building construction, timbers which are shortened for installation in areas less than the full height of others.

Critical Path Method (CPM)
A construction scheduling device and management tool in the form of a diagram showing all the tasks on a job in the proper sequencing of work, with parallel operations indicated, and times required for each task. Each task or activity is given an optimum start and finish time. The diagram indicates which operations are critical to the completion of the others.

Cross bracing
Diagonal bracing between floor joists, rafters, or other structural members to stiffen the structure; often offset to allow for end nailing.

Cross bridging
Transverse rows of small diagonal braces or struts set in pairs, and crossing each other between the timbers.

Cross section
A transverse section cut at right angles to the longitudinal axis of a piece of wood, or the view of a cut off section of a steel member.

Cross vaulting
Vaulting formed by the intersection of two or more simple vaults.

Crossbeam
A beam that runs transversely through the centerline of a structure; any transverse beam in a structure such as a joist.

Crossbuck door
A door made up of two vertical stiles and three horizontal rails, with two diagonal rails crossing in the lower half, resulting in four triangular panels in the lower section, and featuring glass in the upper half of the door.

Cross-cut saw
A hand saw used for cutting transversely across the grain of the wood.

Cross-gable roof
Two gable roof planes that intersect each other at right angles, forming a cross.

Crosshatch
Use of a series of parallel lines to indicate materials in a cross-sectional drawing. There are conventions for showing different materials.

Cross-hatching
The shading produced when a series of parallel lines cross each other; used to indicate certain materials or emphasize certain parts of a design.

Cross-sectional area
The area of a section cut transversely to the longitudinal axis of a member.

Crowbar
A heavy pinch bar made of a piece of round iron which is flattened to a chisel-like point at one end; can be used as a lever.

Crown
Any uppermost or terminal features in architecture; the top of an arch including the keystone; the corona of a cornice, often including the elements above it.

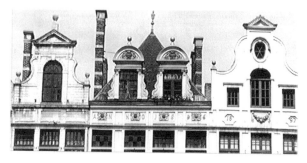

Crown glass
Glass made by blowing a mass of molten material, which is then flattened into a disk and spun into a circular sheet.

Crown molding
Any molding serving as a corona or otherwise forming the crowning or finishing member of a structure.

Crown post
Vertical member in a roof truss, especially a king post.

Crowstep gable
A masonry gable extended above the roof with a series of setbacks; often found in European medieval architecture, especially Dutch architecture.

Crowstone
The top stone of the stepped edge of a gable.

CRSI
Abbreviation for Concrete Reinforcing Steel Institute.

Crucks
Pairs of large curved timbers used for the principal framing of barns and primitive houses. They form a pointed arch, taking the place of both column and beam.

CSI's MasterFormat
A classification that is used as the basis for most commonly used specifications and estimating databases. MasterFormat numbers are also used to organize the information in a construction cost estimate and for filing design-related project data.

CSI's UniFormat
A classification system for construction systems and assemblies; used to develop preliminary project descriptions, preliminary cost classification, and a detailed filing system. It defines eight basic organizing systems: Substructure, Shells, Interiors, Services, Equipment and Furnishings, Building Site Work, Other Building Construction, and General Requirements, including bidding contracts and estimates.

Cubic content
The number of cubic feet contained in a space; used as a basis for estimating the cost of materials and construction. It is also important when estimating the cost of installing heating, lighting, and ventilating systems.

Cull
Any building material that is rejected as being below standard quality, and discarded as unsuitable for sound construction.

Cullet
Large irregular chunks of glass, produced by the slag from a glass furnace. When the glass cools, it is chipped off the sides of the furnace and later used as a catalyst in the mixture of the new batch of glass.

Culling
Sorting and grouping masonry units or other items by size and shape.

Cupola
A small structure projecting above a roof that provides ventilation or is used as a lookout.

Curing
The process by which plaster, adhesives, paint, and concrete reach full strength and hardness. Curing times vary from hours, days, months, and even years.

Curing of concrete
The maintenance of an appropriate humidity and temperature in freshly placed concrete to ensure the satisfactory hydration of the cement and proper hardening of the concrete. In cold weather it may be necessary to provide a source of heat such as a salamander or electric heater, and covering the concrete with a protective tarpaulin.

Curing time
The time required for initial application of a material to attain its design properties.

Current
The flow of electrical energy measured in amperes, or amps. Devices use the power in wattage, measured in watts, which is determined by multiplying the amperage times the voltage.

Current assets
Cash and other assets that will be converted or consumed within a 1-year period.

Current liabilities
Liabilities in a business or personal account that are to be paid within 1 year.

Current-carrying capacity
The maximum-rated current in amperes that an electrical device is allowed to carry.

Curtail
A spiral scroll-like termination of any architectural member, as at the end of a stair rail, or at the ends of the arms of a bench.

Curtain wall construction
A method of construction in which all building loads are transmitted to a metal skeleton frame, so that the non-load-bearing exterior walls of metal and glass are simply a protective cladding.

Curtainwall joints
The joints in this form of construction are not load-bearing, and occur between units of material supported independently. They must be composed of a flexible material to expand and contract in relation to the materials around it.

Cushion
In foundation construction, a capping to protect the head of a pile which is to be sunk into the ground with a pile driver.

Cut and fill
Excavating soil from one area of a site and depositing it on a different area to change the grades in accordance with a landscape or foundation plan.

Cut glass
A glass that has been decorated by grinding figures or patterns on its surface by abrasive means, followed by polishing it.

Cut stone
Any stone cut or machined to a specified size and shape to conform to drawings, for installation in a designated place.

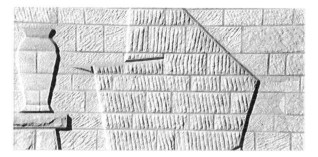

Cutaway corner
A corner formed by the meeting of three wall surfaces; produced by one short wall cutting across on the diagonal; often embellished with corner brackets.

Cut-in box
An electrical outlet box with clamps on the sides that can be easily installed during remodeling. The box does not have to be attached to a stud, but can be slipped into a hole cut in drywall and fastened in place by tightening screws which secure it to the drywall.

Cycle
The flow of alternating current, first in one direction and then in the opposite direction in one cycle. In a 60-cycle circuit, direction changes 60 times a second.

Cylinder lock
A lock with a central cylinder that rotates when the key lifts the internal tumblers.

Cylinder test
A standard laboratory test to determine the compressive strength of concrete from a cylinder-formed sample.

Cyma molding
A molding that has a profile with a double curvature.

Cyma recta molding
A molding of double curvature that is concave at the outer edge and convex at the inner edge.

Cyma reversa molding
A molding of double curvature that is convex at the outer edge and concave at the inner edge.

Cypress
A moderately strong, hard, and heavy softwood. Its heartwood is naturally decay-resistant and is used for exterior and interior construction where durability is required.

Dado
A rectangular groove cut across the full width of a piece of wood to receive the end of another piece.

Dado joint
A joint formed by the intersection of two boards, usually at right angles, the end of which is notched into the side of the other for a distance of half the latter's thickness.

Damages
A monetary compensation that a court awards for loss or injury suffered by a plaintiff.

Damages for delay
An amount of money payable by the contractor for the late completion of building works in order to compensate the client for any reasonable loss; sometimes termed liquidated damages or penalty. Found in the general conditions section of the contract.

Damp course
A course of masonry material on the ground that prevents moisture from penetration upward by capillary action. See *Capillary action*.

Damper
An adjustable metal plate, inside a flue or air duct that regulates the draft of a stove, fireplace, or furnace or controls the flow of air inside the duct. In the event of a fire, the damper operates automatically to close off the duct.

Dampproofing
The special preparation of a wall to prevent moisture from permeating through it. Material used for this purpose must be impervious to moisture.

Darby
A hand-operated straightedge, used in the early leveling stage of concrete placement, preceding floating and finishing. Also, a stiff straightedge of wood or metal used to smooth the surface of wet plaster.

Database
A computer software program that permits the categorization, sorting, manipulation, and retrieval of information in a variety of ways. Information can be sorted in various combinations of categories and hierarchies, and then listed in any desired format. It is useful for client information, marketing information such as mailing lists, and project data. In a building automation system, the database consists of names and descriptions such as temperature set points and operating information such as programs and passwords.

Date nail
A nail driven in a structure, with a stamped date on its head as a permanent indicator of when construction was completed.

x

Date of agreement
The date on the face of the agreement when it was signed.

Date of commencement of work
The date established in the notice to proceed, or the date established in the contract for work to begin.

Date of original construction
The date or period in which construction was either commenced or completed on a building. Methods used to determine this may include documentary evidence, date stone, building department records, or in the case of lack of any records, radiocarbon dating.

Date of substantial completion
The date certified by the architect when the work or a designated portion of it is sufficiently complete, in accordance with the contract documents, so that the owner may occupy it.

Date stone
A stone that is carved with the date of completion of the structure and embedded in the walls; found in many European medieval buildings, and American colonial buildings.

Datum
A point with a given coordinate in space from which other heights and depths can be measured.

Datum level
A basic level or line used as a reference for determining heights and depths of points or surfaces in building construction. Within any given city, the established datum level is recorded in the building codes that control the building standards for that city.

Datum point
A point of elevation reference established by the city from which levels and distances are measured.

Daub
To cover or apply a rough coat of plaster to a backing material.

Daubing
A rough coating of plaster given to a wall by throwing plaster against it.

Daylighting
Lighting of a space with daylight, either from a skylight or with direct or indirect sunlight.

Dead air space
Unventilated air space between structural elements, which is used for thermal and sound insulation.

Dead bolt
A bolt with a square head controlled directly by the key when moved in either direction.

Dead end
The termination of a piping system, such as closing off a line with a cap.

Dead load
The weight of all permanent and stationary construction materials or equipment included in a building.

Dead load deflection
The vertical deviation of a member caused by its own weight, plus the weight of permanently attached members.

Deadening
Installing materials in a building that will inhibit the transfer of sound waves through the use of insulation and other construction techniques, such as discontinuous construction of walls and floors.

Deadlock
A type of lock in which a bolt slides into a receptacle in the door jamb at the turn of a key, or turn piece.

Deadman
An anchor for a guy line, usually a beam, block, or other heavy item buried in the ground to which the line is attached.

Debris
Remains of material that are generally useless.

Debt service
The periodic repayment of loans, including interest and a portion of the principal.

Decay
The decomposition of timber brought about by a fungus. The fungus causes a breakdown of the cellular structure, which softens and weakens the wood.

Deciduous
Pertaining to trees which shed their leaves annually.

Deck
The flooring of a building or other structure; a flat open platform, as on a roof.

Deck paint
Enamel paint that is very resistant to wear; used on such surfaces as porch floors, outdoor decks, and in concrete stairwells.

Decking
Thick floor boards or planks used as a structural flooring, usually for long spans between joists. Also, light-gauge sheets of metal, which are ribbed, fluted, or stiffened for use in construction of concrete floors and roofs.

Declination
The position of the sun at solar noon, which varies with the time of year; used in the calculation of solar heating systems.

Decontaminate
To remove contamination from; to purify.

Decorated gypsum wallboard
Drywall panels with a factory-applied finish, such as decorative vinyl or paper.

Decoration
A combination of materials, textures, or wallpaper applied to the surface of a structure; includes gilding, stenciling, painting, and marbleizing. Also called *ornament*.

Decorative concrete block
A concrete masonry unit having special treatment of its exposed face for architectural effect. Such effects may consist of exposed aggregates or beveled recesses for a patterned appearance, especially when illuminated obliquely.

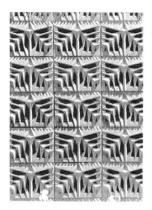

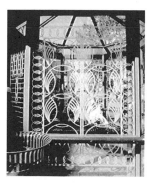

Decorative glass
Glass that has been embellished for a decorative effect. Embossing and sandblasting techniques create a subtle form of ornamentation. Etching and beveling are also used to create ornamentation in glass.

Decorative metal fencing
Ornamental fencing made from metal bar, pipe, and/or other metal shapes; they are welded together into sections of fencing, installed as connecting units.

Decorator
A person primarily engaged in the application of surface coverings, fittings, furniture, and fixtures in building interiors.

Dedication
A ceremony that officially begins the occupation and use of a building. A dedication ceremony may be held for the donation of land to the public for a road or other form of easement.

Deductible
The dollar amount that a policyholder agrees to pay before the insurance kicks in. The insurance company pays the amount over the deductible up to the amount of the policy.

Deduction
The amount deducted from the contract sum by a change order.

Deed
A written legal instrument that transfers the title of property from one person to another. A warranty deed guarantees that the title is without flaws. Also called *ownership document*.

Deed restriction
A statement included in the deed to a piece of land, placing limitations on the use of the property.

Default
A failure to perform the requirements of a contract.

Defect
In lumber, an irregularity occurring in or on wood that will tend to impair its strength, durability, or utility value.

Defective work
Any work that does not meet the standards implied in the contract documents.

Deflection
The deformation or displacement of a structural member as a result of loads acting on it.

Deformation
An act of deforming or changing the shape; an alteration in form that a structure undergoes when subjected to the action of a weight or load.

Deformed bar
A reinforcing bar made with a pattern of protruding ridges to produce a better bond between the bar and the concrete.

Degradation
A loss of the original characteristics, or weakening of an element by erosion. Also, a disintegration of paint by heat, moisture, sunlight, or natural weathering. Also, harmful action caused by human activity, such as vandalism.

Degree of difficulty factor
A factor that considers difficult working conditions when evaluating the time to complete a task, as compared to the time required under normal working conditions to complete the same task. The value obtained is used in scheduling a project.

Dehumidifier
A mechanical device that removes water vapor from the air inside a building, thereby lowering the dew point.

Dehydrate
To extract moisture from a material.

Delamination
Coming apart layer by layer; as in a separation of plies in a plywood panel, either through failure of the adhesive or through failure at the interface of the adhesive and the lamination.

Delay
Any action or item that delays the completion of the job., whether it be labor or materials related. If it is not the fault of any party, an extension of time to complete it is usually granted. If it is the fault of any party, damages may be assessed, such as back charging or other means. See also *Back charge*.

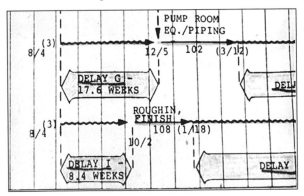

Delinquent payment
Funds due for certified payments to the contractor, subcontractor, or architect who are not paid within the stipulated time period.

Demand
The electrical load integrated over a specific time period; usually expressed in watts or kilowatts (kw).

Demand load
The total water, space heating, electrical current or the like that is required to operate a building's mechanical or electrical system.

Demolition
The deliberate and systematic disassembly or destruction of a structure. In restoration work, demolition may include only partial removal of partitions and other structural elements and mechanical or electrical systems.

Demolition as improvement
Strategic demolition can create new exterior façades, or an interior glassed-in atrium, by selectively reconfiguring the spaces within.

Demolition by neglect
The exact opposite of preservation by maintenance. Any building or site that is not taken care of on a regular basis is a potential candidate for the eventual disuse, disrepair, and ultimate need for demolition.

Demolition delay
A temporary halt to planned demolition; obtained by preservationists, often by a court injunction to allow for a period of negotiation.

Demolition permit
Written legal authorization by the appropriate building authority to proceed with demolishing any part or all of a structure.

Demountable partition
A temporary partition that can be disassembled and relocated.

Density
1. A planning or zoning unit of measurement used to express the ratio of buildings per acre or occupants per gross square foot of floor area. Density is calculated according to the type of zoning for a particular area under consideration, such as commercial, residential, or rural.

Density
2. The standard unit weight per unit volume of material, usually expressed as pounds per cubic foot. In urban planning, the number of people dwelling on an acre of land.

Dentil
A series of closely spaced ornamental rectangular blocks resembling teeth, used as moldings; most often found in continuous bands just below the cornice.

Department of Health and Human Services (DHHS)
The federal agency responsible for setting health and safety standards for the protection of all persons.

Department of Labor (DOL)
The federal agency that oversees all laws associated with hiring, employing, and protecting workers.

Deposition
A formal method of obtaining information relevant to a lawsuit by verbally asking an individual questions under oath.

Depository
A location where bids are deposited and received by an awarding authority.

Depreciated property
Real estate that has declined in value. Most property depreciates over the years, unless it is improved along the way, due to wear and tear and changing development patterns.

Depreciation
The reduction in the value or worth of an asset, such as a building, through physical deterioration over time and general obsolescence.

Depth of cut
The distance that a drill, saw blade, or other cutting device is set to cut into the work.

Deputy inspector
A person hired by a builder and approved by the building department to continuously inspect the work on a project.

Derelict
Land or buildings that have been deserted or abandoned, or damaged by serious neglect, vandalism, or other processes.

Derrick
Any hoisting device used for lifting or moving heavy weights. Also, a structure consisting of an upright or fixed framework with a hinged arm that can be raised and lowered and swung around to different positions for handling loads.

Desalinization
A process that removes salt from masonry.

Design
To compose a plan for a building or renovation. Also, the architectural concept as represented by plans, elevations, renderings, and other drawings; any visual concept of a constructed or reconstructed object.

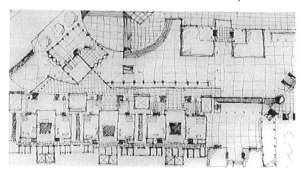

Design and construct
A form of project delivery that includes both the design and construction of a project. See also *Design-build*.

Design controls
Regulations by local governments regarding alterations to existing structures in historic towns or districts; usually restricted to the exterior use of materials and overall design style.

Design development
The second phase of the architect's basic services: drawings that describe the character of the project as to structural, mechanical, and electrical systems; materials and all other essentials; and probable construction costs.

Design development phase
The second phase of the architect's basic services, which includes developing more detailed plans and elevations, developing structural, mechanical, and electrical drawings, specifying materials, and estimating the probable cost of construction.

Design drawing
Any of the drawings made to aid in the visualization, exploration, and evaluation of a concept in the design process.

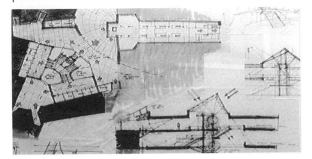

Design guidelines
Criteria for rehabilitation or new construction developed by preservation commissions, to identify design concerns in a historically significant area and to protect the character of designated buildings or districts.

Design load
The capacity required of air-conditioning equipment to produce specified conditions inside, when specified conditions of temperature and humidity exist outside. The equipment should have the capacity equal to the design load. Also, the total load on a structural system under the worst possible loading conditions.

Design professional
A term used to refer to architects; civil, structural, mechanical, electrical, plumbing, and heating, ventilation, and air-conditioning (HVAC) engineers; interior designers; landscape architects; and others whose services require licensing or regulations by the state in which they practice.

Design review
Determining whether modifications to historic structures meet the standards previously established by a review board or preservation commission.

Design specification
A type of specification that describes the materials and methods to be used for the performance of the contract.

Design study drawing
A drawing executed as an educational exercise produced as a preliminary to a final work or made to record observations.

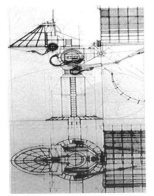

Design symbols
The representations of different building materials by graphic symbols.

Design-bid-build
An approach that allows the design to be fully developed and periodically reviewed by the owner before bidding and construction begin. A finalized design becomes the basis for pricing. This delivery formula is ideally suited to the fixed-price contract method. See also *Design-build* and *Fixed-price contract*.

Design-build
A project delivery approach that combines the design and construction into a single entity. It works on very large complex projects that can be defined in phased bid packages. On projects of large scale it is advisable to have a program manager (design professional) and a construction manager (contractor). The owner gains savings by an earlier finish date, shorter construction loans, and earlier startup for the operations of the project. Maintaining the schedule is the biggest challenge. Long lead items must be ordered, shop drawings must be prepared, permits and inspections must be scheduled and coordinated. Materials must be ordered to be available when needed. In a guaranteed maximum price contract often used in this method, the owner knows the costs beforehand.

Designer
The person who draws, lays out, or prepares a design.

Dessicant
A chemical agent that removes water or water vapor from the air.

Dessicate
To dry thoroughly or to remove the moisture content as in the seasoning of lumber by exposing it to heat in a kiln.

Destruction
The partial or complete loss of a structure; generally connoting a sudden or unplanned occurrence such as a fire, earthquake, or accident, as opposed to demolition.

Destructive probe
A method of determining the condition inside the walls of a structure by removing a portion of the element under investigation. The removed portion should be large enough for adequate inspection, but minimal for repair. See also *Borescope*.

Destructive testing
Materials testing methods that destroy the material in the process, such as compression tests of concrete, tensile tests of steel, and other load tests of structures.

Detail
A large-scale architectural or engineering drawing indicating specific configurations and dimensions of construction elements. If it differs from the general drawings, the large-scale drawing takes precedence.

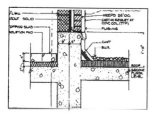 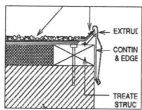

Detail design drawing
An elnargement of a section of a drawing showing a small part of a structure or component at a large scale.

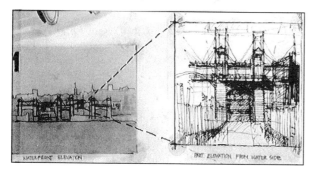

Detailed estimate of construction
A forecast of the construction cost based on unit prices of materials, labor, and equipment in contrast to a square-foot-area estimate.

Detailer
A draftsperson who primarily develops detailed drawings for specific parts of a building; a shop detailer who makes shop drawings for fabrication of specified fixtures.

Deterioration
A worsening of a structure's condition, generally attributable to exposure to weather, normal wear and tear, aging, or lack of maintenance.

Developer
A person or organization that controls and manages the process of the construction of buildings or other facilities by the arrangement of financing for the project, hiring the architect or contractor, obtaining zoning, regulatory approvals, and building permits, and that leases, sells, or manages the completed property.

Development
The process of improving property through the construction of roads, sewers, and electrical service and the construction of residential, commercial, or industrial buildings.

Development potential
The projected future use of a property compared to the existing use.

Device
A mechanism or piece of equipment with a specific purpose.

Dew point
The temperature of air at which its moisture content will begin to condense, forming droplets of water; the dew point varies with the moisture content of the air.

Dewatering
To remove water from the ground or excavations that hinders construction from an area of the site, with pumps or drainage systems.

Diagonal board fence
A style of fence design in which the boards are installed diagonally between the top and bottom rails.

Diagonal chimney stack
A group of chimney stacks that are square in cross-section and set on a diagonal alignment. They are often corbeled and joined at the top.

Diagonal compressive stress
One of the stresses that results from the combination of horizontal and vertical shear stresses in a beam.

Diagonal cutters
A plier-type wire cutter, where the cutting edge is parallel to the axis of the handles.

Diagonal rib
In a rib vault, the intersecting ribs extending from one corner of the compartment to the one diagonally opposite.

Diagonal rib

Dichromatic brickwork

Diagonal sheathing
A covering of wood boards placed over exterior studding at a diagonal with respect to the vertical; provides a base for the application of wall cladding.

Diagonal tensile stress
One of the stresses that results from the combination of horizontal and vertical shear stresses in a beam or slab.

Diagram
A plan, sketch, drawing, chart, or graph, not necessarily representational, that explains, demonstrates, or clarifies the arrangement and relationship of the parts to a whole.

Diamond mesh
Expanded metal lath produced by cutting slits in the metal and pulling it apart, creating diamond-shaped openings.

Diamond point chisel
A V-shaped metal cutting tool with a sharp cutting edge; used to cut grooves.

Diamond saw
A circular saw, with industrial diamonds on the cutting edge of the blade; commonly used for cutting brick and other hard material.

Diamond work masonry
Masonry construction in which pieces are set to form diamond-shaped patterns on the face of the wall.

Diaphragm
A relatively thin element in a structural member, which is capable of withstanding shear in its plane. It stiffens the structural member.

Diaphragm action
The action of a stressed-skin panel on a structure that provides stiffness and resistance to movement that might distort the squareness of the unit.

Dichromatic brickwork
Patterns formed by using two different colors of brick.

Die
In the extrusion process of forming metal or plastic members, the die is the piece having the shaped opening that the material is pushed through.

Dielectric union
A special fitting for joining copper and galvanized pipe, and preventing electrolysis, a corrosive chemical reaction. The fitting contains a washer and sleeve which keeps the two dissimilar metals from contacting.

Differential leveling
Determining the difference in elevation between two points using a level and a rod.

Differential settlement
In the design of foundations, settlement of different parts of a building at different rates; caused by the varying compressibility of the underlying soil.

Diffuser
A device in the ceiling or wall that directs heat or cool air into a room from the ductwork. Also a device used to alter the distribution of light from a luminaire; some are designed to reduce the brightness of the lamp.

Dimension
The measured distance between two points; which when shown on a drawing, is to become the precise distance between two points in a building.

Dimension line
Two lines on a drawing that are perpendicular to the object being dimensioned that identifies the distance between the two points.

Dimension timber
Rough-sawn wood with a rectangular or square cross-section that exceeds the nominal dimensions of 4 by 5 inches.

Dimension work
Masonry built with stone cut to exact size and shape, as in ashlar masonry walls.

Dimensional stability
Applies to a material that has little moisture movement and creep, since thermal and elastic deformation are unavoidable.

Dimensioning
Measurement and placement of dimensional information during the drawing of plans, elevations, and details.

Dimple
A slight depression in gypsum wallboard where the nail heads are located; later filled with joint compound.

Direct costs
The labor, material, subcontractor, and heavy equipment costs directly incorporated into the construction.

Direct current
A form of current in which the electricity flows in one direction only, such as in a dry cell battery. See also *Alternating current*.

Direct expense
All items of expense that are directly chargeable to a specific project, assignment, or task.

Direct gain system
A type of passive solar system where the building itself is oriented so as to be warmed by direct sunlight through windows, skylights, and greenhouses.

Direct labor
Wages earned by employees working on a specific job.

Direct lighting
The use of luminaires that direct most of the flux toward the surface being lit, as opposed to indirect lighting.

Direct nailing
Nailing perpendicular to the work surface.

Direct overhead
Overhead costs that are related to a specific job.

Direct selection
A situation where the owner selects a contractor directly based on the contractor's experience, availability, and capability. The terms of the contract are reached by negotiation rather than by competitive bidding.

Direct tap
A device that clamps around the main service line, such as a water main, so that a branch line can be drilled and tapped off, without taking the main line out of service.

Disc sander
A motor-driven portable tool designed to edge finish floors and other small areas.

Disconnect
A switch or current breaker adjacent to a piece of electrical equipment to disconnect power to the equipment for servicing.

Discontinuous construction
Any of several construction methods, such as the use of staggered studs or double walls to break the continuous path through which sound may be transmitted.

Discovery
A pretrial procedure that collects all the facts and documents related to a contract dispute, including depositions amd production of documents.

Dismantle
To take apart a structure piece by piece, often with the intention of reassembling it or moving it elsewhere for reconstruction.

Dismissal
The act of dropping a lawsuit.

Displacement
The removal or relocation of individuals, businesses, or industries from properties or neighborhoods because of real estate activities.

Dispute procedure
The administrative procedure for processing a contract dispute with the U.S. government. This procedure is provided for in the Contract Dispute Act.

Disrepair
The condition of being in need of repair, a state of neglect, dilapidation.

Dissolve
To make a solution by combining a solid or liquid substance with a liquid which absorbs it.

Distemper
A cheap paint with a binder of casein or some other glue; it is heavily pigmented and thinned with water.

Distributed load
A load spread over the surface. Unless otherwise described, it is usually considered uniformly distributed.

Distribution board
An electric switchboard or panel enclosed in a box, which contains circuit breakers and switches; used to distribute electricity within a building.

Distribution box
In an electrical system, a small metal box which allows accessibility for connecting branch circuits. In septic systems, the concrete box from which effluent is distributed to the field tiles.

Distribution duct
A raceway of various cross-sections, placed within or just below the floor and from which the wires and cables serve a specific floor area.

Distribution lines
In electricity, the main feed line of a circuit to which branch circuits are connected.

Distribution panel
An insulated board or box containing circuit breakers, from which connections are made between the main feeder lines and branch lines. Also called *power panel*.

Distribution tile
The pipe used in configuration with a septic tank system.

Ditch
A long narrow excavation in the earth for installing foundations, sewer systems, drainage systems, electrical cable lines, and utilities. Also called *culvert, channel.*

Divestment
The opposite of reinvestment; occurs when private and public investment is withdrawn from high-risk areas.

Divided light
A fixed window with several smaller panes of glass.

Divider strips
Strips of metal, plastic, or other suitable material that are set in a flooring material, such as terrazzo or concrete, to control cracking and to serve as screed surfaces.

Dividers
A measuring device consisting of two metal points with hinged legs, used for setting off distances, or dividing into equal lengths. They may also be used to scribe a line on a piece of wood to match an irregular surface of masonry.

Division
One of the 16 basic project specification classifications when MasterFormat is used. See also *MasterFormat.*

Document
A written, typed, or drawn record.

Documentation
Information used to accompany a completed National Register application form that records the prior history of an existing building or site; such as maps, site plans, drawings or photographs, or written historic references as to its physical appearance.

Dog's-tooth course
A decorative masonry band forming a zigzag pattern; created by laying rows of bricks at a 45 degree angle to the face of the wall.

Dogleg stair
A stair with two flights between stories, connected midway by a rectangular half-space landing. The two outer strings may be tenoned to a common newel post.

Dolly
A small truck used for moving heavy timbers and structural members, such as beams, girders, and columns. One type has a set of wheels on an axle in the center of the dolly; others have casters on each corner.

Dolomite
Limestone consisting principally of the mineral dolomite.

Dome
A curved roof structure that spans an area on a circular base, producing an equal thrust in all directions. A cross-section of the dome can be semicircular, pointed, or segmented.

Dome light
Any window or opening in a dome.

Domical vault
A rib vault in which each rib has the same radius, beginning from the apex and continuing from one side of the vault to the other.

Door
A hinged, sliding, tilting, or folding panel for closing openings in a wall or at entrances to buildings, rooms, cabinets, or closets.

Door buck

A metal or wood surface set in a wall, to which the finished frame is attached.

Door casing

The finished frame surrounding a door; the visible frame.

Door closer

A device to check a door and prevent its slamming when it closes.

Door frame

An assembly built into a wall consisting of two upright members (jambs) and a head (lintel) over the doorway; encloses the doorway and provides support on which to hang the door. Also called *buck*.

Door head

The uppermost member of a door frame; a horizontal projection above a door.

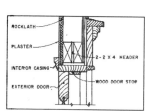

Door jack

A constructed wooden frame used by carpenters for holding a door horizontally while it is being planed and the edges fitted to the size of the opening.

Door jamb

The vertical member located on each side of a door.

Door knocker

A knob, bar, or ring of metal, attached to the outside of an exterior door to enable a person to announce his or her presence, usually held by a hinge so that it can be lifted to strike a metal plate.

Door light

Glass area in a door.

Door lock

A mechanism for opening and closing doors, with or without a locking device.

Door louvers

Blades or slats in a door to permit ventilation while the door is closed; may or may not be adjustable.

Door mullion

The center vertical member of a double-door opening set between two single active leaves, usually the strike side of each leaf.

Door muntin

An intermediate vertical member used to divide the panels of a paneled door.

Door panel

A distinct section or division of a door, recessed below or raised above the general level, or one enclosed by a frame.

Door pocket

The opening in a wall that receives a sliding door, which is installed on tracks during the rough framing stage.

Door pull

A handle which is commonly mounted on a metal plate, designed for attaching to a door to facilitate opening and closing of the door.

Door rail

A horizontal cross member connecting the hinge stile to the lock stile, both at the top and bottom of the door and at intermediate locations; may be exposed as in panel doors or concealed, as in flush doors.

Door schedule

A table located on a sheet of interior elevations, which gives the symbols used for each type of door. It also includes the quantity, type, and size.

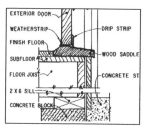

Door sill

The horizontal member; usually consisting of a board covering the floor joint on the threshold of a door. Also called *threshold, saddle*.

Door step

A step before an outer door. Also, several steps leading from an outer door to the ground or street level.

79

Door stile
One of the upright structural members of the frame that is located at the outer edge of a door.

Door surround
An ornamental border encircling the sides and top of a door frame.

Door threshold
A strip fastened to the floor beneath a door, usually required to cover the joint where two types of floor material meet; may provide weather protection at exterior doors.

Door transom
A crossbar separating a door from a light or window that is located above it.

Door trim
The casing around an interior door to cover the break between the material and the door frame.

Doorknob
The rotating handle of a lockset.

Doorstop
A strip against which a door shuts in its frame; a device placed on a wall behind a door or mounted on the floor to prevent the door from opening too wide.

Doorway
The framework in which the door hangs, or the entrance to a building: the key area of interest in a façade as a natural focal point and design element giving human scale, and containing the street number.

Doorway

Dormer
A structure projecting from a sloping roof, usually housing a vertical window which is placed in a small gable, or containing a ventilating louver. Also called *gable window.*

Dormer cheek
The vertical sides of a dormer.

Dormer horizontal cornice
A horizontal exterior trim installed at the head of a dormer window.

Dormer rafter
The roof rafters framing a dormer roof.

Dormer rake cornice
Exterior trim on the sloped edge of a dormer roof.

Dotted line
In an architectural drawing, a line consisting of short dashes indicating some concealed member represented on the drawing.

Double dome
An outer dome with a separate inner dome. The outer dome is usually constructed of masonry materials, and the inner dome framed with wood, often supporting a suspended ceiling. The system is used to either provide a supporting structure for the outer dome or provide a different shape or architectural treatment for the inner one, which is exposed to view.

Double door
A pair of swinging doors with hinges on each jamb, meeting in the middle.

Double glazing
A double pane of glass in a door or window, manufactured with an air space between the two panes which are sealed hermetically; provides sound and temperature insulation.

Double header
A structural member made by nailing or bolting two or more timbers together for use where extra strength is required, as in the opening around stairs.

Double lancet window
A window with two lancet windows that are side by side; found in Carpenter Gothic, Collegiate Gothic, and Tudor revival styles.

Double partition
A partition with two rows of studs that are alternately offset to form a cavity for soundproofing.

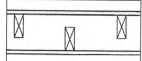

Double payment
Duplication of payment by an owner to a subcontractor or supplier to avoid liens, when the initial payment to the prime contractor was not paid to the subcontractor for work performed.

Double tenon
Two tenons side by side arranged within the thickness of a member; used for thick members to increase the glue line for added strength.

Double vault
A vault, usually domical, consisting of an inner shell separated from a higher outer shell.

Double-acting door
A door that opens in both directions, typically fitted with a double-acting hinge.

Double-acting spring hinge
A door hinge having two sets of springs which push the door back toward a closed position, but at the same time allow it to be opened in either direction.

Double-bar reinforcement
Short sections of reinforcing steel that extend from one concrete pour into the next, to increase the strength at the joint.

Double-decking
Insertion of a mezzanine or extra floor in a building with a high ceiling or a two-story space. The purpose of double-decking is to increase the usable area.

Double-faced door
A door with a different face detail on either side to match the decoration of the room or area in which each side faces. Normally constructed as two thin doors fixed back to back.

Double-framed floor
A floor that has separate floor and ceiling joists within the same cavity between floors.

Double-framed roof
A roof-framing system in which both longitudinal and lateral members are used; similar to one that uses purlins for support.

Double-headed nail
A special nail used in temporary construction, such as formwork and scaffolds. This type of nail has an extra head below the first one, to allow easy withdrawal with a claw hammer.

Double-pitched roof
A roof having two flatter slopes on each side of a steep central ridge; similar to a gambrel roof.

Double-pitched skylight
A skylight in a roof that slopes in two directions, such as one installed over a ridge in a roof.

Double-pole scaffold
A scaffold with two rows of uprights independent of an adjacent wall or support.

Double-sunk
Recessed or lowered in two steps, as when a panel is sunk below the surface of a larger panel.

Double-tier partition
A partition that is continuous through two stories of a building.

Doubling
Two structural members nailed together to provide additional strength.

Douglas fir
A strong, medium-density, medium-textured softwood; widely used for plywood and as lumber in construction.

Dovetail cramps
A device, usually of iron, bent at the ends, or of dovetail form, used to hold structural timbers or stone together.

Dovetail cutter
A rotary power tool that shapes dovetail joints and mortises.

Dovetail joint
A splayed tenon, shaped like a dove's tail, broader at its end than at its base. The joint is formed by such a tenon fitting into the recess of a corresponding mortise.

Dovetail saw
A small tenon saw used for preparing dovetails.

Dowel
A small pin inserted into two abutting pieces of wood; in stone or masonry construction, a wooden or metal pin placed between the different courses to prevent shifting.

Dowel gauge
A tool for locating and guiding drill bits to the correct position for drilling dowel holes.

Dowel lubricant
A lubricant applied to dowels placed in adjoining concrete slabs to allow longitudinal movement in expansion joints.

Doweling
A method of securing two members together through the use of dowels.

Down payment
An initial payment, which is a portion of the total price, made at the time of purchase of a piece of property.

Down zoning
Additional restrictions placed on existing zoning to either limit density or building height; may be used to protect historic districts from future development.

Down-feed system
A water-supply system where water is pumped to storage tanks on the roof, then fed downward by gravity to the building's fixtures.

Downtime
The amount of time that a piece of equipment cannot be used because of failure, repair, or maintenance.

Draft
A preliminary sketch of a design or plan, executed with the idea of potential revision or refinement.

Draft

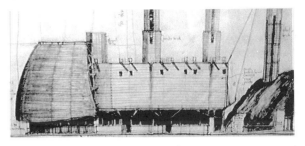

Draft hood
A cap that fits over a chimney flue to prevent downdrafts.

Drafted margin
A narrow dressed border around the face of a stone, usually about the width of a chisel edge.

Drafting
Drawing by using tools such as triangles, parallel rules, and drafting machines, as opposed to free-hand sketching, or using the computer to draw the lines.

Drafting machine
Although outmoded by computer drafting, a device attached to a drafting table that combines the functions of a T-square, parallel rule, triangle, scale, and protractor on a moveable arm and track that reaches every corner of the table.

Drafting service
An individual or firm offering drafting services to supplement an architect's or engineer's staff, or to work directly for clients. Since they are not licensed professionals, their services are restricted.

Drag
To move an object by pulling it.

Dragon beam
A beam of a traditional timber-framed house that is set diagonally at the corner to support the corner post and floor joist when the building jetties on two sides.

Dragon piece
A diagonal tie across the wall plate at the corner of a hipped-end roof for receiving the thrust of the hip rafter.

Drain
A channel, conduit, or pipe used to remove rain, wastewater, or sewage.

Drain field
A system of trenches filled with sand, gravel, or crushed stone, and a series of pipes to distribute septic tank effluent into the soil.

Drain tile
Pipe used at the bottom of foundation walls and footings to allow drainage of groundwater; typically made of terra-cotta with either a circular or hexagonal cross-section.

Drainage
An assembly of pipes and fittings, in the ground, used for the removal of wastewater or rainwater from a building or site.

Drainage hole
A hole in a retaining wall; an open joint in masonry, to drain unwanted water. Also called weephole.

Drainage system
All the components that convey the sewage and other waste to a point of disposal.

Drainpipe
Any pipe used to convey drainage liquids; includes both soil pipes and waste pipes.

Drawing
A sketch, design, or other representation by lines.

Drawing room
A large formal space for entertaining.

Drawings
A graphic representation of the projected construction, consisting of four main elements: plans, elevations, sections, and details.

Drawknife
A woodworking tool with a blade and handle on each end at right angles. It is used to smooth a surface by drawing the knife across it.

Dress
To prepare or finish a wood member by planing, or cutting a stone piece by chipping away at the irregularities.

Dressed lumber
Wood members having one or more of its faces planed smooth.

Dressed size
The true dimensions of lumber after sawing and planing, as opposed to nominal size. See also *Nominal size*.

Dressed stone
Masonry that has been worked to a desired shape. The faces to be exposed are smooth, ready for installation.

Drift
The horizontal displacement, lateral deflection, of a structure subjected to wind or earthquake loads.

Drift pin
A round spikelike tool used in the erection of structural steel to align holes in members to be joined. The tapered round end is inserted through one hole to be matched, while a bolt is placed into an adjacent hole.

Drill

A small portable electric tool used to bore holes in wood or metal, for fastening builder's hardware.

Drill gauge
A plate with holes of various sizes, used to determine the size of drill bits.

Drill saw
A round drill-like tool with a toothed surface, used for enlarging holes of various shapes and sizes for receptacles or switch boxes.

Drip
A groove on the underside of a projecting sill or other element that causes water to fall off instead of running down the wall.

Drip cap
A horizontal molding fixed to a door or window frame to divert the water from the top rail, causing it to drip beyond the outside of the frame.

Drip edge
Metal edging placed around the edge of a roof, prior to installing the roof material. It prevents water from running back under the eaves.

Drip molding
Any molding so formed and located as to act as a drip.

Dripstone cap
A continuous horizontal cap containing a drip molding on a masonry wall.

Dripstone course
A continuous horizontal drip molding in a masonry wall.

Driving home
In shop work, the placing of a nail or screw in its final position by driving it with a hammer or screwdriver.

Drop
Any one of the guttae attached to the underside of the mutules or triglyphs of a Doric entablature.

Drop chute
A metal chute that is used whenever concrete is dropped more than 4 feet, which prevents separation of the aggregate.

Drop molding
A panel molding recessed below the surface of the surrounding stiles and rails.

Drop panel
The portion of a flat slab or flat plate that is thickened throughout the area surrounding the top of the column, to reduce the magnitude of shear stress.

Dropped ceiling
A nonstructural ceiling suspended below the structural system; usually containing a light system in a modular grid pattern. Also called *hung ceiling*.

Drum
A cylindrical or polygonal wall below a dome, often pierced with windows. Also, a cylindrical module of a stone column.

Dry construction
Building without the use of plaster or mortar, which speeds construction and allows earlier occupancy.

Dry masonry
Stonework laid up without mortar.

Dry rot
A fungus that feeds on, and destroys, damp rather than wet timber. This fungus most often develops in damp, poorly ventilated, under-floor spaces and roof areas. Dry rot causes timber to lose strength, develop cracks, and finally become so dry and powdery that it is easily crumbled.

Dry seam
A fracture in stone that, if left untreated, may expand and eventually result in structural failure.

Dry well
A rock-and-gravel-lined hole in the ground designed to receive wastewater from the house but not sewage. Also called *cistern, catch basin*.

Dry-pipe sprinkler system
A sprinkler system whose pipes remain empty of water until the system is activated by a fire; used when there is concern for freezing of the pipes.

Dry-pressed brick
A clay brick made with only a small amount of water, and compressed under high pressure, which results in a very uniform brick with sharp edges and a surface sheen. These bricks are often used as face bricks, although their fragile edges are subject to erosion due to the high clay-to-water ratio.

Drywall
An interior wall constructed with a material such as gypsum board or plywood; usually supplied in large sheets or panels, which do not require water to apply.

Drywall hammer
A hand tool with a flat striking surface on one end of the head and a hatchet-like surface on the other. The dull hatchet blade is used for prying rather than chopping.

Drywall knife
A flat-bladed tool that comes in a variety of widths; also called a putty knife or taping knife.

Drywall tools
A set of tools specifically designed for the installation of gypsum wallboard or other types of wallboard; includes drywall hammers, squares, tape dispensers, knives, spreading and finishing tools.

Duct
A nonmetallic or metallic tube for housing wires or cables; may be underground or embedded in concrete floor slabs. A duct usually fabricated of metal is used to transfer air from one location to another. Also called *vent, raceway, plenum*.

Duct boards
Wooden slats placed on a roof to provide walking access to roof-mounted equipment, without walking on the roof surface itself, or any board laid over muddy ground to form a walkway.

Ductility
The property of a metal that allows it to be deformed. Also, the degree to which a metal can be deformed before reaching its elastic limit. The opposite of brittleness.

Ductwork
An assembly of ducts and duct fittings, usually of sheet metal, arranged for the distribution of air in air-conditioning and mechanical ventilation systems.

Dummy joint
A joint in concrete sidewalks and patios that is nonfunctional and strictly for design.

Duplex box
Electrical box for wiring switches or duplex receptacles.

Dust mask
A protective mask worn when working in areas of high dust density.

Dutch bond
Same as English cross bond or Flemish bond.

Dutch door
A door consisting of two separate leaves one above the other. The leaves may operate independently or together.

Dutch gable
A gable, each side of which is multicurved and surmounted by a pediment.

Dutch gambrel roof

A type of gambrel roof that has two flat surfaces on each side of the ridge, each at a different pitch. The top slope is the flatter of the two, while the lower slopes often end in a flared eave.

Dutchman
In carpentry, any odd piece of wood used to fill an opening in a makeshift manner, such as to correct a mistake, but not always of the same material.

Dwarf wall
A short wall that does not go all the way to the ceiling.

DWV system
An abbreviation for drain, waste, vent; refers to a home's complete system for the removal of waste. The entire system must work on the flow of gravity. Each part works independently of the other two.

Dynamic load
A load on a structural system that is not constant, such as a moving live load or wind load.

E

Early finish
The earliest time that an activity can be finished, as depicted on a Critical Path Method (CPM) chart. See *Critical Path Method*.

Early start
The earliest time that an activity can be started, as depicted on a Critical Path Method (CPM) chart. See *Critical Path Method*.

Early strength
The strength developed within 3 days of pouring concrete.

Earned income
A billable amount for work that has been completed.

Earnest money
A good faith commitment toward a purchase, by placing a deposit along with the offer to buy.

Ears

Projections on the sides of the upper part of door and window surrounds. Also, in plumbing, projections on a metal pipe, to allow fastening it to a wall.

Earth pigments
Mineral pigments that come directly from the earth; used to color concrete, and in the manufacture of paints.

Earth pressure
In foundation design, pressure caused by the weight of the earth acting against a retaining wall, or foundation wall.

Earthquake
A shaking motion of the surface of the earth, caused by a slippage of plates inside the earth's crust. The magnitude is classified by the Richter Scale, which uses a nonlinear scale from 1 to 10. Each numerical number is ten times as strong as the previous one. Building codes require buildings in areas subject to earthquakes to be designed to withstand a statistically anticipated magnitude for that area.

Earthwork
Any construction that involves moving, forming, cutting, or filling earth.

Easement
An interest in property sold or given by the owner to another party, either for profit or for the public benefit; the owner retains the remaining interest. Types include façade easement, to protect the exterior from alterations; open-space easement, to limit or prohibit development in dedicated open spaces; preservation easement, to limit change of appearance or use of a building or landscape feature; and utility easement, to allow for the future installation or maintenance of services. Also called *right of way*.

Easement rights
Laws governing the use of land owned by someone else. Utility companies commonly have easement rights, as utilities often need to cross private property.

Easing
The process of planing the closing edges of doors and windows that are too tight within their frames.

Eaves channel
A channel or small gutter along the top of a wall; conveys the roof rainwater to downspouts, or discharges it through gargoyles.

Eaves channel

Eaves flashing
A strip of flashing placed in an eaves gutter to keep overflowing water from running down the wall. See *Eaves gutter*.

Eaves gutter
A continuous wood or metal trough built into the eaves of a roof .

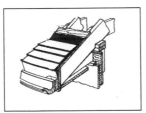

Eaves lath
A wooden strip placed under the last bottom course of roofing tile to raise it to conform to the same slope as the rest of the courses on the roof.

Eccentric load
A load on a column that is not in line with its axis, and introduces bending in the column.

Economic viability
The extent that a property or development plan is feasible and sustainable.

Edge beam
A beam at the edge of a shell plate structure; providing stiffness that increases the load-bearing capacity.

Edge clamp
A C-clamp that uses three adjustable setting screws, one at the top and bottom, and one in the middle of the C. When the top and bottom are attached to a countertop, the middle clamp is adjusted to apply pressure to the edge trim.

Edge joint
A joint formed by uniting the edges of two boards.

Edge joist
The joist at the inside edge of a wall.

Edge laid
Paving or flooring that is installed edge-to-edge length-wise.

Edge molding
A molding made on the edge of a board with a shaping cutter on a power saw.

Edge to edge
Two surfaces that butt together but do not overlap each other.

Edgenailing
Nailing diagonally into the edge of a board. See also *Facenailing*.

Edging
The finishing operation of rounding off the edges of a slab to prevent chipping or damage.

Edifice
A building, especially one of imposing appearance or size.

Efflorescence
In masonry work, white deposits on walls caused by soluble salts that crystallize on the surface.

Effluent
Liquid sewage discharge from a septic tank after having passed through any stage in its purification.

Egress requirement
Fire safety regulation in the building code that determines the number, location, and size of exit doors, corridors, and stairs in a building.

Elastic deformation
The deformation that occurs instantly when a load is applied and is instantly and fully recovered when the load is removed.

Elastic limit
The limit of stress beyond which the material cannot fully recover.

Elasticity
The ability of a material to deform instantly under load and to recover its original shape instantly when the load is removed.

Elastomer
A description of a polymer that will return to its original form once it has been released from the stress that caused deformation.

Elastomeric
Any material having the properties of being able to return to its original shape after being stressed; such as a roofing material that can expand and contract without rupture.

Elbow
Sharp corner in a pipe or conduit, as opposed to a bend, which has a larger radius of curvature.

Electric boiler
A tank controlled by an electrical current that heats and stores hot water.

Electric fixture
An electrical device, located on a wall or ceiling, and used to provide light to an area.

Electric furnace
A heating device controlled by an electrical current.

Electric handsaw
A portable electrically powered saw that accommodates interchangeable blades and other attachments, such as masonry cutting, tuck pointing, and wood trimming.

Electric heating
A system of heating that uses an electrical current to heat an element of resistance within the unit.

Electric outlet
A receptacle that receives an electric current and powers lights, appliances, power tools, motors, and other electrically powered devices.

Electric panelboard
A cabinet that houses fuses, switches, and circuit breakers; installed in or against a wall and accessible only from the front of the cabinet.

Electric radiant heat
A method of heating using the heat produced by passing an electric current through a resistive material. The most common are baseboard and wall convectors. Electric heat is fast, but expensive.

Electric screwdriver
A hand held electrically operated screwdriver, usually cordless and run with batteries. Some are shaped like a screwdriver, others are shaped like pistols, and many have variable-speed motors.

Electric service
The electric power supplied by a utility company, either by aboveground or underground service.

Electrical insulator
A component or device made from material with enough resistance to the flow of electric current to be considered a nonconductor.

Electrical layout
Plans that show the wiring layout, the type of electrical equipment and placement, and the locations of all electrical fixtures.

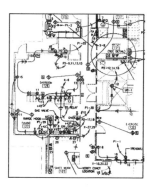

Electrical raceway
A conduit or molded trough through which electrical wires are run.

Electrical schematic diagram
A single line wiring diagram indicating the location of all wiring.

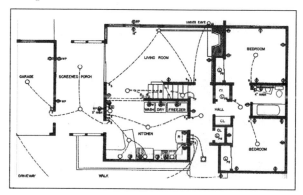

Electrical system
The complete system for delivering and distributing electricity in a structure; includes transformers, meters, cables, circuit breakers, wires, switches, fixtures, and outlets.

Electrical wiring
Copper wire covered with insulation that carries an electric current from the main panel box and through metal conduit throughout the structure to various outlets and fixtures.

Electrician
The skilled and licensed person or company who installs and maintains electrical systems.

Electrician's hammer
A long-nosed hammerhead, with a claw at the other end for pulling nails.

Electrician's pliers
Pliers with insulated handles, and built-in wire cutters.

Electronic stud finder
A device for locating studs behind an existing wall, using either a magnetic or ultrasonic sounding device, signaling the presence of a stud.

Element
An integral part of the substructure or superstructure having its own functional requirements such as a foundation, wall, floor, roof, stairs, and structural framework.

Elevated slab
A roof or floor slab above the ground level, supported by a structural frame.

Elevated water tank
A water tank supported on the roof of a structure to obtain the required pressure. They are usually built within an enclosure, but often left exposed.

Elevator
A platform or enclosure that can be raised or lowered in a vertical shaft that transports people or freight. The hoisting or lowering mechanism that serves two or more floors is equipped with a cab or platform that moves in vertical guiderails for stability. Also called *hoist, lift*.

Elevator car
A cab that includes the platform, framework, controls, and gate or door.

Elevator override
In the event of a fire, elevator operation can be controlled by a building's fire safety system, whereby the elevator car automatically returns to the ground floor, and can only be operated by the fire department.

Elevator pit
A depression that extends below the level of the lowest floor served by the elevator, to accommodate any operating mechanism under the cab.

Elliptical stair
A stair that winds around an elliptically shaped well, or whose shape in plan is that of an ellipse.

Elm
A tough, strong, moderately high-density hardwood of brown color; often has a twisted interlocked grain; used for decorative veneer, piles, and planks.

Embankment
A sloped area of earth abutting a structure.

Embed
To place an object inside another, as in placing a metal plate in the concrete forms to become a place to attach other objects once the concrete has hardened.

Embedded column
A column that is partly, but not wholly, built into a wall.

Embedded reinforcement
Any bar, rod, wire, or other steel member that is placed in concrete in such a way as to add strength to the concrete.

Emergency exit
A door leading to the outside of a structure, normally equipped with emergency exit hardware; used only when other exits fail or are rendered inaccessible due to a fire or other hazardous situation.

Emergency generator
A packaged standby unit including an electric generator and associated controls and equipment to provide power if the normal source fails. Most often used in hospitals and data centers.

Emergency lighting
Temporary lighting devices operated by battery that provide light when the power is interrupted.

Emergency power
Emergency standby generators may also supply power in facilities such as hospitals, where loss of power may pose a life-threatening situation; or data centers, where even the slightest loss of power to computers can cause untold financial damage to on-line systems and networks.

Eminent domain
The power of a government to condemn and acquire private property for the public benefit after payment of reasonable compensation to the owner.

Employee benefits
Customary or mandatory personnel benefits in addition to salary or remuneration may include health insurance, sick leave, holidays, vacations, pensions, or other retirement packages.

Employer's Liability Insurance
Protection for the employer against claims by employees for damages from injuries or diseases sustained in the course of the work. Based on common law negligence rather than on liability under workers' compensation acts.

EMT conduit
Abbreviation for electrical metallic tuning conduit; used for running wires. It is easier to handle than rigid conduit, and installed more quickly due to the nonthreaded type of fittings used to connect it.

Emulsion paint
A paint consisting of small particles of synthetic resin and pigments suspended in water. When the water evaporates, the resin particles form a film binding the pigments.

Enamel
A paint with an extremely high gloss and hard finish.

Encapsulation
An abatement technique for trapping asbestos fibers in a dense chemical compound.

Encased beam
Iron and steel beams that are encased in a variety of materials for protection against fire.

Encaustic tile
Tile whose colored decoration has been fixed by the application of extreme heat. They have been used since the Middle Ages.

Encroachment
Personal property of one part that is situated on land owned by another party.

Encumbrance
Any right or interest in land that diminishes the value of the fee but does not prevent the conveyance of the fee by the owner. Taxes, mortgages, and judgments are liens; restrictions, reservations, and easements are encumbrances, but are not liens.

End grain
The face of a piece of timber exposed when the fibers are cut transversely; exposure of this surface to the elements eventually causes deterioration.

End stiffener
A vertical angle connected to the web of a steel member with bolts, to stiffen the beam and transfer the end shear to other supports.

End to center
On working drawings, the dimension from the end of one object to the center of another; a common form of measurement, such as from the corner of a building to the center of windows, or walls. See also *Center to center*.

End-lap joint
A joint formed between the ends of two pieces of timber, normally at right angles; each piece is notched equal to the width of the other piece, to form a flush surface in the assembled joint.

Energy audit
A study of the energy components of an existing building, including orientation and exposure, building materials and components, and existing mechanical systems; usually performed as a means to determine ways to reduce energy costs.

Energy efficient
A generic term applied to any structure or appliance within it that minimizes the use of the energy delivered to it.

Energy system
The total machinery and processes in a building that use energy, including space heating and cooling, water heating, and the like.

Engineer
A person trained in one of a number of technical areas: civil engineers are involved in the design of buildings, bridges, highways, and airports; electrical engineers design electric power distribution and lighting systems; foundation engineers specialize in foundation design; mechanical engineers design plumbing systems, heating, ventilating, and air-conditioning systems, process piping, and related mechanical components of a building; structural engineers are civil engineers who specialize in the structural calculations for the building's framework.

Engineer's scale
A measuring scale based on decimals of an inch instead of fractions of an inch on an architect's scale. An inch is divided into 10, 20, 30, 40, 50, or 60 parts.

Engineer's transit
An instrument used for surveying differences in elevation and direction.

Engineered fill
Earth that has been compacted into place following specified and tested installation procedures.

English bond
Brickwork that has alternate courses of headers and stretchers, forming a strong bond that is easy to lay.

Entrained air
Microscopic air bubbles intentionally blown into mortar or concrete during mixing.

Entrapped air
Any air void in concrete that is not purposely put there.

Envelope
The imaginary shape of a building indicating its maximum volume; used primarily to check the plan, setback, and other restrictions regarding zoning regulations.

Environment
The combination of all external conditions that may influence, modify, or affect the actions of a person, piece of equipment, or any system.

Environmental codes
Regulations governing building that have an impact on the environment. See also *Building code.*

Environmental conditions
Natural elements that act upon a building, such as earthquakes, wind, rain, sunlight, and humidity.

Environmental damage
The damage caused by the interaction of the building with its environment, such as sun, wind, heat, cold, rain, and water infiltration.

Environmental design
Services rendered by a design professional related to the human physical environment, including architecture, landscape architecture, and urban planning.

Environmental impact
Includes all the social and physical effects of a development or government policy on the natural and built environment.

Environmental impact statement
A detailed analysis of the probable environmental consequences of proposed federal legislation, or large-scale construction making use of federal funds, likely to have significant effects on environmental quality.

Environmental planning
The person or professional whose job it is to determine the future physical arrangement and conditions of a community; involves an appraisal of current conditions, a forecast of future requirements, a plan, and proposals to implement the plan.

Environmental Protection Agency (EPA)
An independent agency of the executive branch of government created in 1970 to coordinate and create government action in controlling the nation's water, air, pesticides, solid waste management, radiation, and noise control.

Epicenter
The point on the earth's surface directly above the focus of an earthquake.

Epoxy
A plastic material that can be used as a filler to replace missing building components.

Epoxy adhesive
A two-part adhesive system using epoxy resin and a hardener; used for installing ceramic tile.

Epoxy binder
A resin with a hardener, which causes a chemical reaction when mixed with epoxy paints, causing it to harden as it dries.

Epoxy joint
In masonry, a visible joint filled with epoxy resin in place of mortar or caulking.

Epoxy paint
A paint that hardens to a gloss by chemical reaction.

Epoxy resin
A group of thermosetting plastics. The uncured resin and hardener are kept separately and mixed just before use. They adhere strongly to metals, glass, concrete, stone, and rubber, and they are resistant to abrasion, weather, acids, alkalis, and heat. They are useful for repairing damaged concrete and for joining new concrete to old; for this purpose they can be mixed into an epoxy resin mortar.

Epoxy weld
In cut-stone fabrication, a joint at an inside angle, connected by an epoxy resin to form an apparent single unit between the two pieces of stone.

EPS forms
Expanded polystyrene panels or foam block, used as formwork for concrete. The forms stay in place after the concrete is hardened and act as insulation. The panels can be linked together with plastic ties, and can be cut with a handsaw.

Equal Employment Opportunity Commission (EEOC)
A government agency that enforces provisions of the Civil Rights Act of 1964, forbidding discrimination by an employer hiring an employee based on race, color, religion, sex, or national origin. It is administered under the Department of Labor.

Equilibrium
A state of loading on a member where all the forces are in exact balance.

Equipment
The devices installed during the construction or alteration of a structure. Architectural equipment is usually fixed within a structure, and is either plumbed or wired to the building's services.

Equipment pad
A thick concrete pad placed under mechanical equipment to disperse the load, and to minimize vibration.

Equity
An interest, commonly expressed in monetary terms, that an owner has in property over and above all liens against the property. See also *Sweat equity.*

Equivalent
Having the same properties, characteristics, or specifications as another.

Erasing shield
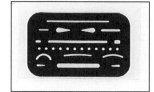
A thin metal plate, die cut with various shapes to allow erasing small portions of a drawing without affecting the other lines on the drawing.

Erecting
Raising the structural members into an upright or final position.

Erection
The hoisting and installing in place of the structural components of a building using a crane, hoist, or any other power system.

Erection bracing

Bracing that is installed during erection to hold the framework in a safe condition until sufficient permanent construction is in place to provide full stability.

Erection drawing
A shop drawing that outlines the components of an installation and details how it is to be erected.

Erection stresses
Those stresses caused by construction loads and by the weight of components while they are being lifted into position.

Erosion
Loss of material or surface due to exposure to the elements, such as rain, sunlight, or harmful polluting elements.

Errors and omissions insurance
A policy of insurance taken out by the architect to protect against errors and omissions in the preparation of the contract documents.

Errors of construction
Includes, for example, mortar joints that were never completely filled, walls that were not tied together, joints between materials that were not properly aligned, metal anchors improperly installed, and reinforcing steel improperly placed too close to the surface.

Escalator
A moving stairway consisting of steps attached to an inclined continuously moving belt for transporting passengers up or down between floors in a structure.

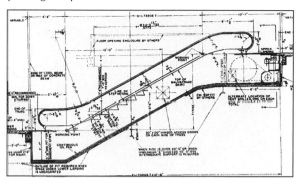

Escrow
Money and papers held by a third party until the conditions in the contract are fulfilled.

Escutcheon

A protective plate that surrounds the keyhole of a door or door handle. Also called *shield, plate, cover.*

Escutcheon pin
Small nail, usually brass, for fixing an escutcheon, often ornamental.

Estimate
The anticipated cost of materials, labor, and equipment slated for a proposed construction project.

Estimate to complete
The estimated total cost to complete a project including hours and cost of materials and overhead.

Estimating
Calculating the amount of material, labor, fabrication, or any combination needed to do the work, and the approximate anticipated cost of the finished product.

Estimator
A person skilled in determining the probable cost of a building project, using certain methods and techniques of estimating.

Evaporative cooler
A large cooling unit in which water is dripped over the thick fiber pads while air is drawn across the pads by a blower. The water absorbs the heat from the air, so the air is cooler and moister. Used primarily in dry climates.

Event
A prescribed activity as shown on a Critical Path Method (CPM) diagram by an arrow or line depicting the start and finish of the event. In a critical path, the event cannot be started until work preceding it has been performed.

Evidence
Documents and testimony introduced in a proceeding to support the claims of the parties.

Excavation
The removal of earth from its natural position; the cavity that results from the removal of earth.

Excavation line
A string stretched between batter boards to indicate the horizontal dimensions of the excavation. See also *Batter boards*.

Excavator
A company or individual who contracts to perform excavation of a building site.

Excess chalking
In painting, a condition caused by the application of too many coats of paint or lacquer to a heavy porous undercoating or the lack of the proper percentage of binder to pigment.

Exculpatory clause
A provision relieving a party of liability.

Excusable delay
A delay in schedule that is beyond the control, fault, or negligence of the contractor.

Executed
A contract that has been signed by both parties and becomes an enforceable contract. Also, work that has been performed and completed.

Exfoliation
Action caused by weathering or salt decay, resulting in the flaking off of surface layers of stone.

Exhaust fan
A fan that withdraws air that is not returned to the central air-treatment center and is exhausted to the outside.

Existing
Any structure that was completed prior to the adoption of a new or revised building code requirement. The structure does not have to be brought up to code, unless work is to be performed either to remodel or renovate the structure.

Existing building
A building built under prior laws and regulations. Current codes will be imposed if the building undergoes modification, additions, or renovations.

Exit control alarm
An alarm that is activated if a fire door is opened.

Exit corridor
An enclosed passageway that connects directly to the outside of a building.

Exit device
A bar across the inside of an emergency exit door; when pushed, it releases the door latch, for quick egress.

Exit sign
An illuminated sign above an exit, installed perpendicular to the wall surface in some corridors, that clearly identifies it as an exit.

Expansion
Stretching of an expanse of concrete due to weather conditions, such as the freezing of water within the concrete.

Expansion anchor
Bolt that is inserted into a hole drilled into masonry or other material, with a device on the end that expands, prohibiting the bolt from being withdrawn.

Expansion attic
An attic left unfinished for possible future expansion to living quarters.

Expansion bit
A boring tool that has an expandable bit for cutting different size holes.

Expansion joint
A joint designed to permit the expansion or contraction caused by temperature changes. It generally extends through the entire structure from the footings to the roof.

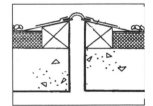

Expansion joint filler
Any material, such as felt, rubber, and neoprene, used to fill an expansion joint.

Expansion loop
A bend in a pipeline in the form of a large loop, to compensate for the longitudinal expansion and contraction in the line due to changes in temperature.

Expansion sleeve
A short length of metal or plastic pipe built into a floor or wall to allow for the expansion or contraction of another pipe that passes through the wall or floor.

Expansion strip
A soft, resilient material used to fill an expansion joint.

Expansion tank
A steel tank used in conjunction with a water well, in which a layer of compressed air in the tank maintains an even water pressure in the system.

Expediter
A person who monitors the arrival of building materials or equipment on site. Also, a person who takes plans and specifications to the building department on behalf of a design firm for the application of a building permit.

Expert witness
A witness in a court case or other legal proceeding who, by virtue of experience, training, skill, and knowledge of a particular field or subject, is recognized as being especially qualified to render an informed opinion on matters relating to that field or subject.

Exploratory demolition
Action prior to remodeling, restoration, or renovation to uncover materials and areas sufficiently to verify the existing conditions of unexposed areas.

Exposed
Any wiring, piping, ductwork, or other equipment that is normally concealed, installed openly along a wall or ceiling.

Exposed aggregate
A decorative finish for concrete; formed by removing the outer surface of cement mortar before it has hardened or by sprinkling aggregate on the wet concrete after placing.

Exposed area
In roofing, the area of a shingle that is not covered by an overlapping shingle, and is exposed to the weather.

Exposed brick
The stripping of plaster from interior walls to expose the brick to make the building appear old. A common practice in the adaptive use of old buildings as restaurants and boutiques, oftentimes changing the building's original character by so doing.

Exposed joint
A mortar joint on the face of a brick, block, or stone wall above the ground level and exposed to view.

Exposure
The amount of actual material exposed to the weather, not including any overlap in the installation. Also, the direction that a building faces determines its exposure.

Extended coverage insurance
An extension to property insurance to include windstorm, hail, riot, and explosion. See also Property insurance.

Extended plenum system
A system of forced-air heating using main ducts and branch ducts; the branch ducts extend from the main ducts to individual spaces.

Extended surface
A series of metal fins on a heating pipe that provide additional surface area for heating.

Extended use
Any process that increases the useful life of an old building through intervention, such as restoration, renovation, or adaptive use.

Extension ladder
A straight ladder with two or more sections, in which the upper section slides up the lower section to extend its height, locking into place at any portion of the extension.

Extension line
A line on a drawing extended away from the points of measurements, so that multiple incremental measurements can also be included between the lines.

Extension rule
A carpenter's rule that can be extended to take measurements between openings for fitting doors or windows.

Exterior
The outside surface of the building. Also called *façade*, *facing*.

Exterior gypsum ceiling panels
Gypsum wallboard panels designed for exterior use in areas with limited exposure to the weather, such as soffits, carport ceilings, or canopies. The panels have a weather-resistant core and are wrapped with a water-repellant paper.

Exterior door
A door on the outside wall of a building that is designed to be exposed to the weather on at least one side.

Exterior finish
The outside finish that is intended primarily to serve as a protection for the interior of the building and for ornamentation; consists of cornice trim, gutters, roof covering, wall material, door and window frames, water tables, corner boards, belt courses, and other ornamentation.

Exterior plywood
Plywood made with a waterproof glue which allows it to be used for exterior siding, roof sheathing, and other applications.

Exterior wall
A wall that is part of the envelope of a building thereby having one face exposed to the weather or to earth. Also called *Outside wall*.

Extra work
Any work performed in addition to the scope specified in the original contract, usually resulting in additional charges, which must be approved in writing by the client before they are paid.

Extruded metal
A metal used for a glass door or window sash that is shaped by being forced through a die with the configuration needed for that particular section. The material comes out in long strips, which are later cut into the appropriate lengths for assembling the doors and windows.

Extruded section
Structural sections formed by the extrusion of light metals through a die, and used for light construction.

Extruded tile
A tile section formed by pushing clay through a die and cutting it into specified lengths.

Extrusion
The process of producing metal shapes of a constant cross-section, by forcing hot metal through an opening in the die that has the desired shape, by means of a high-pressure ram. The process produces a linear element, which is later cut into smaller pieces.

Eye protection
The protection of a worker's eyes with safety glasses, or face shields, usually made from strong acrylic plastic. See also *Face shield*.

Eye screw
A wood screw shank that is bent into a circle at one end.

Eyebar
A metal tension member having an enlarged end, and containing a hole used to make a pinned connection to another part of the structure.

Eye bolt
1. A threaded shank with a looped head, designed to accept a cable, rope, or hook; used as an anchoring device.

Eyebolt
2. A bolt having its head in the form of a loop.

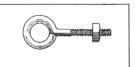

Eyebrow
A curved molding over the top of a window or door, often referred to as a *hood*.

Eyebrow dormer
A low dormer on the slope of a roof. It has no sides; the roof is carried over it in a continuous wavy line.

Eyebrow eave
An eave that is carried over a door entry in a wavy line.

Eyebrow lintel
A lintel above a window and carried in a wavy line.

Eyebrow window
A bottom-hinged, inward-opening sash located in the window of an eyebrow dormer.

F

Fabric
A connotation relating to the physical aspects of a building, structure, or city.

Fabricate
To make by assembling a standard or customized part.

Fabricating
Shop work on reinforcing steel, such as cutting, bundling, and tagging.

Fabrication
In sheet metal work, the construction of metal ducts in an air-conditioning system.

Façade
The exterior face of a building, particularly one of its main elevations, almost always containing an entrance and characterized by an elaboration of stylistic details.

Face
The front façade of a building or the finished surface of an exposed member.

Face block
A concrete block that has a glazed or stone face bonded to the surface; used for ease of cleaning and durability.

Face brick
A brick made or selected to give an attractive appearance when used without rendering of plaster or other surface treatment of the wall; made of selected clays or treated to produce the desired color.

Face grain
The grain on the face of a plywood panel.

Face mark
In woodworking, a mark placed on the surface of a piece of wood to indicate that part as the face.

Face measure
A measurement taken across the top of a wood member, not including rabbets, tongues, or laps.

Face nailed
Nails driven in perpendicular to the surface being nailed. Also called *direct nailing*. See also *Edge nailing*.

Face nailing
Nailing perpendicular to the surface of the pieces to be joined.

Face putty
The putty that is formed at an angle after the glass has been secured in the sash with glazing points.

Face shield
A protective covering with a transparent eye panel, worn to safeguard a worker's entire face while using a grinder, sander, or any other device which can throw small particles into the face or eyes. Face shields designed for welding are opaque with a dark glass eye panel to protect the worker's vision from the bright arc light of the welding torch.

Face side or edge
The side or edge of a piece of timber that has the best appearance. The face is also the first to be prepared and serves as a datum from which the piece may be brought to a final width and thickness.

Face size
The portion of the dressed or finished piece that is exposed to view when installed in place.

Face string
An outer string, usually of better finish than the rough string that it covers; may be part of the actual construction or applied to the face of the supporting member.

Faced
A condition in which one material is faced with a different one.

Faced wall
A masonry wall in which one or both sides are faced with a different material from the body of the wall, but bonded so they will act as a unit under load. See also *Veneered wall.*

Facilities planning
Long-term planning for the use of a building, which may include furnishings, equipment, operations, maintenance, renovation, expansion, and life-cycle planning.

Facility audit
A review and assessment of a facility's physical condition and functional performance.

Facility life cycle
The stages that a facility passes throughout its life; these include planning, entitlement, design, construction, operation, and disposal, renovation, or adaptive use.

Facing
A veneer of nonstructural material forming part of a wall and used as a finishing surface of a rougher or less attractive material, such as stone, terra-cotta, metal, stucco, plaster, and wood.

Facing hammer
In masonry work, a special type of stone hammer with a short stubby handle, and a double-tapered head on each end, with teeth on the chisel-like ends for shaping the surface of stone or cast concrete.

Factor of safety
A factor used in structural design to provide a margin of safety against collapse or serious structural damage. It allows for any inaccurate assumptions in the loading conditions, inadequate control over quality of workmanship, and imperfections in the materials.

Factored load
A load that has been adjusted by the safety factors used in the design of reinforced concrete members.

Factory finish
A product that has been stained and finished as part of the manufacturing process.

Factory-built
Construction that is built, or partially preassembled, in a factory instead of being constructed on site. Some factory-built structures are constructed in two or more modules with self-contained fixtures, and delivered to the site where final assembly takes place. Final finishing is done after the modules are assembled.

Failure

A condition when a structure or material ceases to fulfill its required purpose. The failure of a structural member may be caused by elastic deformation, fracture, or excessive deflection. The nonstructural failure of a material may be due to weathering, abrasion, or chemical action.

Fair Labor Standards Act (FLSA)

A law enacted by Congress in 1936, and amended numerous times. Today it is commonly referred to as the Minimum Wage Law, which established a minimum wage for all workers except agricultural workers, and set a 40-hour week as the maximum for straight time pay for hourly employees.

False

Any architectural element that does not function as it appears, such as a false arch, false window, or false door on a façade, or false ceiling in a room.

False ceiling

A ceiling suspended or hung from the floor above, which hides the underneath and provides a space for cables and ducts.

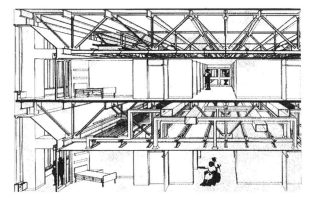

False front

A front wall that extends beyond the sidewalls and above the roof of a building to create a more imposing façade.

False joint

A groove in a solid masonry block that gives the appearance of a true joint.

False window

The representation of a window that is inserted in a façade to complete a series of windows or to give the appearance of symmetry.

Falsework

Temporary shoring, formwork, beams, or lateral bracing to support the work in the process of construction.

Fan

During construction or demolition of a building, an upward projecting arrangement of scaffolding and netting that is intended to catch any falling debris.

Fan coil unit

In air-conditioning, a package unit consisting of a fan, cooling coils, and air filters. Hot water, cold water, or a refrigerant are circulated through the coils to provide the heating or cooling as air is blown over the coils. Electric resistance coils are also used for heating.

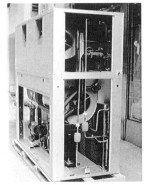

Fanlight

A semicircular window, usually over a door with radiating bars suggesting an open fan, or a wooden panel with the same radiating pattern.

Farenheit

A scale used for recording temperature where freezing is 32 degrees above zero and boiling is 212 degrees.

Fascia

Any flat horizontal member or molding with minimal projection; any narrow vertical surface that is projected or supported on elements other than a wall below.

Fastener

A mechanical device, weld, bolt, pin, or rivet for holding two or more parts, pieces, or members together.

Fast-track

An accelerated method of design and construction management of new construction or rehabilitation, under which sequential contracts for specialized trade work are awarded as plans and specifications are ready, while design is continuing on the other work. The object is to shorten the time between the beginning of design and the completion of construction.

Fast-track construction
A method of project delivery in which construction is begun on a portion of the work for which the design is complete, while design on other portions is being completed. Also, long-lead items are purchased and stored in order to lock in the best prices at the time the contract is let. This overlapping of design and construction activity expedites the occupancy of the facility by the owner and saves money.

Fat mortar
A mortar or concrete mix that contains a high cement content. It is worked more easily than a mixture that has the minimum amount of cement.

Fatigue
A weakening of the structure or a material caused by repeated loads. Fatigue might cause defects in the materials or result in total collapse of the structure.

Fatigue
The tendency of materials to fracture under many repetitions of a stress considerably lower than the ultimate static strengths.

Fatigue failure
Rupture that occurs when a material is subjected to repeated loadings, even though the stresses are substantially less than the ultimate strength.

Fault
In electrical work, a defect caused by poor insulation, improper connections, grounding, or shorting. Also, a shifting along the planes in a rock formation in the earth's crust that causes displacement. Earthquakes are caused by slippage along these fault lines.

Feasibility evaluation
A detailed evaluation of a project's potential, which includes four key areas: market support and economic evaluation, site and location evaluation, structural considerations, and architectural and historical aspects.

Feasibility study
An analysis of a proposed project to evaluate and determine appropriate uses for a structure, including physical conditions, anticipated costs, construction time, procedures, and projected revenues. Adaptive use feasibility studies generally analyze several possible courses of action.

Feather
A small piece or strip of wood which is inserted in the grooved edge of two pieces of wood to make a tight joint.

Featheredged
Anything that slopes off to a thin edge, such as a coping on a wall.

Featheredged coping
A coping stone which slopes steeply in one direction on its top surface.

Federal Acquisition Regulations (FAR)
Procurement regulations binding on all federal agencies adopted in 1984; replaces a series of previous regulations from different government agencies.

Federal employer identification number
A number assigned by the Internal Revenue Service to identify a business for tax purposes. In the case of self-employed individuals, a social security number is used in lieu of an employer identification number.

Federal Home Loan Mortgage Corporation
A government-sponsored organization that provides a secondary market for mortgages; nicknamed "Freddie Mac."

Federal Mediation and Conciliation Service
An agency of the U.S. Department of Labor, which acts as a mediator in the settlement of disputes, as provided in the National Labor Relations Act of 1935 and the Labor Management Relations Act of 1947.

Federal National Mortgage Association
An association created under the National Housing Act to provide a secondary mortgage market organized by private individuals, and operating under federal charter and supervision for Federal Housing Administration (FHA) insured and Veterans Administration (VA)-guaranteed home loans. Nicknamed "Fannie Mae."

Federal specification number
Numbers made up of two nonsignificant groups of letters followed by numbers used in U.S. government specifications, which describe the technical requirements for the purchase of items, materials, or services for use by the federal government. Reference to these specifications are mandatory for government procurement.

Fee
Payment for professional services, excluding payment for direct, indirect, or reimbursable expenses if based on a fee plus expenses agreement. Also, an amount paid to a contractor as compensation for management services on a cost-reimbursable contract.

Feed pipe
A main pipe which carries a supply directly to the point where it is to be used or to a secondary line. Also called a *feeder*.

Feeder
In electric wiring, any conductor in a wiring system between the service equipment and the branch circuit, or connecting directly to equipment. In plumbing, known as a feed pipe.

Feet per minute
A unit that is used to measure the velocity of air and fluid; used in calculations for heating, ventilation, and air-conditioning (HVAC) systems, piping systems, pump capacity calculations, and other systems where flow measurements are needed.

Felt
An interwoven fabric composed of matted fibers that are impregnated with tar. Sometimes covered with a thin metal backing. Also called *building paper, tar paper, sheathing paper.*

Felt papers
Sheathing papers used on roofs and sidewalls as protection against dampness. Felt papers applied to roofs are often infused with tar, asphalt, or other compounds for waterproofing.

Female threads
The threads on the inside diameter of a fitting or nut.

Fence
A guide on a saw against which the work is positioned, for precise cutting. Also, an enclosure or barrier around an area. They are made of a wide variety of materials and designs and are used to outline the property line.

Fence boards
Wood boards used in making a wooden fence.

Fender pile
An outside row of wooden piles that protects a pier or wharf from damage.

Fenestration
The design and placement of windows and other exterior openings in a building.

 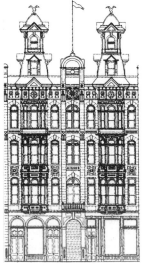

Ferrocement
Concrete made with several layers of finely divided reinforcement, instead of the conventional larger bars.

Ferrous metal
A metal in which iron is the principal element.

Ferrule
A short metal spike used for fastening gutter sections to a building. The ferrule adds structural support.

FHA
Abbreviation for Federal Housing Administration; a government agency regulating federal housing policy.

FHA loan
A loan insured by the government against default. A private lending agency grants the loan, but the federal government ensures that the lender will not lose on the loan. This ensures that much larger loans can be obtained with smaller down payments. The Federal Housing Administration (FHA) inspects the progress of construction in relationship to the terms for payments.

Fiber stress
The direct longitudinal stresses in a beam, such as tension and compression.

Fiberboard
A generic term for building board made from felted wood or other fibers and a soluble binder; includes particleboard and insulating board. Also called *composition board, particle board.*

Fiberglass
The generic term for a material consisting of extremely fine filaments of glass that are mixed with a resin to give the desired form in a mold. Layers of this combination are laid or sprayed into the mold.

Fiberglass-reinforced plastic
A coating of glass fibers and resins applied as a protective layer to plywood used in concrete formwork.

FICA
Abbreviation for Federal Insurance Contributions Act, a federal law which imposes a social security tax on employees, employers, and self-employed individuals.

Field
In brickwork, the expanse of wall between openings and corners.

Field applied
The application of a substance in the field, as opposed to being applied as part of the manufacturing process; the assembly of components in the field.

Field engineer
A representative of a governmental agency who oversees projects at the site. Also, an engineer who works primarily at the job site, as opposed to the home office. Also called a *field representative.*

Field inspection
An inspection of lumber or plywood at the job site, to verify that it is the product that was specified.

Field order
A written order from the architect to the contractor to make a minor change in the work that does not require an adjustment in the contract price or the schedule.

Field photography
Photographic documentation of existing conditions, construction progress, or completed works in the field, using small-format or digital cameras.

Field records
Information gathered from a site or existing building survey, including sketches and measurement notations, as well as small-format or digital pictures.

Field supervision
Supervision at the job site by the appropriate individual.

Field welding
Welding performed at the job site, using gasoline-powered equipment.

Field work
Any work performed at the job site.

Fieldstone
Loose stone found on the surface or in the soil, flat in the direction of bedding and suitable for drywall masonry.

Figure
The pattern produced in a wood surface by annual growth rings, rays, knots, and deviations from the regular grain.

File
A tool with teeth, used for finishing wood or metal surfaces.

Fill
Earth taken from the site or imported from elsewhere, used to raise the existing grade level. Also called *backfill*.

Filled insulation
A loose insulating material poured from bags or blown by machine into walls.

Filler
Any substance in paste form that is used to fill cracks and imperfections in wood or marble.

Fillet
A strip of wood connecting two surfaces that meet at an angle, covering the joint between them.

Fillet molding
A molding consisting of a narrow flat band, often square in section. The term is loosely applied to almost any rectangular molding, usually used in conjunction with other moldings or ornaments.

Fillet weld
A weld made in the interior angle where the members meet at a right angle.

Fill-type insulation
A loose-fill insulation material which is poured in place from bags, or blown in by a pneumatic machine.

Filter
A component of an air-cleaning system to remove particles of dust, dirt, and other debris.

Final acceptance
The formal acceptance by the architect of a contractor's work, notifying the owner that the work conforms to the contract documents and that final payment may be made.

Final completion
A term denoting that the work is complete and all contract requirements have been fulfilled by the contractor.

Final design phase
The planning of architectural services that follows preliminary design and precedes the production of construction documents.

Final inspection
A final review of the project by the architect before the issuance of the final certificate for payment.

Final payment
A payment made by the owner to the contractor, of the entire unpaid balance of the contract sum as adjusted by any change orders, upon issuance by the architect of the final certificate for payment.

Fingerjoint
Joints in woodworking that interlock like interlocking fingers, such as dovetail or mortised joints.

Finish
The texture, color, and other properties of a surface that may affect its appearance.

Finish carpenter
A highly skilled carpenter that installs paneling, trim, cabinets, casework, moldings, and other finishing surfaces, normally in the interior.

Finish carpentry
A term applied to practically all finish work performed by a carpenter, except that classed as rough finish. It includes casings, laying finish flooring, stairs, fitting and hanging doors, fitting and setting windows, baseboards, and other finish material.

Finish flooring
The final floor covering, such as terra-cotta tile, vinyl tile, cork tile, linoleum, hardwood or other wood parquet flooring, marble, or other masonry such as slate or encaustic tile.

Finish grade
The level above a datum when all site work is completed.

Finish hardware
Hardware, such as hinges, door handles, and locks, that has a finished appearance.

Finish nail
Available in length from 2d (penny) to 20d (penny), with a barrel head and slight recess at the top; used for finish work where the final appearance is of importance, such as trimming and moldings and cabinetwork. The small nail head is sunk into the wood with a nail set and covered with a fill compound.

Finished floor level
The final level or position of the finished floor, including any tiles, as opposed to the level of the concrete or wood subfloor surface or floor joists.

Finishing
In carpentry, the final addition of trim and moldings. In concrete flatwork, tooling of a surface to produce the desired appearance. In plastering, the application, smoothing, and texturing of the finish coat.

Fink truss
A commonly used roof truss, suitable for spans up to 50 ft, composed of two trussed rafters, each divided into four parts by purlins, using a tie across the bottom chord.

Fir
A softwood of the temperate climates including Douglas fir, white fir, silver fir, balsam fir; used for framing and interior trim.

Fire alarm
An electrical system, installed in a building as a protective measure against fire, by sounding an alarm when activated by a fire-detection system.

Fire barrier
Any element in a building so constructed as to delay the spread of fire from one part of a building to another; includes fire-resistant doors, enclosed stairways, and other similar obstructions.

Fire blocking
In wood frame construction, solid timbers that are of the same dimension, placed between the floor joists and studs.

Fire damper
A louver that closes automatically in an air duct in the presence of smoke or fire.

Fire detector
An automatic device that signals the presence of heat or flame in a structure.

Fire door
A self-closing door made of fire-resisting material; typically designed to slide across a doorway, delaying or preventing the spread of fire by confining it to one area.

Fire escape
An unobstructed path of egress from a building in the event of a fire. The metal platforms and ladders found on the exterior of older buildings are no longer permitted by building codes.

Fire extinguisher
A device for suppressing fires that consists of a canister containing a fire-suppressing material under pressure. When activated, the material can extinguish the flames.

Fire hazard
Any source of risk or danger from fire, such as the improper installation of wires for an electrical system, the use of combustible materials around fireplaces, and open spaces between floor joists that may create a draft and allow fire to spread; also anything that may obstruct or delay the operations of the fire department or the egress of occupants in the event of a fire.

Fire hose cabinet
A cabinet placed in stairwells at specific intervals, containing 75 feet of 1½-inch hose with a nozzle that is connected to a wet standpipe pipe system, containing water under pressure.

Fire indicator panel
A control panel that indicates a signal from a fire alarm and identifies the zone where the signal was initiated.

Fire labels
The labels placed on fire doors as proof that they meet the fire-resistive time period indicated on the label.

Fire marshal
A person employed by a state, whose duties are to enforce fire prevention laws, make investigations, and coordinate fire prevention activity.

Fire resistance
The capacity of a material to withstand fire or give protection from it; characterized by its ability to confine fire or to continue to perform a structural function.

Fire resistive
A designation applied to materials that are not combustible in the temperatures of ordinary fires and that will withstand such fires without serious impairment of their usefulness for at least 1 hour, called a 1-hour rating.

Fire retardant
A chemical applied to lumber to slow combustion.

Fire stair
A stairway that is enclosed with fire-resistive materials, and is continuous from top to bottom of a structure, entered on each floor level through a fire-rated doorway, balcony, or vestibule, so designed that smoke is prevented from entering the stairway. Often, fire hose connections are provided at each floor level. Often the stairway is enclosed in a masonry tower.

Fire stop
Obstructions across air passages in buildings that prevent the spread of hot gases and flames, such as the solid blocking between studs and floor and ceiling joists.

Fire tower
A stairway which is enclosed with fire-resistive construction and is entered by way of a vestibule of fire-resistive construction at each floor level; so designed that smoke is prevented from entering the stairway.

Fire wall
Any fire-resistant wall that separates one building from another or that subdivides a large building into smaller spaces; usually continuous from the foundations extending above the roof. See also *Fire barrier*.

Fire zone
A building code subdivision of a city or jurisdiction into areas, or zones, that has a certain level of fire risk associated with it as defined in the building code; the relative risk is predicated on density, land use, and existing type of construction in the area.

Firebox
A metal enclosure in a fireplace that contains the fire.

Firebrick
Brick made of a ceramic material that will resist high temperatures; used to line furnaces, fireplaces, and chimneys.

Fire-cut
An angular cut at the end of a joist that is anchored in a masonry wall. In the event of a fire, the joist will collapse without forcing the wall to fall outward.

Fireplace
An opening at the base of a chimney; usually an open recess in a wall, in which a fire may be built.

Fireplace arch
The arch over the front of a fireplace that supports the chimney breast above.

Fireplace back
The rear wall of the firebox; usually constructed of firebrick and sloped forward to reflect heat back into the room, and provide room for a smoke shelf above it.

Fireplace cheeks
The splayed sides of a fireplace.

Fireplace jamb
The interior sides of the firebox; frequently splayed to reflect heat back into the room.

Fireplace trim
Any finish or trim consisting of relatively incombustible materials.

Fireplace unit
A manufactured metal unit that contains a special heating chamber, firebox, throat damper, downdraft shelf, and smoke chamber. It is set up on a hearth of fireproof material. Cool air enters an inlet near the base of the unit and is heated in a double-walled chamber, and returns through an outlet at the top of the unit. Therefore heat is trapped and returned before it has a chance to escape through the chimney, as in a regular fireplace, thus increasing the heating capacity. If covered with masonry it will look like any other fireplace.

Fireproof construction
A method of building that employs noncombustible materials, such as a steel frame covered with a fire-resistant material.

Fireproofing
Material applied to structural elements or systems, which provides increased fire resistance, usually serving no structural function.

Fire-rated brick
A brick that has been graded for use in construction requiring specific fire-resistive characteristics.

Fire-rated door
A door that has been rated by testing its resistance to a fire over a period of time.

Fire-resistance classification
A standard rating of fire resistance and protective characteristics of a building construction or assembly.

Fire-resistance grading
The grading of building components according to the minutes or hours of resistance in a standard fire test.

Fire-resistance rating
Refers to the time in hours that a material or construction will withstand exposure to fire.

Fire-resistant panels
A panel of Type X gypsum wallboard which contains fiberglass and other heat-resistant materials, added to the core to increase its ability to withstand fire.

Fire-resistive construction
Building construction in which the structural members, walls, partitions, floors, columns, and roof are noncombustible materials having fire endurance ratings at least equal to those specified by the appropriate authorities.

Fire-retardant chemical
Chemicals used to reduce flammability or retard the spread of flames.

Fire-retardant coating
A material applied to the surface of a building component to increase its resistance to combustion along the surface; also, a covering applied on a material to delay ignition and combustion of the material.

Fire-retardant paint
A paint based on silicone, casein, borax, polyvinyl chloride, or some other similar substance. A thin coating reduces the rate of flame spread of a combustible material. When applied to wood it increases the wood's resistance to combustion by producing a foaming action when exposed to heat, which stifles the oxygen needed to support combustion. It does not make the wood fireproof

First mortgage
The mortgage on a piece of real property that takes precedence over all other mortgages.

Fish plate
A short piece of board or metal used to hold a joint together.

Fish tape
Flexible steel tape that is run through electrical conduit and the wires are attached and pulled through.

Fitting
Manufactured device that is used to join pipe sections; any piece of sheet metal ductwork of a heating and air-conditioning system other than the straight sections.

Fixed assets
Any asset that is not readily converted to cash, such as real property.

Fixed costs
Applies to items of overhead, such as office rent, administrative salaries, insurance, and office supplies.

Fixed fee
Professional services that are paid for on a lump-sum basis, and not affected by project scope or any other variable, unless specified otherwise.

Fixed glazing
A window or an area of a window that does not open; glazed directly into a fixed frame.

Fixed sash
A fixed window frame that does not open.

Fixed-end beam
A beam that is securely fixed at one end, permitting no rotation.

Fixed-price contract
A contract specifying that the work will be carried out for a fixed lump sum without rise and fall cost adjustments; usually used for newer and short-duration projects.

Fixed-rate mortgage
A mortgage in which the rate of interest remains the same throughout the period of the mortgage.

Fixture
Any item that is fixed permanently to a building, such as lighting and sanitary fixtures.

Fixture schedule
A listing of fixtures on a drawing that identifies the details of all electrical fixtures to be used at various locations.

Fixture supply
The pipe connecting a plumbing fixture to the supply line. The supply line usually contains a shutoff valve in the event of repair or replacement of the fixture.

Flagstone
A naturally thin flat stone, normally used as a stepping stone or as outdoor paving; sometimes split from rock that cleaves easily.

Flammable
Describes a material that burns with a flame.

Flange
A projecting collar, edge, rib, rim, or ring on a pipe, shaft, or beam.

Flange pipe
A pipe that is cast with flanges at the ends to attach to other pipes or connections.

Flare
A fitting operation done on the end of copper tubing to widen the mouth before it is joined to another piece.

Flared eaves
An eave that projects beyond the surface of the wall and curves upward toward its outer edge.

Flash
To use a metal flashing to make a joint weatherproof.

Flashing
A thin impervious material placed in construction to prevent water penetration or provide water drainage between a roof and vertical walls and over exterior doors and windows. *Also called vapor barrier.*

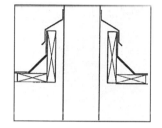

Flashing cement
A mixture of fibers, bitumin, and a solvent, which is applied with a trowel.

Flat plate collector
A style of solar collector consisting of a black, heat-absorbing panel encased in an enclosure with insulation below the panel, and covered with two layers of glass or acrylic plastic. Once sunlight enters, it will be absorbed by the panel and reflected back as heat, which will not pass through the glass, thus becoming trapped inside, where it can be stored for later use.

Flat roof
A roof having no slope, or one with only a slight pitch so as to drain rainwater; a roof with only sufficient slope to cause drainage. Also called *horizontal roof.*

Flat seam
In sheet metal roofing, a seam that is formed to be flat against the surface of the roof.

Flat skylight
A skylight that has a flat profile, rather than one that has a curved profile. Glass skylights are always flat.

Flat slab
A concrete slab reinforced in two or more directions and supported directly on column capitals.

Flatwise
Refers to studs that are placed so that drywall is nailed to the wide, flat side, instead of on the edge; used when a staggered partition is installed. See *Staggered partition.*

Flatwork
Concrete slabs, such as floors, walks, patios, driveways, and sidewalks.

Flaw
A defect in a wood member, or any other structural component, which may eventually cause failure of a building or any part of it. See also *Failure.*

Flemish gable
A masonry gable extended above the roof with setback stages that may be stepped or curved profiles in any of a wide variety of combinations.

Flexible cable
A cable consisting of insulated, stranded, or woven conductors used in electrical work; a hoisting cable made up of steel wire strands.

Flexible connector
In ductwork, plumbing, and electrical work, a connection that permits movement from expansion, contraction, and vibration.

Flexible insulation
A type of insulation consisting of mineral wool, or other substance, that comes in blankets with a vapor barrier on one side. It can fit various installation conditions.

Flexible metal conduit
A spiral-wrapped steel tube that can be threaded through existing spaces; the wiring is pulled or threaded through it after the conduit is in place.

Flight
A continuous series of steps with no intermediate landings.

Flight rise
The vertical distance between the floors in a flight of stairs.

Flight run
The horizontal distance between the bottom and top riser in a flight of stairs.

Flitch
A portion of a log sawed on two or more sides and intended for remanufacture into lumber or sliced or sawed veneer. Also, a complete bundle of veneers after cutting, laid together in the sequence in which they were sliced or sawed.

Flitch beam
A built-up beam formed by two wood members with a metal plate sandwiched in between, bolted together for additional strength.

Float

A tool made of wood, aluminum, or magnesium used in finishing operations to give an even, but not smooth, texture to a plaster or stucco wall.

Float coat

A coat of finishing cement put on with a float.

Float finish

A rather rough concrete finish, obtained by finishing with a wooden float.

Float glass

A flat glass sheet that is extremely smooth and nearly distortion free; manufactured by pouring molten glass onto a surface of molten metal and allowing it to cool slowly.

Float scaffold

A platform scaffold, suspended by ropes or cables from overhead.

Float time

In a Critical Path Method (CPM) of scheduling construction, a method of indicating slack time in the schedule; the amount of time that an activity can be delayed without impacting on the completion of the job.

Floater

A tool used to smooth and finish cement work.

Floating

In concrete work, an intermediate step usually done after edging and jointing and before troweling. If a coarsely textured surface is desired, floating may be the last step.

Floating floor

The floor is separated from the rest of the building by supporting it on sleepers or a built-up structural system, to provide sound insulation or space for high-tech flexible electrical service, independent of wall locations.

Floating foundation

A special type of foundation made to carry the weight of a superstructure that is to be erected on unstable soil. Such a foundation consists of a large raft-like slab composed of concrete, reinforced with steel rods.

Floatstone

In masonry, a type of stone used by bricklayers to smooth gauged brick.

Floor

The horizontal plane that forms a surface for walking in a building, consisting of boards, bricks, stone, clay, tile, or other material. Also called *decking*.

Floor brick

Smooth, dense brick, highly resistant to abrasion; used as a finished floor surface.

Floor drain

A fixture providing an opening in the floor to drain water into a plumbing system.

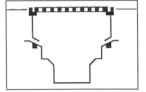

Floor finish

A final coating of a protective film on floors; may include varnish, wax, polyurethane, stain, or paint.

Floor framing

Consists of all structural supports, joists, bridging, and subflooring.

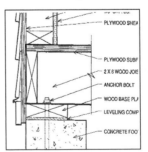
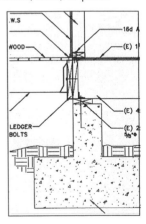

Floor furnace

A heating unit specially adapted for small houses that have no basement or cellar. It is installed directly underneath the floor of a room.

Floor jack

A screw-type jack placed under the floor framing to provide temporary support for alignment or repair.

Floor joist

Any joist or series of joists that support a floor.

Floor level
A designation for the height above a prescribed or established datum; or the location of the floor within the building itself, such as basement or first floor.

Floor lining
A layer of paper, felt, or similar material laid between the subfloor and the finish floor.

Floor load
The total weight on a floor, including the dead weight of the floor itself, and any line or transient load. Permissible loading may be stated in pounds per square foot.

Floor plan
A drawing representing a horizontal section taken above a floor to show, diagrammatically, the enclosing walls of a building, its doors and windows, the arrangement of its interior spaces, dimensions, room designations, and other notations.

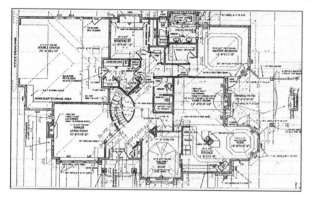

Floor receptacle
An electrical outlet set flush with the floor.

Floor register
A register for warm air that is set flush with the finished floor.

Floor sander
A heavy-duty machine for surfacing wood floors with sandpaper.

Floor sealer
A liquid such as urethane, chlorinated rubber, or acrylic, used to seal the surface of concrete floors to prevent dusting off the surface.

Floor sink
A sink installed in the floor; similar to a floor drain, only larger to handle a greater volume of water.

Floor tile
A ceramic tile that can be used as a floor finish, such as encaustic tile, quarry tile, and glazed tile.

Floor underlayment
A surface on which to lay the finish floor; consisting of particleboard, plywood, waferboard, or similar products.

Floor ventilation
The free movement of air beneath a structure; obtained by providing adequate vents in the foundation walls.

Floor-area ratio
The ratio between the total floor area of all floors of a building that is permitted by code and the area of the lot on which the building is constructed.

Floorboard
The close boarding fixed to the floor joists to provide a surface; normally either timber, plywood, or chipboard.

Flooring
Materials such as boards, bricks, planks, tile, or marble used for the surface of a floor.

Flooring nail
A steel nail with a mechanically deformed shank, often threaded helically, having a countersunk head and a blunt diamond point.

Flow chart
A graphic representation and schedule of the activities of a job from start to finish.

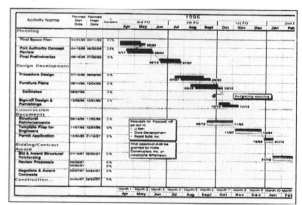

Flue
An incombustible and heat-resistant enclosed passage in a chimney to control and carry away products of combustion from a fireplace to the outside air. Also called *chimney, smokestack*.

Flue grouping
The gathering and grouping of multiple flues into one chimney, to limit the number of fireproof vertical stacks through a structure.

Flue lining
Fire clay or terra-cotta pipe, either round or square, usually in 2-foot lengths of varying size, used for the inner lining of chimneys.

Fluorescent lamp
An electric lamp, consisting of a tube with an inside coating of fluorescent powder, which converts a low-voltage electric charge through mercury vapor into visible light.

Fluorescent light fixture
A lighting fixture containing a series of fluorescent lamps in a reflector, either suspended from the ceiling, or housed in the surface of a ceiling, with diffusing grilles that can be lowered to replace the lamps.

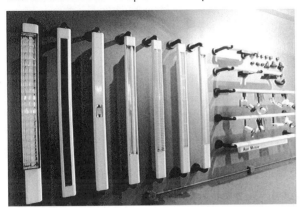

Flush bead molding
A molding whose surface is on the same plane as that of the wood member or assembly to which it is applied.

Flush bushing
In plumbing, a bushing engineered to fit flush into the fitting without a shoulder.

Flush door
A smooth-surfaced door that has faces in the same plane as the surface and that conceals its rails and stiles or other structural features.

Flush eaves
The eaves fascia is set against the wall surface and is attached directly to it.

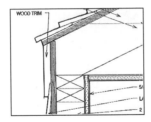

Flush joint
Any joint finished even or level with the surrounding surfaces.

Flush molding
A molding whose surface is in the same plane as that of the wood member or assembly to which it is applied.

Flush panel
One whose surface is in the same plane as the face of the surrounding frame.

Flush paneled door
A paneled door in which, on one or both faces, the panels are finished flush with the rails and stiles.

Flush siding
Tongue-and-groove boards that are laid flush on sidewalls.

Flux
Acid or rosin fluid or paste applied to metal surfaces to remove any oxide film in preparation for soldering, brazing, or welding operations.

Flying façade
The continuation of the façade wall above the roofline of a building.

Flying form
A system of formwork that can be moved intact in large sections; after the concrete hardens, the formwork is attached to the last pour and moved up to the next pour.

Flying scaffold
Staging suspended by ropes or cables from outrigger beams, or specially curved hangers that go over a cornice and hook on the parapet wall.

Foam core
Plastic foam between the veneers of a plywood panel.

Foam rubber
A lightweight rubber produced by entrapping large quantities of air in bubbles within the material.

Foamed-in-place insulation
A plastic foam used for thermal insulation, poured or sprayed into cavities in walls. Also eutethane foam sprayed onto existing walls and ceilings, filling all the voids, and creating a well-insulated roof.

Folding casement window
One of a pair of casements, with rabbeted meeting stiles, that is hung in a single frame without a mullion and hinged together so that it can open and fold in a confined space.

Folding door
One of two or more doors that are hinged together so that they can open and fold in a confined space.

Folding partition
A method of opening or closing off an area, by using panels hung from a ceiling track that stack together in the open position. Also, a series of thin slats of wood, connected at their vertical edges with a flexible material, or continuous hinge, and hung from a track in the ceiling. The door opens and closes like the bellows of an accordion. Also called an *accordion door*.

Folding rule
A wooden rule used by carpenters that pivots and folds in sections.

Folding stair
A stairway that folds into the ceiling; used for access to areas of a building that are not in general use. It is fixed with hinges at the upper end.

Foot
The lowest part of an object, such as the end of a rafter where it meets the top plate.

Foot plate
In framing, the lowest horizontal timber of a partition or wall to which the studding is nailed.

Footbridge
A narrow bridge structure that is designed to carry pedestrians only.

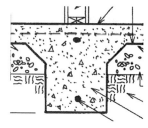

Footing
That portion of the foundation of a structure that transmits loads directly to the soil; may be enlarged to distribute the load over a greater area to prevent or to reduce settling. Also called *anchorage*.

Footprint
The projected area of a building or piece of equipment on a horizontal surface.

Force
Anything that changes or tends to change the state of rest of a body. Common in buildings are the weight of the materials from which they are built, the weight of the contents, and the forces due to wind, snow, and earthquakes.

Forced circulation
Movement of a fluid by pumping as opposed to gravity circulation.

Forced fit
The fitting of a structural member in place by means of force, so that the parts become joined as a unit.

Forced-air heating
The circulation of hot air within a building using fans to move the air within the system of ducts that connects to the furnace.

Foreclosure
The transfer of title back to the lender if the owner fails to pay the mortgage.

Foreclosure sale
The optional right of a lending institution to sell mortgaged property, if the owner fails to make payments.

Foreman
An overseer who organizes and supervises the work of others in the building trades; is usually responsible to a superintendent or manager.

Fork lift truck
A truck with a pair of forks on the front, which can be slid under a load or pallet of materials, and raised so that the truck can move it elsewhere. The trucks are powered by gasoline motors or battery-operated electric engines and can stack materials up to 20 feet or higher.

Form anchor
Any metal device used to attach new concrete forms to existing concrete.

Form coating
A liquid or oil applied to the inside of formwork to allow easy release of the forms from the concrete.

Form deck
A corrugated steel decking used as an integral and permanent formwork for reinforced concrete floors.

Form insulation

Thermal insulation used in cold weather to prevent freezing of the concrete; consists of an airtight seal and is applied to the exterior of the forms.

Form lining

The lining of concrete formwork, which can be used to impart a smooth or patterned finish to the concrete surface; to absorb moisture in order to obtain a drier surface; or to apply a set-retarding chemical, which allows the aggregate to be exposed.

Form lumber

In building forms, any lumber or boards used for shaping and holding green concrete until it has set and thoroughly dried.

Form pressure

Lateral pressure acting on vertical surfaces, resulting from the fluid-like behavior of wet concrete.

Form stop

In concrete work, a plank nailed to a 4 × 4, placed in the form to hold the wet concrete at the end of a day's pour.

Form stripping

A process of removing the formwork from concrete after it has set. See also *Climbing form*.

Form ties

Metal rods or similar devices used to space two forms apart and to keep them from spreading due to the pressure of the wet concrete. The forms are either removed or left embedded in the concrete.

Format

In construction, the standard arrangement of a project manual as set forth by the American Institute of Architects (AID), containing bidding information, contract forms, conditions of the contract, and the 16 subdivisions of specifications.

Formica

A trademark name for a plastic laminate used for facing countertops.

Formwork

The total system of support for freshly placed concrete, including the mold or sheathing which contacts the concrete, as well as all supporting members, hardware, and necessary bracing.

Formwork

Foundation

The lowest division of a building that serves to transmit and anchor the loads from the superstructure directly to its earth or rock, usually below ground level.

Foundation bolt

A bolt or device used to anchor structural parts of a building to the foundation on which it rests. Also called an *anchor bolt*.

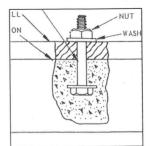

Foundation engineering

The branch of engineering concerned with the evaluation of the soil and the design of the substructure needed to support the construction above.

Foundation plan

A plan view showing the layout of the foundation, footings, and piers.

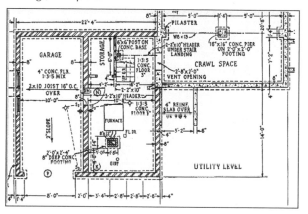

Foundation vent

A screened opening in a foundation wall to ventilate the substructure.

Foundation wall

A wall below, or partly below, grade to provide support for the exterior walls or other parts of the structure.

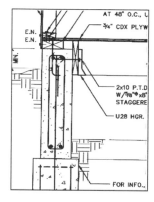

Fountain

An architectural setting that incorporates a continuous or artificial water supply, fed by a system of pipes and nozzles through which water is forced under pressure to produce a stream of ornamental jets.

Fracture

1. In masonry, the separation of the continuous part of a wall of brick or stone, caused by a sudden shock or excessive strain, resulting in a separation from the mortar and cracks apprearing on the surface of the wall.
2. Structural failure of a material by breaking, cracking, or splitting.

Frame

The timberwork, steel, or concrete frame that encloses and supports all the other structural components of a building.

Frame construction

Any type of construction in which the building is supported mainly by a frame, and not mainly by load-bearing walls. Balloon-framed timber houses, steel-framed buildings, and reinforced-concrete-framed buildings all belong in this category.

Frame house

One in which the forms and support are constructed of framed timbers, then sheathed with clapboards or shingles, or the frame may be filled in with brick and plaster. See also *Half-timbered wall*.

Frame of a house

The framework of a house, which includes the joists, studs, plates, sills, partitions, and roofing; all the parts that make up the skeleton of the building.

Framework

Composed of individual parts that are fitted and joined together as skeletal structures designed to produce a specific shape, or to provide temporary or permanent support.

Framing

A system of rough timber structural woodwork that is joined together in order to support or enclose, such as partitions, flooring, and roofing. Any framed work, as around an opening in an exterior wall. Also called *rough carpentry, skeleton*.

Framing

Framing anchor
A metal device consisting of a piece of bent metal plate, with holes in each fold to be used in connecting pieces of timber together. They are made in a variety of shapes and sizes.

Framing in
The process of framing the complete framework of a structure.

Framing plan
A drawing showing the structural framing members such as joists, rafters, beams, and girders in a plan view. It also shows bearing walls, columns, and supports, and their relationship to the floor plan.

Framing sawhorse
An X-shaped frame for holding rough lumber during the process of sawing.

Framing square
A right-angle steel tool used for measuring structural material for framing, roof framing, and stair building.

Free float time
In project management, planning, and scheduling using the Critical Path Method (CPM), the amount of time by which an activity can be delayed without affecting the start of any upcoming activities in the network.

Freemason
Traditionally a term applied to stonemasons who were able to work or carve freestone.

Freestone
Any stone, such as sandstone, that can be freely worked or quarried; used for molding, tracery, and other work required to be executed with the chisel.

Freight elevator
In a building, an elevator with an extra-heavy platform, reinforced side braces to keep the platform from tipping, extra-rigid car frames, and additional guide-rail brackets to anchor the guide rails more securely to the building structure; used for transferring freight from one floor level to another.

French door
A door having a top rail, bottom rail, and stiles, which has glass panes throughout its entire length; often used in pairs.

French window
A type of casement window, similar to a door, where the sash swings from the jamb of the opening.

Fresh-air inlet
In a plumbing system, a connection made to a house drain above the drain trap leading to the outside air, to bring fresh air into the system to eliminate foul gases.

Friction connection
A connection between two or more structural steel members, clamped together with sufficient force using high-strength bolts so that the loads are transmitted between them by friction along the connecting surfaces.

Friction latch
A device consisting of a spring and plunger contained in a casing inside a cabinet door that engages a similar-shaped socket when the door is closed. A slight push inward on the door releases the catch.

Friction tape
A tape coated with a black adhesive compound; used as insulation on spliced joints.

Frieze
An elevated horizontal continuous band or panel that is usually located below the cornice; often decorated with sculpture in low relief.

Frieze-band window
A small window in a continuous series that forms a horizontal band directly below the cornice, usually across the main façade.

Frilled
An ornamental edging such as a scroll that has added decorative carving along its projecting edges.

Front elevation
In an architectural set of drawings, the front view of a building.

Frontage
The extent of land along a public highway, stream, or city lot; also, the extent of a building along a public street, road, or highway.

Front-end loading
The practice of pricing the work to be accomplished at the front end of the job at a higher rate than the work at the end of the job, so that the contractor or subcontractor can submit larger requests for payments at the front end of the job.

Front-entrance door
Any exterior door, specially designed to close a front entrance or doorway.

Frost heave
Swelling of the soil due to the expansion of the groundwater when it turns into ice. It usually causes uplift, since the soil is more restrained in other directions.

Frost line
The level above which the ground is frozen in winter. Foundations should go below the frost line to avoid being heaved up by the freezing action.

Frosted glass
Glass that has been surface-treated to simulate frost, and thus soften and scatter the light.

Full-size details
A design which is drawn to the actual size of the object; used on shop drawings for installation of certain fixtures.

Function
The natural or proper use that a building supports in its design, layout, and construction.

Funded debt ratio
The ratio of working capital from borrowed funds to the working capital from equity.

Furnace
An apparatus in which heat is generated and maintained by burning fuel.

Furring
The addition of spacing members such as wood or metal that are attached to the framing members so that the finish material can be plumb or level.

Furring brick
A hollow brick grooved or scored on one face to provide a key for plastering.

Furring channel
Small metal channels used to hold the metal lath in a plaster ceiling.

Furring strip
A thin piece of wood used to build up areas to align panels.

Fuse
A safety device in an electrical system, which will melt if there is an overload, causing an interruption in the current; mostly replaced by circuit breakers. See also *Circuit breaker.*

Fuse box
A box that holds fuses, circuit breakers, or a service board or panel. Also called *power panel.*

Fusetron
A special type of fuse with a time lag, that will carry the momentary current of motors starting up without interrupting the circuit. Also called a *fusestat.*

Fusible link
A link on the holding device of a fireproof door or window that melts when subject to extreme heat, allowing the door or window to close.

FUTA
An abbreviation for Federal Unemployment Tax Act. A federal law that imposes an unemployment tax on employers.

G

Gable
The entire triangular end of a wall, above the level of the eaves, the top of which conforms to the slope of the roof that abuts against it; sometimes stepped and sometimes curved in a scroll shape.

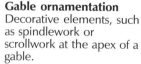

Gable ornamentation
Decorative elements, such as spindlework or scrollwork at the apex of a gable.

Gable post
A post that supports the intersection of the bargeboards located under the ridge of a gable roof.

Gable vent
A screened vent or louver installed in the apex of a gable end of a house, used to let warm air escape from the attic space.

Gable wall
A wall that continues to the roof line on the gable end of a structure.

Gabled tower
A tower that is finished with a gable on two or all sides, instead of terminating in a spire.

Gablet
A small gable; usually found over a dormer window or at the apex of a gable wall.

Gage
In sheet metal work, the thickness is usually specified by gage number, commonly ranging from 32 to 10, in increments of 2; the gage number decreases as the thickness increases. Thus 32 is considered a light gage, and 10 considered a heavy gage.

Gallons per minute (gpm)
A unit of measurement of the rate of flow of a liquid.

Galvanic action
A chemical reaction that takes place when two dissimilar metals come into contact in the presence of moisture. The more chemically active metal corrodes by transferring ions to the more passive metal, which remains unchanged.

Galvanized
The coating of iron or steel with a thin layer of zinc by dipping it into molten zinc; protects iron and steel from rust.

Galvanized steel
Steel coated with zinc to make it weatherproof.

Gambrel roof
A roof that has its slope broken by an angle, so that the lower part is steeper than the upper part.

Gang drilling
The process of drilling holes in a number of stacked and aligned panels or other material at the same time, so that the holes are placed in the identical place in each panel or object.

Gang form
A series of prefabricated forms connected together to make large reusable units, that can be moved by crane or rolled to the next location.

Gang milling
The process of milling with multiple cutting heads, or milling two or more pieces at the same time.

Gang operations
Processing, drilling, or cutting several identical pieces of wood at the same time.

Gang saw
A power saw using multiple blades to make parallel cuts in a piece of wood at the same time.

Gangway
A temporary walkway made of planks and used as a passageway on a construction job.

Gantry
A bridge-like structure, similar to the support for a bridge crane.

Gantry crane
A portal crane with four legs running on rails. It can pass over complete houses under construction or renovation. It is the most expensive type of crane, and used only for large building projects.

GAO
The U.S. General Accounting Office which, under the direction of the Comptroller General, has jurisdiction over bid protests.

Garnet paper
An abrasive paper used for polishing and finishing surfaces of woodwork.

Gas heater
A gas-fired space heater, installed in a wall, or a gas-fired heater used to heat water in a storage tank.

Gasket
In plumbing, the hemp wound around the spigot end of a pipe in a joint; forced into the socket of the mating pipe with a curved tool to form a tight joint. Heated lead was then poured into the joint for a watertight seal.

Gasoline portable tools
Saws, hammers, drills, and the like, that are operated by gasoline; used where electric power is not available.

Gate

A passageway in a fence, wall, or other barrier that slides, lowers, or swings shut.

Gate valve

A flow control device, commonly located at the utility service entrance, consisting of a wedge-shaped gate, which can be raised or lowered in the slot provided.

Gauged brick

Brick that has been cast, ground, or otherwise manufactured to exact and accurate dimensions.

Gauging block

A block of wood used to align and level concrete forms, or layers of brick or concrete block, by suspending it along a string line between the corners of the forms.

Gear

A toothed wheel which interlocks with other toothed or chain-driven mechanism to transmit power and motion as it turns.

General Conditions

Generally occurring prior to the specifications, they represent an extension of the contract agreement and contain contractual requirements, as opposed to the specific technical requirements contained in the 16 subdivisions of the specifications. They include such items as methods of payment, responsibilities of the contractor and the owner, insurance requirements, and other legal statements to avoid disagreements between the owner and the contractor. The most commonly used General Conditions are those published by the American Institute of Architects. Supplementary General Conditions are modifications to satisfy the requirements for a particular construction project.

General contract

In a single contract system, the agreement between the owner and the general contractor.

General contractor

The prime contractor who oversees and is responsible for all work on the site, and to whom all subcontractors on the same job are responsible.

General foreman

The person who is the general contractor's on-site representative, and who coordinates the work of all trades and oversees all labor performed at the site. Also called *superintendent*.

General obligation bonds

Issued to investors by a subdivision of government, following a public referendum, they promise payment by the government. In return, funds are supplied to investors and used to pay for the construction of publicly owned buildings or other public works projects.

General partnership

An association of two or more parties, who share all aspects of the business, including assets and liabilities, and management responsibility.

General requirements

The title of Division 1 in the Construction Specifications Institute's Uniform System. General requirements usually include overhead items and equipment rental.

General Services Administration (GSA)

Owns or manages most federal buildings except those of the military, Veterans' Administration, and Postal Services. They transfer surplus historic public buildings to state and local governments for reuse. They are also required to locate federal offices in buildings of historical, architectural, or cultural significance when possible. They also commission works of art for federal buildings.

Geodetic survey

A survey of large land areas; these calculations can accurately specify points from which other surveys can be controlled.

Geotechnical investigation

Soil boring and laboratory sampling and testing to determine the subsurface conditions, such as the relative compressive strengths of various strata that would have an effect on the design of the foundations and structure of the building.

Ghost mark

An outline on the exterior or interior of a building that shows earlier construction that was either removed or altered. These include outlines created by missing architectural elements, different paint colors, missing plaster, and patched holes.

Gin pole
A vertical guyed pole used for supporting lifting tackle.

Gingerbread
The highly decorative and often superfluous wood-work applied to a Victorian-style house or commercial structure.

Girder
A large or principal beam used to support concentrated loads at isolated points along the length of the span. Also called *beam*.

Girt
In a braced frame, a horizontal member at an intermediate level between the columns, studs, or posts; a heavy beam, framed into the studs, that supports the floor joists.

Girth
The distance around a column and the circumference of a circular object.

Glass
A hard, brittle, usually transparent or translucent substance, produced by melting a mixture of silica oxides. While molten, it may be easily blown, drawn, rolled, pressed, or cast to a variety of shapes. It can be transparent, translucent, or mirrored; and it can be made nonglare, pigmented, or tinted. It can be shaped by casting, rolling, pressing, or baking, adding patterns and textures at the same time. It can also be bonded to metal for use as an exterior cladding.

Glass block
Composed of two sheets of plate glass with an airspace between them, formed into a sealed modular hollow block; laid up with mortar, similar to masonry blocks as a modular material; comes in several distinct styles, patterns, and degrees of transparency and translucency.

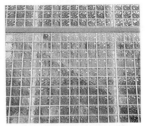

Glass door
A door consisting of heat-strengthened or tempered glass, with or without rails or stiles; used primarily as an entrance door for retail stores.

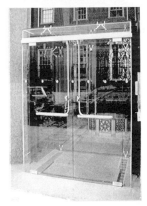

Glass wool insulation
A kind of insulating material composed of glass fibers that are formed into lightweight blankets of uniform thickness, fastened securely to heavy paper or vapor barrier; manufactured in standard widths to go between the studs in a wall or joists in the ceiling.

Glass-fiber-reinforced concrete
Alkali-resistant glass fibers added to concrete to strengthen it.

Glass-fiber-reinforced plastic
A molded, lightweight material used to match existing stone or terra-cotta elements, as replacement parts.

Glazed brick
Brick or tile having a ceramic glaze finish.

Glazed work
Brickwork built with enameled brick or glazed brick.

Glazier
A worker whose business is that of cutting panes of glass to size and fitting them into position in frames for doors and windows.

Glazier's points
Small metal triangular fasteners used to hold glass in its framework. They are pushed into the wood frame and against the glass, and later covered over with glazing compound.

Glazier's putty
A mixture of whiting and linseed oil forming a plastic substance used for fixing panes of glass into frames.

Glazing
A clear or translucent material such as glass or acrylic that admits light into a building.

Glazing bar
A bar of wood or metal that holds panes of glass in place. Also called *astragals, muntin, sash bar.*

Glazing fillet
A narrow strip of wood or plastic fastened to the rebate of a glazing bar; used instead of face putty to hold the glass in place.

Glazing gasket
A narrow prefabricated strip of neoprene used as a dry alternative to glazing compounds. The gasket is impervious to moisture and temperature and is often used with large sheets of glass.

Gliding window
A window that slides back and forth in tracks. Same as a sliding window, or patio door.

Globe
A spherical ornament, fabricated out of solid wood or a metal shell, usually found on the top of steeples and cupolas.

Globe valve
A valve that shuts off the flow in a pipe with a rounded disc.

Gloss
A property of paint finish that determines its reflective quality; either shiny, semireflective, soft finish, or flat.

Gloss enamel
A finishing material that forms a hard coating with maximum smoothness and a high shine.

Glue
An adhesive substance; types include liquid glue, casein glue, animal glue, epoxy resin, vegetable glue, synthetic resin, cellulose cement, and rubber compounds.

Glue block
A wood block usually triangular in cross-section, glued to an angular joint between two members at right angles to stiffen the joint.

Glue injector
A metal syringe with a small pointed nozzle for injecting the glue into a joint or through a very small hole.

Glue line
The line of glue visible on the edge of a plywood panel; also applies to the layer of glue itself.

Glued floor system
A method of floor construction where a plywood underlayment is both glued and nailed to the floor joists for a stronger bond.

Glue-laminated arch
An arch made from layers of wood that are joined with adhesives. The glued joints transmit the shear stresses, so the structure acts as one piece capable of use as a structural arch and long-span beam.

Glulam
Glue-laminated lumber; normally a structural timber member, glued and laid up from fairly small sections and lengths to form either large cross sections, long lengths, curved shapes, or a combination of these.

Good one side
A grade of sanded plywood with a higher grade of veneer on the face than on the back; used where appearance of the face is important.

Gouge
A cutting chisel with a U-shaped or V-shaped cutting end; used to make a groove in the material being chiseled.

Governing codes
All federal, state, and local codes that are applicable to a specific project.

Grade
The designation of the quality of a manufactured piece of wood; also the level of the ground in relation to the building. Also called *ground level, grade line.*

Grade beam
A reinforced concrete horizontal beam supported on each end that supports an exterior wall of the super-structure; normally placed directly on the ground.

Grade level
The elevation of the ground surface around a building at a construction site.

Grade mark
A marking rolled onto a reinforcing bar to identify the grade of steel in the bar.

Grade of steel
A means by which a design engineer specifies the strength of the steel required in each part of the structure.

Grade rod
A measuring rod used by surveyors to determine the difference in elevation from the last measurement with a transit to the point at which the rod is located. The rod is marked off in feet and decimals of a foot.

Grade stake
In earthwork, a stake that designates the specified level at that point.

Grade stamp
A mark or series of marks, placed on the back of lumber, plywood, or other material, that indicates the classification or quality of the material.

Grade strip
A thin wooden strip nailed to the inside of a concrete form, to indicate the finished level of the concrete pour.

Grader
A gasoline-operated vehicle with a large blade underneath, used for grading and leveling the ground.

Gradient
The slant of a road, piping, or the ground; expressed as a percentage of slope from true horizontal.

Grading
Preparing the ground level of a building site to the proper elevation and contour.

Grading plan
Similar to a site plan, but showing the desired contours and related earthwork as to how the site is to be graded.

Grain
The pattern of fibers found on the cut surface of wood, ranging from fine-grained to coarse-grained.

Graining
The painting of a surface to imitate the grain of wood or the veining of marble.

Grandfather clause
A structure, code, ordinance, or procedure in use prior to the adoption of a new building code, and therefore allowable for continued use unless altered or renovated, in which case it must be brought up to the current code.

Granite
An igneous rock having crystals or grains of visible size; consists mainly of quartz and mica or other colored minerals. Also called *stone*.

Granular fill insulation
A granulated insulation that can be easily placed or poured into place, such as vermiculite or perlite.

Graph
A diagram illustrating ideas by graphic means, usually on paper that is ruled into small squares prepared for that purpose. The squares are available in certain scales, such as a ¼-inch graph, similar to the scale of an architectural drawing.

Graphite paint
A black painting compound consisting of powdered graphite and oil; used to coat metallic members and to inhibit corrosion.

Graphitization
A corrosion of cast iron caused by leaving the metal unpainted for long periods, or when caulked joints fail and acidic rainwater corrodes them from the backside. When affected, they retain their shape but lose their structural integrity and must be replaced.

Grate
A frame that consists of parallel metal bars, attached by crossbars at regular intervals; used as a grille or security device. Also called *spaced bars*.

Gravel
Small pieces of stone that are of varying sizes; used as an ingredient in concrete.

Gravel fill
Crushed rock, pebbles, or gravel deposited at the bottom of an excavated wall, or footing, to ensure adequate drainage of water.

Gravel roof
A roof built up with a layer of pebbles embedded in the hot tar undercoating. The pebbles protect the tar and break up raindrops.

Gravel stop
A continuous upright or slanted metal strip that prevents gravel on a built-up roof from being washed off.

Gravity retaining wall
A retaining wall that relies on the weight of the masonry or concrete for its stability.

Gravity ventilator
A device without a fan that is installed in an opening and activated by the air passing through it.

Green architecture
Traditionally thought of as formal picturesque gardens that are closely related to buildings, or where landscape and architecture come together. The term also currently represents buildings that are designed according to energy-saving and/or pollution-reducing criteria, and that use sustainable, natural, or recyclable materials in the construction.

Green concrete
Concrete that has set initially, but has not yet hardened to the desired strength.

Green design
Initially, the term meant incorporating passive and active solar design, daylighting, and natural ventilation. Construction materials, such as wood, wood products, rubber, linoleum, and natural stone were preferred to more durable but more energy-consumptive materials like concrete, masonry, asphalt, and metals.

Green lumber
Boards cut from green or unseasoned logs; lumber that has not been dried or seasoned and that has a moisture content over 20 percent.

Green terminal
A green screw terminal on an electrical device which indicates a grounding terminal and which is usually connected to a green insulated wire.

Greenbelt
A belt of green land around urban areas conserved so as to prevent further expansion. They are kept open by severe and normally permanent planning restrictions.

Greenboard
Water-resistant drywall, which gets its name from the green paper covering it. It is not waterproof, but can be used in bathrooms as a backing for tiles.

Grid foundation
A foundation consisting of several intersecting continuous footings that are loaded at the intersections.

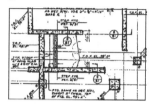

Grid systems
A method of laying out an area in a grid, using squares, or any other shape to make it easier to manage.

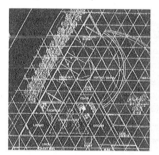

Grillwork
Materials arranged with voids to function as, or with the appearance of, a grille.

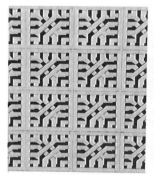

Grind
To reduce any substance to powder by friction; to wear down or sharpen a tool by use of an abrasive.

Grinding wheel
An abrasive wheel used to sharpen tools or to shape materials.

Grindstone
A flat rotating wheel made of sandstone and used for sharpening tools or wearing down materials by abrading or grinding them.

Grit number
An indicator of the coarseness of abrasives; the higher the number, the finer the grit.

Groin
The curved area formed by the intersection of two vaults.

Grommet
A metal eyelet used primarily in awnings, or along the edge of tarpaulins, used to cover work from rain.

Groove
A continuous recess formed centrally along the edge of a timber board in order to accommodate a tongue.

Gross floor area
The area within the perimeter of the outside walls of a building as measured from the inside surface of the exterior walls without reduction for hallways, stairs, closets, and thickness of the walls.

Gross margin
A percentage produced by dividing gross profits by total revenues.

Gross profit
Profit after direct costs are deducted, and before expenses are deducted.

Ground
A piece of wood or metal embedded in and flush with the plastering of walls to which moldings, skirting, and other joiners' work is attached. Also used to stop plastering around door and window openings.

Ground anchor
A device inserted into the ground, by screwing it in like an auger or by excavating and backfilling; used for stabilizing a retaining wall or for resisting uplift.

Ground beam
A reinforced concrete beam cast directly on the ground, either horizontally, or on a slope; used to tie footings together, or to support a wall above.

Ground course
A horizontal course, usually of masonry, laid on the ground.

Ground cover
Low plants that will spread to form a thick mass, thus preventing erosion of the soil under them.

Ground glass
Glass whose surface has been roughened with an abrasive, diffusing the light passing through it; produced by sandblasting or etching with acid.

Ground joint
A closely fitted joint in masonry, usually without mortar. Also, a machined metal joint that fits tightly without packing or employing a gasket.

Ground lease
A lease on property limited to the land only.

Ground line
The ground level or natural grade line from which measurements for excavating are taken. Also called *grade, ground level.*

Ground story
The part of a building that lies between the ground and first floor.

Ground water
Water that is naturally contained in, or passing through, the ground or subsoil.

Ground wire
A wire that does not carry any current during normal operation, but is used to ground the system.

Grounding
The method of connecting electrical circuits to the earth, such as connecting a grounding conductor to water pipes which generally are installed in earth outside the building.

Grounding plug adapter
An electrical device into which a three-prong plug can be inserted; it contains two prongs and a wire or metal loop for a grounding connection, and can be inserted into a two-slot outlet.

Groundsill
In a framed structure, the sill that is nearest the ground or on the ground; used to distribute the concentrated loads to the foundation.

Groundwork
Site work that takes place on the ground, such as excavations, drain laying, pathways, and driveways.

Grout
Mortar containing a considerable amount of water so that it has the consistency of a viscous liquid, permitting it to be poured or pumped into joints, spaces, and cracks within masonry walls and floors. Also called *caulking compound.*

Grout injection
Stabilizing or waterproofing the ground by injecting a liquid cement slurry under pressure. Grout-injected piers are made by drilling into sandy or unstable soil and inserting the grout through the hollow drill stem as the auger is withdrawn.

Grouted masonry
Concrete masonry construction composed of hollow units when the hollow cells are filled with grout.

Grouting
Injecting cement grout into foundations and decayed walls for reinforcing and strengthening them.

Guarantee
A written assurance that a stated event will occur, and the consequences provided if it does not.

Guaranteed maximum cost
The amount established in an agreement between owner and contractor as the maximum cost for performing specified work on the basis of the cost of labor and materials plus overhead expenses and profit.

Guaranty bond
A bond that secures payment and performance; types include a bid bond, labor and material payment bond, performance bond, and a surety bond.

Guard
A security person to provide protection at a construction site, during and after hours of work. Also, bars or fence around an excavation, equipment, or materials stored on a construction site.

Guard rail
A horizontal rail of wood, metal, or cable fastened to uprights around the edges of platforms, or around excavations.

Guestimate
The educated guess or estimate of an experienced person, such as the approximation of total costs without having undertaken detailed calculations.

Gum
A moderately high-density hardwood, whitish to gray-green in color and of uniform texture; used for low-grade veneer, plywood, and rough cabinetwork.

Gunite
The trademark name of construction material composed of cement, sand, or crushed slag, and water mixed together and forced through a cement gun by pneumatic pressure.

Gunny
A coarse jute cloth material, which is soaked with water and used to cover concrete to prevent moisture loss during curing.

Gusset
A plate used to connect two or more members, or add strength to a framework at its joints.

Gusset plate
A plate used to connect members of a truss or to connect several steel members in a common joint.

Gut rehab
The removal, or gutting, of the interior elements in a structure, leaving only the structural elements standing.

Gutter
A shallow channel of metal or wood at the edge of a roof eave to catch and drain water into a downspout. Also called *channel*.

Gutter hook
A light metal strap used to secure or support a metal gutter.

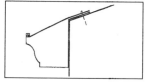

Guy cable
A cable anchored at one end that stabilizes an object at the other end.

Guy rope
A rope that secures or steadies a load lifted by a crane or derrick, or ties and secures a temporary structure.

Gypsum
A natural rock used in the manufacture of drywall and plaster.

Gypsum block
A fire-resistant gypsum block that can be used in non load-bearing applications.

Gypsum board
A wallboard having a noncombustible gypsum core; covered on each side with a paper surface. Also called *dry wall, sheetrock, wallboard, building board.*

Gypsum board nail
Short, stubby nail used for applying both rock lath and gypsum board to stud walls and ceiling joists.

Gypsum plaster
Ground gypsum mixed with a retardant; used as a base coat plaster.

Gypsum roof deck
A structural roof deck of gypsum concrete.

Gypsum wallboard
Panels composed of a gypsum rock base sandwiched between two layers of heavy paper; commonly used on the interior walls of a building in drywall construction. Available in standard and fire-resistant panels.

H section
An H-shaped structural member used primarily for columns and piles due to the ability of the section to withstand rotation; usually square in its outer dimensions, it is also used for beams with the flanges installed in a horizontal position.

H-section

Hack
Any rough manner of cutting.

Hacksaw
A lightweight handsaw with a narrow, fine-toothed blade held in an adjustable metal frame; used for cutting pipe and other metals.

Hairpin
In steel construction, light hairpin-shaped reinforcing bars.

Half baluster
A baluster that projects from the surface to which it is attached, by about one-half its diameter.

Half bat
One-half of a building brick. See also *Brick bat.*

Half round
A molding with a cross section in the shape of a cylinder cut in half along its length.

Half section
A form of drawing where one half the object depicts the object's exterior, and the other half shows a section of the interior.

Half-glass door
A door with a glass pane above the middle rail.

Half-landing
A landing located halfway up a flight of stairs.

Half-lap dovetail joint
A dovetail joint where each member is cut away so that the surfaces are on the same plane when joined.

Half-lap joint
A joint formed by cutting away half the thickness of the face of one piece and half the back of the other piece, so that when they are joined the outer surfaces will be flush.

Half-pitched roof
A double-pitched roof in which the rise is half the span.

119

Half-round file
A piece of wood that has one flat face and one face that is curved like half of a cylinder.

Half-round molding
A convex strip or molding of semicircular profile.

Half-space landing
A stair landing at the junction of two flights, reversing its direction, making a turn of 180 degrees. Such a landing includes the width of both flights plus the well.

Half-timbered wall
Descriptive of buildings of the sixteenth and seventeenth centuries, built with strong timber foundations, supports, knees, and studs, and walls filled in with plaster or brick.

Halved joint
A timber-lengthening or angle joint formed by cutting away half the thickness of each piece and fitting them together so they are flush.

Hammer
A tool for driving nails, pounding metal, or other purposes. All types of hammers have a solid head set perpendicular to the handle, regardless of the use.

Hammer beam
A short horizontal member, attached to the foot of a principal rafter, located within a roof structure in place of a tie beam.

Hammer brace
A bracket under a hammer beam to support it.

Hammer-beam roof
A roof without a tie beam at the top of the wall.

Hammerhead key
A piece of hardwood shaped into a dovetail on both ends and driven into similarly shaped recesses in the two members being joined.

Hand
Referring to either left or right to designate how a door is hinged and the direction it opens.

Hand brace
A hand-operated tool, commonly used with a wood bit to bore holes.

Hand drill
A hand-operated tool for drilling holes.

Hand file
A hand tool used in finishing flat surfaces.

Hand lever punch
In sheet metal work, a hand tool for punching holes.

Hand sawn
Wood that has been sawn by hand, as opposed to sawn in a mill.

Hand screw
A clamp held together and adjusted by two screws.

Hand tools
Any tool which is operated and guided by hand.

Hand-hewn
Wood beams that have been trimmed with hand tools, such as the adze; typical of early barn timbers.

Handicap door-opening system
A door equipped with a knob or latch and handle located approximately 3 feet above the floor, for the convenience of people in wheelchairs.

Handicapped access
Retrofitting a building to ensure that facilities are made available to persons with limited mobility and other handicaps. This may not apply to converted historic buildings and museums if the revisions are not within the building's historical and architectural integrity.

Handrail
A rail providing a handhold and serving as a support at the side of a stair or elevated platform.

Handsaw
Any saw operated by hand instead of electricity; may be either a cross-cut, ripsaw, or keyhole saw used to cut wood by carpenters, or a hacksaw used to cut metal or plastic pipe by plumbers.

Hand screw
A clamp with two parallel jaws and two screws used by woodworkers. The clamping action is provided by means of the screws, one operating through each jaw.

Hanger
A strap or rod attached to an overhead structure to support a pipe, conduit, or the framework of a suspended ceiling; a stirrup bracket used to support the end of a beam or joist at a masonry wall or girder. Also called *drop support*.

Hanger bolt
A bolt used for attaching hangers to woodwork; it consists of a lag screw at one end with a machine-bolt screw and nut at the other end.

Hanging gable
A small extension of the roof structure at the gable end of a barn or house.

Hanging gutter
A sheet metal gutter shaped in cross section like a half-moon; attached to the eaves by metal straps or cast-iron hangers.

Hanging scaffold
A suspended scaffold supported by cables at each end and raised or lowered by a small electric motor located on the cable.

Hanging stile
The stile of a door to which the hinges are fastened, or the uprights of a window to which the casements are hinged.

Hard costs
Hard project costs include land acquisition, easement rights, construction cost for labor, materials, equipment, utility permits, demolition, testing, furnishings, hazardous material abatement, and off-site amenities. See also *Hidden costs, Life cycle costs,* and *Soft costs.*

Hard hat
A protective helmet that consists of a hard shell with a shock-absorbing webbing suspended inside to cushion any blow received.

Hardboard
A building material manufactured from wood fibers compressed into sheets; one type is called Masonite.

Hardener
A chemical applied to concrete floors to reduce wear and dusting.

Hardness
A measure of the resistance of a material to abrasion.

Hardpan
A hard, dense layer of clay in soil that is difficult to excavate, but is an excellent stratum on which to place foundations and footings.

Hardware
Fastenings used for the installation of doors and windows, such as hinges, catches, lifts, and locks.

Hardwired
An electrical appliance or machine that is wired directly into an outlet.

Hardwood
Lumber produced from deciduous trees, as opposed to conifers, but having no bearing on the hardness of the wood itself. The types are: alder, ash, aspen, basswood, beech, birch, buckeye, butternut, cherry, chestnut, cottonwood, elm, gum, hickory, locust, magnolia, maple, oak, sycamore, walnut, willow, and yellow poplar.

Hardwood floor
A finished floor consisting of strips of hardwood, such as oak, and varnished or otherwise sealed.

Hasp assembly
A fastener for a door consisting of a hinged metal strap that fits over a loop, and is secured by a pin or a locking device.

Hatch
A covered opening in a floor or roof.

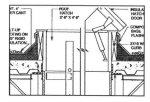

Hatchet
A small hand tool with a short handle; used for splitting or rough-dressing of lumber.

Haul
To move a load from one location to another.

Haunched beam
A beam whose cross section is thicker at the supports than in the middle of the span.

Hazardous area
Any part of a building where highly toxic chemicals, poisons, or highly flammable substances are stored.

Hazardous material
Any material, such as asbestos, used in building construction that can be harmful to the construction workers or future occupants of the building.

Hazardous waste
A material defined by statute or regulations as likely to be harmful or cause an adverse health effect to humans.

H-clip
A metal clip that holds adjacent edges of plywood in alignment.

Head casing
The casing or trim over a window opening which serves as a stop for the wall material. An exterior head is usually topped by a drip, which throws rainwater away from the wall.

Head joint
A vertical joint which joins bricks at their ends. See also *Bed joint*.

Head lap
The distance that the bottom of a shingle or siding overlaps the top of the row preceding it.

Header
A framing member supporting the ends of joists, transferring the weight of the latter to parallel joists and rafters. Also called *lintel*.

Header bond
A brickwork bond pattern consisting entirely of headers; usually offset from the course above and below by one-half the width of one header.

Header course
A continuous row of bricks composed of headers, usually separating several rows of stretchers.

Headroom
The clear vertical distance between a floor and ceiling, or stair tread and overhead obstruction.

Hearing
A proceeding conducted by an arbitrator or a judge, who listens to evidence presented by both sides in a dispute.

Hearth
That part of the floor directly in front of the fireplace, and the floor inside the fireplace on which the fire is built; made of fire-resistant masonry.

Hearthstone
A single large stone forming the floor of a fireplace; also, materials such as firebrick and fireclay products, used to form a hearth.

Heartwood
The center portion of a tree trunk that is no longer growing or carrying the sap; often harder, denser, and of a different color.

Heat balancing
A condition of thermal equilibrium in a building where heat gains equal the heat losses.

Heat exchanger
A device for transferring heat from one fluid to another in a cooling system.

Heat gain
Migration of heat into a space by conduction, radiation, or exchange of air.

Heat loss
Migration of heat from a space by conduction, radiation, or exchange of air.

Heat pump
A type of heating and air-conditioning installation where a powered ventilator operates as an air-conditioning device where summer heat is drawn out and released; the cycle is reversed for heating the outside air.

Heat recovery
The extraction of heat from any source that is not designed primarily to produce heat, such as the lights in a room.

Heat resistance
The ability of an insulation material to resist the transfer of heat through it. It is expressed as an R-value. The higher the R-value, the better the insulation.

Heat storage
The ability of rocks, salt, water, and other materials to absorb heat and retain it until needed.

Heat transfer
A generic term for thermal conduction, convection, and radiation.

Heat-absorbing glass
Glass whose solar transmittance is reduced by adding various coloring agents to the molten glass. The most common colors are bronze, gray, and green.

Heat-actuated fire door
A fire door designed to shut automatically in the presence of smoke or heat.

Heater
Any appliance for heating a room or building, such as a radiator, stove, or furnace.

Heating
Raising the temperature of an interior space, either by a fire in a fireplace, hot air from a furnace, gas heater, electric heater, or radiator.

Heating load
The amount of energy required to fulfill a building's space heating or water heating requirements.

Heating plant
Any system for heating a building, such as a furnace, boiler, pipes, and fixtures.

Heating, ventilating, and air-conditioning (HVAC)
Control of the interior temperature and moisture, through a mechanical system of heating and cooling units and accompanying ductwork.

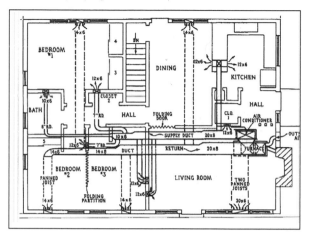

Heat-reflective glass
Window glass that has been treated with a transparent metallic coating to reflect substantial portions of the radiant heat striking it.

Heavy timber
A type of construction called mill construction, which requires noncombustible exterior walls with a minimal fire rating of 2 hours, solid or laminated interior members, and heavy plank or laminated wood floors and roofs.

Heavy-timber construction
Fire-resistant construction obtained by using wood structural members of specified minimum size; wood floors and roofs of specified minimum thickness, and exterior walls of noncombustible construction.

Heel
The lower end of an upright member resting on a support.

Heel joint
A gusset plate at the main support of a roof truss.

Helical stair
A stair whose treads are wrapped around a helix; commonly called a *spiral stair*.

Hemlock
Wood of a coniferous tree; moisture-resistant, soft, coarse; uneven textured, splinters easily, inferior for construction use.

Herculite
The trade name for a type of thick tempered plate glass; used for commercial installations and installed without framing members around the door.

Heritage
Any legacy or tradition from the past that has meaning and value for the present and future.

Herringbone matched
The assembly of wood veneers from the same flitch, so that successive sheets are alternated face up and face down. Side-by-side sheets show a symmetrical mirror image at the joints. See *Flitch*.

Hex head
A bolt head with six sides.

Hex nut
A threaded nut having six sides.

Hickey
A portable conduit-bending tool with a side opening jaw and a long stiff handle to act as a lever in bending the pipe.

Hickory
A tough, hard, strong wood; has high shock resistance and high bending strength.

Hidden costs
Costs that will not show up on the project estimate, because they result from the basic approach to the project. They include project phasing, contract selection methods, project delivery methods, and managing roles.

Hidden line
A dashed line on a drawing that represents that which is hidden below the surface that is being shown.

Hide glue
A glue widely used in the woodworking industry, as a ready-to-use strong liquid.

Hiding power
The ability of a paint or other coating to obscure the surface beneath it.

High chairs
A manufactured device used to hold up the welded wire frame at approximately one-half the thickness of the cement slab during placement of the concrete.

High gloss
A paint that dries with a lustrous, enamel-like finish.

Highbay lighting
A system of lighting located high above the floor level.

High-early-strength cement
A type of portland cement that sets or hardens to its full strength in a shorter period of time; frequently used when the temperature is below freezing.

High-limit control
A temperature-operated switch used for warm air, hot water, or steam systems, which prevent the systems from overheating.

Hinge
A movable joint used to attach, support, and turn a door about a pivot, consisting of two plates joined by a pin that supports the door and connects it to its frame, enabling it to swing open or closed.

Hinge strap
An ornamental metal strap fastened to the surface of the door to give the appearance of a strap hinge.

Hip
The external angle at the junction of two sloping roofs or sides of a roof; the rafter at the angle where two sloping roofs or sides of a roof meet.

Hip rafter
A rafter located at the junction of the sloping sides of a hip roof.

Hip roll
A rounded piece of tile, wood, or metal used to cover, finish, and sometimes add a decorative effect. Also called a *ridge roll*.

Hip tile
A convex-shaped tile used to cover a roof hip, installed overlapping along the edge of the hip.

Hip-and-valley roof
A hip roof with valleys at the inside corners of all changes in direction of the roof.

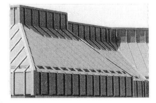

Hipped dormer
A dormer whose roof has a miniature hipped appearance in front, dying into the main roof at the back.

Hipped end
The sloping triangularly shaped end of a hipped roof.

Hipped gable
The end of a roof formed into a shape intermediate between a gable and a hipped roof. The gable rises about halfway up to the ridge, resulting in a truncated shape, the roof being inclined backward from this level. Also called *Jerkinhead roof*.

Hod
A V-shaped trough with a perpendicular handle, used to carry bricks and mortar placed in the trough and balanced on a worker's shoulder.

Hoist
A projecting beam with block and tackle, used for lifting goods; often seen above openings in the upper stories of medieval houses. Also, a mechanisn for lifting building materials up the outside of a structure under construction. Also called *lift*.

Hold harmless clause
A clause in the contract documents whereby one party agrees to hold another party harmless for damages or claims brought against them. An agreement by an insurance carrier that they will assume a contractual obligation made by their named insured and be responsible for certain acts which might otherwise be the obligation of the other party to the contract.

Hole saw
A cylindrical cap with a sawtoothed edge, used as an attachment on a power drill to cut material out as a cylindrical plug.

Hollow block masonry
Extruded block of concrete or burnt clay, which consists of voids and consequently is a good insulator. It is used for walls and as a backing for brick.

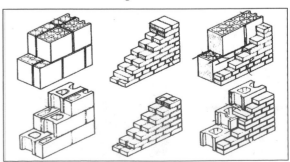

Hollow masonry unit
A unit of brick, concrete block, or clay tile block whose cross-sectional area in any given plane parallel to the bearing surface is less than 75 percent of its gross area in the same plane.

Hollow metal door
A metal door fabricated of sheet metal and reinforced by light metal channels; has a hollow core, which is sometimes filled with a fireproof insulating material if it is a fire door.

Hollow tile
A structural clay tile unit with vertical hollow cells; used to build interior masonry partitions and as a backup block for brick veneer.

Hollow-core door
A wood flush door having a framework of stiles and rails encasing a honeycombed core of corrugated fiberboard or a grid of interlocking horizontal and vertical wood strips. Also called *veneered door*.

Hollow-tile floor
A reinforced concrete floor that is cast over a formwork of hollow clay tile blocks, the concrete filling the voids between the tiles.

Homogeneous beam
A structural beam composed of only one material.

Honeycomb brickwork
A brick bond characterized by the absence of certain bricks for decorative purposes or to allow ventilation or provide a screened effect.

Honeycombed concrete
Concrete with voids caused by failure of the cement mortar to fill all the spaces between the particles of the coarse aggregate.

Hood
A projection above an opening, such as a door or window, serving as a screen or as protection against the weather. Also called *cover*.

Hoodmold
The projecting molding of the architrave over a door or window, whether inside or outside; also called a *dripstone*.

Hook
A semicircular or 90 defree turn at the free end of a bar to provide anchorage to the next pour of concrete.

Hook knife
A knife with a blade in a hook shape; used to cut linoleum. Also called a *linoleum knife*.

Hooked bar
A concrete reinforcing bar whose end is bent to improve its anchorage, generally through bending into a 90 degree angle.

Hoop reinforcement
Closed hoops around the main or longitudinal reinforcement of columns to restrain the buckling of the longitudinal steel.

Hopper window
A window that opens toward the interior of the building, by tilting inward from a pivot at the sill line.

Horizontal
A condition parallel to the horizon, as indicated in a bubble level.

Horizontal application
A method of installing gypsum wallboard with its length horizontal to the floor, and perpendicular to the framing members.

Horizontal cornice
The horizontal member of the pediment under the two inclined members.

Horizontal roof area
The area of a roof taken horizontally as a flat plane, regardless of the slopes of any section.

Horizontal sliding window
A window with sashes that slides horizontally in tracks.

Horizontal wood siding
Wood boards used as an exterior surface on framed construction, often overlapped to shed water more efficiently.

Horsepower
A unit of power or work. An electrical horsepower is equal to 746 watts.

Hose bibb
A water faucet which is threaded so that a hose may be attached to it.

Hot mop
Applying molten tar over felt paper on a roof or other area that requires waterproofing.

Hot water boiler
A heating unit in a hot water heating system.

Hot wire
Any wire in an electrical system that carries a current, most commonly color-coded black or red. A green wire is the ground and does not carry any current. See also *Ground*.

Hot-air furnace
A heating unit that warms the air, which is drawn into ducts and dispersed throughout a building, or portion thereof.

Hot-water heating
A system of heating a building by means of hot water circulating through pipes, coils, or radiators.

House drain
A horizontal piping system within a building, which receives waste from the soil stack and carries it to the sewer.

House museum
A museum whose building, furniture, or history itself is of historical or architectural significance.

House sewer
The part of a drainage system which extends from the building to the main sewer in the street.

House trap
A large, U-shaped trap with cleanout plugs at the top of both legs, located in the main sewer line to act as a trap for the main building drain.

Housed joint
Any fitted joint such as a mortise and tenon, where a space is cut in the end of one piece to receive the tongue cut on another piece.

Housing code
Minimum requirements for light and ventilation, room size, security, and fire egress of dwelling units.

Housing tract
A large parcel of land broken up into individual building lots where individual homes are constructed, usually by one builder or developer.

Howe truss
A truss having upper and lower horizontal members, between which are vertical and diagonal members. The vertical web members take tension, and the diagonal web members are under compression.

Hub
In plumbing, the enlarged end of a pipe which is made to provide a connection into which an adjoining pipe will fit.

Human scale
A combination of qualities in architecture or the

landscape that provides an appropriate relationship to human size, enhancing rather than diminishing the importance of people.

Humidifier
A device for adding moisture into the air, activated by a humidistat.

Humidistat
An automatic regulating device for controlling humidity, actuated by changes in the air.

Hung ceiling
A nonstructural ceiling, supported entirely from above on a grid system of members that incorporates the ceiling tiles, lighting fixtures, and air diffusers. Also called *dropped ceiling*.

Hung sash
A sash whose weight is counterbalanced by weights encased in the window frame, allowing it to be raised easily.

HVAC
Abbreviation for heating, ventilation, and air-conditioning.

Hydraulic cement
A cement that will harden even in water, used to repair cracks and holes in cement that have active water leaks.

Hydraulic elevator
An elevator powered by the energy of a liquid under pressure in a cylinder that acts on a piston or plunger to move the elevator car up and down on guide rails.

Hydraulic jack
A lifting device operated by a lever from the outside and put into action by means of a small pump using oil to provide the lifting pressure.

Hydrochloric acid
A very strong liquid acid usually diluted with water that is commonly used in the industry for cleaning purposes. It is being replaced for building cleaning by a milder acidic solution. See also *Phosporic acid*.

Hydrostatic test
A pressure test of a system or component using water equal to or greater than the pressure in the final system.

Hypalon
A type of rubber-based roof coating that is abrasion-resistant and fire-resistant; usually applied wet in two applications.

Hypalon roofing
An elastomeric roof covering that is more resistant to thermal movement and weathering than neoprene; available in liquid, sheet, or caulking consistency compound.

I beam
An I-shaped structural member, used for beams with the flange in the upright position.

IAPMO
Abbreviation for the International Association of Plumbing and Mechanical Officials, authors of the Uniform Plumbing Code. See *Uniform Plumbing Code.*

ICBO
Abbreviation for International Conference of Building Officials, authors of the Uniform Building Code. See *Uniform Building Code.*

Ice dam
A buildup of ice at the edge of a roof caused by the refreezing of melting snow from the roof surface above.

Icon
An image of sacred personages that are objects of veneration. Icons are often found on buildings, and venerated buildings are referred to as "icons."

Icynene foam
A sprayed foam insulation with a high R-value, forming a complete seal in the cavity.

Imitation
The representation of one material with another, generally copying the color and surface appearance of another material. Common forms of imitation are wood graining and marbleizing.

Impact damage
A loss that impacts on the overall cost or schedule of a job, such as delays or lost labor productivity.

Impact load
The effect of a moving load upon a stationary structure.

Impact resistance
Capacity of a material to resist loads suddenly applied.

Impact wrench
A pneumatically operated wrench which provides an impact rotation to the socket for fast tightening of bolts.

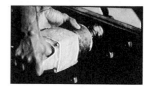

Impedance
The resistance to the flow of current in an alternating current electrical circuit, measured in ohms. One ohm produces a decrease in voltage of 1 volt with a constant current of 1 ampere.

Impermeable
Resistant to penetration by fluids or vapor.

Impervious
Resistant to water.

Implied contract
A contract that is inferred from actions rather than by a legal agreement.

Import fill
In earthwork, fill material which is taken from one location and deposited in another final position. Fill that is removed from a site is said to be exported.

Imposed load
The weight of any movable load in a building or structure, such as wind, rain, and snow, occupants, or furniture and other belongings.

Impregnation
The treatment of a wood product using oil, mineral, or chemical, under pressure; usually for preservation.

Impregnation of timber
The process of saturating timber with a preservative, such as creosote oil.

Improved land
Building sites that have water and sewage connections available and access to streets and telephone, gas, and electrical services.

Improvement
Any changes made in a project that tend to increase its value, such as the addition of a building for a home. An improvement can also be made by installing drainage, utilities, infrastructure, or by removing unsightly objects or growths. An improvement is any act that serves to add utility, beauty, or increase the value of the property.

Improvements on land
Any addition to a site that increases its value or utility, such as erecting buildings and retaining walls, fences and driveways. Also, any addition that is not embraced within the boundaries of a property, such as water mains, sewers, street lighting, sidewalks, and curbs.

In situ
A term meaning "in position"; applied to building elements and improvements that are assembled or cast in their permanent position on site rather than prefabricated elsewhere; for example, cast concrete rather than precast concrete.

In situ pile
A concrete pile cast in its final location, with or without a casing, as distinct from a pile that is precast and subsequently driven.

In the clear
The uninterrupted linear measurement of a space; not including the structural parts themselves.

Inadequate
A condition that exists when the work does not meet the plans and specifications.

Incandescent light
A lamp from which light is emitted when a tungsten filament is heated to incandescence by an electric current.

Incentive
A discount, contribution, or amenity offered to a lessee of a property or facility.

Incentive clause
A clause in the contract between the owner and contractor that outlines savings shared proportionately between the guaranteed maximum price and the actual work performed on the basis of cost plus fee, with a guaranteed maximum price.

Inching
The process of moving a crane hook or trolley in short increments. Also called *jogging*.

Incombustible
Material that does not burn in a standard test in a furnace.

Income property
A building or group of buildings that generates income for the owner, either residential, commercial, or industrial.

Income statement
A financial statement for a specific period that shows revenues, expenses, and the resulting profit. Also called a *profit and loss statement*.

Indemnification clause
A clause in a contract that protects an individual from damage or loss.

Indemnify
To provide security through contract clauses or bonds to protect against damages or loss.

Indemnity
The act of holding a person harmless from liability or loss.

Indemnity bond
A bond that guarantees compensation to a party who suffered a loss.

Indented
A gap left by the omission of stone, brick, or block units in a course of masonry; used for bonding future masonry.

Indented bar
A reinforcing bar with indentations pressed in the rolling process, to improve the bond between the steel and the concrete. Also called *deformed bar*.

Indented bolt
A bolt that has been forged with indentations to improve its anchorage in concrete.

Independent contractor
A person who performs work for another party, and who accepts sole responsibility for the results of such work.

Indirect expense
Costs that are not applicable to the completion of any specific project, such as overhead. See also *Direct expense*.

Indirect gain system
A passive solar system where heat from the sun is stored in one part of the structure, and through natural movement heats other parts of the structure.

Indirect lighting
Lighting reflected from the ceiling or other surface, not received directly from a luminaire.

Indirect luminaire
A lighting fixture designed to reflect its light onto a surface above the fixture, instead of directing it downward.

Indirect system
A system of heating or air-conditioning where the heating or cooling is done in an area different than the area served, and circulated through pipes or ducts to the area served.

Industrial archeology
Studying the remains of, and saving,landmark examples of American engineering, such as factories, bridges, railroads, steel plants, and mills.

Industrial hygienist
A qualified professional who is knowledgeable in monitoring the air in asbestos abatement and other safety-related tasks, and deals with occupational health hazards, in terms of recognizing, evaluating, and developing controls for treatment.

Industrial park
A contiguous grouping of industrial-zoned sites, including streets and utilities, where a developer may sell lots or construct speculative industrial buildings for sale or lease.

Industrial waste
Liquid chemical waste from manufacturing or processing plants.

Industrial wood floor
A floor composed of thick wooden blocks laid on end. Used for heavy loads and traffic.

Industry specification
A specification approved for use by federal agencies, prepared by technical or industry associations.

Industry standard
Published specifications from information readily available from technical reports, test procedures and results, codes, and other data.

Inert material
Any material that will not enter into a chemical reaction with another material.

Infilling
Material used to fill the space in a framework; also the process of placing additional buildings between existing ones.

Infiltration
The passage of outside air into a room or conditioned space through cracks, joints, damaged areas, or openings in the building's enclosure.

Infrared spectography
The process is a chemical analysis technique used to characterize the chemical nature of a material.

Infrastructure
The service part of the built environment that includes gas, electric service, water and sanitary sewer systems, roads, and railroads.

Inhibitor
A material used to reduce the corrosion of metals embedded in concrete, such as a rust inhibitor.

Injection molding
The molding of liquid plastics, liquid metals, or other material by injection into a mold.

Inorganic fiberboard
Board made from inorganic fibers, such as fiberglass, as opposed to organic fibers.

Insect infestation
Attack on a material, usually wood, by insects such as beetles, termites, and carpenter ants.

Insert
A plug or patch used to replace a defect in laminated timber or plywood veneer.

Inset dormer
A dormer that is partially set below a sloping roof, leaving a level area in front of the window.

Inside finish
Includes all the fittings, door trims, window trims, and shutters; most commonly used to denote woodwork but is sometimes extended to more elaborate and permanent work, such as marble, tile, and other items.

Inside trim
The finishing of trim around window and door openings. Also called *casing*.

Insolation
The total amount of solar radiation that strikes a collector, including direct, diffused, and reflected.

Inspection
An examination of the work in progress or completed, conducted by a public official or owner's representative, to verify that it is in accordance with the contract documents.

Inspection aids
Sophisticated tools for inspection including surveying, photogrammetry, or controlled perspective photography.

Inspection card
A card that is issued with a building permit and posted at the job site. It is signed by the building inspector as various portions of the work are completed.

Inspection certificate
A certificate issued by a building inspector stating that the work is in accordance with the regulations in the appropriate building code.

Inspection list
A list of items of work to be completed or corrected by the contractor, commonly called a *punch list*.

Inspector
One who checks the work performed by someone else for quality or compliance to a building code.

Installation
The assembly of building components on site and affixed in position for use.

Instruction to bidders
A detailed list of information pertinent to the project that is given to selected and qualified bidders in the bid package.

Insulate
To reduce sound or heat transfer through an element of construction normally by the inclusion of lightweight porous material, dense material, or discontinuous construction.

Insulated metal roofing
A light-gauge flexible metal roofing panel filled with mineral fiber or foamed plastic.

Insulated steel door
A steel frame covered with steel panels over a core of foam insulation, offering good thermal and security protection.

Insulating board
Any board suitable for insulating purposes; usually manufactured from vegetable fibers.

Insulating concrete
A lightweight concrete produced with lightweight aggregates, used as insulation from heat, cold, fire, and sound.

Insulating glass
Glass that has insulating qualities, made by sandwiching two layers of glass separated by a vacuum-sealed edge.

Insulation
A material that reduces the transmission of sound, heat, electrical current, or the like.

Insulation batt
Flexible glass fiber insulation with an aluminum foil or kraft paper backing on one or both sides,; made to standard widths to fit between studs.

Insulation board
Any type of building board used to prevent the passage of heat, cold, or sound through walls and floors.

Insulator
An object that will not carry an electrical current, used as a covering or support for a current-carrying conductor. Also, any device which serves as a nonconductor of electric current, such as glass or porcelain.

Insurance
A method of protection offered by an insurance company. The most common types in the building industry are Builder's Risk insurance, providing protection during construction against fire, theft, wind, and vandalism; Professional Liability insurance, to protect the architect or engineer against malpractice; Title insurance, to protect a property against encumbrances not stated in a title report; and Workers' Compensation insurance, required of employers to protect employees against job-related accidents.

Integral porch
A porch within the main structure of the house and covered with the same roof.

Integrated ceiling
A suspended ceiling system in which acoustical, illumination, and air-handling components are combined as an integral part of a grid.

Intelligent building
A building that has some control over heating, ventilation, and air-conditioning (HVAC) systems; fire safety and security access systems; or telecommunication systems.

Interim financing
The financing of a construction project from the start of excavations through its completion, after which time permanent financing is arranged by the owner. Also called a *construction loan*.

Interior decoration
The surface treatments applied to the inside of a building, including furniture, floor coverings, and artwork.

Interior decorator
One who works primarily with furnishings, fixtures, and wall coverings.

Interior designer
One who designs the finishes and furnishings of the interior spaces; may also design space with nonstructural partitions, especially in office buildings.

Interior door
A hollow-core or solid-core door that is soundproof.

Interior finish
The final appearance of all exposed interior surfaces: floors, walls, ceilings, and all finish materials, such as tile, marble, plastic laminate, wood, and paint.

Interior lot
A property, or lot, that is bounded by a street or highway on only one side.

Interior plywood
Plywood made with a water-resistant glue, but not suitable for exterior applications.

Interior trim
A general term for all the finish molding, casing, and baseboard.

Interior wall
Any wall within a building; entirely surrounded by exterior walls.

Interlocking joint
A form of joggle in which a protrusion on one member complements a slot or routed groove in another; a joint formed between sheet-metal parts by joining their preformed edges to provide a continuous locked piece.

Interlocking shingles
Roofing shingles with interlocking tabs on the top of the shingle to fit into adjacent shingles on each side.

Interlocking weatherstripping
A type of weatherstripping used on sliding glass doors that consists of a metal channel on the door that interlocks with one on the frame, providing an effective seal.

Intermediate rib
A subordinate vault rib between primary ribs.

Intern architect
A person pursuing a training program under the guidance of practicing architects with the objective of qualifying for registration as an architect.

Interpolate
To go between two known or fixed points and approximate a location within them.

Interpret
To clarify or explain the significance of structures.

Interpretive restoration
Replacement of existing elements based on knowledge rather than exact physical evidence or documentation.

Interrogatory
A written question that a person involved in a lawsuit must answer under oath.

Intersecting arcade
Arches resting on alternate supports in one row, meeting on one plane at the crossings.

Intersecting vault
Where two vaults, of either semicircular or pointed form, meet at right angles.

Intersection
The point where two elements cross over each other, such as the junction of two members in a truss, or the junction of two streets.

Interstices
Spaces or intervals between parts of a structure or between components.

Interstitial
Forming a narrow or small space between parts of other elements, or between floors in a structure.

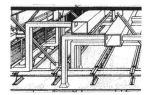

Interstitial condensation
Condensation that occurs within spaces inside the construction, as opposed to surface condensation.

Intervene
To occur or come between two periods or points in time, as to hinder or modify actions.

Intonaco
The fine finish coat of plaster made with white marble dust to receive a fresco painting.

Inverse
Reversed in position or direction.

Investment architecture
Major comprehensive planning, redevelopment, and architectural schemes associated with complex design problems in the early 1950s which involved coordinating various talents to resolve complex design issues.

Investment property
Property or buildings purchased for the purpose of producing rental income, plus income from investment tax credit. Substantial rehabilitation expenses may be deducted after taxes, for qualified rehabilitation of income-producing property more than 30 years old.

Invisible hinge
A hinge installed so that no parts are exposed when the door is closed.

Invitation to bid
A portion of the bidding requirements soliciting bids for a privately financed construction project.

Invited bidder
One of those selected by the architect and owner as the only one allowed to submit a bid on a project.

Iron
A metallic element found in the earth's crust, consisting of a malleable, ductile, magnetic substance from which pig iron and steel are manufactured.

Iron framing
A system of structural ironwork for buildings.

Ironwork
Objects made of cast-iron or wrought iron; most often with utilitarian form in colonial America, but thereafter elaborate and ornamental.

Isolation
Reduction of vibration or sound; usually involving resilient surfaces or mountings or discontinuous construction.

Isolation joint
A joint that separates one concrete section from another so that each one can move independently; found in floors, at columns, and at junctions between the floor and walls.

Isolation system
A structural system which includes isolators and all connections to structural members which transfer the forces between elements of the isolation system.

J

Jack
A mechanism for raising loads short incremental distances, by means of a screw operated by a lever, or hydraulic press, or air pressure.

Jack beam
A vertical strut used to support another beam or truss, thereby eliminating the need for a fixed column.

Jack hammer
An electric or pneumatic tool for breaking concrete or pavement. It has a chisel or pointed bit, and drills into the material with a vibrating action, loosening pieces of the material.

Jack post
A screw jack with a wide base, with a wide plate on top for supporting sagging beams or joists.

Jack rafter
Any rafter shorter than the full length of the sloping roof, such as one beginning or ending at a hip or valley.

Jack stud
A short stud that does not extend from the floor to the ceiling, such as the studs under a window. Also called a *cripple*.

Jack truss
A truss in the end slopes of a hipped roof; usually smaller than the main trusses.

Jacket
A covering applied to exposed heating pipes. Also, the outer protective sheath or casing on cables and wires that provides additional insulation to the individual wires within.

Jacking plate
A steel bearing plate that transmits the load of the jack to the pile during jacking operations.

Jackscrew
A mechanical device operated by a screw; used in lifting weights and for leveling work.

Jalousie window
A window consisting of a series of overlapping horizontal glass louvers that pivot simultaneously in a common frame and are actuated by one or more operating devices. Also called *louvered window*.

Jamb
The vertical member at the side of a window, door, chimney, or other exterior opening.

RATED FRAME
MASONRY ANCHORS - MIN. 3 PER SIDE
5 7/8"
1 15/16"
2"

Jamb anchor
A steel anchor used to fasten a steel fire door to a wall.

Jamb shaft
A small shaft having a capital and a base, placed against the jamb of a door or window.

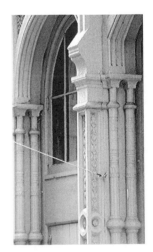

Japanese lacquer
A hard-wearing, deep colored varnish from the Japanese varnish tree.

Jerkinhead
Gable end that slopes back at the top to form a small hipped roof end; also called a *hipped gable*.

Jerkinhead roof
A combination of gable and hipped roof. The gable rises up the ridge, but at some point the roof is tilted back, as in a hipped roof.

Jerry-built
Traditionally applied to building speculators who built houses between the first and second World Wars, using shoddy materials and short-cut methods to secure a quick profit.

Jettied house
A building having a second story that overhangs the lower one.

Jetty
The upper story that juts out over the lower story of a timber-framed house.

Jib
The arm of a crane that holds the pulley and hoisting mechanism.

Jib boom
The hinged extension that extends the reach of the crane or the height of the boom. It is attached to the upper end of a crane's boom.

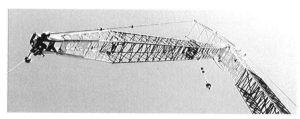

Jib crane
A crane which has a projecting arm from the top of the vertical shaft.

Jigsaw
A power woodworking saw with a reciprocating thin blade suspended vertically in a frame. The thin blade allows sharper cuts than a band saw, and is used to cut complex curves in thin material, such as that used for ornamental fillers in gables, bargeboards, and other brackets and scrollwork.

Job captain
A member of the architect's staff normally responsible, on a given project, for the preparation of drawings and their coordination with other elements.

Job requirements
A list of tasks required to complete the structure within the scope of the contract documents. Also called *general requirements*.

Job site
The area defined by the boundaries that the construction activities occupy.

Job site security
Protection of tools and materials stored on the job site from theft, vandalism, fire, or other damage.

Job site storage
An area set aside on the job site for the storage of the contractor's materials, tools, and equipment.

Jog
A change in direction in a joint or member.

Joggle joint
A notch or projection in one piece of material, which is fitted to a projection or notch in a second piece, to prevent one piece from slipping past the other.

Joggle post
A post made of two or more pieces joggled together.

Jogglework
A stone keyed by joggles.

Joiner
A woodworker skilled in wood finishing, such as moldings, stairs, windows, doors, and interior trim.

Joinery
The craft of woodworking, especially the finishing and trimming of doors, paneling, sashes, cabinets, and other trim.

Joint
The space between the stones in masonry or between the bricks in brickwork. In concrete work, joints control the shrinkage on large areas and isolate independent elements.

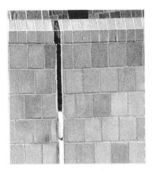

Joint cement
A compound either dry or premixed, used to embed joint tape, cover nails, and finish gypsum wallboard.

Joint compound
A material used to fill the gaps between drywall, or for general patching and repairing. It shrinks as it dries, so larger cracks may need more than one application.

Joint covers
A process of protecting joints in masonry after repointing, by installing metal covers over the joint, joints with an elastomeric sealant.

Joint failure
Movement resulting in a crack or void that allows moisture to enter, causing deterioration.

Joint reinforcement
Steel wire, bar, or fabricated reinforcement that is placed in horizontal mortar joints.

Joint venture
A legal arrangement joining two or more parties to share the work and responsibilities of a design or construction project on an agreed-upon basis of each other's involvement and compensation, similar to the legal characteristics of a partnership.

Jointing
In masonry, the finishing of joints between courses of bricks or stones before the mortar has hardened.

Jointing compound
In plumbing, any material such as paste or cement, used to achieve a watertight seal in pipes and joints. In drywall construction, a premixed finishing paste applied over joint tape and holes to be sanded to a smooth finish when dry.

Joist
One of a series of parallel timber beams used to support floor and ceiling loads and supported in turn by larger beams, girders, or bearing walls.

Joist anchor
A metal tie used to anchor a beam or joist securely to a masonry or concrete wall.

Joist hanger
A metal angle or strap used to support an individual joist against a beam or girder. The hanger is fastened to the beam, and the joist is fastened to the hanger.

Journeyman
The intermediate level of development of proficiency in a particular trade or skill, by a craftsperson who has finished apprenticeship in a trade and qualifies for wages but remains employed by others.

Judgment
A final decision of a court in a legal dispute.

Jumbo brick
A brick that is larger than standard brick.

Junction box
In electrical work, a box in a street distribution system, where one main is connected to another main; also a metal box where a circuit is connected to a main.

Jurisdictional dispute
A disagreement among labor unions over which one has the right to perform the work in a particular area.

K

Kalamein door
A fireproof door with a metal covering.

Keene's cement
In plastering, a specially processed type of gypsum plaster that produces a very hard, smooth finish coat.

Kelvin
A scale for measuring temperature where 0 degrees represents absolute zero.

Kerf
A series of grooves, or kerfs, cut down to about two-thirds of the thickness of the wooden piece so that the piece can be bent around curves.

Key
A tapered or wedge-shaped piece that locks pieces of timber together.

Key activity schedule
A schedule of the milestone events that are shown on a Critical Path Method (CPM) schedule. See also *Milestone activity* and *Critical Path Method*.

Keyhole saw

A small hand saw with a thin blade tapering to a sharp end, designed for cutting small rounded openings, such as a keyhole. Keyhole saws are also used by carpenters to enlarge holes and notch structural members for cables and conduit.

Keying

The process of inserting a piece in a notch, recess, or mitered joint; used to strengthen the joint.

Keying in

The process of tying a new brick or concrete block wall into an existing one.

Keynotes

In working drawings production, the substitution of specific notations on materials and components by the use of a numbering system representing those items. The keynote table is printed on the page in tabular form and the keynote notation number is placed on the drawing. The advantages are that it saves repetitive drafting notation, it simplifies the drawing, making it more readable, and it produces clarity of notation. The keynotes can be coordinated with the 16 category CSI MasterFormat and linked with the written specifications. See also *CSI's MasterFormat.*

FLOOR PLAN KEYNOTES

REF #	KEYNOTE	CSI #
	DIVISION 3 – CONCRETE	
3.1	CONCRETE SLAB	03300
3.3	CONCRETE WALL	03302
	DIVISION 4 – MASONRY	
4.1	BRICK	04210
4.3	FACE BRICK	04215
4.5	CONCRETE BLOCK	04220
4.7	GLASS BLOCK	04270
4.9	STONE	04410
4.11	STONE VENEER	04450
4.13	MASONRY FIREPLACE	04550
4.15	HEARTH	04550
	DIVISION 5 – METALS	
5.1	STEEL HEADER ABOVE	05120
5.3	STEEL BEAM ABOVE	05121
5.5	METAL POST	05123
5.7	METAL STAIR	05510
5.9	METAL RAILING	05521
5.11	HANDRAIL	05521
	DIVISION 6 – WOOD & PLASTIC ROUGH CARPENTRY	
6.1	WOOD POST	06101
6.3	WOOD BEAM ABOVE	06101
6.5	PLYWOOD DIAPHRAGM	

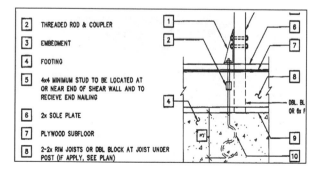

2	THREADED ROD & COUPLER
3	EMBEDMENT
4	FOOTING
5	4x4 MINIMUM STUD TO BE LOCATED AT OR NEAR END OF SHEAR WALL AND TO RECIEVE END NAILING
6	2x SOLE PLATE
7	PLYWOOD SUBFLOOR
8	2–2x RIM JOISTS OR DBL BLOCK AT JOIST UNDER POST (IF APPLY, SEE PLAN)

Keyway

A groove in one concrete pour that is filled with concrete from the next pour.

Kicker

A thin wood block or board, attached to the formwork at an angle to provide lateral support to the form.

Kickplate

A metal plate placed along the lower portion of the door to prevent marring the door by show marks.

Kiln

A large oven used for the artificial seasoning of lumber, for the firing of brick, and for the burning of lime.

Kiln dried

Wood that has been seasoned by the heat of a kiln, rather than dried in the air.

King bolt

A vertical tie rod from the lower chord of a truss to the upper apex, taking the place of a king post.

King closure brick

A rectangular brick, one end of which has been cut off diagonally to half the width of the brick. It is used as a closer in brickwork.

King post

A vertical member extending from the apex of the inclined rafters to the tie beam between the rafters at the lower ends of a truss, as well as in a roof.

King truss

A triangular truss with two inclined members, joined at their apex, and a horizontal tie beam that connects their lower ends, with a vertical central post that connects them.

Kiosk

A small ornamented pavilion or gazebo, usually open for the sale of merchandise or to provide cover or shelter for travelers.

Kip

A unit of weight or force exerted on a member equal to 1,000 pounds.

Kitchen cabinet

A unit of built-in furniture in a kitchen with shelves, drawers, and doors; used for storage of kitchen utensils, and china; made of particleboard covered with a plastic laminate or metal.

Knee

A piece of wood with a bend; either natural or artificially set.

Knee brace

A diagonal corner member for bracing the angle between two joined members. Being joined to each other partway along its path serves to stiffen and strengthen the joint.

Knee pads

Protective padded coverings worn on the knees by bricklayers, tile layers, and carpet installers.

Knee wall
A low wall resulting from one-and-a-half-story construction.

Kneestone
A stone that is sloped on top and flat on the bottom that supports inclined coping on the side of a gable; also, a stone that breaks the horizontal joint pattern to begin the curve of an arch.

Knob and tube
In electrical work, a means of concealing electrical wiring. This was one of the earliest methods used for wiring houses. When structures are wired this way, insulated wires are supported with porcelain knobs and tubes when passing through wood construction members of a floor or wall. It is the oldest type of installation, and it still meets the requirements of the National Electric Code (NEC), but it is not approved by many local ordinances. It is still used for many temporary installations, such as construction shacks.

Knob insulator
A porcelain knob to which electrical wires may be fastened.

Knocked down
Any object that is prefabricated but delivered disassembled, requiring assembly according to instructions at the job site.

Knocker
A metal fixture, hinged at the top, on the exterior face of a door.

Knockout
Removable metal discs in an electric box to allow cables to be pulled through. They may be pried out with a screwdriver.

Knot
A hard, cross-grained section in a piece of timber, where a branch had formed in the trunk of the tree.

Knotty pine
Boards used for interior wall paneling and cabinets, with a series of exposed knots.

Knuckle
The part of a hinge containing the holes through which the pin passes.

KSI
Kips per square inch; a unit of measure of the force acting on a member. A kip is equal to 1,000 pounds.

L

Label
A molding or dripstone that extends horizontally over a door or window opening, then bends vertically downward a certain distance; often containing an ornamental device at the bottom of each end called a label stop. See also *Label stop.*

Label stop
The termination of a hoodmold or arched dripstone in which the lower ends are turned in a horizontal direction away from the door or window opening.

Labeled door
A door with a fire rating from the Underwriters Laboratories, Inc.

Labeled frame
A door frame that has received certification from the Underwriters Laboratories, Inc.

Labeled window
A fire-resistant window that carries a fire rating based on testing by the Underwriters Laboratories, Inc.

Labor and material payment bond
A bond that guarantees that all labor and material will be paid for by the general contractor who secures the bond.

Labor burden
The nonwage expenses associated with the employment of labor; includes payroll taxes, workers' compensation insurance premiums, employees' benefits, and other similar costs.

Labor union
An organization of workers with similar skills who are joined in a common cause, such as collective bargaining with employers, for working conditions, wage rates, and employee benefits.

Laboratory testing
Tests performed under laboratory conditions. Includes durability during freeze/thaw cycles, stability under exposure to ultraviolet light, hardness, water absorption, and compressive strength. Coatings can be tested for adhesion.

Lacing course
A course of brick or tile inserted in a rough stone or rubble course as a bond course.

Lacquer
Any gloss enamel which dries quickly, used as a decorative wood finish and as a clear protective coating on brass and other polished metals; highly resistant to weathering.

Ladder
A wooden object consisting of two side pieces connected to each other at regular intervals by rungs; used for climbing up or down during construction or renovation, or used as a temporary stair.

Lag bolt
A bolt with a square or hexagonal head, threaded at one end similar to a lag screw, and used for the same purpose. See also *Lag screw*.

Lag expansion shield
A lead expansion plug that accepts a lag bolt. The shield is tightened in the hole by expanding as the screw is tightened.

Lag screw
A heavy-duty screw with a square head without a slot, so tightening is done with a wrench.

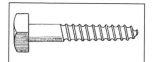

Lally column
A proprietary name for a cylindrical column that is filled with concrete; used as a structural column to provide support to beams or girders.

Lamb's tongue
The end of a handrail that is turned out or down from the rail and curved to resemble a tongue.

Laminate
Material that has been bonded into several layers, with adhesives under pressure, and sometimes with nails or bolts.

Laminated
Any construction built up out of thin sheets or plates that are fastened together with glue, cement, or other similar adhesive.

Laminated arch
A structural arch built up from multiple layers of smaller timbers.

Laminated floor
A structural floor that is constructed using a continuous series of lumber set on edge and nailed together.

Laminated glass
Two or more plies of flat glass bonded under heat and pressure to inner layers of plastic to form a shatter-resistant assembly that retains the fragments if the glass is broken; also called *safety glass*.

Laminated wood
An assembly of pieces of wood with the fibers or grain in each piece parallel to the fibers of the other pieces. The wood is built up in plies or laminations and joined with glue or mechanical fasteners. The layers are held together under pressure until the glue sets. Also called *plywood*.

Laminating
The process of bonding laminations or thin plates of material together with an adhesive.

Lamp post
A vertical support for an external light or luminaire, containing a complete internal wiring system.

Lanai
A living room or lounge area that is entirely, or in part, open to the outdoors.

Land reclamation
Gaining land that was previously submerged, by draining, filling, or a combination of these procedures, or reclaiming land that was otherwise unusable due to chemical waste or other hazard, by removing the affected earth and replacing it.

Land subdivision
A general area that has been divided into blocks or plots of ground, such as residential, commercial, industrial, or agricultural sites, with suitable streets, roadways, and open spaces.

Land survey
A survey made to determine the lengths and directions of boundary lines and the area of the tract bounded by these lines.

Land surveyor
A professional who establishes the length and direction of boundary lines on existing property, or new boundaries resulting from the division of larger parcels of land into smaller lots.

Land use
The specified permitted use of a property or district. Typical categories of use include residential, commercial, industrial, institutional, and agricultural.

Land use analysis
The study of an existing pattern of use within an area, to determine the nature and magnitude of deficiencies which might exist, and to assess the potential of the pattern relative to the community's development goals.

Land use plan
The projection of a future pattern of use within an area, as determined by development goals.

Land use regulation
Restrictions imposed on development by governing agencies, such as zoning, architectural review boards, or public participation in the planning or review process, which may result in hinderances to development.

Land use survey
A study and recording of the way in which land is being used in an area, usually classified as commercial, industrial, residential, or rural.

Landfill
The alternating burial of waste and approved landfill.

Landing
The horizontal platform at the end of a stair flight or between two flights of stairs.

Landmark
Any building or place which has a special character or special historical or aesthetic interest or value as part of the development, heritage, or cultural characteristics of a city, state, or nation. In New York City, any improvement 30 years or older that has a special character, historical interest, or aesthetic value as part of the development, heritage, or cultural characteristics of the city, state, or nation.

Landmark protection ordinances
Typically deals with the protection of isolated landmarks located outside the confines of a historic district, and provides for a stay of demolition for periods varying from 90 days to 1 year.

Landmark site
A parcel on which a designated landmark is situated.

Landmarks Commission ordinances
Grants landmark jurisdiction over an entire area such as a city, but its power generally applies only to single buildings within that area. Some have authority over historic districts.

Landmarks Register
A listing of buildings and districts designated for historical, architectural, or other special significance. Local registers are often modeled after the National Register of Historic Places and maintained by a preservation commission.

Landscape
The built or human-influenced habitat, including topography, plant cover, buildings, or other structures.

Landscape architect
The professional whose job it is to design, arrange, or modify the features of a landscape or garden for aesthetic or practical purposes.

Landscape fencing
Boundary or property lines defined by the use of trees or shrubbery.

Landscape window
A double-hung window in which the upper sash is divided into small panes of colored glass. The lower sash contains a larger single pane of clear glass.

Landscaping
The process of arranging trees and shrubbery on a specific site.

Land-use analysis
A planning process that studies an area by documenting existing conditions and patterns of use, then identifies patterns of potential future use. The analysis and recommendations include such items as traffic patterns, zoning, roads and sewer services, water supply, air quality, and environmental conservation factors.

Lantern
A tower or small turret, with windows or openings for light and air, crowning a dome or cupola.

Lantern light
A small turret crowning a roof or dome, often glazed to provide light or ventilation.

Lap
The length by which one piece of material overlaps another.

Lap joint
A joint in which one member overlaps the edge of another and is connected.

Lap siding
Refers to any siding that overlaps, such as clapboards.

Lap splice
(1) A splice made by placing one piece on top of another and fastening them together with pins, nails, screws, bolts, rivets, or similar devices. (2) In reinforced concrete construction, the ends of steel reinforcing is overlapped a certain dimension, based on the diameter of the bar, and tied with wire. Although it is the simplest method of splicing, it does not provide as much continuity as other splices, and has been shown to fail under severe loading, such as seismic forces.

Lap weld
A simple weld applied at the junction of two pieces of metal that are overlapped.

Lapis lazuli
A decorative variety of calcite, stained a deep blue by trace minerals; used as a stone veneer and in powdered form as the original ultramarine pigment.

Larch
A fine-textured, strong, hard, straight-grained wood of a coniferous tree; heavier than most softwoods.

Large-format photography
Pictures taken with a format of 4 by 5 inches or larger in cameras with tilts and swings for perspective controlled documentation of existing buildings.

Laser
A thin, concentrated beam of light; used in surveying for precise alignment.

Laser beam cutting
Using the concentrated beam of a laser to cut through wood or metal.

Laser beam welding
Using the heat generated by a laser beam to join metals.

Latch
A simple fastening device having a latch bolt but not a dead bolt; with no provisions for locking with a key, and usually operable from both sides.

Latch bolt
A spring bolt with a beveled edge, so that when the door is closed it springs back into a fixed notch.

Late finish
In a Critical Path Method (CPM) diagram, the latest that an event can be completed without adversely affecting the rest of the schedule. See also *Early finish*.

Late start
In a Critical Path Method (CPM) diagram, the latest that an event can be started without adversely affecting the rest of the schedule. See also *Early start*.

Latent defect
A construction defect that is not apparent or noticeable by visual inspection.

Lateral load
Forces that act on a structure from a horizontal direction, such as wind or seismic forces.

Lateral support
Temporary bracing that provides support from side-to-side forces. Also, roof and floor framing provides permanent lateral support for walls, columns, and beams.

Lateral thrust
In masonry, the pressure of a force which acts against its sides.

Latex
A water-based emulsion used in adhesives and coatings, composed of a synthetic rubber or plastic produced by polymerization.

Latex paint
A polymer-based paint that can be thinned with water.

Lath
Originally a rough-sawn strip of wood fixed to timber framing with small gaps between adjacent laths as a ground for plaster. Now applied to other materials used for the same purposes, such as metal lath.

Lathe
A machine for turning metal or wood. The piece to be turned is mounted between two chucks that rotate, and the cutting tool can slide back and forth on a track and be moved closer or farther away from the wood, allowing a variable profile to be cut.

Lattice structure
An open girder or open-web joist, column, cylindrical shell, dome, or other structural type, built up from members intersecting diagonally to form a lattice; used to span long distances with a lightweight structure.

Lattice truss
A truss consisting of upper and lower horizontal chords, connected by web members that cross each other, usually stiffened by joining at the intersection of the braces.

Latticework
Reticulated or netlike work formed by the crossing of laths or thin strips of wood or iron, usually in a diagonal pattern.

Lauan mahogany
Very thin sheets of wood, most commonly Philippine Mahogany.

Lavatory
A wash basin or, by extension, a room containing a wash basin and a water closet.

Lawsuit
A legal proceeding brought about to settle a dispute between two or more parties.

Lay up
To place materials in the relative position they will occupy in the finished building.

Laying out
Marking or laying the actual materials in their location before they are permanently installed or laid up.

Laying out the bond
The process of laying loose brick along the area to calculate how many bricks will be needed for the wall, and eliminating the need for cutting a lot of extra bricks.

Laylight
A glazed opening above or below a skylight to admit light, either natural or artificial, to a space below.

Layout
A diagram indicating the pattern of construction. Also, used to determine the exact position on a site by defining the outer perimeter of the foundation with stakes or batter boards. See also *Batter boards*.

Layout line
A pencil line on the surface of a board to indicate where to cut or drill, or a chalk line on a floor indicating the location of a partition or other object.

Layout tee
In carpentry, a simple method of ensuring that all cuts made on similar rafters are identical, by construction of a small T-shaped template with angle cuts on the stem of the tee. It can be placed over a rafter and the angle of the cut marked or scribed onto the rafter with a pencil.

Leaching
The process of percolation, whereby liquid effluent seeps into the surrounding soil.

Leaching cesspool
In plumbing, a cylindrical chamber in the ground lined with stones without mortar that allows liquids to seep out into the soil.

Leaching field
A system of underground tile or pipes arranged in trenches filled with gravel on the downhill side of a septic tank. The waste is discharged into the tile bed and seeps into the soil along the lengths of the feeders.

Lead
A soft, malleable, heavy metal that has a low melting point and a high coefficient of thermal expansion; very easy to cut and work. Created by building up a section of masonry wall, which is racked back on successive courses; a line is attached to the leads as a guide for constructing the wall in between them.

Lead masonry
The process of building up sections of masonry and racking back on successive courses. A line is stretched to the leads as a guide for constructing the wall in between them.

Lead paint
Usually associated with oil-based paint or paint containing white lead. They are now considered a long-term health hazard and must be removed wherever found among habitable spaces.

Lead plug
A cylinder of lead inserted into a hole in masonry. It is hollowed out to accept a screw or eye hook; when screwed in, the lead expands and holds the screw or eye hook firmly in place.

Lead poisoning
A condition arising from breathing the fumes of lead compounds or ingesting lead paint and water contaminated by lead pipes.

Lead wool
A fine steel mesh used to plug enlarged screw holes in wood. The screws grip the wool when they are turned, compressing it into a tight mass.

Leaded glass
Dates from the Middle Ages when glass was set into malleable lead frames.

Leaded joint
A joint made in cast-iron piping by pressing oakum into the opening between the bell and spigot, and pouring hot lead into the joint. See also *Oakum.*

Leaded light
A window with small diamond-shaped or rectangular panes of glass set in cames.

Leader
A vertical pipe that carries rainwater from the roof gutter to the ground or drain system.

Leader head
An enlarged collector at the top of a leader for receiving a large volume of rainwater at a narrow area where a gutter is not practical.

Lead-free paint
A paint that does not contain any lead compounds.

Leak
An opening, such as a crack or hole in a roof, where water from rain or snow can enter the building. In plumbing, a hole in a pipe which permits gas, water, or other liquid to escape.

Lean-to
A shed or building having a single pitched roof, with its highest end against an adjoining wall or building.

Lean-to rafter
A rafter that extends from the top plate on the low wall to the top plate on the high wall of a lean-to roof.

Lean-to roof
A roof structure that has only one slope.

Lease
An agreement granting permission for the use of a property for a specified time period, usually for a specific amount of rent, without transferring ownership.

Leaseback
A transaction that occurs when a property owner sells property to another party, who subsequently leases possession of the same property back to the original owner.

Leasehold improvement
An improvement to a piece of property by a tenant, which has value for that specific tenant for the period of the lease, but could be forfeited upon termination of the lease.

Leaves
Hinged or sliding components, as in a door.

Ledger
A wood strip nailed to the lower side of a girder to provide a bearing surface for joists.

Ledger strip
A strip of wood nailed along the bottom side of a girder to support the joists. If the joists are the same height as the girder, they must be notched to fit over the ledger strip, so that they remain flush with the top side of the girder.

LEED program
A federal program to promote recycling in a major way. The U.S. Green Building Council's Leadership in Energy and Environmental Design program establishes guidelines for documenting sustainable design practices for existing buildings.

Leeward
The side of the structure that is sheltered from the wind.

Legal description
A written documentation of the location and boundaries of a parcel of land. A legal description may be based on a metes and bounds survey or the rectangular system of survey, or it may make reference to a recorded plot of land.

Let in
To cut into one member to allow for the passage or connection of another member.

Let-in brace
A diagonal brace that is cut into the studs the depth of its own thickness, to provide a flush surface for the finished siding or panels.

Let-in bracing
Diagonal bracing placed into cut-in slots in the studs to align the outside face of the bracing flush with the surface of the wall.

Letter of agreement
A written document stating the terms of an agreement between two or more parties, which is often sufficient to qualify as a legal document when signed by the recipient.

Level
A device for determining the horizontal or vertical attitude of a member. It consists of one or a series of horizontally and vertically placed glass tubes nearly filled with alcohol or ether, leaving an air bubble inside. When the bubble is centered in the tube, the object is true and level.

Leveling board
A long, straight board used to support a level on top, to allow leveling over a greater distance than the level can cover by itself.

Leveling rod
A tall rod, graduated in feet and inches; used to determine the differences in elevation as seen through the eyepiece of a level; records the elevation above the last measured benchmark.

Leverage
The use of fixed-cost funds to acquire property that is expected to produce a higher rate of return either through rental income or appreciation.

Liability
A situation whereby one party legally assumes the loss or damage by another party.

Liability insurance
Protection from liability arising from injury to another person or another person's property.

Library of Congress
Serves as the national library of the United States; maintains collections of manuscripts, photographs, maps, and related historical documents; preserves its own building; and produces publications and exhibits. It is the repository for Historic American Building Survey (HABS) and Historic American Engineering Record (HAER) documentation.

License
The permission by an authority to practice or offer a service that would otherwise be unlawful to practice or offer without it.

Licensed contractor
A person or business entity authorized by governmental authority to provide and perform contracting services for others.

Lien
A legal charge against property that is made securely for the payment of a debt or for the performance of an obligation.

Lien release
A document which releases a lien on a property upon satisfaction of the amount claimed in the lien.

Lien waiver
A document in which a party gives up the right to place a lien in the future.

Life cycle
In a building, the expected useful life of the structure and its fixtures before requiring restoration or replacement.

Life cycle cost
The initial capital outlay, cost of construction, and cost of maintenance throughout the estimated useful life of the facility.

Life cycle costing
The analysis of the total cost of a building or structure over an extended period of time, including the initial cost, maintenance costs, and replacement costs based on the life expectancy of its components; usually compares alternative components and systems.

Life safety
Items in general building codes that deal with aspects of life safety, such as fire protection.

Life safety code
A code dedicated to saving lives from fire; developed by the international organization NFPA Committee of Safety to Life.

Lift
An enclosed platform made to travel up and down in a vertical framework or shaft, to move materials during construction. Also called *hoist*. See also *Elevator*.

Light
An opening through which daylight is admitted to the interior space of a building; an individual pane of glass, window, or compartment of a window.

Light fixture
A luminaire secured in place or attached as a permanent appendage or appliance. It consists of a lighting unit, with lamps and components to protect the electrical circuits from the weather, and other devices to spread the light in a prescribed pattern.

Light fixture

Light framing
Lumber that is less than 4 inches wide, used to frame the skeleton of small structures.

Light well
A small court commonly placed in large buildings to admit daylight into interior areas not exposed to an open view.

Lighthouse
A tall structure topped by a powerful light used as a beacon or signal to aid marine navigation. Now automated or replaced by automatic light towers, lighthouse complexes were built to be instantly recognizable.

Lighting fixture schedule
A listing on the drawings of the lighting fixtures needed as represented on the electrical plan, or reflected ceiling plan.

Lighting maintenance factor
A factor used in the calculation of the number of luminaires needed to light a space. It refers to the extent of cleaning and replacement that will take place once installed.

Lightning conductor
A metal cable or rod running from the highest point on the roof, and insulated from it to a water pipe or other conductor to the ground.

Lightweight concrete
A type of concrete that is composed of any lightweight aggregate, such as sand.

Limba
A straight-grained, fine-textured wood used for interior paneling.

Lime stucco
A stucco composed of lime, sand, and aggregate; may also contain pigments and waterproofing materials.

Limestone
Rock of sedimentary origin composed principally of calcite, dolomite, or both; used as a building stone or crushed-stone aggregate, or burned to produce lime.

Limit of liability
A preset limit that an insurance company will pay in the event of loss, damage, or injury

Limit switch
A switch which opens an electric circuit when a device, such as an elevator, reaches the limit of travel. Also, an electrical switch that cuts off power on a piece of equipment, if the operator fails to do so; used on cranes and similar moving equipment.

Limited partnership
A form of ownership in which the general partners manage the operations and bear full responsibility, and the limited partners, whose obligation is limited, have no control over the partnership.

Line graph
A graphic representation of a situation over time, using a line that connects points on a graph. Comparisons can be made by using a series of lines charting the same information, but with information resulting in different coordinate points.

Line item
An item listed on a plan or specification with unit price and quantity needed.

Line level
A bubble level designed to hook over a string; used when laying foundations, tile pipe, determining grades, or in establishing level masonry courses along the run of masonry work.

Lineal foot
A running foot, as distinct from a square foot or a cubic foot.

Lineal measure
One-dimensional measurement of a piece of material or object.

Linear diffuser
An air-conditioning device that distributes air to a space from a linear slot, often at the terminals of the duct but also along the run.

Lineman's pliers
Pliers with a tapered blunt nose and side cutters as part of the jaws.

Lining
Material that covers any interior surface, such as a framework around a door or window or boarding that covers interior surfaces of a building.

Link
An appendage that connects one building to another, or an addition to an existing building.

Linoleum
Floor covering made from jute or similar fabric that is impregnated with oxidized oils, resin, and a filler, such as cork.

Linoleum knife
A knife with a hooked blade, curving back toward the handle; used for cutting linoleum, vinyl flooring, or for trimming drywall.

Lintel
The horizontal beam that forms the upper structural member of an opening for a window or door and supports part of the structure above it. Also called *header*.

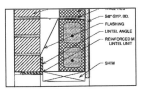

Lintel course
In stone masonry, a course set at the level of a lintel. It is commonly differentiated from the wall by its greater projection, its finish, or thickness, which often matches that of the lintel.

Liquid roofing
A liquid or semiliquid material put on with a mop or roller to create a seamless waterproof membrane.

Liquid system
A solar heating system where water is circulated through a collector to a storage tank, then back in an open or closed loop. The pipes pass through convection heaters or blowers to transfer heat into the building.

Liquidated damages
An amount of money charged against the design firm or construction company reflecting real loss, such as loss of operations, additional lease charges, late fees, or loss of rental income. Usually limited to 1/2 to 1 percent of the contract amount.

List
A series of words or numbers that organizes elements into a comprehensive sequence. Also applies to a vertical member leaning to one side, or off plumb.

List of materials
A list on a fabrication drawing that shows the materials needed to build the object shown on the drawing.

Listed
An electrical product that has been tested by the Underwriters Laboratory and verified that it performs the way it was designed to.

Litigation
The taking of a matter under dispute before a court of law where evidence is given under oath and becomes a process of determining liability or resolution, through submission to the jurisdiction and procedures of federal or state courts.

Live
An electrical circuit that has a positive current running through it.

Live load
A load that is not permanently applied to a structure, as compared with a dead load representing the building component's permanent weight. Also called *moving load*.

Live load deflection
The sagging of a beam or joist under the weight of a vertical live load, or the displacement of a vertical member due to a horizontal live load, such as wind.

Load
The force or forces that act on a structural member, or system of members.

Load center
In an electrical system, the distribution center for electrical power; also called a *panel box*.

Load factor
A factor used in structural design to adjust the working load to determine the ultimate load. Also, in an air-conditioning system, the ratio of the average air-conditioning load on the system at its maximum capacity.

Load-bearing wall
A wall capable of supporting an imposed load in addition to its own weight.

Loader
A tractor with a bucket on the front for scooping material from excavations and loading it onto trucks. Also called a *front end loader*.

Loading dock
The area of a building accessible from the street, and convenient to the transportation systems within the building, that provides for the loading and unloading of commercial vehicles.

Loan-to-value ratio
The ratio between the amount of a mortgage loan and the appraised value of the property.

Lobbying
A group of private citizens engaged in influencing politicians to take action for or against their cause, or in favor of some special interest.

Local buckling
Crinkling of a strut or of the compression flange of a beam because it is too thin; particularly liable to occur in thin-walled sections.

Lock
A device that fastens a door, gate, or window in position; may be opened or closed by a key or a dead bolt.

Lock nut
A type of secondary nut placed on a bolt to prevent the first nut from turning.

Lock seam
In sheet metal work, a seam that is formed by bending each adjoining edge into a hook, and pressing them together to make a tight joint.

Lock set
A complete lock, including knobs, trim, escutcheon plate, and screws.

Locking pliers
Pliers with an adjustable screw and lever that can be locked into place over the desired object.

Locust
Wood of the black and red locust tree; coarse-grained, strong, hard, decay-resistant, and durable.

Lodge
The workshop and living quarters for the stone masons set up when major medieval buildings were being constructed. The term now refers to any meeting place with living and dining accommodations.

Loft building
A former commercial or industrial building containing large open floor areas; used currently for conversion into residential units.

Log building
A structure built from cut and stacked horizontal logs rather than dressed lumber; one of the earlier forms of dwellings in many parts of the world. The log cabin became a symbol of the pioneering westward movement.

Log cabin siding
Wood siding with a bulging, rounded profile, designed to resemble the logs of a log cabin.

Loggia
An arcade or colonnaded structure, open on one or more sides, sometimes with an upper story; an arcade or colonnaded porch or gallery attached to a much larger structure.

Logistics
The science of coordinating the activities involved in construction in the proper sequence and time; such as figuring labor and materials to do the job, hiring laborers and subcontractors, coordinating their arrival at the job site, and arranging the delivery of the materials in a sequential manner to properly construct the building.

Long house
A dwelling used by Native American tribes, constructed of poles lashed together in the form of a barrel vault; approximately 16 feet wide and up to 100 feet long, with inside compartments that open onto a continuous aisle.

Long span steel joist
A joist made up of steel angles, or steel angles and steel rods in a triangular pattern.

Long term
Refers to events or liabilities that will come due beyond 1 year.

Longitudinal bracing
Stiffening or bracing by members or panels that run in the direction of the length of a structure, as opposed to vertical or diagonal bracing.

Longitudinal reinforcement
Reinforcing steel that is placed parallel to the long axis of a structural member.

Long-lead item
A condition where there is a long period of time between placing an order for equipment or materials, which includes the time required to manufacture, assemble, and deliver the item to the job site.

Long-nose pliers
Pliers used for grasping items in tight places. They have long narrow jaws that taper to a point.

Long-term deflection
Total deflection, consisting of both the elastic deflection and the creep deflection over a long period of time.

Long-term liabilities
Obligations that are payable beyond 1 year.

Long-term monitoring
A method of determining suspected movement in a façade, or its elements, by using crack gauges that record minute movement over a period of time. Changes in the pattern of heat emanating from a building can be recorded using time-lapse thermography.

Lookout
A rafter or joist that projects beyond an end wall of a building; may be ornamental or supporting an over-hanging roof or cornice.

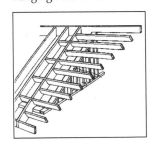

Loose-fill insulation
A material that can be blown into an area, such as an attic space, and provides insulating qualities by the air pockets created within the material.

Loose-pin hinge
A hinge on a door that can be separated by removing a vertical pin that holds it together, allowing the door to be taken out of its frame, or assembled into a frame.

Loss of use insurance
Protection against financial loss during the time required to repair or replace property damaged or destroyed by specific actions covered in the policy.

Loss payable clause
A protective clause in an insurance policy for mortgage holders, whereby any payments for loss will be made payable to both the policyholder and the mortgage company.

Lot
One of the smaller portions of land into which a village, town, or city block is divided or laid out; also, a parcel of a subdivision, described by reference to a recorded plot or by definite boundaries. Also a portion of land in one ownership; if two or more lots are occupied by a single building unit, then such a plot is considered a single lot.

Lot line
The line that bounds a plot of ground described as a lot in the title to the property. The line is represented on paper and may be expressed on the property by boundary markers at corners, a fence, stone wall, or other means of delineation.

Louver
A window opening made up of overlapping boards, blades or slats, either fixed or adjustable, designed to allow ventilation in varying degrees without letting the rain come in. See also *Jalousie window*.

Louvered door
A door having a louvered opening, usually with horizontal blades, that allows for the passage or circulation of air while the door is closed.

Low bid
A bid that conforms with the bidding documents that offers the lowest price among two or more bidders for performance of the work.

Low voltage
Any voltage less than 12 volts, not hazardous, and commonly used for doorbell wires.

Low-density concrete
A concrete that is up to one-third lighter than normal concrete; produced by mixing it with a lightweight aggregate such as vermiculite, or foaming agents, which create air pockets within the concrete.

Low-emissivity glass
Glass that transmits visible light while selectively reflecting the longer wavelengths of radiant heat; made by a coating either on the glass itself or by the transparent plastic film in the sealed airspace of insulating glass.

Lower-tier subcontractor
A sub-subcontractor, or one who contracts with a subcontractor for a specific portion of the work.

Lowest responsible bidder
The bidder who has submitted the lowest qualified bid. The owner and architect must have agreed in advance whether or not the lowest bid will be the only condition for granting the work.

Lucite
The trade name for a clear plastic sheet material; often used for glazing where breakage of glass might be a hazard.

Lug sill
A window sill in a brick or stone wall that extends beyond the width of the window opening.

Lugs
In electrical work, the terminals placed on the ends of conductors to enable the wire to be attached or detached quickly.

Lumber
Timber that is sawn or split in the form of beams, boards, joists, planks, or shingles; refers especially to pieces smaller than heavy timber.

Lumber-core plywood
A plywood made with a core of boards encased in a thin top and bottom layer, covered by two thin facing layers.

Lumber defects
Blemishes and fissures which degrade the quality of lumber; including knots, checks, shakes, and splits.

Luminaire
A device for providing mechanical support and electrical connections to a lamp or lamps; fixed to a support, such as a wall, or recessed in a ceiling.

Luminous ceiling
A lighting system in which the whole ceiling is translucent with lamps that are installed above and suspended from a structural ceiling.

Lump sum
A bid or proposal that is priced as a total unit rather than broken down into components or categories.

Lump sum bid
A bid of a set amount to cover all labor, equipment, materials, overhead, and profit necessary for construction of an improvement to real estate.

Lump sum contract
A stipulated sum that is to be paid to the contractor, which has been determined in advance and written into the contract.

Lump sum proposal
A proposal to do the work, or any designated portion of it, for a specified sum of money.

Luster glass
An iridescent glass, of the type made by Tiffany.

LVL
Abbreviation for Laminated Veneer Lumber, manufactured by gluing parallel laminations into thicknesses common to solid sawn timber. It is also called *engineered lumber*.

M

M roof
A roof formed by the junction of two parallel gable roofs with a valley between them.

Machine bolt
A metal bolt with a square or hexagonal head, with threads on the lower end for attaching a nut.

Machine room
A space that houses machinery and equipment, such as elevator equipment, generators, boilers, or air-conditioning equipment.

Machine screws
A threaded screw with a flat end instead of a pointed one; used for the assembling of metal parts.

Machine-sanded
Sanded by a drum sander to remove manufacturing marks or defects or to remove an existing finish.

Magnetic stud finder
A metered device that can detect the metallic nail or screw heads used to construct the stud wall initially, as it passes over the finished wall.

Magnetized hammer
A hammer that can hold a nail or tack on its magnetized head, so that the worker can hold material in place with the other hand.

Mahogany
A straight-grained wood of intermediate density, pinkish to red-brown in color; used primarily for interior cabinetwork and decorative paneling.

Main
In electrical work, the current from which all other branch circuits are taken.

Main beam
In floor construction, one of the principal beams that transmits loads directly to the columns.

Main breaker
A protective device at the service entrance to a building, that trips when there is an overload to the main service line, or needs to be turned off for service inside.

Main disconnect switch
A switch in the service panel that can shut off all electricity to a building at one time.

Main rafter
A roof member extending at right angles from the plate to the ridge.

Main runner
A metal supporting member which is suspended from the ceiling above by wires, and which in turn supports the cross-tees that hold ceiling tiles.

Main stack
In plumbing, a vent pipe that runs vertically from the building drain up to the roof.

Main Street program
Encourages economic revitalization through preservation of central business districts in small to medium-sized communities. These programs are aided by local, state, and federal private and government organizations, such as the National Trust for Historic Preservation's Main Street program.

Main tie
The lower tension member of a roof truss that connects the feet of the principal rafters.

Maintain
To keep in a state of proper repair, and prevent deterioration by constant or periodic attention, such as cleaning, painting, or refinishing.

Maintenance
Providing upkeep, repair, and care for a building's structural integrity and appearance after acquisition or after restoration, at an acceptable level to enable it to fulfill its function over time and to prevent deterioration.

Maintenance bond
A guarantee to the owner that any defects in materials or workmanship that show up within a prescribed period of time will be replaced at the contractor's expense.

Maintenance period
The period after completion of the construction during which the contractor is obligated to repair any defects in workmanship and materials.

Male nipple
A short section of pipe with threads on the outside of both ends.

Male thread
A thread on the outside of a fitting or pipe. See also *Female thread*.

Malleability
The property of a metal that allows it to be shaped by bending, hammering, or extruding without cracking or rupturing.

Mallet
A small wooden or rubber hammer with a thick barrel; used for striking other tools, such as a chisel or other cutting tools. See also *Maul*.

Malpractice
A negligent act or intentional omission by a professional.

Management
Directing the activities of others in the planning and carrying out of a task; also, those responsible for such direction.

Managing partner
The person in a partnership responsible for decisions affecting all projects, or projects assigned to him or her, on behalf of the partnership. Also called *partner-in-charge*.

Mandatory
Required by code or specification.

Mandatory improvements
Changes required by regulatory codes when a building is altered, and especially when changed to a new use with greater inherent hazard.

Manifest
A list of items contained in a shipment.

Mantel
The frame and shelf surrounding the fireplace; often used to denote just the shelf.

Mantelpiece
The fittings and decorative elements of a mantel, including a cornice and shelf carried above the fireplace.

Manual
Any action or task that is accomplished by hand, as opposed to being assisted by an electrical or gasoline-powered tool.

Manufactured building
A building which is manufactured in a plant and which often includes structural, electrical, plumbing, heating, ventilation, and air-conditioning (HVAC), or other service systems in the structure before delivery to the site for installing or erection.

Manufactured roof
A finished roof system totally manufactured in a factory or plant.

Manufactured wall
A finished wall system totally manufactured in a factory or plant.

Manufacturer
An enterprise that constructs, fabricates, or assembles products from raw materials, or assembles products from unfinished materials supplied by others that are incorporated into their own products.

Map
A vertical graphic description of a defined geographic area showing legal boundaries and physical features. Examples include a site map, land-use map, subdivision map, topographic survey map, and U.S. Geodetic Survey (USGS) map.

Maple
A hard, tough, moderately high-density wood, with a uniform texture; used for flooring and wood trim.

Marbeling
The process of painting a wood surface so that it will resemble marble.

Marble
Metamorphic rock made up largely of calcite or dolomite; capable of taking a high polish and used especially in architecture and sculpture. Numerous minerals account for its distinctive appearance.

Marbleized
Painting wood or plaster to look like marble by a special technique of simulating the veining of the stone.

Margin
An amount of money added to the cost of materials.

Margin light
A narrow pane of glass at the edge of a sash window or door.

Margin trowel
A rectangular masonry trowel that has a flat end rather than a pointed one.

Marine glue
A waterproof glue used on exterior applications using plywood or other wood products.

Mark out
To delineate where cuts are to be made on lumber.

Market analysis
An economic examination and analysis of the potential for development of a particular project, including demographic studies and projected income and return on investment.

Market evaluation
Part of a feasibility study that includes community market dynamics, social and demographic characteristics, recent development trends, specific markets, the competition, and geographic factors.

Market rent
The current rental value of a property, which varies according to local or national market conditions.

Market research
Investigation to determine specific aspects of a marketplace, such as the potential prospects in an area, or the number of competing firms in the same area.

Market valuation
A valuation of the current market rent of a property, obtained by comparison with equivalent properties.

Marketing
The process of promoting an individual, firm, or company that provides a professional service or product.

Marking
A reference number of other nomenclature marked on each component in a delivery to the job site. If it is a specialty item, it is keyed to its position in the structure as found in the drawings or specifications.

Markup
A percentage amount of money that may be added to the total cost of materials or other direct costs, to make up a final bid or contract price. These are applied mainly to the fixed overhead costs, contingencies, and the anticipated profit.

Marquetry
Inlaid pieces of a material, such as wood or ivory, fitted together and glued to a common background.

Masking
A method of covering an area with a removable protective adhesive material, to protect adjacent work from damage; such as that used in plastering, painting, or spraying compounds.

Masking tape
An adhesive-backed tape for covering the edges of an area to be painted or sprayed with other material; available in rolls of various widths. Once removed, it leaves a clean sharp line.

Mason
A craftsperson skilled in shaping and joining pieces of stone or brick together to form walls and other parts of buildings and structures.

Mason's measure
A method of estimating the masonry required for a job by counting the corners twice, and disregarding small openings.

Mason's scaffold
A strong self-supporting scaffold that can hold the weight of the total number of masons working, the masonry units, and the tubs to hold the mortar during construction.

Masonite
The trade name for brand of dense compressed tempered board, made from wood fibers in a binder. It has a hard smooth finish on one side, and is used as an underlayment for vinyl flooring. Also called *hardboard*.

Masonry
Includes all stone products, all brick products, and concrete block units, including decorative and customized blocks.

Masonry anchor
A metal device attached to a door or window frame that ends up embedded in the mortar joint of the masonry.

Masonry bond beam
A beam made by placing reinforcing bars in a specially designed concrete block that is hollow on the top, and used as a course in a concrete block wall. Concrete is placed in this top block forming a continuous beam around the perimeter of the wall.

Masonry field
In brickwork, the expanse of wall between openings, composed principally of stretchers.

Masonry joints
Usually consist of mortar which is part of the wall system, and act as adhesives, and must take the same tensile, compressive, and shear stresses as the material itself, so expansion and contraction forces will not affect them differently.

Masonry lintel
A lintel over doors and windows made of precast concrete or concrete block filled with reinforcing bars and cement; used where a matching appearance is desired.

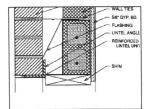

Masonry nail
A short, stubby, hardened steel nail of specialized design, used for fastening wood to masonry work or concrete.

Masonry panel
A prefabricated section of masonry that is constructed on the ground, or in a factory, and shipped to the site for erection by crane.

Masonry reinforcing
Consists of steel rods placed in the grouted voids, and lateral rods laid between the horizontal courses.

Masonry saw
A portable electrically powered handsaw, similar to a circular saw, with a variety of blades, such as diamond and other abrasive masonry-cutting blades, used to cut concrete, and concrete block.

Masonry toothing
Leaving alternate masonry units out of a wall in order to provide a bond for new courses.

Masonry veneer
A single wythe of masonry used as a facing over another backing material.

Masonry wall
A load-bearing or non-load-bearing wall consisting of hollow masonry units.

Massing
The overall shape of a building, as differentiated from wall treatment and fenestration.

Mast
The vertical shaft of a tower crane. Also, a broadcasting antenna located on the top of a structure.

Master
In the building trades, a term that signifies the third and highest level of achievement of a person, and who has been issued a license to practice the trade without supervision, such as is required with the journeyman or apprentice level of skill.

Master builder
An individual of broad experience and training, who is distinguished in the craft of building.

Master plan
A plan drawn on a small scale, supplemented with written material depicting all the elements of a project or scheme. Applications include site planning and proposed land use improvements.

Master plumber
An individual licensed to contract for the installation of plumbing and accept responsibility for its performance.

Master switch
In electrical work, a switch that controls two or more circuits.

MasterFormat
The copyrighted title of a uniform indexing system for construction specifications, created by the Construction Specifications Institute. It outlines a numerical system of construction-related data, based on a format with 16 major divisions. See also *CSI and CSI MasterFormat*.

Mastic
A jointing compound that dries on the surface but remains permanently plastic underneath; used to seal joints between precast concrete panels, curtain walls, windows, and pipes. Usually inserted into the joint with a pressure gun or hand applicator. Any heavy-bodied, doughlike adhesive compound; a sealant with puttylike properties used for applying tiles to a surface or for weatherproofing joints.

Match
To make equal to a sample or adjoining piece; as to quality, color, texture, thickness, width, surface treatment, or joints.

Matched lumber
Any lumber that has been edge-dressed and shaped to make a tongue-and-groove joint on the edges when laid edge to edge.

Matched veneer
Installations of wood or stone veneer where the patterns of the grain of adjoining pieces are aligned at the edges, either in a herringbone or book-matched pattern.

Matching
Used to describe the arrangement of timber veneers, such as book-matching, slip-matching, and quarter-matching.

Material deficiency
Defective material or workmanship of a magnitude that requires correction. Also, a shortage of specified materials delivered to the job site.

Material safety data sheet
A form published by manufacturers of hazardous materials that describes the hazards of the product and the proper uses and precautions.

Materials cage
A metal platform or cage on a hoist; used for lifting materials to the upper floors of a building under construction.

Materials list
A list of the type and quantity of all materials that will be required on a specific project. Also called a *bill of materials*.

Material schedule
A listing on the drawings of the materials needed on a project.

Materials symbols

Various standardized symbols used by architects and builders to designate specific kinds of materials to be used in the construction.

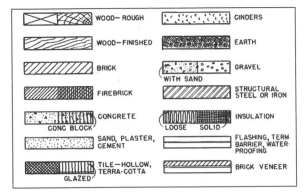

WOOD – ROUGH	CINDERS
WOOD – FINISHED	EARTH
BRICK	GRAVEL WITH SAND
FIREBRICK	STRUCTURAL STEEL OR IRON
CONCRETE CONC BLOCK	INSULATION LOOSE SOLID
SAND, PLASTER, CEMENT	FLASHING, TERM BARRIER, WATER PROOFING
TILE—HOLLOW, TERRA-COTTA GLAZED	BRICK VENEER

Matte surface

A surface that redistributes the incident light uniformly in all directions, so that the luminance is the same and without sheen, even when viewed from an oblique angle.

Maul

A heavy hammer used for driving stakes or wedges.

Maximum demand

In electrical design, the largest anticipated electrical load on the entire electrical system during a specific period of time. In plumbing design, the largest anticipated load on a sanitary system during a specific period of time.

Maximum rated load

The sum total of the greatest live load and dead load that a scaffold is going to carry, plus an additional safety factor.

Maximum size of aggregate

The maximum size permitted in reinforced concrete design, determined by the thickness of the slab and the distance of the reinforcement from the face of the finished concrete.

Measure

To find the dimensions of an object or area.

Measured drawings

An architectural drawing of an existing building drawn to scale from field measurements.

Mechanic

A person skilled in the maintenance and repair of mechanical equipment.

Mechanical bond

A physical bond formed by keying or interlocking, such as plaster keying into expanded metal lath, or concrete interlocking with the deformations of the reinforcing bars, as opposed to a chemical bond by adhesion.

Mechanical code

Regulations that apply to the design of heating, ventilating, plumbing, and air-conditioning systems.

Mechanical drawing

A graphic representation constructed with drafting instruments; a plan showing the layout and details of plumbing and heating, ventilation, and air-conditioning (HVAC) systems.

Mechanical engineer

A person trained, skilled, or professionally engaged in a branch of engineering related to mechanical equipment, particularly heating and air-conditioning systems.

Mechanical equipment

The equipment used in water; gas; heating, ventilation, and air-conditioning (HVAC); and other utilities, such as furnaces, hot water heaters, ducts, vents, and piping.

Mechanical fastener

Any device for making a physical connection between two objects, such as screws, nails, bolts, pins, cleats, and split-ring connectors. It does not include glue or cement or similar method of bonding.

Mechanical joint

A plumbing joint that uses a clamping device to secure the sections, such as screws or nuts and bolts.

Mechanical pencil

A pencil used in drafting that holds replaceable leads, and feeds them in as needed.

Mechanical room

A room containing a permanently installed air-conditioning system, boiler, or furnace, with all the accompanying plumbing and ductwork.

Mechanical services

Building services such as heating, ventilating, air-conditioning, and gas installations.

Mechanical systems

Construction or renovation of heating, ventilating, air-conditioning, plumbing, and fire suppression systems.

Mechanics lien

A lien filed by a contractor or tradesperson for unpaid work performed on a project, which becomes an encumbrance on the property until released by agreement, paid, or dismissed by action in the courts.

Mediate
To bring about a resolution to a dispute, using a neutral third party, such as an arbitrator or mediator.

Mediation
A method of resolving disputes by using an impartial intermediary who suggests solutions to settle the dispute, rather than imposing a decision on the parties.

Mediumscope
A term established by the Construction Specifications Institute (CSI) to outline a section of the specifications that describes a group of related materials and applications.

Meeting rail
One of the horizontal rails of a double-hung sash.

Member
Any individual element of a building, such as an entablature, cornice, column, beam, rafter, or any other framing member; also one of the individual shapes that make up a molding, such as a cornice or a water table.

Membrane curing
Controlling the curing of concrete by covering the surface with vinyl sheeting,

Membrane waterproofing
A sheet material placed over a subfloor to provide a waterproof barrier under a finished floor of tile that is set into a mortar bed.

Membrane waterproofing
Applying a layer of impervious sheet material to a foundation wall.

Mercury switch
An electrical switch that uses a small sealed tube of mercury to complete the circuit; the switch is noiseless when operated.

Meritless claim
An obvious insufficient claim made without merit or substantiation that should be rejected without argument or proof.

Mesh
An arrangement of intertwining material making up a screen or sieve.

Mesh reinforcement
Welded wire fabric used as reinforcement for concrete, particularly in slabs.

Metal building
A metal structure, usually constructed or fabricated in a factory, and erected at the job site. Also applies to a metal structure that is constructed totally at the site.

Metal chimney
A vertical metal shaft from a fireplace that encloses a flue that carries smoke into the outside air.

Metal clad cable
An electrical conduit with a flexible steel jacket wrapped around insulated wires.

Metal crating
Open metal grating or flooring for pedestrian traffic over openings in the sidewalk or other walkways.

Metal deck
Sheet-metal sections that are formed with ridges for strengthening, and used in flat roof systems.

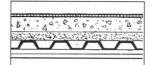 

Metal decking
Preformed light-gauge metal sheets used for decking over metal joists. Some are formed with enclosed channels in which electrical cables can be run. These types are usually embedded in a concrete floor.

Metal ductwork
Lightweight sheet-metal ductwork used to carry heat and cooling in an air-conditioning system; sometimes exposed of the ceiling.

Metal gutter
A type of attached gutter; prefabricated of sheet metal; usually obtainable in two styles: either half round or with an ornamental profile resembling a cornice molding.

Metal lath
Sheets of metal which are slit and stretched, forming a series of diamond-shaped openings; used as a backing for plaster.

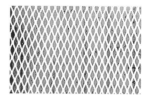

Metal pan
A square or rectangular pan that is placed upside down on plywood forms, adjacent to other forms on all sides, to act as formwork for poured concrete. When the plywood and pan are removed, the underside of the slab shows a wafflelike surface. See also *Pan forms*.

Metal roofing
Sheet metal used for roofing, either as a batten or standing-seam design.

Metal stud
A unit of vertical support in a drywall installation, made from light-gauge metal in the form of a channel with a turned-in edge, with preformed holes for electrical conduit and pipes. The edges are creased so that the metal screws used to fasten the wallboard will not drift off the edge of the stud. They are screwed into metal channels at the top and bottom. They are also used for installing gypsum board onto a suspended ceiling.

Metal trim
Any ornamental feature made out of pressed-metal sheeting, such as metal strips around door or window openings.

Metal valley
A V-shaped valley or gutter between two roof slopes, lined with pieces of lead, zinc, copper, or sheet metal to prevent water from entering.

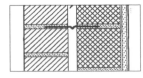

Metal wall tie
Strip of corrugated metal used to tie a brick veneer wall to a framework.

Metal wall ties
In masonry, a steel tie which is coated with portland cement and used to bond two separate walls in cavity-type walls.

Metal-clad door
A flush door having face sheets of light-gauge steel bonded to a steel channel frame; or a door having a structural wood core clad with galvanized sheet metal.

Metes and bounds
A method of defining boundary lines when describing the location of land in terms of directions and distances from one or more points of reference.

Metric measure
A decimal system of measure, which uses the meter for length and the kilogram for weight, unlike the system used in the United States, which uses inches and yards for length and pounds and tons for weight.

Mews
An alley or courtyard in which stables are or once were located or have been converted into residences.

Mezzanine
A low-ceilinged story located between two main stories; it is usually constructed directly above the ground floor, often projecting over it as a balcony.

Mildew
A mold or discoloration on wood caused by fungi.

Milestone activity
A key item of major significance in the life of a project under design or construction, as represented on a Critical Path Method (CPM) diagram.

Mill construction
A type of construction historically used for mills and factories, consisting of masonry walls, heavy timber, and plank floors.

Milled-each-end pipe
Asbestos cement pipe in fixed lengths that has a smooth surface on each end for joining. The rest of the pipe is left rough.

Milled-overall pipe
Asbestos cement pipe that has been milled smooth from end to end. It can be cut to any length and joined with existing pipe.

Miller Act
A federal labor law that protects subcontractors and suppliers by requiring that the general contractor working on federally funded projects obtain performance bonds and labor and materials payment bonds.

Milling
In stonework, the processing of quarry blocks, through sawing, planing, turning, and cutting, to produce finished stone.

Millwork
Wood products, such as cabinets, moldings, door and window frames, panels, built-ins and stair components that are manufactured by machines. Also called *trim, finish work.*

Mineral fiberboard
Mats of fiberglass or rock wool fiber with a stiff paper-board face; used primarily for roof insulation.

Mineral wool
A type of material formed from mineral slag, such as glass wool and used for insulation and fireproofing in buildings, which includes rock wool and glass wool.

Minimum wage law
A common term to describe the Fair Labor Standards Act of 1938, establishing a minimum wage for workers, and the 40-hour workweek.

Minor changes in the work
Any change in the construction, issued by a field order written by the architect, that does not involve an extension of time or a charge for such work, as long as it is consistent with the intent of the contract documents. See also *Field order.*

Miscellaneous iron
Steel pieces, such as lintel angles, plates, braces, and other structural shapes attached to or embedded in reinforced concrete.

Mismatched
A bad fit at a joint, poor grain, or imperfect color matching of veneers.

Mission parapet
A low, free-standing wall at the edge of a roof, frequently curved; found in many Spanish missions of the south-western United States.

Miter
The line formed by the meeting of moldings or other surfaces that intersect each other at an angle. Each member is cut at exactly half the angle of the junction. Also called *beveled.*

Miter box
A device used used on a workbench for guiding a handsaw at the proper angle for cutting a miter joint in a piece of wood. Can be made of wood, using precut slots on the sides to hold the saw, or metal, which has an adjustable carriage to change the angle of the miter.

Miter cut
In carpentry, a cut made at an angle for joining two pieces to form an angle.

Miter joint
A joint between two members at an angle to each other. Each member is cut at an angle equal to half the angle of the junction, usually at right angles.

Miter saw
A deep saw with a stiffening piece along the upper edge or back; often used in adjustable miter boxes.

Mitered joint
A joint that is cut on an angle.

Mixed use
A zoning classification permitting a variety of autho-rized activities in an area or a building, as distinguished from the customary isolated uses and required planned separation between them.

Mixed-use development
A large-scale real estate project under one coherent plan that includes three or more significant uses (retail, office, residential) with functional and physical integration of the project's components.

Mobile hoist
A platform hoist that can be towed around a site and used to lift workers or material.

Mobile home
A dwelling manufactured in a factory with all the services and fixtures installed, intended for transporta-tion in one or more sections, and erected on blocks or a continuous foundation.

Mobilization
The process of assembling machinery and equipment for movement to a job site.

Mockup
(1) A model of a construction assembly, built to scale or full size, and used to analyze construction details, strengths, appearance, and workability. (2) A model of an object in the course of design, as in a cross-section of a window or its parts; built to scale or full size, for studying installation details in renovation work, judging its appearance, and/or testing performance.

MOD 24
A framing system that accommodates the modular dimensions of plywood and other panels, by using 24-inch centers instead of 16. It provides an in-line transfer of structural loads through a direct load path.

Model
A three-dimensional scaled representation of an object, system, or building; executed at a small scale; used to study the massing, design, structure, mechanical layout, or aesthetic appearance of a proposed project or renovation.

Model home
A complete living unit, usually furnished, to serve as a model for other dwellings in a particular development.

Modeling
The shaping of three-dimensional forms in a soft material, such as clay, to produce replacement parts for sculptural elements in a restoration.

Modernization
Redesign of an existing structure to make it look new, or contemporary in style, as opposed to restoration.

Modernize
To make modern in appearance, style, or character. To adapt to a modern style.

Modification
A written change in the contract; consisting of a change order, field order, or other written interpretation issued by the architect.

Modillion
A horizontal bracket or console, in the form of a scroll with acanthus, supporting the corona under a cornice.

Modillion cornice
A cornice supported by a series of modillions, often found in Composite and Corinthian orders.

Modular brick
A brick with nominal dimensions based on a 4-inch module.

Modular construction
Construction in which the size of all building materials is based on a common unit of measure.

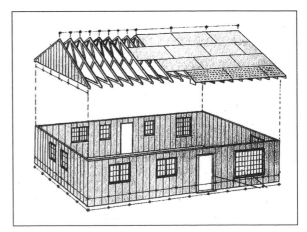

Modular dimensions
Building material that is based on a common unit of 4 inches or another dimension that fits standardized building panels.

Modular house
A factory-built house in complete modular sections, which can be transported to the job site on a trailer or truck, and erected on a prepared foundation. See also *Factory-built house.*

Module
A simple ratio by which all parts of a building are related as part of an ordered system. Also called *standard unit.*

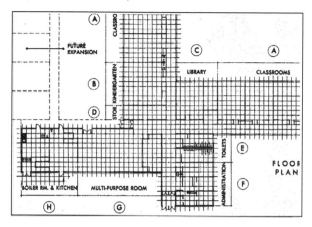

Modulus of elasticity
A measure of the unit stress in a material to the unit strain acting on a material.

Moisture barrier
Any material, such as specially treated paper or plastic sheeting, that is impervious to water; used in walls and other areas to stop moisture from entering and thus prevent condensation. Also called a vapor barrier.

Molded brick
Bricks that are pressure molded into various shapes before firing; used for cornices, moldings, and other ornamental brickwork.

Molded insulation
Thermal insulation, such as fiberglass or urethane foam, that is premolded to fit plumbing pipes and fittings.

Molded plywood
A plywood panel that has been permanently bent to a desired shape.

Moment connection
A rigid connection between members that is resistant to rotation, as opposed to a pin connection, which allows rotation.

Moment connection
A totally rigid connection between structural members which transfers rotational forces from one member to the other, as opposed to a pin connection, which can only resist shear forces.

Monochromatic
Consisting of only one color.

Monolith
An architectural member such as an obelisk or the shaft of a column that consists of a single stone.

Monolithic
Shapes usually formed of a single block of stone, or cast in one piece without construction joints. They are massive and uniform.

Monolithic column
A column whose shaft is of one piece of stone, wood, concrete, or marble as opposed to being made up from several components.

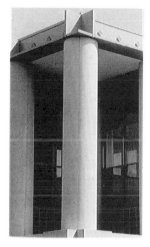 

Monument
A stone, pillar, megalith, structure, or building erected in memory of the dead, an event, or an action. Also a permanent marker, such as a boundary stone used for locating a property line or corner.

Mopping
Applying hot bitumen or other synthetic polymers with a mop or roller.

Mortar
A mixture of portland cement, sand, and water that can be placed with a trowel, and which hardens in place. Also, the mixture of fine cement paste and fine aggregate which fills the voids in the coarse aggregate in concrete. Also called *cement matrix.*

Mortar board
In masonry work, a small square board with a handle underneath that holds the mortar for the mason.

Mortar hoe
A hoe used in the mixing of mortar, or the placing of concrete. The hoe has two large holes in the blade, to assist in the mixing, and to make it easier to draw the hoe through the mixture.

Mortar mixer
An electrical or gasoline-powered mechanical device for mixing mortar.

Mortgage
A lien against real property that secures payment of a debt, usually involving the property.

Mortice
A rectangular slot cut into one piece of timber, into which a tenon or tongue from another piece is fitted to form a joint.

Mortise and tenon
A joint between two members, formed by fitting a tenon at the end of one member into a mortise cut into the other.

Mosaic
(1) A design created by inlaying pieces of tile, glass, stone, or wood into an adhesive bed to form a pattern, design, or representational picture.

(2) An aerial photographic map pasted up from individual overlapping photographs, often obtained by the use of photogrammetry. See also *Photogrammetry*.

Mosaic tile
Tiles arranged in decorative patterns and attached to a netlike backing; when installed, mosaic tiles are grouted just like regular tiles.

Mucking
The adjustment of steel bars during the placement of concrete.

Mud
A term used for the joint cement used for wallboard; also used to describe wet mortar, concrete, stucco, or similar materials.

Mud jacking
A process of raising a concrete slab on the ground where it has settled or been depressed; a hole is drilled through the slab, then a mixture of mud and cement is pumped under pressure under the slab, thereby raising it. The same process can be used to pump mortar under pressure to stabilize rubble masonry.

Mudsill
A foundation timber placed directly on the ground or on the foundation. Also called *foundation sill*.

Mullion
A dividing piece between the lights of windows, usually taking on the characteristics of the style of the building. Also called *window divider*.

Multicurved gable
A gable having an outline containing two or more curves on each side of a central ridge, as in a Flemish gable.

Multiple of direct expense
A factor applied to the cost of professional services that accounts for the cost of salaries, benefits, overhead, and profit. Also called a *multiplier*.

Multiple prime contract
A system of contracting when one or more contractors are used on the same project, either sequentially or at the same time.

Multiplier
A factor by which an architect's or engineer's direct personnel expenses and reimbursable expenses are multiplied to determine the amount billed to the client. It is used to cover other fixed costs, such as overhead.

Multiplier
A method used to determine compensation for direct personnel salaries and benefits, overhead costs, or other reimbursable expenses. The total costs are then multiplied by a percentage factor to arrive at the total billable amount.

Multistory frame
A building framework of more than one story, in which loads are carried to the ground by a system of beams and columns.

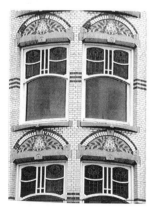

Muntin
A secondary framing member to hold panes in a window, window wall, or glazed door; an intermediate vertical member that divides panels of a door. Also called *glazing bar, sash bar*.

Muriatic acid
A commonly used cleaner for brick.

Museum village
A site in which structures have been restored, rebuilt, or moved from another location, that interprets a historical setting, often using the trades and activities of a previous era. Often called an outdoor museum, or village museum.

N

Nail
A slender piece of metal pointed at one end for driving into wood and flat at the other end for striking with a hammer; used as a board fastener. The size of the nail is indicated by the term "penny" and the letter "d," which now refers to the length of the nail and range from 2d (1 inch) to 60d (6 inches).

Nail bags
A leather, canvas, or nylon pouch on a wide belt, used by carpenters to carry nails when working.

Nail puller
A small bar with a V-shaped or forked end which can be slipped under the nail head.

Nail punch
A small knurled steel rod with a smooth tapered end; used by carpenters to drive the nail head below the surface of the wood. Also called a *nail set*.

Nailed-glued roof truss
A truss with plywood gusset plates that are spread with casein glue, then nailed to hold them in place. After the glue dries, the strength of the bond depends entirely on the glue.

Nailer
A block of wood installed within construction to provide a means of attaching other pieces of wood or other materials.

Nailing machine
A manual nailing device which holds staples or nails and is operated by striking a plunger knob with a mallet; used for applying underlayment to floors, and for installing finish flooring.

National Archives and Records Administration
A government body that administers the collections of the National Archives and provides grants for the publication of historical papers and preservation projects.

National Association of Homebuilders (NAHB)
An organization of builders of single family and multi-family dwellings.

National Building Code
An old building code published by the American Insurance Association. It is not as widely adopted as other model codes.

National Center for Preservation Technology and Training
A National Park Service center whose mission is to promote technology and training for historic preservation professionals and conservators; provides training and information management in architecture, archeology, and landscape architecture.

National Electric Code (NEC)
A nationally accepted guide to the safe installation of wiring and equipment; unrelated to design specifications but rather to safeguarding persons and buildings and contents from the hazards arising from the use of electricity for heat, light, and power. It is published by the National Fire Protection Association with participation from the National Electrical Manufacturers Association.

National Environmental Policy Act
Legislation passed in 1969 that set up the Council on Environmental Quality to require environmental impact statements for all major federal actions and federal legislation affecting the quality of the human and built environment.

National Fire Protection Association (NFPA)
An association that develops standards and codes governing fire safety in building structures, and also establishes standards for electrical safety, which are published annually as the National Electrical Code (NEC).

National Historic Landmark
A designated district, site, or building, listed in the National Register of Historic Places that is of architectural or historic significance to the country as a whole, rather than just to a particular state or locality.

National Historic Landmarks Program
Established by the National Sites Act of 1935; surveys sites of national significance based on a series of theme studies, including prehistoric archeology, architecture, politics, religion, and science. The effort is to promote a set of general concepts on what is worth saving.

National Historic Preservation Act
Legislation passed in 1966 expanding the National Register of Historic Places to a nationwide inventory of districts, sites, structures, and objects of state and local as well as national importance, maintained by the National Park Service, U.S. Department of the Interior. The act also created the Advisory Council on Historic Preservation to advise the president and Congress on historic preservation matters. The council is authorized to comment on federally funded plans for highway or utility construction, if they are likely to have any adverse effect on historic structures, or historic districts.

National Historic Sites Act of 1935
Legislation that authorized the secretary of the interior to acquire national historic sites and to designate sites and buildings as National Historic Landmarks.

National joint guidelines
A set of guidelines adopted by the Associated General Contractors of America (AGC), Association of Specialty Contractors (ASC), and the American Subcontractors Association (ASA), to assist and advise members of the construction industry as well as owners, architects, engineers, and subcontractors, in efficient methods for

administering construction projects. The same organization develops policy statements to be followed in effecting efficient working relationships among members, insurance companies, and governmental agencies.

National Labor Relations Act (NLRA)
A law enacted by congress in 1935, mandating the procedures and regulations by which labor-management relations are to be conducted.

National Labor Relations Board (NLRB)
An organization that enforces the National Labor Relations Act.

National Park Service
Conducts research and salvage programs in archeological areas as well as historic site surveys for the National Historic Landmarks Program.

National Plumbing Code
A code issued by the American National Standards Institute (ANSI) in 1955, and used in a limited degree.

National Preservation Week
In 1973 the National Trust for Historic Preservation succeeded in making preservation official for at least 1 week held annually in early May. The activities include tours and seminars, exhibits, film showings and children's programs, and ceremonial starts and finishes to preservation projects.

National Register of Historic Places
A list, maintained by the National Park Service, of U.S. places of significance in history, archeology, architecture, engineering, and culture, on a national, state, or local level.

National Trust for Historic Preservation
A nonprofit organization chartered by Congress in 1949 that is the leader of the national preservation movement, committed to saving America's diverse historic environments and to preserving and revitalizing communities nationwide. It has seven regional offices, owns 18 historic sites, and works with thousands of community groups in all 50 states. It has programs designed to increase public awareness and encourage participation in preservation activities, and it advises on all preservation issues from organizing to fund-raising. It offers financial support, publishes extensively, maintains properties, offers information services, and provides guidance through the National Main Street Center.

Natural cleft slate
A thin piece of slate that has been split along its natural cleft or seam. It usually has a rougher surface texture than slate that is machine-split.

Natural convection
The natural movement of air caused by differences in temperature and density, such as hot air rising, and cold air falling.

Natural environment
Includes all natural land forms, rivers and lakes, trees and plants, but does not include the built environment.

Natural grade
The profile and elevation of the undisturbed surface of the ground on the site.

Natural stone
A stone that has been quarried and cut but not crushed into chips and reconstituted into cast stone.

Natural ventilation
Movement of air without the use of mechanical power; achieved by the suitable location and arrangement of windows, doors, and built-in vents.

Neat
Expression for building or excavating to the exact dimensions. Also used to describe a material which is prepared for use without the addition of any material other than water, such as neat cement.

Neat cement
A cement used without sand, as opposed to cement mortar.

Needle
A short heavy timber or steel beam which is passed horizontally through a hole in a wall to support the end of a shoring timber; used in underpinning work.

Needle beam
A steel beam used to support an existing structure while it is being repaired, or to provide support when moving a structure or when removing a portion of the wall below the beam; usually installed by removing a section of the wall or area and inserting it into position.

Needle-nose pliers
Pliers that have tapered jaws that come to a point.

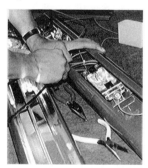

Negative reinforcing
Steel reinforcing to compensate for negative bending forces in a reinforced concrete structural member.

Negligence
The failure of a party to conduct the performance according to the standards of care required by law or building codes.

Negotiate
The act of bargaining through discussion in the hopes of coming to a settlement or agreement.

Negotiated contract
An agreement between a design professional and owner, or between a contractor and owner, reaching a mutually agreed-upon price based on the scope of professional services or the extent of construction work.

Neoprene
A synthetic rubber material used for roofing and flashing, vibration, and sound absorption. It has a high resistance to sunlight and petroleum products and is long lasting; used for gaskets in curtain-wall systems.

Neoprene membrane
An impervious membrane used for roofing and waterproofing installations, made of an oil-resistant synthetic rubber.

Neoprene roof
A roof surface covered with a sheet of synthetic rubber.

Neoprene sealant
A rubber sealant with good weathering capabilities, and fair elasticity and shrinkage. However, it does not retain its elasticity in cold weather.

Nest of saws
A set of saw blades intended for use with the same handle, which is detachable; often used for small saws such as keyhole saws.

Net
A screening used to cover the outside of a scaffold while cleaning or restoration is taking place. Also, a safety device slung from a scaffold to protect passersby from falling debris.

Net floor area
The floor area of a building that is occupied, excluding hallways, elevator shafts, stairs, toilets, and wall thicknesses; used for determining fire-code requirements and rental space.

Net income
In accounting, the income or profit left after deducting all expenses.

Network schedule
An integrated scheduling process whereby construction activities are programmed into a sequential network on the basis of starting and finishing dates.

Neutral arbitrator
An arbitrator who remains unbiased to either party in a dispute.

Newel
The central post or column that provides support for the inner edges of the steps in a circular staircase and around which the steps wind.

Newel cap
The terminal feature of a newel post, often molded or turned in a decorative manner.

Newel post
A tall post at the head or foot of a stair supporting the handrail, often ornamental.

Niche
A recess in a wall; usually semicircular at the back, terminating in a half-dome, or with small pediments supported on consoles; often used as a place for a statue.

Night seal
A temporary sheet membrane made of synthetic material, used to cover a roof opening, until it is closed with permanent material. Also used to cover material stored on site and protect it against moisture.

Nipple
In plumbing, a short piece of pipe which is threaded on the outside to connect to other pieces of similar sized pipes which have threads on the inside to accept the nipple.

No-damage-for-delay
A clause in a construction contract permitting time extension but no monetary damages for delays that are not the fault of the contractor.

Nogging
Brick or miscellaneous masonry material used to fill the spaces between the wooden supports in a half-timber frame.

Noise pollution
Noise caused by traffic, car alarms, boom box radios, aircraft, industry, or other human-made inventions.

Noise reduction
Reducing the level of unwanted sound by any of several means of acoustical treatment.

Nominal size
The measurement used in naming a component, not necessarily its actual size when finished, for example, a "2 × 4" actually measures 1 5/8 × 3 5/8 inches.

Nominal size of timber
The size of timber before it is dressed, and usually before it is seasoned. Size of timber is usually given in nominal size, and the actual size is slightly smaller.

Nonbearing partition
A wall that divides a space into rooms or areas, but does not carry any of the structural load from above.

Noncombustible
In building construction, a material that will not ignite, burn, support combustion, or release flammable vapors when subjected to fire or heat.

Noncombustible material
Any material that has fire-resistive properties and will not support combustion.

Noncompensable delay
A delay whereby the contractor will not be compensated for delay-related costs from the owner, but receives an extension to the schedule.

Nonconductor
A material that will not carry an electric current; such materials are generally used as insulators.

Nonconforming building
Said of any building that does not comply with the requirements set forth in the applicable codes, rules, or regulations.

Nonconforming use
A building use that is not consistent with an area's zoning regulations. Nonconforming use may be "grandfathered" in subsequent zoning changes, but upon conversion to a new or adaptive use, the owners will be required to adhere to the applicable regulations, unless they are granted a variance.

Nonconforming work
Any work that does not meet the plans and specifications, or violates the applicable building code.

Nondestructive investigation
Examination of the existing conditions of a structure without damaging or destroying it in the process.

Nondestructive probe
A method of determining the condition inside the walls of a structure without causing a condition that requires repair. One method is the acrylin-headed hammer or mallet to tap and sound areas of the façade. Another is the penknife for testing wood and mortar joints. A moisture meter can determine areas that are damaged by water. A magnet can determine which metals are iron or steel and subject to rust. A metal detector can locate supporting structures, cramps, and dowels for stone or terra-cotta projections, or masonry ties. Other sophisticated methods include thermography, x-ray photography, ultrasonic, and pulse wave testing.

Nondestructive testing
Testing that does not destroy the object being tested. Techniques include the use of strain gauges, x rays, and ultrasound, which makes use of very high frequency sound waves to locate flaws in metal.

Nonhabitable area
The area of a building that cannot be utilized; includes the structure, partitions, and ducts.

Non-load-bearing wall
A wall subject only to its own weight and wind pressure.

Nonmetallic sheathed cable
An electrical cable consisting of two or more individually insulated wires, and usually a bare ground conductor, wrapped together in a flexible plastic outer covering. Commonly referred to by the trade name Romex.

Nonrecoverable costs
Includes the leasing commission, legal fees, and owner's contribution to marketing funds that are not charged to the tenants.

Nonrestrictive specification
A specification that does not restrict the product used in the building to a specific manufacturer or material supplier.

Nosing
The rounded edge of a horizontal surface that projects beyond the vertical surface below, such as the projection of a tread beyond the riser.

Notary public
A person authorized to authenticate documents, affidavits, and signatures with a seal.

Notched trowel
A trowel with a serrated edge, used to apply mastic or mortar for a tile bed. The mastic or mortar goes down in ridges, and the tile is pushed into the mastic, spreading it out evenly.

Notching
In carpentry, a method of joining timbers by cutting notches at the ends of a piece, then overlapping the notched pieces to form a joint.

Notice of completion
A notice filed by the owner with the county recorder, indicating that construction is complete, ready for occupancy, and that all construction bills have been paid. This sets up the time limit for subcontractors or material suppliers to file a lien in the event they have not been paid.

Notice to proceed
A written notice to the contractor from the project owner, authorizing the work to begin on a specified date.

Null
No longer having a legal or binding force, such as a condition resulting from an invalid contract.

Nylon
A class of thermoplastics characterized by extreme toughness, strength, and elasticity and capable of being extruded into filaments, fibers, and sheets.

O.C.
Abbreviation for on center. See also *On center.*

Oak
A tough, hard, high-density wood; coarse-textured, ranging in color from light tan to pink or brown; used for both decorative and structural applications, such as framing timbers, flooring, and plywood.

Oak floor
A floor consisting of small slats of tongue-and-grooved oak; used as a finished floor.

Oakum
Hemp or twisted rope used for caulking joints in cast-iron pipes. See also *Leaded joints.*

Obscure glass
Glass that has one or both faces acid-etched or sandblasted and allows the transmission of light, but does not show objects on the other side, such as frosted or ground glass.

Observation of the work
Periodic site visits by the architect during the progress of the work to determine if the work is being performed according to the plans and specifications.

Observatory
A structure in which astronomical observations are carried out; also a place such as an upper room that affords a wide view; a lookout.

Obsidian
A natural volcanic glass, usually black with a bright luster, that is transparent in thin slabs.

Obsolescence
Items or buildings that become out of date or practice and fall into disuse; also impairment of a building resulting from a change in the design or from external influences that tend to make the property less desirable for continued use.

Obstruction
An object or other obstacle that prevents passage from one area to another, or a blockage in a piping system.

Occupancy
Acquiring title to a property by taking possession of it; the act of taking over anything that has no owner.

Occupant load
The total number of persons in a given area at the same time.

Occupational accident
A mishap or accident that occurs while one is on the job site, and is caused by hazards inherent to the job.

Occupational Health and Safety Administration (OSHA)
A U.S. federal agency concerned with the safety of workers; issues safety regulations.

Octagon roof
A roof that fits over an octagonal-shaped structure.

Octagonal house
An eight-sided house, usually two to four stories high.

Off site
Materials or equipment stored away from the main construction site.

Off center
Applies to a structural member that is not properly centered.

Off-center splice
A connection between two members of unequal length that occurs other than at the center of the span.

Office of Federal Contract Compliance (OFCC)
An agency that administers the affirmative action program for equal rights of employees under the Civil Rights Act of 1964.

Office partition
Stationary walls in an interior that partition off a space for use as an office.

Off-white
White with the addition of a small amount of another color, but insufficient to identify any color other than white, with either a cool or warm color in appearance.

Oil stain
A thin oil paint with very little pigment; used for staining timber.

Oil-based caulking
An inexpensive but less substantial compound with low elasticity and a short life span of only 5 years, that will bleed through paint if not properly sealed. Good for back-sealing with a bead behind shingles and around windows. See also *Acrylic latex caulking, Butyl rubber,* and *Silicone acrylic caulking compounds.*

Oil-fired boiler
A device for heating water that is operated by burning oil as a fuel.

On center
Refers to the measurement from the center of one member to the center of another, especially those in a series, such as studs or joists.

On grade
A building component placed and supported directly from the ground.

One-hour rating
A fire rating indicating that a material can be exposed to flame for an hour without losing structural integrity.

One-way floor system
In reinforced concrete construction, consists of a flat slab supported by reinforced girders running parallel and supported by columns.

One-way joist construction
A concrete floor or roof construction whereby the joists are cast integral with the slab, and are supported on girders, which in turn are supported by columns.

One-way slab
A concrete slab designed to span in one direction only.

Opal glass
Glass containing calcium phosphate, derived from bone ash which renders the glass white and opaque.

Opalescent glass
An iridescent multicolored glass; first used by Louis Comfort Tiffany in the late nineteenth century, and now called Tiffany glass.

Open bid
A proposal by a contractor to perform the work, but reserving the right to lower the bid to compete with a lower bid.

Open bidding
A procedure where bids are accepted from all interested parties, rather than from a list of selected bidders.

Open boarding
A form of roof sheathing where spaces are left between adjacent boards, allowing better ventilation.

Open construction
A building component or assembly that is manufactured in such a manner as to be open to inspection at the installation site, without being disassembled. See also *Closed construction.*

Open decking
A deck constructed with the joists exposed on the underside.

Open defect
A hole or check in lumber, plywood, or veneer that has not been filled or patched.

Open eaves
Overhanging eaves where the rafters and underside of the roof are visible from below.

Open excavation
A process of excavating without the use of piles, shores, or other sheeting to hold back the earth.

Open grain
Wood having a coarse texture.

Open joint
A joint that is not entirely tight or flush.

Open pediment
A broken pediment.

Open plan
A building floor area that has few interior partitions.

Open riser
The space between the treads of a staircase that does not have solid risers.

Open shop
A company whose employees are not bound by, or covered by, collective bargaining agreements.

Open space
An area such as a plaza, park, greenbelt, or easement that is not occupied by buildings or transportation networks.

Open space easement
Used to save a structure from contiguous development that would change or interfere with its visual surroundings. Generally an easement runs with the land, as a permanent interest. Holders of easements, such as preservation groups or government bodies, are also qualified to enforce the protective restrictions.

Open stair
A stair or stairway whose treads are visible on one or both sides and open to a room in which it is located.

Open timbered
Heavy timber work that is exposed and not concealed by sheathing, plaster, or other covering.

Open web beam

A truss with parallel top and bottom chords formed by a pair of angles, employing a web of diagonal struts and used as a beam. The struts connecting the top and bottom chords are also composed of steel bars or rods.

Open-end mortgage

An arrangement that allows the party to borrow additional money for the repair and upkeep of the property, thereby extending the mortgage.

Open-frame girder

An open-web girder or truss built with only vertical members connecting to the top and bottom chords.

Opening light

The portion of a sash or casement window that may be opened for ventilation rather than a dead light, which is fixed.

Open-string stair

A staircase whose profile of treads and risers is visible from the side. The treads support the balusters.

Open-web joist

A lattice joist welded from light steel sections and mass-produced to certain standard lengths; used to support floor or roof loads.

Open-well stair

A stair built around a well, leaving an open space.

Openwork

Any work characterized by perforations, especially of an ornamental nature.

Operable transom

A panel of glass light above a door, which may be opened for ventilation.

Operable window

A window that may be opened for ventilation, as opposed to a fixed light.

Optical coatings

Sheet material applied to glazing to reduce the transmission of sunlight, or to reflect infrared radiation back to the heat exchanger

Option

A stipulation granted for money received, allowing a party to purchase or rent property within a specified time limit.

Oral agreement

An agreement that was made in conversation between the parties and was not reduced to writing.

Orange peel

In painting, a term applied to a pebble effect in sprayed coats of paint or lacquer similar to the peel of an orange; may be caused by too much pressure by holding the spraying device too close to the surface, or using a thinner that dries too quickly and prevents the proper flow of solids.

Orangeburg pipe
The trade name for polyvinyl chloride (PVC) pipe, a common plastic piping used for cold water service system

Orbital sander
A power tool for finish sanding that uses an oscillating motion to move the sandpaper, so that the work is sanded in all directions.

Ordinance
A law or regulation enacted by a city or county pertaining to the construction and use of a building.

Ordinary construction
A type of construction where the exterior materials are of stable noncombustible material with a 2-hour fire rating, and the interior may be of wood frame or other combustible materials.

Organic
Descriptive of materials produced from vegetable or animal sources.

Organic soil
A soil with a high organic content, that is very compressible and unstable soil for construction due to its inability to support heavy loads.

Orientation
The placement of a structure on a site with regard to local conditions of sunlight, wind, drainage, and with an outlook to specific vistas.

Oriented strand board (OSB)
A building board manufactured similar to plywood, using pressed strands of wood into thin sheets, with alternate layers laid perpendicular to the one before it, and then pressed together with phenolic resin. It is stronger than randomly placed strand board. See also *Waferboard*.

Original construction
The remains of a structure that still exist, without having been subsequently altered or obscured by a later addition.

Original grade
The level of the ground at a job site prior to any excavation or fill.

Ornament
Anything that embellishes, decorates, or adorns a structure, whether used intentionally and integrated into the structure or applied separately to enhance the building's form and appearance.

Ornamental cast iron
Decorative architectural elements molded from cast iron; used for railings, brackets, and ornamental columns and screens.

Ornamental plaster
Decorative details cast in plaster, such as ceiling medallions and cove moldings.

Ornamental stone
Carved or shaped stone used for ornamentation and trim, as opposed to building or facing stone.

Ornate
Elaborately decorative.

OSHA
Abbreviation for the Occupational Safety and Health Act of 1970 or Occupational Health and Safety Administration.

Outbuilding
Any building separate from the main house, but with an ancillary use; includes carriage house, garage, shed, stable, smokehouse, and outhouse.

Outer string
The string at the outer and exposed edge of a stair, away from the wall.

Outlet
In an electrical wiring system, a point at which current is used to supply appliances or lamps.

Outlet box
A metal box located at the end of a conduit, where electric wires are joined to one another, and to the convenience outlet or fixture.

Outlet ventilator
A louvered opening in the gable end of a building that provides ventilation.

Outline specifications
An abbreviated form of specifications used during the schematic or design development stage.

Outlooker
A member that projects beyond the face of a gable and supports the over-hanging portion of a roof.

Out-of-plumb
A structural member that is not properly aligned in a true vertical fashion.

Out-of-square
A condition that exists where members that are supposed to be square and true are not, or that a true 90-degree angle does not exist.

Out-of-true
In woodworking, a place in a form where there is a twist or other irregularity in the alignment; also, a varying from exactness in a structural member.

Outside air intake
An opening in the exterior wall through which outside air is drawn into a boiler room or air-conditioning system.

Oval window
A window in the shape of an ellipse, or in a shape between an ellipse and a circle.

Overall dimension
A total outer dimension of a building, including any projection.

Overdesign
In structural calculations, adherence to requirements beyond normal service demands, to compensate for unknowns.

Overflow pipe
A pipe installed to prevent flooding in plumbing fixtures, or to remove excess water from buildings.

Overhanging eaves
The eaves of a roof that project past the line of a building rather than flush.

Overhead
Indirect expenses that are part of operating a business, and are not connected with any particular job; such as record keeping, rent, utilities, telephone, advertising, legal services, office salaries and benefits, office supplies, proposals and presentations, transportation and entertainment, taxes, and other costs associated with bidding. The costs to conduct business that occur whether or not there is any specific project. It becomes part of the bidder's markup, or the design professional's multiplier. See also *Markup*, and *Multiplier*.

Overhead concealed closer
A door closer that is installed within the door head, exposing only the arm that closes the door.

Overhead door
A door of either the swing-up or the roll-up type constructed of one or several leaves. When open, it assumes a horizontal position above the door opening.

Overhead door
Any door which opens by lifting vertically, including roll-up and sectional doors.

Overlay flooring
A finish wood flooring consisting of thin strips of maple, mahogany, oak, or other hardwood.

Overload

In electricity, more than a normal amount of electric current flowing through a device or machine, or a load greater than the device is designed to carry. Also an excess of electrical power, current, or voltage in an electrical circuit or device that is not designed to handle the extra load.

Overrun

The amount above the estimated cost or quantity, or the amount beyond the estimated schedule. The condition that exists when the cost of the project to a specific date exceeds the value of the work performed to that same date.

Overtime

An amount of extra payment for labor—normally at 1½ times the hourly rate. Work on Sundays and holidays usually requires payment of double time, depending on the union contract.

Owner

The person or entity that typically owns or leases the site, and who retains prodessional services for building design and contracts for the construction of the building, and acquires furnishings, fixtures, and equipment for installation in it.

Owner's inspector

A person hired by the owner to inspect the progress of the work.

Owner's liability insurance

Protection for the owner against claims arising out of the operations performed by the contractor for the owner, or the owner's general supervisor.

Owner's representative

The person designated by the owner to be the official representative in all matters relating to the project; may be an architect, engineer, or contractor.

Owner-architect agreement

A contract between the owner and architect for professional design services.

Owner-builder

An owner of property that undertakes the total construction, addition, renovation, or remodeling of a building without the assistance of a general contractor. The owner acts as his or her own contractor, and can hire subcontractors if desired.

Owner-contractor agreement

A contract between the owner and contractor for the performance of construction on a project, or a portion of it.

Oxidation

A corrosion process that occurs when cast-iron is exposed to air and moisture, leading to cracking of the metal. Also called *rusting*, which traps and holds liquid corrosive agents. Cast-iron will corrode if it is adjacent to lead or copper. See also *Galvanic corrosion*.

P

P trap

In plumbing, a trap used in sanitary pipes shaped like the letter P, with a horizontal outlet.

Package deal

A project wherein one company contracts to provide a complete single-responsibility design, construction, and financing service for a client. It differs from a turnkey job which generally involves design and construction only.

Packaged air conditioner

A factory-assembled air-conditioning unit ready for installation in an opening through a wall, a window, or for mounting on a roof.

Packaged boiler

A factory-assembled water or steam boiler with all controls and auxiliary equipment already hooked up ready for installation on the job site.

Packaged chimney

A complete prefabricated chimney unit, usually made of metal, which comes in a range of specifications and types. Some are coupled with a prefabricated fireplace unit.

Packaged equipment

A complete equipment package delivered to the site for final assembly, such as a boiler, or air-conditioning equipment. The disadvantage to this method is the large size; equipment is often shipped in components that are assembled on site.

Packaged lumber

Lumber that has been cut to standard lengths and milled to fit its use, strapped with steel, or wrapped in paper or plastic.

Pad

An isolated mass of concrete forming a foundation.

Paint

A protective finish for architectural elements, most often composed of a coloring agent ground in linseed oil or other synthetic base.

Paint analysis
Determining the approximate date of application and sequence of multiple layers of paint; used to arrive at the original historic color at a particular time.

Paint remover
A liquid solvent used to remove dry paint by softening it to the point where it can be scraped off with a scraper or putty knife, or brushed with a wire brush.

Paint thinner
A liquid, such as turpentine, used to thin heavy-bodied paints for easier application.

Painted glass
Plain glass painted with enamel, then fired in a kiln at a high temperature.

Painter
A craftsperson skilled in the preparation and application of paint, lacquer, and varnishes to wood, plaster, and other surfaces, either for new construction, renovation, or restoration.

Painter's putty
A plastic substance made from a mixture of whiting and linseed oil; used for fixing panes of glass in window frames, as well as nail holes and defects in wood prior to painting.

Palladian motif
A door or window opening in three parts, divided by posts, featuring a round-headed archway flanked by narrow openings with a flat lintel over each side; the arched area rests on the flat entablatures.

Pan floor
In concrete construction, a floor made up of pan-formed joists or small beams, or waffle-like series of coffers and small beams.

Pan forms
Panlike metal or fiberglass structures used as forms for the bottom side of concrete floors. Reinforcing bars are placed in the recesses between the pans, which become an integral part of the structural system. The voids are then filled with concrete to form a wafflelike slab.

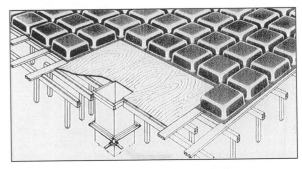

Pane
A relatively small piece of window glass set in an opening; also known as a *light*.

Panel adhesive
Similar to construction adhesive, used primarily for wood paneling, various types of tile, and foam.

Panel box
A box in which electric switches and fuses for branch circuits are located.

Panel wall
A non-load-bearing wall between columns or piers in skeleton construction; such walls are supported at each story of the building frame.

Panelboard
In electrical work, the board to which the fuses or circuit breakers are attached. Also called a *panel box*.

Paneled ceiling

A ceiling divided into compartments by raised moldings, often containing paintings or other ornamentation within the panels in classical and revival styles.

Paneled door

A door having a framework of stiles, rails, and muntins that form one or more frames around thinner recessed panels.

Paneling

A surface that is either sunken or raised, plain or ornamental, and surrounded by a border or frame of wood or other material.

Panelized construction

Large panels used mainly for flat roof construction; consisting of plywood secured to a structural frame.

Panic device

A horizontal bar that releases a latch and opens a door when the bar is pushed. Also called *panic hardware*.

Panic hardware

Door hardware that can be released quickly by pushing a horizontal bar; required for certain exit doors by building codes.

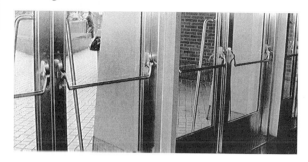

Paperhanger

A painter or decorator who specializes in hanging wall coverings.

Par lamps

Parabolic aluminum reflector lamps, which offer excellent beam control, from a very narrow spot to a wide flood; can be used outdoors unprotected because they are made of hard glass that can withstand adverse weather.

Parapet

A low protective wall or railing along the edge of a raised platform, bridge, roof, balcony, and above cornices; may be straight, stepped, curved, solid, or with decorative openings. Also called *curb*.

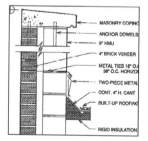

Parapet gutter

A gutter that is located behind a parapet wall.

Parapet wall
The portion of any exterior wall, party wall, or fire wall which extends above the roof line.

Parapeted gable
A gable end wall that projects above a roof; may follow the roof line in a straight, stepped, or curved profile.

Parcel
A piece of land with its own metes and bounds.

Parge coat
In masonry, a coarse coat of plasterwork applied over a masonry wall, as protection for damp-proofing.

Parging
The application of mortar to the back of the facing material, or the face of the backing material. Also called *back-plastering*.

Parking area
An area, usually paved, set aside for the parking or storage of vehicles.

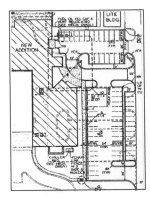

Parking garage
A garage for passenger vehicles only, exclusively for the purpose of parking or storing of automobiles and not for automobile repairs or service work.

Parking lot
An open area on the ground for short-term storage of vehicles.

Parquet
A flat inlay pattern of closely fitted pieces, usually geometrical, for ornamental flooring or wainscoting; often employs two or more colors or materials such as stone or wood.

Parquetry
Small pieces of wood fitted together to form a geometrical design.

Partial occupancy
Occupation and use of a structure before it is finally completed.

Particleboard
A processed wood usually made into panels; made from dry wood chips and particles that are bonded together by pressure and heat with a resin bond. Also called *composition board, fiberboard*.

Partisan arbitrator
An arbitrator who is appointed by, or partial to, one party in a dispute.

Partition
An interior wall dividing a room or part of a building into separate areas; may be either non-load-bearing or load-bearing. Also called *wall*.

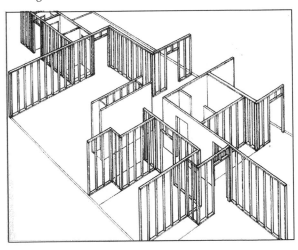

Partnership A legal business relationship between two or more persons, contractually associated as joint principals in a business as co-owners, where assets and liabilities are shared. See also *Limited Liability Partnership*.

Party wall
A wall used jointly by two parties under an easement agreement, erected upon a line dividing two parcels of land, each one a separate real estate entity. Also called *common wall*.

Passageway
A space that connects one area of a building with another.

Passenger elevator

An elevator used to convey people from floor to floor in a multistoried building.

Passive solar system

Providing solar heat and/or cooling to a building through architectural design, rather than by mechanical means, through the choice of materials, placement of windows, and other natural ventilation devices. See also *Active solar system*.

Patent defect

A defect that is noticeable in materials or workmanship through observation, as opposed to latent defect, which cannot be detected by observation. See also *Latent defect*.

Patina

A greenish-brown crust produced by oxidation that forms on the surface of copper and bronze, often multicolored and considered decorative; any thin oxide film that forms on a metal or other material.

Patio

An outdoor area, often paved and shaded, adjoining or enclosed by the walls or arcades of a house.

Patio door

A panel door, usually constructed of glass in aluminum, PVC, or wood frames, that slides in tracks at the floor and head of the door. They are often designed in two-, three-, or four-panel units, with one or more panels stationary.

Pattern

(1) A template for producing duplicate designs; used for repetitive designs in woodwork, concrete, or concrete block. (2) The juxtaposition of repetitive elements in a design, organized so as to produce an arrangement of parts that are viewed as a unit; may occur at various scales and sizes.

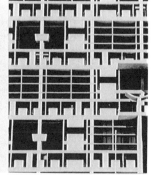

Pattern staining

Discoloration of plaster ceilings of composite construction, caused by the different thermal conductance of the backing. The air circulates more freely over the warmer parts, and deposits more dust on them.

Patterned block

Concrete block with a customized, recessed decorative pattern on the front face.

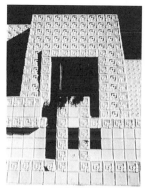

Patterned brickwork

Bricks with more than one color or texture that are laid in different directions, so as to form decorative designs.

Patterned brickwork

Patterned glass
Glass that has an irregular surface pattern formed in the rolling process to obscure vision or to diffuse light; usually on one side only, with the other side left smooth.

Pavement
The durable surface of a sidewalk or other outdoor area, such as a walkway or open plaza.

Pavement light
Thick, translucent glass disks or prisms, set into a section of pavement to transmit light to a space below.

Paver
A paving stone, brick, or tile.

Pavilion
An open structure or small ornamental building, shelter, or kiosk used as a summer house, or as an adjunct to a larger building; usually detached and used for specialized activities and often located as a terminal structure. Also called *belvedere, gazebo.*

Pavilion porch
A structure projecting out from a veranda or porch with a peaked roof, similar to a gazebo.

Paving
The surface covering of walkways, sidewalks, roadways, and parking areas.

Paving brick
A hard vitrified clay brick with resistance to abrasion.

Paving stone

A block or slab of natural stone used as a paver.

Paving unit

A preshaped unit used to pave a surface.

Payment bond

A type of security purchased by a contractor to guarantee that the contractor will pay all costs of labor, materials, and all other costs related to the contract for the project.

Payment clauses

Clauses in a contract or agreement that pertain to billing of progress and final payments, and reviews and certifications relating to conditions affecting payments, and liens.

Payment schedule

A schedule that specifies the times and amounts of payments due for construction services.

Payments withheld

A provision of the American Institute of Architects (AIA) general conditions which provides that the owner may withhold payment if the contractor falls behind schedule, or if the work deviates from the contract documents in any other manner.

Payroll

The document outlining the wages, salaries, fringe benefits, and deductions paid to employees by an employer.

Payroll deduction

An amount withheld from gross pay by the employer to cover federal and state taxes, including union dues and medical insurance if applicable.

Peak load

The maximum demand over a specified time period on systems or devices, such as heating, ventilating, air-conditioning, or electrical systems.

Peak-head window

A window that goes to the underside of a gable dormer; most often found in Gothic Revival architecture.

Pediment

A low-pitched triangular gable above a façade, or a smaller version over porticos above the doorway or above a window; a triangular gable end of the roof above the horizontal cornice; often decorated with sculpture.

Peg

A tapered cylindrical wooden pin that is driven through a hole to hold two or more members together.

Pegboard

A hardboard that has been perforated by a pattern of holes drilled during its manufacture. These may serve a decorative or acoustic purpose, or they may be used with special hooks to support shelves and other fixtures.

Pegged frame

A type of framing used in early medieval houses and barns, consisting of a timber frame with diagonal corner braces secured with pegged mortise-and-tenon joints.

Penalty clause

A clause in a construction contract by which a contractor is assessed with a monetary penalty for delay in the completion of a project; usually figured on a daily basis. See also *Bonus clause.*

Penalty/Bonus clause

Contracts frequently include penalties for failure to meet the schedule. Some offer bonuses for early completion. Generally, a penalty clause must be accompanied by a bonus clause, although the amount for each need not be equal.

Pendant

A hanging ornament or suspended feature on ceilings and vaults.

Pendentive
The curved triangular surface that results when the top corner of a square space is vaulted so as to provide a circular space for a dome.

Pendil
The projecting exposed lower end of a post of the overhanging upper story or jetty; often carved.

Penny
A measure used to describe the size of nails; originally determined by the weight of 100 nails that equaled a certain number of English pennies, designated by (d).

Pentachlorophenol
A toxic compound often included as a compound in stains and wood preservatives for shakes and shingles. It repels water and prevents decay and mildew.

Penthouse
A structure on a flat-roofed building, occupying usually less than half the roof area.

Percentage complete
A measure of the status of the project, to the projected completion; determined by measuring the materials in place, or hours worked, in comparison to those planned initially.

Percentage fee
Compensation based on a percentage of the construction cost.

Percentage of completion accounting
An accounting method whereby any payment received will not be counted as earned income until the work is actually completed. Until then, the percentage of completion determines the percentage of payment declared as earned income; the remaining balance is declared as unearned income.

Percolation test
A 12-inch hole is dug to the depth that the drain tile will be placed, and filled with water. The rate of absorption is recorded on an hourly basis to determine the suitability of the soil for a septic system of drain tiles, or a cesspool. An absorption of 1 inch per hour is the minimum acceptable rate.

Perforated pipe
A pipe consisting of a series of holes along its length; used for providing drainage of groundwater or moisture alongside building foundations.

Perforated tape
A paper tape used in drywall installations to cover the joints between the wallboard. The joint compound is applied over the tape and smoothed over with a taping blade.

Performance bond
An undertaking by a surety which guarantees that a contractor will perform according to a contract.

Performance criteria
Criteria against which the performance of a party to a contract is measured to determine if that party's obligations are fulfilled.

Performance specification
A specific description and evaluation criteria for the performance of a product, material, assembly, or piece of equipment.

Performance specifications
Specifications that delineate the results to be achieved rather than the specific methods or materials to be used.

Perimeter foundation
A continuous footing and foundation wall around the outside of the structure.

Perimeter heating
A system of heating where ducts radiate from a central plenum chamber and carry warm air through registers located along the outer walls.

Perimeter heating system
A system that incorporates outlets for warm-air ducts on the outside perimeter of a room, with the return vents near the ceiling.

Period costume
A reproduction of the actual clothing worn during a specific historical period, and worn at a house museum, or other period setting.

Period exhibit
A display that portrays a historical period of time, either in the furniture and wall coverings or in a reconstructed setting depicting a historic time.

Period room
A collection of original furniture and furnishings depicting a specific period in the past; usually re-created in a historical structure, house museum, or art museum.

Peristyle
A colonnade surrounding either the exterior of a building or an open space.

Permafrost
A permanently frozen layer of soil.

Permanent bracing
Bracing incorporated into the framing or structure, such as diagonal bracing or shear panels designed to resist lateral loads.

Permanent formwork
The formwork that is not struck, but is left permanently in position after the concrete has been cast.

Permanent loan
Long-term financing that replaces a short-term construction loan.

Permeability
A characteristic of substances that permits the passage and absorption of fluids.

Permeable
If the voids in a material are connected, it is said to be permeable, capable of absorbing moisture or liquid.

Permit
A document that allows building activity on a site, such as a building permit.

Perpendicular
A line or plane that meets another at right angles.

Personal injury insurance
Protection against personal bodily injury or damage to the character or reputation of a person.

Personal protective equipment
Specialized equipment worn by workers against injury from environmental hazards.

Personnel lift
An elevator attached to the outside of a building to take workers to floors above the ground level.

PERT
An acronym for project evaluation and scheduling, used by the military and in industrial production. It is often confused with the scheduling method of preference in the design and construction industry, known as the Critical Path Method (CPM). See also *Critical Path Method*.

Phantom line
A dashed line on a drawing that signifies an object that is below the level being shown on a plan, or is hidden behind the surface on an elevation or sectional view.

Phase
To implement in stages.

Phased application
The application of a material at two or more different times, such as in painting, plastering, and poured concrete, wherein succeeding applications can only be applied after the previous one has dried, or cured.

Phased building
New construction or renovation that proceeds over a period of time in such a manner that portions of the project are completed in sequence or phased stages. Some projects are arranged in continuous phases where other phases may be separated by years. Also called *phased development*.

Phillips-head screw
A type of screw having a cross slot cut into the head for driving or removing the screw with a special Phillips-head screwdriver.

Photogrammetry
A two-stage recording process involving the photography and survey control on a site and secondly, the orientation of the photograph and measurement or plotting in the laboratory using a stereoscopic plotting device.

Physical depreciation
The reduction in the property value due to deterioration of the physical fabric because of wear and tear, inadequate maintenance, weathering, and decay.

Piano hinge
A very long, narrow continuous pin hinge that is used in cabinetry to hinge large or heavy panels.

Pick
A word used in the construction industry to refer to anything that is picked up and moved by a crane, usually offloaded from a truck to be installed higher up in the structure, such as on the roof.

Pickled finish
The white finish that appears when old paint is removed.

Pickling
An acid wash used to clean metal surfaces and to remove corrosion.

Pickup truck
A light truck with an open back, low sides, and a tailboard that lowers for loading material.

Picture rail
A molding fixed to an interior wall. Pictures may be suspended from it by means of small metal hooks, which fit over the top of the molding.

Pie chart
A graphic diagram using a circle or oval to indicate the whole object, with wedge-shaped pieces within that represent the proportionate divisions of related items.

Pier
A free-standing support for an arch, usually composite in section and thicker than a column but performing the same function. Also, a thickened part of a wall used to provide lateral support or bear concentrated loads. *Also called support abutment.*

 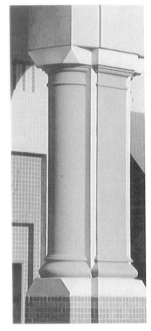

Pier footings
Created by digging holes in the ground and filling them with concrete. Support posts are installed later resting on the concrete. Preformed tubes resist frost heave and result in less movement.

Pigment
A pulverized substance made of organic matter that becomes paint when combined with a liquid such as linseed oil or other synthetic material.

Pigtail splice
A splicing method of connecting two electrical wires by placing them side by side and twisting them around each other.

Pilaster
A partial pier or column, often with a base, shaft, and capital, that is embedded in a flat wall and projects slightly; may be constructed as a projection of the wall itself. Also called *wall column*.

Pilaster strip
A slender pier of minimal projection.

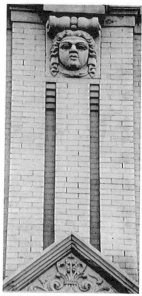

Pile
One of a series of large timbers or steel sections driven into soft ground down to bedrock to provide a solid foundation for the superstructure of a building.

Pile

Pile driver
A machine for driving piles, consisting of a framework for holding the pile, a hammer, and a method of providing power to the hammer.

Pile foundation
A field of piles and pile caps that transmits the load of the structure to a bearing soil below.

Piled underpinning
A method of underpinning existing foundations by driving piles on each side of a wall supported by inadequate foundations. A concrete needle is inserted into a hole in the wall and bears on the top of the two piles, thus transferring the loads to the piles.

Pillar
A column or post supporting an arch or other superimposed load. Clustered or compound pillars consist of a central shaft with smaller shafts that are grouped around it. Also called *post, column*.

Pilot hole
A puncture or small hole to guide a nail or screw.

Pin
A peg or bolt of wood, metal, or any other material that is used to fasten or hold something in place or to serve as a point of support.

Pin joint
A flexible joint connected by a pin through a hole in each of the members to be joined; used primarily for large spans where complete freedom to rotate is required, such as roof forms secured with pin-joint buttresses as the main support.

Pine
A wood of a number of species of coniferous evergreens; may be divided into two classes: soft pine and hard pitch pine; an important source of construction lumber and plywood.

Pinholing
In painting, a defect in a spray-painted surface caused by holes due to bubbles that persist until the film has dried. The bubbles may be caused by sealed air pockets, moisture or oil in the air lines, or porous undercoating, or use of thinner that dries too quickly.

Pintles
Square metal devices used to transfer loads of columns on upper floors by passing the loads through intervening beams and girders to metal column caps on the column below.

Pipe
A long, tubular vessel used to carry a fluid or gas from a supply source to fixtures, or from plumbing fixtures back to sewer lines.

Pipe chase
A vertical shaft or space in a building where pipes can be run.

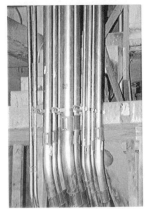

Pipe column
A steel pipe between 3 and 6 inches in diameter used as a column with a base and top plate; often contains a mechanism for adjusting its length, such as an integral screw jack; also called a *lally column*.

Pipe coupling
In plumbing work, a short collar consisting of a threaded sleeve used to connect two pipes.

Pipe fitting
In plumbing, refers to ells, elbows, and various branch connectors used in assembling pipework.

Pipe hanger
In plumbing, applies to various types of supports, such as clamps and brackets, for soil pipes.

Pipe insulation
Insulation that is wrapped around pipes to reduce heat loss or gain.

Pipe joint compound

A nonhardening liquid sealing compound used on the external pipe threads to prevent leaks, yet still allow disassembly for repair or replacement.

Pipe wrench

An adjustable wrench for gripping pipe, with serrated jaws. The movable jaw is set at a slight angle to the fixed jaw, so that force on the handle tightens the grip on the pipe. Also called a *stilson wrench*.

Pipefitter

A person who installs piping for steam systems; hot water heating, cooling, and other systems.

Pipework

An assembly of pipes and fittings used for the conveyance of fluids.

Pitch board

In stair building, a piece of wood cut in a right-angled triangle, with the shortest side representing the height of the riser, and the longer side representing the width of the tread. This piece of wood is attached to another piece at right angles, and can be used as a template for marking the cuts for risers and treads on a stringer.

Pivoted door

A door hung on center or offset pivots as distinguished from one hung on hinges or a sliding mechanism.

Pivoting window

A window that opens and closes by rotating on two pivots, either horizontally or vertically. Generally located in the center of the window, or at the bottom in the case of a transom.

Plain bar

A reinforcing bar without deformations.

Plain masonry

A masonry wall without reinforcement, or one with only light steel for shrinkage.

Plain sawing

Cutting lumber parallel to the squared side of a log, producing a long, flat grain pattern.

Plan

A two-dimensional graphic representation of the design and dimensions of a project, or parts thereof, viewed in a horizontal plane from above.

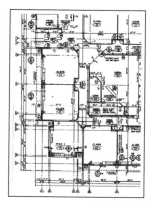

Plan and profile sheets

Drawings used by the crew doing the earthwork and grading; consists of a plan view that shows the area to be graded, and a profile, or vertical cut through the area to be graded.

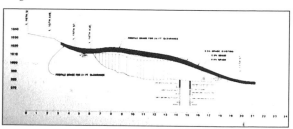

Plan room

A room that contains plans for projects under consideration for bids; a service provided by some organizations in the construction industry.

Plan view

In architectural drawings, a top view of a horizontal section taken at a distance above the floor. See also *Floor plan*.

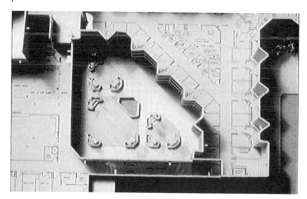

Plane

A hand held woodworking tool used for shaping and smoothing wood surfaces. An adjustable blade determines the depth of the cut.

Planimeter

A mechanical device for measuring areas on a site map.

Plank

A long, flat piece of wood measuring at least 2 inches in thickness and more than 8 inches in width; used for flooring and sheathing.

Plank flooring
A floor constructed of wide boards with tongue-and-groove edges. The planks are often fastened to the floor with screws, and wood plugs inserted in the holes to simulate a wood-pegged floor.

Plank house
A type of timber construction consisting of sawn planks laid horizontally and notched at the corners.

Plank truss
A roof or bridge truss consisting of heavy timber members such as planking.

Plank-frame
A type of house in colonial America constructed of heavy wood planks erected vertically into grooves in a sill plate, and drilled and pegged together.

Planned maintenance
A planned regular preventative maintenance program to keep a building and its services in good working order.

Planned unit development (PUD)
A zoning process that allows a developer to offer public amenities, such as building roads, schools, or providing open space in exchange for looser restrictions on density or building heights.

Planner
The person and/or professional in architecture or interior design who deals with the layout, design, and furnishings of spaces within a proposed or existing structure.

Planning
The establishment of the project activities and events, their logical relations and interrelations to each other, and the sequence in which they are to be accomplished. Also, the process of studying the layout of spaces within a building or other facility, or installations in open spaces, in order to develop the general scheme of a building or group of buildings.

Planning commission
A committee of citizens, appointed or elected, who have the vested authority to set and rule on zoning matters for a city or county, and review applications for variances.

Planning grid
An arrangement of one or more sets of regularly spaced parallel lines, with the sets at right angles or any other selected angles to each other, and used like graph paper to assist with modular planning.

Plans
The official approved plans, profiles, typical cross-sections, working drawings, and supplemental drawings, which show the location, character, dimensions, and details of the work to be performed.

Planter
A permanent, ornamental container for planted pots or boxes, integral with the finish of a building.

Planter

Plaques and markers
Used by many state historic programs to identify historic sites, National Register properties, and significant restoration projects; usually affixed to the exteriors of buildings.

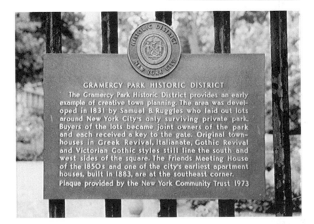

Plaster
A mixture of lime or gypsum, sand, portland cement, and water used to produce a pastelike material that can be applied to the surfaces of walls and ceilings and that later sets to form a hard surface.

Plaster lath
Thin narrow strips of wood nailed to ceiling joists, studding, or rafters as a groundwork for receiving plastering.

Plaster of paris
A gypsum substance especially suitable for fine ornamental plasterwork because it fills a mold completely and dries quickly.

Plasterboard
A building board made of a core of gypsum or plaster, faced with two sheets of heavy paper. Also called *drywall, sheetrock.*

Plastic
Any of the various synthetic complex organic compounds produced by polymerization; can be molded, extruded, or cast into various shapes or drawn into fibers.

Plastic anchor
A preformed hollow insert for use in drywall or plaster to hold light loads. A metal screw is inserted into the anchor, expanding it into the material.

Plastic conduit
In electrical work, a conduit made from polyvinyl chloride (PVC) or other plastic material. It is more economical and easier to work with than metal conduit.

Plastic laminate
A laminate consisting of paper, cloth, or wood covered with a phenolic resin; used for countertops and cabinets that require a washable finish.

Plastic mortar
A mortar of a consistency that allows it to be readily used without disintegrating; plasticity can be improved by additives called *plasticizers.*

Plastic pipe
Pipe made from various types of plastic for use in plumbing, including tubing and fittings. Types include: CPVC pipe, made from chlorinated polyvinyl chloride, and used to convey hot water; PB pipe, a flexible tubing made from polybutylene, and used for hot and cold water; PE pipe, a flexible tubing made of polyethelene, and used for cold water; PP pipe, a hard pipe made from polypropylene, and used for plumbing traps and drainpipes; PVC pipe, a rigid pipe made from polyvinyl chloride; and SR pipe, made from styrene rubber, and used primarily for underground applications.

Plastic skylight
A skylight made of transparent or translucent acrylic, set into a raised frame for installation on a roof.

Plastic veneers
Flexible plastic films with adhesive backing used to cover various surfaces on which a hard, fine finish is desired.

Plastic wood
A paste of wood flour, synthetic resin, and a volatile solvent; used for filling holes and cracks in wood; dries soon after application.

Plasticity
The characteristic of being workable; to be able to be molded, or shaped.

Plasticizer
Admixture to mortar or concrete that increases its workability.

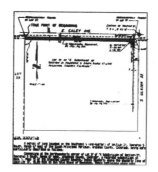

Plat map
A map that shows land subdivisions within a specified area; includes lot lines, streets and improvements, easements, geographical features, elevation measurements, survey bench marks, and often a written legal description of the property.

Plate
In wood frame construction, a horizontal board connecting and terminating posts, joists, or rafters; a timber laid horizontally on the ground to receive other timbers or joists.

Plate girder
A steel beam built up from vertical web plates and horizontal flange plates.

Plate glass
A high-quality float glass sheet, formed by rolling molten glass into a plate that is subsequently ground and polished on both sides after cooling.

Platform
A raised floor or terrace, open or roofed; also, a stair landing. Also called *balcony, ledge, gallery.*

Platform framing
Wooden structures framed with studs that are only one story high. The floor joists rest on the top plates of the story below; bearing walls and partitions rest on the subfloor of each successive story. Also called *western framing.*

Playhouse
A place of assembly for dramatic presentations; also, a small building serving children as a make-believe home.

Plaza
A public square or similar open area within a town or city.

Pleadings
Documents that are filed with a court accusing a party of negligence or wrongdoing, or defending a party against such accusations.

Plenum
The airspace in an integrated ceiling, which may be above atmospheric pressure if used for the air supply or below atmospheric pressure if used for the air exhaust. Also called *duct, raceway, vent.*

Plenum chamber
An air compartment maintained at a pressure slightly above atmospheric, to deliver and distribute the air to one or more ducts or outlets.

Plenum system
A method of heating or air-conditioning where air forced into the building is at a pressure above atmospheric.

Plexiglass
A clear plastic used for windows and lighting fixtures.

Pliers
A small pincerlike tool having a pair of long, retractable broad jaws that are roughened for gripping and bending wire or for holding small objects.

Plot
A parcel of land consisting of one or more lots or portions thereof, which is described by reference to a recorded plot by survey. Also called *lot, property, site.*

Plot plan
A plan showing the size and configuration of the lot on which the building is to be located; containing all the necessary data before excavation for the foundation is begun.

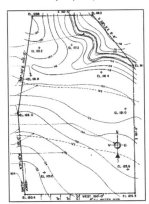

Plot ratio
The gross floor area of a building divided by the area of its site. The basic ratio permitted is frequently modified, by providing a bonus for arcades, setbacks, and plazas, as well as the incorporation of existing buildings of architectural significance.

Plug
In plumbing, a threaded fitting used to close the end of a valve, union, or coupling.

Plug cutter
A saw used on a drill press that cuts cylindrical wood plugs to be used to fill holes in wood.

Plumb
Any method of lining up the building elements in a true vertical direction.

Plumb bob
A weight attached to a line that is used to test perpendicular surfaces for trueness to establish vertical lines or to locate a point.

Plumb cut
A straight vertical cut.

Plumb line
A strong, heavy string or cord with a weight on one end; used to establish a perpendicular alignment.

Plumber
The skilled craftsperson who installs and maintains pipework and appliances.

Plumbing
The installation of pipes, fittings, and fixtures for bringing water into a structure, and to remove wastewater from the building, including venting of the entire system.

Plumbing code
A building code regulating the design of plumbing systems.

Plumbing fixture
A device that uses water and discharges wastewater, such as sinks, lavatories, water closets, and drinking fountains. Does not include pipe fittings or valves.

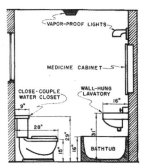

Plumbing symbols
Shapes used on a plumbing layout denoting specific fittings and other items.

Plumbing system
The combination of supply and distribution pipes for hot water, cold water, and gas and for removing liquid wastes in a building. Plumbing systems include the water supply distribution pipes; fixtures and traps; the soils, waste, and vent pipes; the building drain and building sewer; storm-drainage pipes; and all connections within or adjacent to the building.

Ply
A thickness of material, used for building up several layers, as in plywood and built-up roofing.

Plywood
An engineered panel of wood composed of an odd number of thin sheets permanently bonded together, sometimes faced with a veneer. Also called *laminated wood.*

Plywood grades
A rating system for the quality of plywood, ranging from Grade 1 with matched grains that can be used for furniture or paneling, to Grade 4, which can have many defects, but is sound enough to be used for construction.

Pneumatic hammer
A portable electric or gasoline-powered pneumatic hammer that operates on a vibrating principle; used for removing defective brick and mortar for repointing, and for cutting and drilling holes in floors, and many other heavy-duty applications such as tamping and cutting.

Pneumatic tools
Tools that are powered by compressed air or gas; such as grinders, impact wrenches, and saws.

Pocket
A recess in a wall to allow passage of a sliding door hanging on a track.

Pocket door
A door that slides in and out of a recess in a doorway wall requiring no room for the door swing.

Pointed surface
The texture of stone showing nicks made into the surface with a pointed tool, such as a pick or geologist's hammer.

Pointing
The finishing operation on a mortar joint, without the addition of surface mortar; the pressing of surface mortar into an existing raked joint. Also called *caulking*.

Pole
A slender log used as a structural member, with or without the bark removed.

Pole structure
A building or structure with a roof supported by round wood columns.

Pole-frame construction
The use of vertical poles or timbers as the main structural system; often used in hillside construction to alleviate the force against continuous foundations.

Polycarbonate
A thermoplastic used for molded parts where high-impact strength and heat resistance are required, such as construction safety helmets and machinery guards.

Polychromatic
Having or exhibiting a variety of colors.

Polychromy
The practice of decorating architectural elements or sculpture in a variety of colors.

Polyester
A type of thermoplastic resin with outstanding weather resistance, transparency, and toughness; also used with fiberglass for laminating or molding corrugated roofing panels or glazing.

Polyester resin
A synthetic resin with excellent adhesive qualities, high strength, and resistance to chemicals.

Polyethylene
A tough, light, flexible thermoplastic used in the form of sheeting and film for packaging and damp-proofing, and for creating a vapor barrier.

Polyethylene film
Large plastic sheets used as a vapor barrier, for waterproofing and to cover fresh concrete so it can cure.

Polymer concrete
A concrete in which a plastic is used as a binder instead of portland cement.

Polypropylene pipe
A plastic pipe with resistance to chemicals and heat.

Polystyrene
A waterproof material commonly called styrofoam, the brand name of one manufacturer. Available in 4- × 8-foot sheets, it can easily be cut to fit between studs or glued to masonry walls or floors. It will burn during a fire, causing caustic fumes. Used as a rigid insulation material with a high thermal resistance value, and for roof decking.

Polysulfide
A thermosetting resin, used as a building sealant.

Polysulfide rubber sealant
Similar to butyl rubber caulking, but has better elasticity, and does not become brittle in cold weather. It also has a long life expectancy.

Polyurethane
A group of plastics used mainly as a light insulating material in the form of flexible or rigid foam and as a sealant.

Polyvinyl chloride
A synthetic vinyl resin commonly used for the manufacture of PVC pipe; used for plumbing and waste lines.

Polyvinyl resin adhesive
An all-purpose glue which sets quickly and dries clear, for use on wood, plaster, and other porous materials.

Ponding
(1) In concrete work, the process of curing concrete by flooding the slab with water. A dyke is first built around the perimeter using sand or other containment.
(2) Shallow pools of water that collect in low spots on horizontal surfaces such as slabs and roofs.

Porcelain enamel
A glassy metal oxide coating bonded to a metal panel at an extremely high temperature and baked onto steel panels for large architectural applications. It is a very durable material that is scratch resistant.

Porch cornice
A continuous band at the cornice of a porch, filled with a spindlework design.

Porch lattice
A network panel of crossed latticework, to screen the underside of a porch that does not have a continuous foundation.

Porosity
The empty space in a material. If the voids are large, the material is more porous than if they are small. If the voids are small enough, water droplets will not penetrate, but water vapor molecules will. Materials which are impermeable, or waterproof, but vapor-permeable, are called *microporous*. See also *Permeability*.

Portal
An entrance, gate, or door to a building or courtyard, often decorated. It marks the transition from the public exterior to the private interior space.

Porthole
A small window, usually circular, in a ship's side or on an exterior part of a structure.

Portico
A range of columns or arches in front of a building, often merged into the façade, including a covered walkway of which one or more sides are open; includes every kind of covered ambulatory. Also called *colonnade*.

Post
Any stiff, vertical upright, made of wood, stone, or metal, used to support a superstructure or provide a firm point of lateral attachment.

Post bracket
A projection at the top of a post.

Post-and-lintel construction
A type of construction using vertical columns, posts, and a horizontal beam, or lintel, to carry a load over an opening, in contrast to structural systems using arches or vaults. Also called *post-and-beam construction.*

 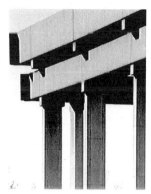

Post-construction services
Design or construction services rendered after the notice of final completion or after 60 days from the date of final completion; usually performed to assist the owner in occupying the facility.

Postoccupancy evaluation
The process of evaluating an occupied facility, considering factors such as its conformance to user satisfaction, functionality, technical performance, and cost-efficiency.

Postoccupancy service
Any service rendered after the final certificate for payment, or more than 60 days after the date of substantial completion; usually involving those services necessary to assist the owner in the use, occupation, and maintenance of the facility.

Post-shore
An adjustable timber support for stabilizing concrete work while it is curing and reaching its final strength.

Post-tensioning
A method of strengthening concrete by drawing steel cables through holes in a concrete slab, and applying tension to plates attached to the cables after the concrete has attained a certain specified strength. This action puts the concrete under a compressive stress, which adds strength to the overall concrete structure.

Poultice
A thick paste used in conservation to draw out toxins and other undesirable substances. Once it dries out, it can be removed with a wooden spatula.

Pour strip
In precast concrete construction, a perimeter strip between the tilt-up concrete panels and the floor slab, to be filled in with concrete, tying them together.

Poured in place
Concrete poured and cured in its permanent location, such as perimeter and slab building foundations.

Power buggy
A gasoline- or diesel-powered cart with a bin to carry wet cement short distances for placement. The bin has a rocker arm for dumping the concrete in place.

Power hammer
A gun that is powered by blank cartridges, for driving fasteners into concrete, where other nailing guns do not have enough force. Each fastener requires a new cartridge.

Power of attorney
A legal right for one party to act as an agent for another.

Power saw
A saw powered either by electricity or compressed air.

Power tool
A device used in construction that is usually powered by electricity.

Power transformer
A device that transfers electricity in an alternating-current electrical system; either stepping up or stepping down the voltage in the process.

Power washing
Cleaning the surface of a building with pressurized water.

Pratt truss
A statically determinate truss, consisting of straight top and bottom chords, regularly spaced vertical compression members, and diagonal tension members; used for medium to long spans in buildings and for small bridges.

Precast
A concrete member that is cast and cured in a place other than its final position in the structure.

Precast concrete
Material that reduces the need for on-site formwork with a process known as tilt-up construction, in which precast panels are lifted into a vertical position and then attached to the structural frame.

Precast pile
A concrete pile that is cast and subsequently driven, as opposed to one cast in place.

Preconstruction
The preliminary design and budgeting phases of a design-build project.

Preconstruction CPM
A plan and schedule that covers the conceptual design phase that precedes the awarding of the contract.

Precut
A piece of timber or other material that is cut to length during manufacturing, to avoid cutting on the job.

Predesign services
Preliminary services provided by an architect to assist the owner in developing the project program, schedule, and budget.

Predrilled
Material that has been drilled at the factory to facilitate the erection or installation with bolts or other fasteners.

Pre-engineered steel building
An industrial-type structure consisting of a rigid frame, girts, purlins, and a metal decking for the roof and walls. They are manufactured to standard designs and engineering.

Prefabricate
To construct all the parts to a structure at the factory so that the final construction consists of assembling and uniting the standard parts on the job site.

Prefabricated construction
A building so designed as to involve a minimum amount of assembly at the site; usually comprises a series of large units or panels manufactured in a factory.

Prefabricated masonry panel
A wall panel assembly of masonry units and a backing material, assembled off-site, and delivered to the job site for erection on the structural frame.

Prefabricated masonry panel

Prefabricated modular units
Units of construction that are prefabricated on a measurement base of 4 inches, or its multiples, and can be fitted together on the job with a minimum amount of adjustments.

Prefinished
Wood products such as plywood, doors, cabinets, window sash, moldings, and trim, that have a finish coat of paint, stain, vinyl, or other material already applied before it is delivered to the job site.

Preformed ductwork
Ductwork fittings that have been factory-shaped for a specific application, such as elbows and tees.

Preglazed
Window sash delivered to the job with the glass fixed in place.

Prehung door
A complete packaged door, frame, trim, and all hardware, ready for installation in its rough opening.

Preliminary CPM
A CPM analysis made before the awarding of contracts to determine a reasonable construction timetable.

Preliminary drawings
Drawings that depict the basic scheme for the project, produced in the early stages of the design process. See also *Schematic design* and *Design development drawings*.

Preliminary estimate
A rough estimate of costs prepared by the architect or contractor during the early planning and development phase of the project, for the guidance of the owner.

Premature demolition
Demolition of a building before official action can be taken, such as waiting for approval of an application; oftentimes by accident or without adequate knowledge of the situation.

Premises
The property, including the buildings, structures, and grounds, that is included in a title to ownership, or a deed of conveyance.

Prepaid asset
Any expense that has been paid ahead of the due date.

Prequalification of bidders
The process of determining the experience, capability, qualifications, competence, integrity, responsibility, and availability of bidders for the proposed project, and then selecting a list of qualified bidders.

Preservation
Keeping in existence, unchanged, natural resources and buildings that have been inherited from the past. The Secretary of the Interior's standards define preservation thus: "to sustain the existing form, integrity, and material of a building or structure, and the existing form and vegetative cover of a site."

Preservation architect
An architect who specializes in the preservation of buildings, particularly those of historical significance.

Preservation by deed
A method used by preservationists to use deed restrictions to curtail development or alteration of a structure or area. A preservation organization may acquire and then sell a property subject to a covenant and reverter clause in the deed that the purchaser must comply with certain restoration guidelines. If not, the property reverts back to the organization.

Preservation commission
A generic term for a municipal agency that designates and administers preservation ordinances and regulates historic districts and landmarks. It may adopt design guidelines or act as an architectural review board.

Preservation master plan
An overall plan for a preservation or restoration project that outlines all the major components required and outlines a key to their relationship, which portion should be dealt with first, and how each phase will be implemented.

Preservation ordinances
Regulations regarding preservation. There are two kinds of statutes: landmark commission ordinances and historic district ordinances. These ordinances define the architectural and historical standards of value in the area based on an architectural survey. Each sets up an agency with authority to review proposals to alter or demolish designated structures and to restrict such actions. Each provides a procedure by which decisions can be appealed by applicants either to a higher administrative authority or zoning board or city council, or made directly to a court.

Preservation plan components
Consist of a historical overview, treatment of architectural styles, construction, description of the community inventory of significant cultural resources, and indication of problem areas; establishment of preservation planning goals and objectives; suggested cultural management program; and identification of potential funding sources.

Preservation restrictions
May involve easements, restrictive covenants, deed restrictions, or leasing restrictions clauses.

Preservation survey
An inventory of property that can be limited to a carefully defined geographic area, such as a neighborhood or enclave of buildings, or it can encompass an entire state, or the nation. It can be limited to places of obvious cultural significance or individual building types, such as commercial, or it can cover all built and natural resources. The amount of information can vary from construction dates and architectural styles, to an in-depth analysis of an individual structure, such as measured drawings, photographs, chain-of-title information, and technical architectural descriptions. Far-reaching surveys can include the area's social and economic factors, development patterns, visual relationships, and design elements. A survey produces a wealth of material: historical data, development statistics, photographs, measured drawings, and maps.

Preservationist
A person or professional who aspires to, agrees with, and takes action to preserve the natural and built environment.

Preservative
Any substance that will poison the food supply of and prevent the action of wood-destroying fungi, insects, and similar destructive life, when the wood has been properly coated or impregnated with it.

Presidential sites
Our past presidents are recognized by scores of historic sites, ranging from the humble to the palatial: birthplaces, residences, monuments, tombs, and libraries for presidential memorabilia.

Pressed wood
In carpentry, a panel manufactured from wood fibers by using heat and pressure.

Pressed-metal ceiling
Thin sheet metal that is stamped with a decorative pattern and used as ceiling panels by nailing them to the underside of beams or furring strips.

Pressure grouting
A method of repairing cracks in brick walls that are not cavity walls. A temporary seal is applied to the crack. Injection ports are inserted at regular intervals, and an epoxy resin compound adhesive is injected into the ports.

Pressure washing
The process of cleaning mortar with a stream of water that is highly pressurized; used to clean a masonry wall, or to prepare it for painting.

Pressure-glued
A method of gluing that places the wood members under high pressure until the glue sets.

Pressure-relieving joint
A horizontal expansion joint at the bottom of precast or preassembled masonry units, to prevent loads from the panels above being transferred to the panels below.

Pressure-treated lumber
Wood injected with chemicals to preserve it from decay and to ward off insects. Once treated, the chemicals are insoluble and resistant to water leaching. Treated lumber often bears a mark indicating the level of treatment, and has a green cast.

Prestressed concrete
A process of anchoring steel rods into the ends of forms, then stretching them before the concrete is poured, putting them under tension. When the concrete hardens, they spring back to their original shape, providing additional strength.

Pretensioned concrete
A method of developing a higher strength in concrete, by putting the reinforcing bars in tension before the concrete is placed. The tension is released once the concrete hardens, adding compressive stresses to the concrete.

Pretensioning
The process of stretching steel wires in the forms before concrete is placed, and keeping the tension on until the concrete has set. After the concrete hardens, the steel remains in tension, adding to the strength of the concrete.

Prevailing wage
The wage set by the federal and state governments for construction work that equals wages paid for similar work in that particular area.

Prevailing wage Law
A law that establishes minimum wages for different job classifications in the construction industry.

Preventative maintenance
Regular maintenance to prevent deterioration below the level of adequate quality.

Primary blasting
The drilling and packing of explosives in the drilled cavities of natural rock, to blow the rock loose.

Primary colors
Hues are red, yellow, and blue. From these three colors, with the addition of white, it is possible to create the full color spectrum.

Primary subcontractors
Subcontractors such as plumbers; electricians; or heating, ventilation, and air-conditioning (HVAC) workers who may perform a major portion of the work, and may also work directly for the owner with their own prime contract.

Prime bid
A bid from a prime contractor or primary subcontractor made directly to the owner, as opposed to a bid from a subcontractor to the general contractor.

Prime contract
An agreement between a prime design or engineering firm, or a general contracting firm, and the owner for a substantial portion of the work on a project.

Prime contractor
The contractor who takes responsibility for the entire project; who may build all of the project, or have subcontractors build the entire project, or may build part of it and subcontract out the rest.

Primer
A paint, applied as a first coat, which serves the function of sealing and filling on wood, plaster, and masonry; inhibits rust and improves the adhesion of subsequent coats of paint on metal surfaces.

Primer coat
A ground coat of paint applied to timber and other materials as a preservative and as a filler for the pores, which serves as a base for future coats of paint. The priming paint is mixed with turpentine to make it thinner than normal consistency.

Principal
The person legally responsible for all the activities and actions of a business, such as architecture, engineering, or construction.

Principal purlin
A massive wood purlin that runs parallel to the ridge of the roof about midway between the ridge and top plate. It is framed into the principal rafters and supports a number of common rafters.

Principal rafter
One of a pair of large diagonal framing members forming a roof truss, framed into a horizontal tie beam. The rafter supports purlins, which in turn support smaller common rafters.

Principal-in-charge (PIC)
The person in a design firm with the responsibility for administering and monitoring services on a particular project. The person is normally an officer of the company, or a principal of the firm.

Prismatic glass
Rolled glass that has parallel prisms on one face. These prisms refract the transmitted light and thus change its direction.

Pro forma

A statement of the economic analysis of the costs and value of a proposed real estate development; usually includes land costs, hard and soft costs, equity, financing, and sales price. See also *Project costs*.

Procurement

Purchasing materials or services. The process as used in construction may include obtaining competitive bids, placing a purchase order, arranging for transportation, and receipt of goods and materials at the job site.

Product standard data

Standards published by the National Institute of Standards and Technology [(NIST), formerly the National Bureau of Standards (NBS)] of the U.S. Department of Commerce, and by various private organizations of manufacturers. The standards usually cover dimensional requirements for standard sizes, technical requirements and specifications, and methods of testing and marking the products.

Productivity

A measure of the effectiveness of work performed per unit of time, such as installing so many square feet of material per hour.

Professional advisor

A design professional hired by the owner for counseling on various design matters, such as conducting a design competition for the project, or advising the client during the programming phase of a project.

Professional engineer

A person who holds a license to perform engineering services, such as mechanical, structural, civil, sanitary, and electrical engineering.

Professional fee

The amount of money charged by a person or company, such as architects' or engineers' fees for professional services performed.

Professional liability insurance

Insurance designed to insure an architect, engineer, or any person or firm undertaking design responsibility, such as a design-build contractor, against claims for damages resulting from alleged professional negligence.

Professional practice

The operation of one of the design professions, whose services are rendered within the guidelines of a recognized code of ethics, standards, and legal requirements.

Profile

An outline of a former structure seen or represented from the side, or one formed by a vertical plane passed through an object at right angles to one of its main horizontal dimensions.

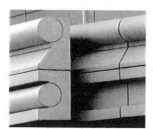

Profile

Profit

The amount of money received for services or work over and above the cost to perform the work.

Profit-sharing plan

A method of distributing a portion of a firm's profit to employees, either short term or long term; used as an incentive to increase performance, hopefully resulting in more profit for the firm and those participating in the plan.

Program

A schedule of work that a contractor plans to undertake in order to complete a project.

Program management

The management of the building and construction program for large-scale public and private projects.

Programming phase

The stage in the development of a project where the owner provides full information to the design professionals regarding requirements for the project.

Progress chart

A modified version of the horizontal bar chart used for the project schedule, wherein individual work items, or phases completed, are filled in or otherwise delineated on the chart.

Progress payment

A prescheduled partial payment made at various times during the work activity, based on percentage of work completed, or monthly in proportion to the percentage of work completed, and often includes payment for materials already delivered to the site or stored in a warehouse.

Progress schedule

A diagram, graph, or other pictorial or written schedule showing proposed and actual times of starting and completing of the various elements of the work.

Progressive scaling

The gradual disintegration of a material from surface scaling to penetration deeper within the material.

Project
The total activity that is to be undertaken, whether a new construction or renovation project, that is, the total amount of construction work to be performed as stated in the contract documents.

Project budget
The amount of money established by the owner as available for the entire project, which normally includes land costs, financing costs, professional services, cost of construction, furniture, fixtures, and equipment, and the cost of owner-furnished goods and services, contingency allowance, and other established costs related directly to the project. See also *Construction budget*.

Project checklist
A list of all services performed by the architect, including all predesign, design, and construction-related increments of the work.

Project closeout
The process that includes final inspection, submittal of all necessary documentation, acceptance of the project, and final payment.

Project control
The ability to determine the project status as it relates to the timeline and schedule.

Project costs
These include the hard costs, soft costs, life-cycle costs, and cost of operation. Hard costs consist of land and property acquisition, easement rights, construction costs for labor, materials, equipment, utilities permits, testing, demolition, site preparation, furnishings, hazardous materials abatement, and off-site amenities. Soft costs include site and property evaluation, real estate options, service and title fees, promotion, owner's insurance, legal counsel, administration, design and construction finance application fees, points and closing costs, title search, and administrative reviews. Life-cycle costs include building maintenance, cleaning and repairing, maintenance of grounds, systems replacement for any building element that wears out, utility costs for ongoing use of the building's systems. Operations costs borne by the owner include property management, leasing and promotion, loss recovery on vacated leases, losses on unleased or unused space, trash and waste removal, water, sewer, utilities, and energy costs.

Project data
Information submitted by the contractor to illustrate a specific product, material, or system for some portion of the work; usually consists of illustrations, performance data, schedules, instructions, brochures, diagrams, and other information.

Project delivery system
The method selected for the performance of all the tasks on a building project; including design, preparation of construction documents, construction, and management of the construction. See also *Design-bid-build* and *Design-build*.

Project management
The practice of developing, planning, procuring, and controlling all the services and activities required for the satisfactory completion of a project according to an agreed time and cost.

Project manager
The person charged with managing the project activities from start to finish. The tasks include both administrative and technical responsibilities. The term applies to the design professional, contractor, or construction management entity.

Project manual
Includes all the documents prepared by the project manager for the project, such as the bidding requirements, conditions of the contract, sample forms, and specifications.

Project overrun
A situation that exists when the latest cost estimate exceeds the original planned cost.

Project record documents
Consists of the certificates and all other information relating to the work, products, assemblies, and equipment, that the contractor gives to the owner prior to the project closeout and final payment.

Project representative
A representative of a design firm, contractor, or owner, who assists in the administration of the construction contract at the project site.

Project team
An assembly of professional individuals chosen to provide various aspects of service or work during the duration of the project.

Project underrun
A situation that exists when the original planned cost is greater than the current cost estimate to complete the project.

Project work plan
A document that delineates the tactics a firm will use in carrying out the project on time, and within the allocated client's budget, as well as the firm's own budget.

Projections
Protrusions from the plane surface of the wall, which serve aesthetic functions, such as emphasizing openings and creating scale and visual interest. They also prevent water from reaching the wall surface. Projections include pediments, cornices, string courses, sills, lintels, balconies, and other ornamentation. When they deteriorate, and their supports corrode, they may become dangerously unstable and fall off the structure. Therefore, they should be checked periodically to keep them stable and in good condition. Many cities have strict ordinances regarding how often and how closely they have to be checked for structural integrity.

Propane torch
A hand-held torch consisting of a nozzle screwed onto a bottle containing pressurized propane gas. When ignited, the nozzle is used to control and direct the flame for preheating, soldering, brazing, and other applications that only require moderate heat; used by plumbers to solder copper tubing joints.

Property
A plot or parcel of land, including buildings or other improvements. Also called *real property, lot, plot, site.*

Property damage insurance
Protection against the destruction of tangible property by other parties, including loss of use as a result. Does not include injury or damage to the property if it is in the care, custody, or control of the insured.

Property insurance
Insurance on the work at the site against loss or damage caused by fire, lightning, wind, hail, vandalism, or other perils that may occur.

Property line
A boundary line between plots of land, such as farms or lots. The location of a property line is recorded in the legal description of the piece of land.

Proportion
The relation of one dimension to another, often described as a numerical ratio.

Proposal
An offering to provide a service or perform work under specified conditions, usually defining in detail the terms of providing the service or work, a schedule for the performance of such work, and often includes the cost of such service or work. If so, it is called a *fee proposal,* or a *cost proposal.*

Proposal schedule
A schedule included in the proposal outlining the general scope and breakdown of tasks and duration of the activities. The timeline is set in the horizontal dimension on the chart, and the activities are set in the vertical column at the left of the schedule.

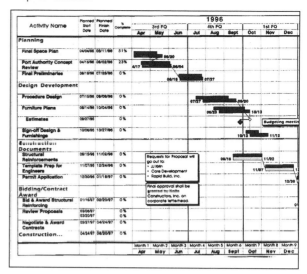

Proprietary specification
A specification that describes a product, material, or piece of equipment by trade name, or by naming acceptable suppliers by name.

Protected membrane
A roofing membrane with a protective surfacing on top, such as roofing felt, which is protected with fine gravel in a built-up roofing system.

Protected membrane roof
A membrane roof with the thermal insulation installed over the waterproof membrane.

Protected noncombustible construction
Buildings with bearing walls that have a minimum 2-hour fire-resistance rating, and roofs, floors, stairways and supports with a 1-hour fire rating.

Protected opening
An opening, such as a window or door, with the same fire-resistance rating as the wall in which it sits.

Protected ordinary construction
Buildings with roofs, floors, supports, and enclosed stairway walls with a 1-hour fire-resistance rating.

Protected wood frame construction
Buildings with all members protected by 1-hour fire-resistance-rated materials.

Protection
A special status applied to some buildings, as defined by the Secretary of the Interior's standards, indicating that the purpose of this status is, "to effect the physical conditions of a property by defending or guarding it from deterioration, loss or attack, or to cover or shield the property from damage or injury." In the case of buildings, it is generally temporary, anticipating future historic preservation treatment.

Protective clothing
Clothing designed to protect workers and reduce the possibility of injury, such as welder's goggles, face guards, aprons, steel-toed shoes, and hard hats.

Protective coating
An outer coating to provide protection against the elements.

Pry bar
A steel bar that has one or both ends flattened, curved, and notched; used for wedging the ends between materials and pulling them apart, or for pulling nails and fasteners. Also called a *crow bar*.

PSF
Pounds per square foot.

PSI
Pounds per square inch.

P-trap
A device in a plumbing system used to maintain a water seal in a drain line to prevent sewer gas from entering the building through the line.

Public building
Buildings of, concerning, or affecting the community of people. Americans live under four systems of jurisdiction: the town or city, county, state, and federal governments. The first federal buildings set a standard of architectural style for the entire country. Each has its own governmental symbols and image: the town or city hall, county courthouse and post office, and the state capitol.

Public Buildings Cooperative Use Act of 1976
Legislation that directed the General Services Administration (GSA) to acquire historic structures for federal office use and promote the mixed public uses of such buildings.

Public housing
Low-cost housing, owned, sponsored, or administered by a municipal or other government agency.

Public liability insurance
Protection against bodily injury or death of persons other than employees of the insured, and/or property damage.

Public space
An area within a building where the public has access.

Public utility
A company that provides a service for the public, such as water, gas, and electricity.

Pull box
In electrical work, a metal box with a cover, placed in a long run of conduit, or where a number of conduits make a sharp bend, to help in pulling the wires, or for the purpose of distributing them to other locations.

Pumped concrete
Concrete that is transported by a truck and deposited through a pipe or hose by a pumping mechanism on the truck.

Punch
A small, cylindrical, pointed steel tool with a sharp end, which is used to punch small holes in metal.

Punch list
A list prepared by the architect and given to the contractor when the building is substantially complete, outlining those items that need to be completed, or defective items that need to be corrected or replaced for total completion.

Punching shear
The shear forces resulting from a vertical support punching through the concrete slab which it supports.

Puncture
To pierce or penetrate a membrane or other seal.

Puncture resistance
The ability of a material such as conduit, pipe, or membranes to withstand a localized force which might puncture through it.

Purchase order
A written order to a vendor to supply material or services, and to bill the person or institution issuing the purchase order at a specified price.

Purlin
A piece of timber laid horizontally on the principal rafters of a roof to support the common rafters on which the roof covering is laid.

Push drill
A hand drill that looks like a screwdriver, but works by pushing the handle in the direction of the work. Helical grooves in the shank turn the drill bit as it is pushed, and a spring returns it to a starting position.

Putty
A type of sealer, kneaded to the consistency of dough, and used in sealing glass in sashes or filling small holes and cracks in wood prior to painting.

PVC pipe
Abbreviation for polyvinyl chloride; piping used in all parts of a plumbing system. Also used for electrical conduits.

Q

Quality assurance
The system for assuring that the contract's technical requirements are met by the contractor. Also, the management of quality at all stages in the manufacture of a product and delivery of services, as standardized internationally by ISO 9000.

Quality control
Tests and sampling techniques to see that the required quality of construction is provided.

Quantity survey
An inventory compiled for the purpose of estimating the amount of material and labor required to complete a construction operation.

Quantity take-off
A listing derived from the plans and drawings, of the total number of items needed to complete a building project, or specific portion thereof; such as all the material needed for a complete plumbing or electrical installation.

Quarry
A small, square or diamond-shaped pane of glass.

Quarry tile
Unglazed ceramic tile, machine made by the extrusion process from natural clay or shale.

Quartered
Lumber that is sawn from a log at a perpendicular angle to the growth rings. The lumber sawn in this manner is easier to dry without warping and shrinking, and it is used for flooring and weatherboards.

Quartered veneer
Veneer for which a log is sliced or sawed so as to bring out a certain pattern of the grain.

Quartzite sandstone
A variety of sandstone composed largely of granular quartz cemented by silica, forming a homogeneous mass of very high tensile and crushing strengths; used as a building stone and as an aggregate in concrete.

Queen closer
A brick cut in half along its length to keep the bond correct at the corner of a brick wall.

Queen post
One of the two vertical supports in a queen-post truss.

Queen truss
A truss framed with two vertical tie rods or posts, as opposed to a king truss, which has only one in the center.

Quick assets ratio
A ratio of current fixed assets to current liabilities; used to quickly ascertain the financial condition of a business.

Quick valve
A valve that can be fully opened or closed with a quarter turn of the stem. Types include plug valves, ball valves, and butterfly valves. They are available in a variety of sizes, materials, configurations, and pressure ratings for different service applications; typically used for gas and other fuel lines.

Quirk
An indentation separating one element from another, such as between moldings.

Quirk bead molding
A molding containing a bead with a quirk on one side, as on the edge of a board.

Quirked molding
A molding characterized by a sudden and sharp return from its extreme projection or set off and made prominent by a quirk running parallel to it.

Quoin
One of a series of stones or bricks used to mark or visually reinforce the exterior corners of a building; often achieved through the use of a contrast in size, shape, color, or material, which may be imitated in non-load-bearing materials. Also called *stone coping*.

Quonset hut
A prefabricated steel structure composed of arched steel ribs covered with corrugated sheet metal, forming a barrel vault. Developed for the military prior to World War II.

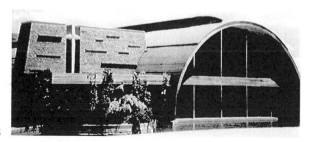

Quotation
A price for supplying materials or labor, or both, that is offered by a contractor, subcontractor, material supplier, or vendor.

R

Rabbet
A long L-shaped channel cut into the edge of a board, to receive another board that is similarly cut and fitted to it at right angles.

Rabbeted
Two members joined together by interlocking grooves cut into each one.

Raceway

An enclosed channel designed to hold electrical wiring or cables; typically made of metal. Types include: one-piece raceway, shaped to resemble a molding; two-piece raceway, consisting of a galvanized steel channel to cover surface-run electrical wiring; and overfloor raceway, with a thin, flat section, designed to be placed on the floor. Also called *duct, plenum, vent.*

Rack
A framework of wood or metal, designed to hold or permanently store materials.

Racking
In laying a stone or brick wall the corners are stepped back so that it is shorter than the course below it. The workers later tie in the courses so that the vertical line at the corner does not crack from uneven settlement.

Racking back
The process of building up the corners of a brick wall first, the middle portion being racked back down to the center, then filled in to completion.

Radial drill
A drill press with a radial arm that pivots.

Radial grating
A metal grating used around the bottom of trees, in which the bars extend from a common center, and the cross bars form concentric circles.

Radial saw
A bench or shop saw with a movable arm holding a circular saw, which can be tilted to different angles.

Radial-arm saw
A circular power saw mounted on an arm above the saw table, which can be raised or lowered or pivoted, so that the blade can cut at various angles.

Radiant heat
Heat transmitted to a body by electromagnetic waves, as distinct from heat transferred by thermal conduction or convection.

Radiant heating
A system of pipes, usually installed in the floor, carrying heat or hot water to radiate heat into the room.

Radiator
A heating unit that transfers heat by radiation; usually fed by hot water or steam.

Radiography
The production of photographs of invisible features, such as defects in welds, by means of x-rays.

Rafter
An inclined member in a roof framing system that supports the sheathing and roof covering. Also called *beam, timber.*

Rafter length
The span of a rafter, measured from the ridge to the outside edge of the wall plate, not counting any overhang.

Rafter level cut
The horizontal cut of a birdsmouth; also a horizontal cut on the bottom of a rafter tail to provide a nailing surface for a closed cornice. See also *Birdsmouth.*

Rafter plate
A plate that supports the lower end of rafters.

Rafter plumb cut
The vertical cut where the rafter meets the ridge, and also at the other end if the rafter is to support a fascia. Also, the vertical cut of a birdsmouth. See also *Bird's mouth.*

Rafter seat
The horizontally cut portion of the bird's mouth that rests on the top plate.

Rafter seat cut
The horizontal cut portion of a bird's mouth, a cutout in the rafter that allows the rafter to sit firmly on the top plate. See also *Bird's mouth*.

Rafter shortening
Cutting the length of the rafter by one-half the thickness of the ridge board. The opposite rafter is shortened by the same amount.

Rafter tail
The part of a rafter that overhangs the exterior wall to support the eaves or gutter.

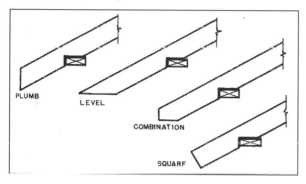

Rail
A bar of wood or other material passing from one support to another; a horizontal piece in the frame or paneling, as in a door rail, or in the framework of a window sash.

Railing
Any open construction or rail used as a barrier, composed of one of a series of horizontal rails supported by spaced upright members.

Rain leader
A pipe that carries storm water from the gutter to a downspout and eventually to the ground.

Raised floor
A false floor, that provides a space for cables or ducts above the structural floor. Floor sections are usually supported on short, adjustable peg columns.

Raising
The process of physically lifting a framework into a vertical position by a team of workers who then connect it to the other timbers. The framework is first assembled on the ground or on the floor decking. This technique is frequently used for building the timber frames of barns.

Rake
The slope, or angle, of inclination. The context usually indicates whether it is measured from the horizontal or the vertical axis.

Raked joint
A joint made by removing the surface of mortar with a square-edged tool while it is still soft. Raking produces marked shadows and tends to darken the overall appearance of a wall. The result is not a weather-tight joint.

Raking cornice
A cornice following the slope of a gable, pediment, or roof.

Raking molding
Any molding adjusted at a slant, rake, or ramp; any overhanging molding that has a rake or slope downward and outward.

Rammed earth construction
A type of construction where the exterior walls are bearing walls, composed of sand, clay, coarse aggregate and moisture, and compacted by pressure into the forms.

Ramp
An inclined plane, useful in complying with modifications to a structure to meet the Americans with Disabilities Act (ADA) requirements.

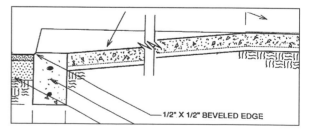

Random
An application of material that consists of a variety of sizes, lengths, or shapes.

Random rubble
Masonry consisting of stones of irregular size and shape with roughly flat faces, set randomly in a wall.

Random shingles
Wood shingles of different widths banded together; often these vary from 3 to 12 inches in width.

Random tab shingles
Asphalt or fiberglass shingles made to resemble wood shingles, by having extra tabs on them that are randomly applied.

Random width
Any material with varying widths.

Random width flooring
Wood flooring made up of various widths, often called a *plank floor*.

Random work
Any type of work done in an irregular manner, such as a wall built up of irregular-sized stones.

Range
In masonry, a course of stonework or a wall laid up in courses.

Rasp
A course file or a filelike tool that has coarse projections for reducing material by a grinding motion instead of by cutting.

Rat tail file
A round, tapered woodworking file used to shape and enlarge holes and cutouts.

Ratchet
A mechanism that allows free movement in one direction, but locks in the direction of the applied force; used with braces, wrenches, and lifting devices.

Raze
To tear down or demolish, to level to the ground.

Razing
The process of demolishing a structure without possible reconstruction.

Reaction
The response in structures to the imposed loads, which are generally developed at the supports; also, the force that is transferred to one structural member from another.

Ready-mixed concrete
Concrete that has all the ingredients mixed before delivery to the job site in special trucks. It is the most common form of concrete, except for very small pours such as sidewalks, where additional water is added at the job site.

Ready-to-assemble
Items shipped in pieces to the job site with all the slots, holes, and hardware needed for on-site assembly; used for furniture, cabinets, and other related items.

Real estate
Land and any improvements to it such as buildings and other site features.

Real Estate Investment Trusts (REITs)
A funding mechanism for development including demolition and environmental cleanup.

Real property
Land with or without buildings, fences, and other features. Also called *real estate*.

Real property inventory
An itemized list and classification of the real property of a person or estate, showing the amount, character, and condition of such property at a given time; also, an objective listing of the supply, character, and condition of all real property in a given area at a certain period of time.

Realtor
An agent who is a member of the National Association of Realtors, and who is licensed to sell real property.

Ream
The process of smoothing the surface of a hole and finishing it to the required size with a reamer; also removing burrs or sharp edges inside the mouth of a pipe with a reamer.

Rebar
A contraction for reinforcing bar, commonly used in the building trades.

Rebuild
To build again; to make extensive structural repairs.

Receivables
Money that is due and payable from clients or customers.

Receptacle
In an electrical system, a device placed in an outlet box to which the wires in the conduit are attached; fixtures plug into the receptacle.

Recess
Receding part or space, such as a cavity in a wall for a door, an alcove, or a niche.

Recessed dormer
A dormer with all or part of the window set back into the roof surface, resulting in the sill's being lower than the roof.

Recessed luminaire
A lighting fixture recessed into a ceiling so that its lower edge is flush with the ceiling, as compared to a surface-mounted fixture. A fluorescent fixture is called a *troffer*.

Reciprocating saw
A handheld power woodworking tool with a reciprocating thin blade clamped to the chuck of the saw; used to do fine curved work; similar to the saber saw.

Recirculated air
In an air-conditioning system, the return air that is reconditioned and distributed again, as opposed to new air.

Reclaim
To bring about a change in land or material from an unusable condition to a usable state, and to restore a structure to use and make suitable for habitation.

Reclamation
Restoring land to a usable state.

Recognition program
A program that recognizes buildings, places, and areas of importance. Giving recognition is a long-standing preservation technique of the National Register of Historic Places. There are also many private-sector programs that identify landmarks and signify their value.

Reconstruct
New construction following the exact forms and details of the original building.

Reconstruction
Rebuilding what has been lost by replacing it with new construction, following the exact form, materials, and details as the original.

Record
An account made in an enduring form.

Record drawings
Construction drawings revised to show significant changes made during the construction process; usually based on marked-up prints, drawings, and other data furnished by the contractor to the architect.

Rectified photographs
Prints of large-format field photography that were made using perspective control devices on the camera. Notes may be added to the photograph and dimensions, if control dimensions were taken in the field.

Rectify
To correct by calculation or adjustment.

Recycle
To extract and reuse useful substances found in waste.

Recycling
The collection and reprocessing of materials to produce new products; can also be applied to the refurbishment or reuse of old buildings.

Red lead paint
Commonly used as a rust-inhibiting primer on steel; has been largely superseded by other primers due to the toxicity of lead.

Redesign
To alter an existing design toward a new scheme.

Redevelop
To restore to a better condition; to reclaim.

Redevelopment
The act or process of redeveloping or renovating a blighted area, such as is the case in urban renewal programs.

Reducer
A fitting which has one of its openings reduced to a smaller diameter to join with a smaller pipe in the line.

Redundant member
Any member in a truss that is not required for the strength or stability of the truss; also, any member in an assembly that does not carry any load.

Redwood
A durable, straight-grained, high-strength, low-density soft wood; especially resistant to decay and insect attack; light red to deep reddish-brown; used primarily for construction, plywood, and millwork. Due to its soft consistency it has been used for ornamental moldings and gingerbread for many Victorian style homes.

Reference standard specification
A nonproprietary specification that uses reference standards to describe equipment or assemblies to be included in the building.

Reference standards
Generic specifications and technical data that has been prepared by organizations that are generally accepted by the construction industry.

Refinish
To apply a new finish to an existing surface.

Reflected ceiling plan
The plan of a ceiling projected onto a flat plane directly below.

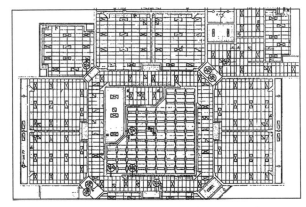

Reflection
The action on the part of surfaces of throwing back rays of light or sound that falls upon them.

Reflective glass
Window glass having a thin, translucent metallic coating bonded to the exterior or interior surface to reflect a portion of the light and radiant heat and light that strikes it.

Reflective glass

Reflective insulation
Metal that reflects infrared radiation and reduces the amount of heat entering a building, particularly via the roof. It commonly takes the form of aluminum foil, backed up by kraft paper.

Reflux
A flowing back to another place or state; to ebb.

Refrigerant
A gas that circulates through a cooling system; the most commonly used is Freon.

Refurbish
To make clean, bright, or fresh again.

Refurbishment
To bring an existing building up to standard, or to make it suitable for a new use by renovation, or by installing new equipment, fixtures, furnishings, and finishes.

Regenerate
To form, construct, or create new.

Regional planning
A profession that began in the United States in the 1970s whose central focus was the physical environment of cities and regions. Includes forces that shape the environment, plans and policies to ease and eliminate urban and regional problems, and the availability of government and private resources. The purpose is to integrate the physical, social, economic, and political aspects of community development in finding solutions to urban and regional problems.

Register
A device at the open end of a duct for warm or cool air, with adjustable fins to direct and adjust the flow of air from an air duct inside a building; often covered with an ornamental grille of metal. Types include baseboard register, ceiling register, floor register, wall register, and a round ceiling register to direct the air in all directions.

Reglet
A flat, narrow molding used to separate panels; also a groove in a wall to receive flashing.

Rehabilitate
To restore to a useful state by repair, alteration, or other modification.

Rehabilitation
Slum areas and substandard buildings brought up to an acceptable living standard. The Secretary of the Interior's standards describe rehabilitation as "returning a property to a state of utility through repair or alteration which makes possible an efficient contemporary use while preserving those portions or features of the property which are significant to its historical architectural, and cultural values."

Reimbursable expenses
Money spent on a project that will be reimbursed by the owner as outlined in the agreement.

Reinforce
To strengthen by adding extra support.

Reinforced concrete
In concrete masonry construction, steel reinforcement that is embedded in such a manner that the two materials act together in resisting forces.

Reinforcement displacement
The movement or relocation of reinforcing bars from their original position in the concrete forms; can be caused by the pouring of the concrete itself, if the bars are not tied or supported properly.

Reinforcement ratio
A numerical ratio of the effective area of the reinforcing bars to the area of concrete, at any given portion of the structural member.

Reinforcing
Steel bars or wire mesh placed in concrete to increase its tensile strength.

Reinforcing bar
A steel bar used in concrete construction that provides additional strength. The bars are deformed with patterns made during the rolling process.

Reinstate
To restore to a previous condition or position.

Reinvestment
A method used to combat deterioration of declining neighborhoods by channeling public and private resources into their development.

Rejection of work
Action taken by the architect that rejects the construction work if it is not carried out in accordance with the requirements of the contract documents.

Rejuvenate
To restore to a youthful appearance.

Release agent
A substance that is applied to formwork in order to prevent adhesion between a concrete surface and the face of the form.

Relief valve
A pressure-activated valve designed to automatically relieve pressure if the equipment exceeds its designed settings.

Relieve
To assist any overloaded member by any construction device, such as a discharging arch placed above an opening.

Relocate
To establish in a new place; the process of moving a building or structure to a new location, usually placing it on a totally new foundation.

Relocation
Forcing households or businesses to move to new locations, necessitated by urban renewal, or other government actions.

Remake
To make new; to reconstruct.

Remedy
The solution that a court or arbitrator brings to settle a dispute between two parties.

Remodel
Revisions within an existing structure without increasing building areas.

Remodeling
The process of modifying an existing building or space for current use; usually involves replacing some of the existing building fabric or adding new components.

Rendering
A drawing, especially a perspective view, of a building or interior space, artistically delineating materials, shades and shadows; done for the purpose of presentation.

Renew
To make new or to restore to a former condition.

Renovate
To restore to an earlier condition by repairing or remodeling.

Renovation
Bringing an existing building back to its former or original condition.

Repair
Any labor or material provided to restore, reconstruct, or renew any existing part of a building, its fixtures, appurtenances, mechanical or electrical systems, or equipment. Also, to bring to a sound condition after damage or injury in a fire.

Replace
To put back in place; to use a substitution in place of the original that was lost, damaged, depleted, or deteriorated.

Replacement value
An item in an insurance policy that establishes the estimated cost to replace damage to an existing building with new construction, based on current construction costs.

Replacing
The renewing or restoring to a former place or condition, as the renewing of parts of a building that have been damaged or impaired by use or by the elements.

Replica
An exact copy of an original building or any building component.

Replicate
To duplicate, copy, or repeat; to reproduce in the likeness of the original.

Repointing
The process of filling a mortar joint after raking out the old mortar and working it to the desired joint profile; carried out for restoration purposes and not part of the original construction.

Repressed brick
Bricks that are pressed again while still in the plastic state, usually with the name of the manufacturer. This procedure produces a slightly denser uniform brick but does not alter its original characteristics.

Reproduce
To produce a counterpart, image, or copy of the original.

Reroofing
The process of applying new roofing material over an existing roof.

Resawn board
Lumber that has been sawn horizontally to produce two thinner pieces.

Researching structures
Examining past evidence of a building's history. Items to look for in researching buildings consist of architectural plans and drawings, assessment records, building inspector's records, deeds, film, videotapes, guide books, household inventories, insurance records, legal resources, magazines, manuscripts, maps, measured drawings, newspapers, oral histories, photographs and slides, postcards, reports and feasibility studies, surveys, and trade catalogs.

Reserve
An amount of money held in a trust account to cover construction changes, or cost overruns in a large construction project. This reserve guarantees to the lending institution that the contractor will be able to cover these costs.

Resident engineer
An engineer that represents the owner on a construction project; used on federal or state projects.

Resilient flooring
A manufactured floor covering, such as asphalt, vinyl, and vinyl asbestos tile, linoleum, and cork tile.

Resin
Obtained as gum from certain trees, or manufactured synthetically, and used in paint or varnish and in making plastics and adhesives.

Resistance
The ability of a building material to resist forces acting upon it, such as compression, tension, shear, or torsion.

Reskinning
The process of removing the existing veneer masonry and installing a new veneer, or installing a new veneer over the existing masonry veneer. This is usually done if the original skin is damaged, and repair is cost-prohibitive or technically impractical, or the original skin is dated and a fresh image is needed.

Resort
A place frequented by people for relaxation and recreation; a customary or frequent gathering place.

Resource
Any valuable component of the natural or built environment.

Respect
To show consideration for; avoid violation of, treat with deference.

Responsiveness
Appropriateness of a bid to the requirements of the solicitation, as to price, quality, quantity, and schedule.

Restaurant
A commercial establishment where food and beverages are served to the public; either in a separate building or within a hotel or other facility.

Restitution
An award by the court that restores the parties to their former financial position.

Restoration
According to the Secretary of the Interior's standards, "accurately recovering the form and details of a property and its setting as it appeared at a particular period of time by means of the removal of later work or by the replacement of missing earlier work." Since authenticity is the primary goal, and this calls for extensive research, study, and money, restoration is frequently restricted to those structures intended for public use or those opened as house museums.

Restoration architect
An architect who specializes in the restoration of existing structures as opposed to new construction.

Restore
To put back into a prior state, condition, or use.

Restrictive covenant
A requirement to adhere to a specific restriction on the use or development of real property, may be incorporated into the deed, and may include how the property may be used, location of improvements, or type of structure.

Retain
To keep or hold in a particular place, condition, or position.

Retainage
An amount withheld from the progress payments, and not released until the final payment, as specified in the owner-contractor agreement.

Retainer
A payment made in advance for services that are to be performed once work is started; typically applies to professional services and not to construction.

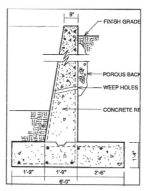

Retaining wall
A wall, either freestanding or laterally braced, that bears against earth or other fill surface and resists lateral and other forces from the material in contact with the side of the wall.

Retarder
In concrete work, an additive that slows down the setting time, allowing more time to place the concrete.

Retempering
In masonry work, restoring the workability of mortar that has stiffened due to evaporation by adding water and remixing.

Retooling
Removing deteriorated stone from the surface of a masonry façade with a chisel.

Retrofit
To add new building materials, mechanical, plumbing, fire safety, or electrical equipment, or other elements and components not in the original; often required to meet current code requirements.

Return air
The air that is brought in from an air-conditioned space and recirculated in order to reduce the energy that would be consumed by using only fresh air as a source.

Reuse
Make suitable for new requirements or conditions through modifications.

Revamp
To patch up or restore.

Revenue
Income received from clients for the performance of services, or capital gains from the sale of long-term assets, such as rents or royalties.

Revenue Act
Legislation passed in 1978 that provided an investment tax credit for the rehabilitation of old buildings used for commercial and industrial purposes.

Reversal
The process of removing damaged brick from a wall and reversing the brick to expose its interior face, if it is not also deteriorated.

Revert
To return to a former condition.

Revise
To change or modify.

Revision
A change or alteration to the original, such as a revision to a contract, or revisions to the contract documents.

Revision block
A table within a drawn block on a drawing, showing the number, nature, and dates of revisions made to that drawing, or portions thereof.

Revitalize
To impart new life or restore vitality in residential or commercial areas through physical improvements and economic programs, such as a main street program.

Revolving door

An exterior entrance door with four fixed panels that rotates on a central pivot, set within a partial cylindrical frame. The panels are set at 90 degrees to one another, so that two panels always maintain a closure.

Rezoning
To divide a municipality or piece of property into new or different zones to permit new uses.

RFP
Abbreviation for request for proposal; usually initiated by the owner.

Rheostat
Having a resistance which can be adjusted, regulating the flow of electric current.

RIBA
Abbreviation for Royal Institute of British Architects.

Ribbed slab
A panel composed of a thin slab reinforced by ribs in one or two directions, usually at right angles to one another; also called a *waffle slab* due to its appearance.

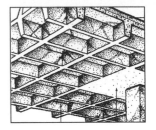

Ribbed vault
A vault in which the ribs support, or seem to support, the web of the vault.

Ribbon strip
A horizontal board that helps to support the ends of rafters or joists; it is set into the studs to provide a flush surface.

Ribbon window
One of a horizontal series of windows, separated only by mullions, which forms a horizontal band across the façade of a building.

Richter scale
A quantitative measurement of the magnitude of an earthquake. The magnitude is the logarithm of the amplitude that would be recorded on a standard seismograph 100 kilometers from the epicenter of the quake. An increase of 1 unit of magnitude equals an increase of ten times the energy released by the earthquake. A magnitude of 5 is potentially destructive; the earthquake of 1906 in San Francisco had a magnitude of 8.6 and destroyed most of the city.

Ridge
The horizontal lines at the junction of the upper edges of two sloping roof structures. Also called *roof peak, ridge pole.*

Ridge beam
A horizontal beam at the upper edge of the rafters, below the ridge of the roof.

Ridge board
A longitudinal member at the apex of a roof that supports the upper ends of the rafters.

Ridge cap
Any covering such as metal, wood, or shingles used to cover the ridge of a roof.

Ridge course
The top course of roofing tiles, roll roofing, or shingles.

Ridge crest
A linear ornamental device; usually composed of metal, attached to the crest of a roof, providing a transition to the sky.

Ridge roll
A wood strip, rounded on top, that is used to finish the ridge of a roof, often covered with lead sheathing. Also, a metal or tile covering that caps the ridge of a roof.

Ridge ventilator
A raised section on a roof ridge provided with vents that admit air currents.

Right to Work Law
A law that states that workers are not required to join a union as a condition of getting or keeping a job.

Right-of-way
A strip of land over which a lawful right of passage exists for the benefit of people who do not own the land; granted by deed or easement for construction or maintenance of specified utilities or transportation corridors. See also *Easement*.

Right-to-know
A right of workers to know the risks and hazards of their work-related exposure to chemicals and hazardous substances; granted by the Occupational Safety and Health Act (OSHA).

Rigid arch
An arch without joints that is continuous and rigidly fixed at the abutments.

Rigid conduit
Nonflexible steel tubing used to carry electrical conductors.

Rigid connection
A joining of two structural members that prevents any end rotation of either member at the joint.

Rigid frame
A structural framework in which all columns and beams are rigidly connected. There are no hinged joints, and the angular relationship between beam and column members is maintained under load.

Rigid frame

Rigid insulation
A type of nonflexible panel of expanded synthetic material, such as styrofoam and urethane foam, as well as rigid processed wood or gypsum panels.

Rigid joint
A joint that is capable of transmitting the full extent of force at the end of the member to the other members framing into the joint.

Rigid metal conduit
A metal pipe of standard weight, for pulling wires and cables in an electrical system. The thickness of the pipe allows for cutting standard threads.

Ringer crane
A crane that has a circular base which allows the crane to rotate a full 360 degrees.

Riprap
Irregularly broken and random-sized large pieces of quarry rock used for foundations. Also, a foundation or parapet of stones thrown together without any attempt at regular structural arrangements.

Ripsaw
A hand saw designed to cut wood parallel to the grain, or lengthwise on a board. The cutting teeth on the saw are set alternately right and left, to avoid tearing the wood. See also *Cross-cut saw.*

Rise
Vertical height of an arch, roof truss, or rigid frame, measured from a base line.

Rise and run
The pitch of an inclined member or surface, such as a roof; usually expressed as the ratio of the vertical rise to the horizontal run.

Riser

The vertical surface under the tread of a step, or the vertical portion of a stair step which may be open. Also, in plumbing, a vertical supply pipe for a sprinkler system, or a pipe for water, drainage, gas, steam, or venting that extends vertically through one or more stories and services other pipes.

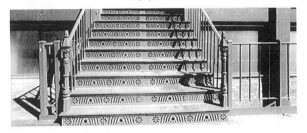

Riser pipe

A vertical pipe that rises from one floor level to another floor level, for the purpose of conducting steam, water, or gas from one floor to another.

Risk management

The management of an activity, accepting a level of risk that is balanced against the benefit of the activity; usually based on an economic assessment.

Rivet

A shank with a head that is inserted into holes in the two pieces being joined and closed by forming a head on the projecting shank. The rivets must be red hot to be formed in such a manner and this method has generally been replaced by welding or bolting.

Rock rash

A patchwork appliqué of oddly shaped stone slabs used on edges as a veneer; often further embellished with small cobbles or geodes.

Rock wool

An insulating material that looks like wool but is composed of substances such as granite or silica.

Rocklath

A flat sheet of gypsum used as a plaster base.

Rockwork

Quarry-faced masonry; any stonework in which the surface is left irregular and rough.

Rod

In surveying, a vertical measuring device, marked off in feet and tenths of a foot; used with a level to measure vertical differences in elevation. By taking a series of measurements from each given point down the slope of the land, the vertical measurement of a sloping site can be calibrated. Also, a thin metal strip used as a stiffener or fastener.

Roll molding

Any convex rounded molding that has a cylindrical or partially cylindrical form.

Roll roofing

An asphalt-impregnated roofing felt, covered with crushed mineral, available in 3-foot-wide rolls. Also called *construction paper, tar paper, building paper.*

Rolled glass

Molten glass from a furnace that is passed through rollers to produce a pattern on one or both surfaces of the glass.

Rolled steel section

Any hot-rolled steel section, including joists, angles, channels, and rails.

Rolling door

A large door consisting of horizontal, interlocking metal slats guided by a track on either side; opens by coiling about an overhead drum at the head of the door opening.

Rolling scaffold

A scaffold on wheels that can be moved around; used on interior work.

Rollover mortgage

A mortgage with a fixed interest rate for a specific period of time, after which it can be extended at the prevailing higher or lower interest rate.

Roll-up door

A door made of small horizontal interlocking metal slats that are guided in a track. The configuration coils around an overhead drum that is housed at the head. The door may be manually or electrically operated.

Romex

A trade name for nonmetallic sheathed cable; used extensively for interior wiring.

Roof balustrade

A railing with supporting balusters located near the eaves of a roof, or at the top flat portion of a mansard roof.

Roof boards

Wood boards used as a roofing underlayment instead of plywood, to allow the roof to breathe.

Roof bond

A guarantee that a roof installed within the proper specifications will be repaired or replaced if it fails within a specified period of time due to normal weathering.

Roof comb

A wall along the ridge of a roof that makes the roof appear higher.

Roof cornice

A cornice immediately below the eaves; also called an *eaves cornice.*

Roof curb
A pitched roof that slopes away from the ridge in two successive planes, as a gambrel or mansard roof.

Roof deck
The structural material between the deck of a roof and the roof covering system; may be metal, wood, concrete, gypsum, or any combination.

Roof drain
A drain designed to receive water collecting on the surface of a roof and to discharge it into a leader or a downspout.

Roof drain strainer
A domed wire cage projecting above the roof, designed to trap debris before it enters the drain pipe.

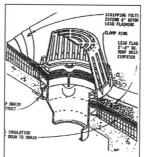

Roof guard
Metal devices installed at various locations on a sloped roof to prevent snow from sliding off; most often close to the eaves.

Roof jack
A cone-shaped sheet-metal flashing mounted on a metal base; used to seal the area where a roof vent or other pipe comes through the roof.

Roof live load
Consists of any external load that may be imposed on a roof, such as wind, snow, construction equipment, and workers.

Roof pitch
The slope of a roof usually expressed as a ratio of vertical rise to horizontal run, or in inches of rise per foot of run.

Roof plate
A plate at the top of a wall that receives the lower ends of roof rafters.

Roof pond
An open filled trough or plastic bag on a roof to capture heat from the sun; they are covered at night to allow the heat to radiate down into the building.

Roof ridge
The horizontal line at the junction of the upper edge of two sloping roof surfaces.

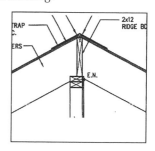

Roof ridge beam
A beam at the upper ends of the rafters, at the ridge of the roof.

Roof ridgecap
Any covering such as metal, wood, shingles, or tile used to cover the top course of materials at the ridge.

Roof ridgeroll
A wood strip, rounded on top, that is used to finish the ridges of a roof; often covered with lead sheeting. Also, a metal, tile, or asbestos-cement covering that caps the ridge of a roof.

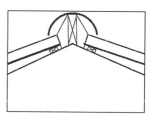

Roof sheathing
Plywood or other sheet material fastened to the roof rafters as a base for shingles or other roofing material.

Roof truss
A built-up structure of wood, consisting of a top and bottom chord and intermediate strut supports.

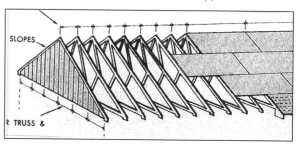

Roof walkway
A permanent pathway for access across a roof surface.

Roofer
One who installs new roofs or makes repairs to existing roofing material.

Roofing felt
Waterproof felt, soaked in asphalt, bitumen, or tar, that is used in built-up roofing.

Roofing nail
Made of aluminum alloy. Roofing nails are short and stubby and have a large, thin, flat head.

Roofing square

A measure of roofing material sufficient to cover 100 square feet when applied in a standard manner.

Rooftop air-conditioner

An air-conditioning system installed on a roof.

Room

An enclosure or division of a house or other structure, separated from other divisions by partitions.

Room air-conditioner

A self-contained machine inserted in a window or exterior wall of a room and used to circulate air cooled by refrigeration into the room while rejecting the heat outdoors. May also be fitted to supply heat if appropriately circuited.

Room finish schedule

Information on the design drawings that lists in the form of a schedule the types of finishes to be given to floors, walls, and ceilings.

NO	ROOM NAME	FLOOR		WALLS								CEILING	
		MTL	BASE	NORTH	C	EAST	C	SOUTH	C	WEST	C	MTL	HEIGHT
106	Commons	CPT1	VB	EXG PLAS P8	--	--	--	--	--	GPDW/CL	P1	EXG	--
107	Abstract	CPT1	VB	GPDW	P1	EXG PLAST P1	GPDW	P1	EXG PLAS P6	ACT	--
108	Vestibule	EXG	EXG	EXG	--	EXG	--	EXG	--	EXG	EXG	EXG
109	Womens Restroom	EXG CT	EXG	EXG	--	EXG	--	EXG	--	EXG	--	EXG	EXG
110	Womens Restroom	EXG	EXG	EXG	--	EXG	--	EXG	--	EXG	--	EXG	EX1
111	Mens Restroom	EXG	EXG	EXG	--	EXG	--	EXG	--	EXG	--	EXG
112	Corridor	CPT1	VB	EXG		EXG PLAS P1	--	EXG PLAS P8	EXG PLAS
113	Janitors Closet	EXG T3	EXG	EXG	--	EXG	EXG	--	EXG	EXG
114	Mens AR Vestibule	EXG CT	EXG	EXG CT	--	EXG	--	EXG	EXG PLAS	EXG
115	Mens Restroom	EXG CT	EXG	EXG CT	--	EXG CT	--	EXG CT	--	EXG CT	EXG PLAS	EXG
116	Corridor	CPT1	VB	--	--	EXG PLAS P1	GPDW	P11	GPDW	P1	ACT	8'0"
117	Cataloging	CPT1	VB	GPDW	P7	GPDW	P1	GPDW	P1	ACT
118	Catalog Office	CPT1	VB	EXG PLAS P7	GPDW	P1	EXG PLAS P1	ACT
119	Aquisitions	CPT1	VB	EXG PLAS P7	GPDW	P13	GPDW	P1	ACT
120	Aquisitions Office	CPT1	VB	EXG PLAS P7	GPDW	P1	GPDW	P1	ACT
121	Corridor	CPT1	VB	GPDW	P1	GPDW	P1	EXG PLAS P6	GPDW	P1	ACT	8'0"
122	Reference Collection	CPT1	VB	EXG PLAS P8	GPDW	P1	--	GPDW	P1	ACT
123	Public Catalog	CPT1	VB	--	--	--	EXG PLAS P8	P1	ACT
124	Microform	CPT1	VB	GPDW	P1	GPDW	P1	GPDW	P1	ACT	8'0"
125	Office	CPT2	VB	GPDW	VVC1	GPDW	VVC1	GPDW	P1	GPDW	P1	ACT	8'0"

ROOM FINISH SCHEDULE

Rope

Strands of fiber that are twisted or braided into a thicker cord, and used to haul or hoist material.

Rotary drill

A hydraulically or motor-driven tool for drilling holes in rock or earth; contains a cutting bit at the end of a metal rod.

Rotary-cut veneer

Veneer in which the entire log is centered in a lathe and turned against a broad cutting knife, which is set into the log at a slight angle.

Rough carpentry

Includes all the wood framing members and sheathing of a building. Also called *framing*.

Rough estimate

An approximation made without a detailed examination.

Rough floor

A subfloor serving as a basis for the laying of the finished floor, which may be of wood, linoleum, tile, or other suitable material. See also *Subfloor*.

Rough grading

The cutting and filling of earth for the preparation of finish grading.

Rough hardware

All the concealed hardware in a building such as bolts, nails, and spikes that are used in the construction and may not be visible in the completed work.

Rough lumber

Lumber that is not dressed; used for rough framing and heavy timber construction. Also called *undressed lumber*.

Rough opening

A rough framed opening in a building wall that is designed to contain a door or window; any unfinished opening in a building.

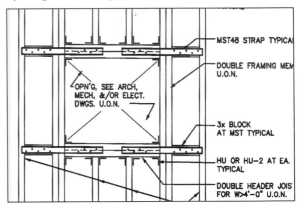

OPN'G, SEE ARCH, MECH, &/OR ELECT. DWGS. U.O.N.

MST48 STRAP TYPICAL

DOUBLE FRAMING MEM U.O.N.

3x BLOCK AT MST TYPICAL

HU OR HU-2 AT EA. TYPICAL

DOUBLE HEADER JOIS FOR W>4'-0" U.O.N.

Rough sawn

Wood that has not been planed or sanded with saw marks left on the surface.

Rough work

In construction, the rough skeleton and rough framing members, including rough openings for doors and windows.

Rough-hewn

Timbers or lumber with a rough, uneven surface made by trimming with an axe or adze; sometimes used for decorative effect.

Rough-in

The early stage of construction in which the framing and rough carpentry are in place, and electrical systems are roughed in, along with ductwork for the heating and air-conditioning.

Rough-in plumbing

Installation of all piping, traps, and vents in preparation for the installation of the finish plumbing fixtures.

Round pediment

A round or curved pediment; used ornamentally over a door or window.

Rout

In woodworking, the gouging out of material with a router; a two-handled tool for smoothing the face of depressed surfaces.

Routing
The cutting away of wood to shape a molding or other piece of millwork.

Row house
One of a series of identical buildings in a continuous row on one or both sides of a street.

Rowlock
A brick laid on its edge so that its end face is visible; one ring of a rowlock arch.

Rowlock arch
A segmental arch composed of full rowlock bricks.

Rubbed brick
A decorative finish that is obtained by rubbing bricks with a stone, brush, or abrasive tool, so as to produce a smooth surface of consistent color; used to highlight door, window, and arcade openings, arches, medallions, bands, and corners of façades.

Rubbed finish
A finish resulting from the use of an abrasive or carborundum stone to remove surface irregularities from concrete. A rotary carborundum sander is also used on concrete.

Rubber-base paint
A paint used in damp areas, and for sealing and water-proofing basements; must be thinned with solvent.

Rubber-insulated wire
A common wire, insulated for heat and water resistance; used for commercial and residential applications.

Rubble
Rough stones of irregular shapes and sizes, used in rough, uncoursed work in the construction of walls, foundations, and paving.

Rubble wall
A rubble wall, either coursed or uncoursed.

Rubblework
Stone masonry built of rubble.

Run
Stonework having irregularly shaped units and no indication of systematic coursework. Also, the horizontal distance covered by a flight of stairs.

Run of rafter
In building, the horizontal distance from the face of a wall to the ridge of the roof; this distance is represented by the base of a right-angle triangle.

Running measure
One-dimensional measurement of a piece of any material; also called *lineal measurement*.

Rust
A substance, usually in powder form, accumulating on the face of steel or iron as a result of oxidation. Rust will ultimately weaken or destroy the steel or iron on which it forms.

Rustic arch
An arch laid up with regular or irregular stones; the spaces between them are filled with mortar.

Rustic brick
A fire-clay brick having a rough-textured surface, used for facing work; often multicolored.

Rustic joint
In stone masonry, a deeply sunk mortar joint that has been emphasized just by having the edges of adjacent stones chamfered or recessed below the surface of the stone facing.

Rustic quoin
A stone quoin, projecting out from the main surface of the wall with rough, split faces and chamfered edges, to give the appearance of rugged strength.

Rustic slate
One of a number of slate shingles of varying thickness, yielding an irregular surface when installed.

Rustic stone
Any rough, broken stone suitable for rustic masonry, most commonly limestone or sandstone; usually set with the longest dimension exposed horizontally.

Rustic woodwork
Decorative or structural work constructed of unpeeled logs or poles.

Rustic work

In ashlar masonry, grooved or channeled joints in the horizontal direction, which renders them more conspicuous.

Rusticate

To give a rustic appearance by beveling the edges of stone blocks to emphasize the joints between them; used mainly on the ground floor level.

Rusticated masonry

Coursed stone masonry where each unit is separated by deep joints. The surface of each unit is usually very rough.

Rusticated wood

Wood incised in block shapes to resemble rough stone.

R-value

A measure of a material's resistance to the transfer of heat at a given thickness of material. The higher the "R" value, the more effective the insulation. The term is the reciprocal of the "U" value. See also *U-value*.

S

Saddle

A ridged piece on the back of a chimney to shed water back toward the main roof surface. Also called *cricket*.

Saddle notch

A round notch cut near one end in either the lower or upper surfaces of a log that forms an interlocking joint when matched with a similarly notched log set at right angles to it; used in log-cabin construction.

Saddle roof

A roof built with a ridge terminating in two gables.

Safe carrying capacity

In construction, the capacity to carry the load; it is designed to support without failing in any way. In electrical work, the maximum current a conductor will carry without becoming overheated.

Safety belt

A belt-like harness to stop a worker during a fall; it is worn around the waist, and is attached to a lifeline at the top of a structure.

Safety glass

Glass containing thin wire mesh reinforcement; glass laminated with transparent plastic; glass toughened by heat treatment, causing it to break into small fragments without splintering.

Safety goggles

A protective eye covering, made with safety glass or impact-rated plastic; to protect workers from eye injuries while operating power equipment, or other work activities.

Safety lintel

A load-carrying lintel placed behind a more decorative one, as over a door or window opening.

Safety net

A meshed fabric that is spread out below construction activity to protect material or workers from falling, and to protect people passing by underneath. The net is supported on poles attached to the building or construction.

Safety net

Safety nosing
Stair nosing with an abrasive nonslip surface installed flush with the surface of the tread.

Safety shoes
A worker's shoes with a steel-protected toe, and nonslip soles.

Sag
To bend in the middle of a beam or other body, either by a load placed upon it or by its own weight.

Salamander
A type of portable temporary heater used on a construction project; used to remove moisture from the air when concrete is drying in cold weather.

Salvage
Building components recovered from partially dismantled or completely razed buildings.

Salvage archeology
Rescue of building material and data threatened by damage prior to destruction, or during the act or aftermath of demolition; also called *rescue archeology*.

Salvage value
A value given to a piece of equipment after its useful life, or at the end of the depreciation period.

Sample soil
A representative specimen of soil from a site; used for testing for compactibility and other characteristics.

Samples
Examples of materials or products requested by the architect to be supplied by the contractor, manufacturer, or supplier, for approval before installation.

Sampling
Obtaining a small amount of material for testing from a representative lot.

Sand finish
Colored, textured plaster surface, similar in appearance to sandpaper.

Sandblasting
Abrading a surface, such as concrete, using a stream of sand ejected from a nozzle by compressed air; used for removing dirt, rust, paint, or cleaning up construction joints, or carried deeper to expose the aggregate for a decorative rough texture.

Sanded
A smooth surface produced by rubbing wood or other material with sandpaper.

Sander
An electric tool designed to smooth wood and remove imperfections and saw marks.

Sand-finished plaster
A finished plaster surface textured with the addition of sand.

Sand-floated
In plastering, a rough sand finish obtained with a wooden float.

Sanding
Finishing surfaces, particularly wood, with sandpaper or some other abrasive.

Sanding wheel
A metal disc, with an adhesive-backed sandpaper affixed to it, mounted on a power saw in place of the circular blade; used to sand wood, to sharpen tools, and to smooth the edges of cut material such as tile.

Sandpaper
An abrasive paper, made by coating a heavy paper with a fine sand or other abrasive held in place with glue; used for polishing surfaces and finished work.

Sandstone
Sedimentary rock that is composed of sand-sized grains naturally cemented by mineral materials.

Sandwich beam
A built-up beam composed of two joists with a steel plate between them. The joists and plate are held together by bolts.

Sandwich construction
Composite construction consisting of a light core of insulation and outer layers of higher-density materials with greater strength.

Sandwich panel
A building panel composed of two sheets of plywood whose surfaces are bonded with an adhesive to a filler material of plastic foam, corrugated paper, or other lightweight material to achieve a fairly high compressive strength. They are used for roof panels, and floor panels.

Sanitary engineering
The part of civil engineering that deals with water supply, sewage, and industrial waste, especially as it relates to the public health and the environment.

Sanitary plumbing
The assembly of pipes, fittings, fixtures, and appliances that removes the sanitary waste.

Sanitary sewer
A disposal system that carries only sewage waste, and not storm or surface water. Also called *storm sewer*.

Sanitary waste
Dirty water from kitchens, bathrooms, and laundries.

Sapwood
The outer layers of the wood of a tree, in which food materials are conveyed and stored during the life of a tree. The sapwood layers are usually of lighter color than the heartwood.

Sash
Any framework of a window; may be movable or fixed; may slide in a vertical plane or be pivoted.

Sash balance
In double-hung windows, a device usually operated with a spring, designed to counterbalance the window sash without the use of weights, pulleys, and cords.

Sash bars
The strips of wood that separate the multiple panes of glass in a window. Also called *glazing bars, muntins*.

Sash window
A window formed with glazed frames that slide up and down in vertical grooves by means of counterbalanced weights.

Sashless window
A window composed of panes of glass that slide along parallel tracks in the window frame toward each other to leave openings at the sides.

Satinwood
A hard, fine-grained, pale to golden yellow wood of the acacia gum tree; used in cabinetwork and decorative paneling.

Saturation
The purity of a hue. The higher the saturation, the purer the color.

Saw
A carpenter's tool for cutting wood, consisting of a steel blade with teeth and a handle. The types include backsaw, bandsaw, coping saw, crosscut saw, dovetail saw, hacksaw, keyhole saw, radial saw, rip saw, table saw, and power saw.

Sawhorse
A portable four-legged support frame to hold material being sawed or fitted; usually used in pairs.

Sawn veneer
Wood veneer that has been cut with a saw, rather than peeled on a lathe, or sliced by a blade.

SBCCI
Abbreviation for Southern Building Code Congress International, Inc. authors of Standard Building Code.

Scab
Short piece of lumber nailed over a splice or joint to add strength or prevent slippage or movement.

Scaffold
A temporary platform to support workers and materials on the face of a structure and provide access to work areas above the ground. Also called *staging*.

Scaffold crane
A small self-contained motorized crane attached to the scaffolding for lifting relatively small loads.

Scaffolding
A temporary structure for the support of elevated platforms for workers, tools, and materials. Adjustable metal scaffolding is often used as shoring in concrete work, to provide support until the concrete cures.

Scaled drawing
A plan made in a small reduced predetermined scale representing the exact proportions and scaled dimensions as the actual work. The scale is indicated on the drawings. See also *Architect's scale* and *Engineer's scale*.

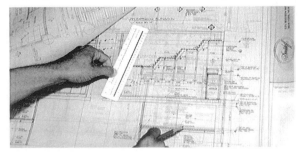

Scaling
Local flaking or peeling away of the outer surface of concrete or mortar. Also, the scaling of dimensions on a plan to determine the full-size dimensions on the job.

Scarf joint
An end joint between two pieces of timber, tapered to form sloping surfaces that match. A stepped or hooked scarf joint has both pieces notched to form matching steps so as to facilitate alignment. The pieces may be glued or bolted together.

Schedule
A table or list of working drawings giving number, size, and placement of items such as doors and windows. Also, a chronological display on a chart, showing the sequence of all the project tasks.

JAN	FEB	MAR	APR	MAY	JUN	JUL	AUG
● DESCRIBE ROLE OF FACILITY		■ PRE-PROPOSAL CONFERENCE					
● ORGANIZATIONAL DEVELOPMENT			■ RECEIPT OF A/E PROPOSALS				
● CERTIFICATE OF NEED				■ SITE VISITS A/E OFFICES			
DATA GATHERING AND APPLICATION					■ SELECT A/E FIRM		
					■ SIGN A/E CONTRA		
					■ INITIATE A/E V		
						■	■
● SELECT CONSULTANT							
● FINANCIAL FEASIBILIY OF PROJECT							
● SOLICITATION OF ARCHITECT							

OWNER

● DEVELOP BLOCK RELATIONSHIPS		■ PRE-PROPOSAL CONFERENCE					
● 3D COMPUTER MODELING			■ RECEIPT OF A/E PROPOSALS				
● PUBLIC RELATIONS RENDERING						FUNCTIONAL SPACE	
● GROSS SQUARE FOOTAGE PROGRAM						REVIEW P	
● PRELIMINARY SITE PLAN						SINGLE LI	
● PRELIMINARY PROJECT COSTS							

Schedule of materials
A detailed listing of materials to be used in a building project under their respective names, such as door schedule, window schedule, finish schedule, materials schedule, fixture schedule, and the like.

FINISH SCHEDULE					
FINISH KEY	FLOOR	BASE	WALLS	CEILING	REMARKS
A	CONCRETE	NONE	CMU	NONE	ROOM 102 NOT TO BE PAINTED
B	CONCRETE W/HARDNER	VINYL	CMU	24" X 24" ACOUSTICALBOARD	OMIT HARDNER IN ROOM107
C	CARPET	VINYL	GYPSUM BOARD	ACOUSTICAL TILE	
D	CARPET	VINYL	GYPSUM BOARD	GYPSUM BOARD	
E	VINYL	VINYL	GYPSUM BOARD CMU	GYPSUM BOARD	
F	TERRAZZO	TERRAZZO	GYPSUM BOARD	GYPSUM BOARD	
G	ACCESS FLOORING	VINYL	WOOD PANELING	GYPSUM PLASTER	SEALER ON CONC. BELOW ACCESS FL
H	BRICK PAVERS	WOOD	WOOD PANELING	ACOUSTICAL PLASTER	
J	CERAMIC TILE	CERAMIC TILE	VINYL WALL COVERING	24" X 48" ACOUSTICAL BOARD	
K	QUARRY TILE	QUARRY TILE	CERAMIC TILE	ACOUSTICAL TILE	

Schedule updating
The regular review, analysis, evaluation, and revision of the Critical Path Method (CPM) or other schedule used to sequence the construction activities.

Scheduling
The sequential planning of items of work on a design or construction project, relating to the length of time for each activity, and planned start and completion dates.

Scheduling software
Computer software used to itemize the sequence of project tasks. Many are interactive, allowing changes in one area to affect changes in other related areas.

Schematic design phase
The phase of design services where the architect prepares design studies and other documents to illustrate the project's design and relationship of components, and present them to the owner. Estimated construction costs often accompany this phase.

Schematic drawing
A diagrammatic or preliminary drawing prepared by the architect, outlining the general concept or scheme for the project; the predecessor of design development.

Scissors truss
A type of truss used to support a pitched roof. The ties cross each other and are connected to the opposite rafters at an intermediate point along their length.

Scope
The extent or intention of the construction activity; Also, the portion of the plans, specifications, and addenda on which the contractor has based its bid.

Scope bidding
A method of bidding based on a description of the general scope of a project as to the architectural design and structural, mechanical, and electrical systems.

Scope documents
Any document among the bidding or contracting documents setting forth the intent that the individual documents indicate only the general scope and performance criteria, and that the contractor shall be required to perform all work and furnish all materials necessary to accomplish construction according to the general scope standards.

Scored block
A stretcher or corner block that has a horizontal groove that resembles a mortar joint, giving the appearance of only half a block.

Scoring
Partial cutting of concrete flat work for the control of shrinkage cracking. Also used to denote the roughening of a slab to develop mechanical bond.

Scratch coat
In three-coat plastering, the first coat of plaster which is scratched with a tool to provide a bond for the second coat.

Screed
A guide placed along the edge of the work at the desired height for leveling concrete.

Screed chairs
The supports used to fix the depth of a slab and to hold the screeds in place.

Screed guide
A wooden framework to be used in leveling off poured concrete to its desired height.

Screeding
Striking off excess concrete during the finishing operation for concrete slab or sidewalk work.

Screen block
An open pattern cast into the block; used for sun and privacy screens.

Screen door
A door intended to allow ventilation but keep out insects; usually consists of a lightweight frame and fine wire mesh screening.

Screw
Mechanical device used to fasten wood or metal parts, consisting of a helix wound around a tapered cylinder.

Screw anchor
A metal shell similar to that used with an expansion bolt, which expands when a screw is driven into it, and wedges itself in the material.

Screw clamp
A woodworking tool with a pair of opposing jaws that can be adjusted by two screws; used for holding pieces of wood while cutting, or to form a glued joint.

Screw jack
A lifting device actuated by square-threaded screws. Its lifting capacity is more limited than a hydraulic jack.

Screwdriver
A tool used for driving in or removing screws by turning them. The tool is made of a well-tempered steel bar or rod flattened at one end to fit into the slot of screw head.

Scribe
The process of cutting or scratching a line along a surface with a sharply pointed steel tool.

Scribing
Marking and fitting woodwork to an irregular surface by holding the piece against the irregular outline and copying the profile to fit.

Scrollwork
Decorative woodwork cut with a jigsaw, and used as exterior ornamentation. Also called *gingerbread*.

Scupper
An outlet in a wall of a building for drainage of water from a floor or flat roof. Also called *wall drain*.

Scuttle
A small opening in a ceiling or roof; usually installed on top of a built-up frame. Also called *hatchway, opening, trap door*.

Seal
To close a small hole or crack with a plastic material, such as caulking, filler, or chinking.

Sealants
Sealants are critical in curtain wall structures, where they weatherproof the joints between the glass panes and the mullions and muntins that support them. They are used to seal joints between large masses of masonry to allow for expansion or contraction, and joints where roofing materials meet the rear surfaces of parapets. Types include oil and resin-based caulks for bearing masonry joints; polysulfide sealants for high-rise masonry and curtain walls; silicone sealants for high-rise metal and glass curtain walls, insulating glass systems and structural glazing, and high-movement joints; urethane sealants for high-rise stone, concrete and brick masonry façades, and paving systems; acrylic and latex sealants for small-scale construction; and butyl sealants for glazing joints and splice seals in window units.

Sealed bidding
A basic method of procurement used commonly on public projects; after a solicitation for bids, they are received at a designated time and place in sealed envelopes, to be opened in public, where an announcement of the lowest responsible bidder is given.

Sealer
A liquid painted on wood or masonry to prevent moisture from entering. Also called *caulking.*

Seam
A method of joining edges of sheet metal which includes lap seam, standing seam, dovetail, leaded, or slip hook.

Season
To dry wood through exposure to the air or the heat of a kiln, thus lowering its moisture content. Also called *air dry.*

Seasoning
Removal of moisture from green wood in order to improve its workability and serviceability.

Seasoning check
Separation of wood extending a few inches in length longitudinally; formed during the drying process; commonly caused by the immediate effect of a dry wind or hot sun on freshly sawn timber.

Seated connection
A simple connection where a steel beam rests on top of a steel angle, which is fastened to a column or girder.

Second mortgage
A mortgage against a property that already has a primary mortgage against it. The second mortgage is behind the first mortgage in terms of recovery, and is generally much smaller to reduce the risk.

Secondary color
In painting, a color produced by mixing two or more primary colors, as the colors obtained by mixing red, yellow, and blue pigments in pairs: Red and yellow make orange, yellow and blue make green, and red and blue make purple.

Secondary colors
The colors green, orange, and purple that result from a mixture of pairs of primary colors.

Secondary element
A nonessential element of a structure, such as the trim around doors and windows, which is essentially a finishing element.

Secondary reinforcement
Any steel placed in concrete other than the main reinforcing bars, such as temperature steel, stirrups, or ties.

Seconds
A lower grade of material or workmanship that does not meet the standard set for it.

Section line
A dashed or solid line drawn on a plan or elevation, with arrows at each end of the line pointing in the direction that the sectional view faces.

Sectional door
An overhead door that lifts vertically and is constructed in panel-like sections that move on tracks mounted at the sides of the door opening.

Sectional elevation
In architectural drawing, a cross-sectional view of a structure showing the details of the construction.

Sectional scaffold
Scaffolding that is composed of hollow metal sections with flattened ends containing a hole or other device for joining. The sections can be stacked as high as needed and are quick to erect and dismantle.

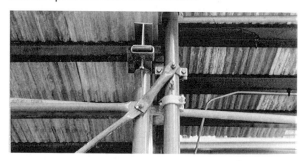

Sectional structure
A building that is put together at its site from prefabricated parts, made previously in a factory, and delivered to the site for erection. It differs from a modular structure, which is a factory-built complete room, or group of rooms. See also *Modular structure.*

Secured loan
A loan made in exchange for an interest in tangible collateral, such as property.

Security
Tangible property or items of value offered as collateral in the event of default on a loan. Also, actions taken to protect property or to limit risk of loss or physical danger, such as watching over a construction site.

Seepage pit
An area where solid wastes are held in a separate tank, and only the effluent passes to the pit for seepage into the soil, like a leaching field. Also called *sewage basin, cesspool.*

Segmental arch
A circular arch in which the intrados is less than a semicircle; an arch struck from one or more centers below the springing line.

Segmental pediment
A pediment above a door or window that takes the form of an arc of a circle.

Seismic
Relating to earthquakes.

Seismic code
Minimum earthquake requirements for a structure; most codes require seismic reinforcing if existing buildings are altered.

Seismic load
An earthquake load which acts both horizontally and vertically. The design value used to calculate the structural connections necessary to resist these loads varies with the locality type of facility and earthquake zone of the area.

Seismic reinforcement
Stabilization of outer walls, reinforcement of overhangs, and tying floors to walls—any or all of these may be required to bring a building up to code if it is renovated or adapted to a new use.

Select structural
A designation given to lumber of high quality in terms of appearance, strength, and stiffness.

Selective bidding
A process of competitive bidding where the owner selects the contractors who are invited to bid to the exclusion of all others, as opposed to open bidding.

Self-climbing crane
A type of crane used on tall buildings, which is moved hydraulically upward as the building is constructed. The building is literally built around the crane, which is supported on each successive floor.

Self-closing door
A door for the control of fire or smoke, which closes by itself by the action of a spring that is held open by a fusible link that melts in a fire, causing the door to close.

Self-supporting partition
A partition constructed of gypsum wallboard fastened to gypsum coreboard only, without any framing members involved. The partition can only support its own weight.

Semidetached house
A houses that shares a party wall with another house.

Semigloss paint
A paint or enamel that when dry, has some luster but is not very glossy.

Semirigid joint
A joint in either steel or concrete that is designed to permit some rotation; also called a *partially fixed joint*.

Separate contract
A prime contract which may be one of several on a building project for different portions of the work; as opposed to a subcontract, given by a prime contractor already contracted for a portion of the work to a sub-contractor.

Septic tank
A concrete or steel tank in which sewage is partially reduced by bacterial action. The liquids from the tank flow into the ground through a tile bed.

Series circuit
An electrical current set up so that the current goes through one load before it can go to the next; used in perimeter security systems. If the circuit is broken, an alarm system is activated.

Service area
An area of a building that supports the operation of the building, such as loading, parking, and waste collection.

Service cable
A cable supplying electricity to a building, either by an overhead wire or in an underground conduit.

Service conduit
A pipe that carries electrical service from the street to the service main in the building.

Service connection
The wiring from the outside power lines to a building's service entrance box.

Service core
A vertical element in a multistory structure, containing the elevators, vertical runs of most of the mechanical and electrical services, and the fire stairs. It is generally the first element to be constructed, and it then is used for vertical transportation during construction.

Service disconnect
A switch for disconnecting an entire building from electrical service.

Service entrance distribution box
The circuit breaker or fuse box located at the main service entrance.

Service entrance door
An exterior door in a building; used for deliveries, removal of waste, or by service personnel.

Service entrance equipment
The electrical equipment that makes up a home's service center; consists of the electric meter, disconnect switch, and distribution panel.

Service head
A type of weatherproof fixture at the top of a conduit on the exterior of a building, bringing electrical service into a building.

Service panel
A cabinet that is the main power distribution center, which receives incoming electricity and distributes it to the branch circuits. The panel contains the main disconnect switch, the grounding and neutral connections for the entire system, and fuses or circuit breakers for the branch circuits.

Service pipe
The section of pipe that connects the services of gas, water, or steam to a point within the building. In electrical work, the conduit or pipe that contains underground electrical service which connects to the meter.

Service stair
A stairway that is not used for general purposes but to provide access to specific areas such as the roof and equipment rooms.

Service switch
The main switch that connects all the lamps or motors in a building to the service wires.

Setback
The minimum regulated distance between a property line and a building. Also called *building line*.

Setting out
The process of establishing pegs, profiles, and levels for excavation and positioning buildings or marking out the position of walls on a floor slab.

Settlement
Movement in a structure due to consolidation of the soil beneath it. Also, a newly colonized region, or small community of homes.

Settling
The uneven vertical downward movement of a structure or parts of a structure, causing cracks in masonry or plaster and doors and windows that will not open easily.

Sewage ejector
An ejector pump used to pump sewage from holding tanks which collect sewage from appliances and fixtures that are installed lower than the adjacent public sewer main.

Sewer pipe
A conduit or pipe for carrying off wastewater or sewage.

Shake
Any thick, hand-split, edge-grained shingle or clapboard; formed by splitting a short log Into tapered sections.

Shank
The main body of a nail, bolt, screw, or other fastener, extending from below the head to the end or point.

Shear
A condition that exists when members meet each other. There is vertical shear in timber construction when the force acts across or perpendicular to the grain. Horizontal shear occurs when the forces cause sections of a member to slide across one another.

Shear panel
A vertical panel that is usually a minimum of 4 feet wide, that resists lateral forces by being anchored to both the bottom and top plate of the framing as well as the framing members on each end of the panel.

Shear panel

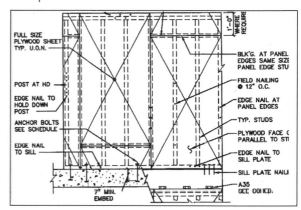

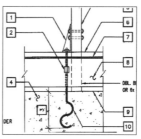

Shear reinforcement
Reinforcement designed and placed to resist shear forces, such as stirrups in reinforced concrete members.

Shear wall
A wall that resists shear forces in its own plane due to wind or earthquake forces.

Shear-plate connector
A type of wood-to-wood connector.

Sheathing
The wood covering placed over the exterior studding or rafters of a building, to provide a base for the application of wall or roof cladding.

Sheathing paper
An asphalt-impregnated or plain kraft building paper, used as an underlayment for walls, floors, and roofs to protect against moisture and the passage of air. Also called *building paper, felt, tar paper, roll roofing.*

Shed
A rough structure for shelter, storage, or a workshop; may be a separate building or a lean-to against another structure; often has one or more open sides.

Shed dormer
A dormer whose eave line parallels the ridge of the roof.

Shed dormer window
A dormer window whose eave line is parallel to the ridge.

Sheet glass
A float glass fabricated by drawing the molten glass from a furnace. The surfaces are not perfectly parallel, resulting in some distortion of vision. Used for ordinary window glass.

Sheet metal
A flat rolled metal, such as galvanized steel, aluminum, or copper, that has been rolled extremely thin, and used in the fabrication of ductwork, flashing, and gutters.

Sheet pile
A pile in the form of a plank, driven in close contact with others to provide a tight wall to resist the lateral pressure of water or adjacent earth.

Sheet piling
A series of piles driven in close contact, or interlocking with one another, to form a tight wall to resist the lateral thrust of earth or water. They are often corrugated in profile for added strength.

Sheet-metal roof
A roof covering of aluminum, copper, stainless steel, or galvanized metal sheets.

Sheet-metal screw
A self-tapping screw used in sheet-metal work. Large screws are driven into prepunched holes, while smaller screws only require a pierced hole. They come in various lengths and diameters. A pan head metal screw has a self-drilling point for fastening metal studs to the metal stud runner.

Sheet-metal worker
A tradesperson who fashions sheet metal into ducts and flashing, and who installs those completed components in the project.

Sheetrock
A proprietary name for gypsum wallboard. Also called *drywall, gypsum board, plaster board, wallboard.*

Shelf angle
A steel angle that supports a brick or masonry veneer.

Shelf life
Maximum interval during which a material may be stored and remain in a usable condition.

Shell
Any incomplete structural framework that is not filled in or occupied.

Shellac
A wood finisher and resin used in varnish, which produces a transparent shiny surface; often used to enhance and protect wood grain.

Shim
A thin piece, usually wedged-shaped, placed or driven into a joint to level or plumb a structural member. Also called *filler.*

Shingle
A roofing unit of wood, asphalt, slate, tile, concrete, asbestos cement, or other material that is cut to stock dimensions and thickness and used as an overlapping covering over sloping roofs and sidewalls.

Shingle nails
Used to install cedar shingles. These nails have small heads and thin shanks to avoid splitting the shingle.

Shiplap siding
Wood sheathing whose edges are rabbeted to make an overlapping joint.

Shoddy
Materials or standards of workmanship that is of a low quality; slang term for any inferior-quality work.

Shoe
A piece of timber, stone, or metal, shaped to receive the lower end of any member; also called a *soleplate.* Also, a metal base plate for an arch or truss shaped to resist the lateral thrust. Also called *plate, sole.*

Shoe mold
The small molding against the baseboard at the floor.

Shop drawing
Detailed drawing, diagram, illustration, schedule, performance chart, brochure, and other data prepared by the contractor, manufacturer, supplier, or distributor, that illustrate how specific portions of the work shall be fabricated or installed.

Shop painting
Painting metal components in a shop before shipping to the job site.

Shore
A temporary support used in compression as a temporary support for excavations or formwork or for propping up unsafe structures. Also called *timber brace.*

Shoring
The use of timbers to prevent the sliding of earth adjoining an excavation. Also, the use of timbers and adjustable steel or wooden devices placed in a slanted position as bracing against a wall, or used as temporary support during restoration.

Short circuiting
In electrical systems, an interrupted circuit.

Shotblasting
Cleaning a steel surface by projecting steel shot against it with compressed air.

Shotcrete
Cement mortar or concrete placed under pressure through the nozzle of a cement gun. Also called *gunnite*.

Shrinkage
A decrease in dimensions occurring when a material experiences temperature changes.

Shrinkage crack
A rift that appears in the surface of building materials such as concrete, masonry, and mortar joints, due to shrinkage.

Shrinkage reinforcement
Secondary reinforcement designed to resist shrinkage stresses in concrete; generally smaller in section than the structural steel.

Shut-off valve
A device used to shut off the flow of water or gas to a building, branch line, or fixture.

Shutter
One of a pair of movable panels used at window openings to provide privacy and protection from the elements when closed.

Shutter

Shutter bar
A hinged bar that can be pivoted around and fastened across the interior side of a pair of shutters.

Shutter box
A pocket on the inside of a window to store shutters when folded.

Shutter fastener
A pivoting device on the exterior side of a window that holds a shutter in the open position; often made of decorative wrought iron.

Shutters
Protective covering for the outside of windows, made of wood, metal, or vinyl. Louvered shutters are used for ventilation.

Siamese connection
A hose connection shaped like the letter Y, for the fire department to use in connecting water to the standpipe, found on the outside of a building, .

Sick building
A building that causes a higher-than-normal level of minor illness to its occupants. Typical symptoms are irritation to the eyes, nose, or throat; shortage of breath; dizziness; and general fatigue. Sick building syndrome is mainly associated with air-conditioned buildings and usually affects those who have no control over ventilation or heating or lighting levels.

Sick building syndrome
A situation in which building occupants experience acute health and discomfort effects that appear to be linked to time spent in a building, but no specific illness or cause can be identified.

Side gable
A gable on one side of a house, perpendicular to the main façade.

Sidelight
A framed area of fixed glass, set vertically on each side of a door, usually made up of a number of small panes.

Sidewalk
A paved walkway flanking a road, or leading to a building. Also called *pavement*.

Sidewalk bridge
A lightweight structural covering over a sidewalk used to protect pedestrians from construction or cleaning of the structures overhead.

Sidewalk elevator
An elevator for hauling materials to a basement, that rises flush with a sidewalk.

Siding
A finish covering of wood, aluminum, or asbestos-cement material, on the exterior walls of a wood-framed building.

Siding shingles
Wood, slate, or asbestos cement shingles installed over sheathing and sheathing paper on exterior walls of wood-framed buildings.

Silicone
A heat-stable compound, chemically inert, and used as sealant, insulator, and lubricator, in water-resistant film, heat-resistant paints, or other resins for electrical insulation.

Silicone acrylic caulking
Silicone is added to an acrylic latex mixture to make it more flexible, and it can be painted over.

Silicone sealant
A sealant that possesses a high degree of elasticity and resistance to weathering and can be applied at any temperature.

Sill plate
A heavy timber plate at the bottom of the frame of a wood structure resting directly on the foundation, and bolted to foundation.

Sill sealer
A waterproof material used to seal the joint between the top of the foundation and the bottom of a sill or soleplate.

Sillcourse
In stone masonry, a stringcourse set at the windowsill level; commonly differentiated from the wall by its greater projection, finish, or thickness.

Simple beam
A beam without restraint or continuity at the supports, as opposed to a fixed-end beam.

Single contract
A contract where a prime contractor is responsible for all the work.

Single-family dwelling
A house that is usually detached and designed to shelter a group of related individuals.

Single-hung window
A window with two sashes, only one of which opens.

Single-phase power
A 2- or 3-wire electrical distribution system, typically used for homes and small commercial buildings.

Single-pitched roof
A roof having only a single slope on each side of a central ridge, as compared to a shed roof, which has a single slope but not a central ridge.

Sinking foundation

A structural situation that occurs when the subgrade was insufficient when the structure was built, or it was improperly compacted. Signs of a sinking foundation are doors and windows that stick, nail pops, cracking at the joint between the ceiling and wall, or tell-tale sag in the roofline. To remedy it, foundations can be shored and undercut. Weak soil can be removed and concrete fill pumped in to stabilize it. The existing structure must be realigned and anchored to prevent further creep caused by the momentum of its misalignment. Underpinning the foundations may provide another solution. See also *Underpinning*.

Sit-down strike

A strike where the workers stay on the job site, but refuse to work.

Site

An area or plot of ground with defined limits on which a building, project, or part is located or proposed to be located; the specific location of a building or buildings. Also called *plot, property, lot*.

Site analysis services

Research and analysis services to determine the appropriateness of the selected site for the intended building program; may include studies of typography, natural features, prevailing winds, drainage, access, traffic flow, sound studies, surveying, and soil investigation.

Site and location evaluation

Part of a feasibility study that includes existing and planned uses of adjoining property; public services, transportation, and jobs; hidden assets of the area; entertainment and social offerings; and real estate sales and rental market.

Site audit

A review of activities and progress at a construction site, which may include videotape recording for posting on Web site intranets.

Site contamination

The degradation of land and buildings due to exposure to materials, processes, or organisms detrimental to health.

Site marker

A plaque or sign located at a historic site or building.

Site plan

A plan of a construction site showing the dimensions and contours of the lot and the dimensions of the building or portion thereof to be erected, including walkways, paved areas, and street frontage.

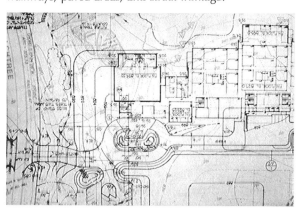

Site planning

The process involved in locating structures on a site, including buildings, parking, walkways, landscaped areas, and other features, such as views and vistas, solar orientation, grading considerations, watercourses, and existing natural site features.

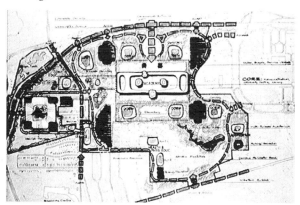

Site relationship

The relationship of a plot of land where something was, is, or will be located to its situation or position in a place, town, or building, especially with reference to the surrounding locality.

Site safety officer

The person responsible for carrying out a health and safety plan on site, and for seeing that the proper safety measures are taken during the progress of the work.

Site testing
Small sample tests carried out on the building, as a sample of how it will work on a larger scale.

Site work
Construction outside a building, including earthwork, landscaping, utilities, and paving.

Site-specific
A set of plans for a structure that is designed for a specific terrain and building lot, as opposed to one which could be built on any lot, such as in a tract development.

Sizing
A thin, pasty substance used as a sealer, binder, or filler; generally consists of a diluted glue, oil, or resin; often required as an underlayment in applying gold leaf.

Skeleton
The frame of a structure before any infill material or glazing is installed. Also called *framing*.

Skeleton construction
A system by which the loads are transmitted to the ground by a frame of columns and girders forming a three-dimensional grid, as opposed to construction with load-bearing walls.

Sketch
A rough drawing that represents the main features of a plan or building; used as a preliminary study.

Sketch plan
A free-hand sketch of a floor plan of an existing building done as part of a site investigation for restoration or renovation; to be translated later into a measured drawing and incorporated into the contract documents.

Skewed
Out of plumb, out of square, off level, or out of line with a standard reference.

Skewed beam
A structural member intersecting another at an angle other than 90 degrees.

Skilsaw
The brand name for a popular circular saw.

Skim coat
An application of a thin coat of joint compound over areas of a rough wall.

Skin
A non-load-bearing exterior wall, such as a curtain wall in an office building.

Skin repair
Repairs to a building's skin can be accomplished by pointing, patching, and cleaning. Other repairs involve replacement of roof elements, spalled materials, crack injections, or building flashings. See also *Reskinning*.

Skintled brickwork
In masonry, an irregular arrangement of bricks, with respect to the normal face of a wall; the bricks are set in and out so as to produce an uneven effect on the wall. Also, a rough effect caused by mortar being squeezed out of the joints.

Skip sheathing
The application of boards over rafters, joists, or wall framing, with a space between them to allow for breathing, as an underlayment for the application of shakes and shingles.

Skylight
An opening in a roof that is glazed with a transparent or translucent material used to admit natural or diffused light to the space below.

Skyscraper construction

A method of construction developed in Chicago, in which all building loads are transmitted to a metal skeleton, so that any exterior material is simply a protective cladding.

Skywalk

A walkway that is located over the ground level and the street; and often connects buildings across a street.

Slab

The upper part of a reinforced-concrete floor, that is carried on beams below. Also, a concrete mat poured on subgrade, serving as a floor rather than as a structural member.

Slab-on-grade

A concrete mat poured directly on the ground, that functions as a floor and not as a structural member.

Slate

A hard, brittle metamorphic rock characterized by good cleavage along parallel planes; used as cut stone in thin sheets for flooring, roofing, and panels and in granular form as surfacing on composition roofing.

Sledgehammer

A heavy hammer with a long handle and two chamfered square heads, used for driving stakes, or breaking rock or concrete, usually requiring the use of two hands.

Sleeper

A horizontal timber laid on a slab or on the ground and to which the subflooring is nailed. Also, any long horizontal beam, at or near the ground that distributes the load from the posts to the foundation.

Sleeve

A tube, or tubelike part fitting over or around another part. Also, a pipe used to provide openings for the installation of electric and plumbing services, used in solid concrete floors through which the services must pass. Also called a *sleeve chase*.

Slenderness ratio

In structural design, the resistance of a structural member to buckling under a compressive load, normally a consideration for a column. It is based on the ratio of the height of a wall, column, or pier to the radius of gyration of the member.

Sliced veneer

Wood veneer for which a log or sawn flitch is held securely in a slicing machine and the wood is sheared off in sheets.

Slide rule

A hand-held scale with a sliding center section, and a sliding clear marking device; used primarily for multiplying and dividing, but can provide more sophisticated calculations, such as square root, cube roots, and trigonometric functions.

Slider

A window with movable sections that slide back and forth to open and close.

Sliding door

A door that is mounted on a track in the floor that slides in a horizontal direction parallel to the wall on which it is mounted.

Sliding sash window

A window that moves horizontally in grooves, or between runners at the top and bottom of a window frame.

Slip form

A form that is raised as the concrete is placed. It can be raised vertically, or moved horizontally.

Slip joint
In brickwork, a type of joint made where a new wall is joined to an old wall by cutting a channel or groove in the old wall to receive the brick of the new wall. This method of joining the two walls forms a kind of telescopic, nonleaking joint.

Slope
The relationship of the vertical rise of a roof to the horizontal distance to the ridge. Thus, if a roof rises 3 feet vertically from the top of the wall plate, and is 12 feet from the outside of the wall plate to the centerline of the ridge, the slope is 3 in 12. Also called *slant, roof pitch*.

Slowdown
An organized action by a group of workers to slow the production of work in order to pressure management for a resolution to their cause, whether it be payment, benefits, or working conditions.

Slump
A measure of the consistency of concrete, mortar, or stucco by using the slump test method. See also *slump test*.

Slump cone
A metal mold in the form of a truncated cone, with an open bottom diameter of 8 inches, open top diameter of 4 inches, and a height of 12 inches.

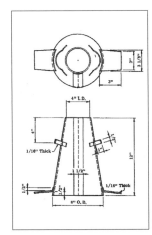

Slump test
Wet concrete, mortar, or stucco is placed in the top of a slump cone, and when full and leveled to the top, the cone is lifted vertically, leaving a cone-shaped pile of material. A ruler is used to measure the drop or slump in the top surface of the material from the original 12 inches of the slump cone. Concrete with a low water-to-cement ratio may have a slump of only 3 inches, while a very wet concrete may slump as much as 5 inches.

Slurry
A mixture of portland cement, slag, or clay in a solution where the particles are suspended in the liquid. It can be pumped into foundation formwork that is heavily reinforced, and fill the voids between the reinforcing.

Slurry wall
A foundation wall in an excavation that is heavily reinforced with steel and filled with a liquid concrete mixture by pouring or pumping.

Slurry wall

Small Business Administration (SBA)
A U.S. government agency that provides assistance to small businesses, including financial and management assistance to qualifying small businesses.

Smoke chamber
The portion of a chimney flue located directly over a fireplace.

Smoke control system
A system to control the movement of smoke during a fire within a building.

Smoke detector
A device that detects the presence of smoke and sounds an alarm.

Smoke vent
A covered opening in a roof which will open automatically when a fusible link melts, and allow the smoke to escape.

Smoke venting
Provision for allowing smoke from a building fire to escape rapidly into the atmosphere.

Snap-off anchor
A self-drilling anchor which is broken off after drilling so a bolt can be screwed into it.

Snips
A type of shears for cutting sheet metal. Also called *tin snips*.

Snow guard
A board, metal frame, or other device attached to portions of a sloped roof to prevent snow from sliding off the roof; often installed in rows, but particularly near the eaves.

Snow load
The superimposed load assumed to result from severe snowfalls in any particular region.

Society for Commercial Archeology
A group that focuses on the preservation of roadside architecture.

Society of Architectural Historians
An organization composed of architectural historians, architects, educators, and others interested in architectural history. The society sponsors a Historic Preservation Committee, promotes preservation of significant architectural landmarks, and conducts tours of historic buildings and districts.

Socket wrench
A wrench with a recessed socket that fits over a bolt, and a ratchet device for tightening the bolt by turning the wrench in one direction to tighten it and returning it for another turn.

Sod roof
A roof composed of a thick layer of earth; frequently pitched or barrel shaped and supported by logs, or by a concrete form with a vapor barrier. Now considered a plus in Green Design criteria.

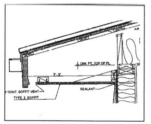

Soffit vent
An opening in the underside of a roof overhang, which provides ventilation to the soffit area.

Soft costs
Development expenses not attributable to the purchase of property or construction, such as interest on borrowed funds, architectural and other fees, marketing costs, and incidental expenses.

Software
Computer programs and associated instructional materials for many business, professional, and construction-related uses.

Softwood
The wood from needle-bearing conifer trees, regardless of the softness or hardness of the wood itself. Types include cedar, cypress, Douglas fir, hemlock, pine, Redwood, and spruce.

Soil gases
Gases that may enter a building generated from the surrounding soil.

Soil investigation
A complete examination and testing of surface and subsurface soil and conditions on a site. The results published in a report may affect the design of the structure.

Soil pipe
A vertical drain pipe conveying waste matter from a water closet to the drainage system of the building. Also called a *soil stack* or *waste stack*.

Soil report
A report from a geological engineer providing specific information on the subsurface conditions that may affect the design of foundations and footings.

Soil sample
A sample of soil taken from a specific location of a construction site, either by boring or other method, to test in a laboratory for its bearing capacity.

Soil stack
The main vertical pipe that receives wastewater from all fixtures in a building.

Soil test
A test to confirm that land for a private septic system can percolate sufficiently, or to indicate the type of septic system to be used. A soil test can determine how land will compact during development. It can be used to gather data for drainage issues, foundation issues, or compaction, particularly in relation to its suitability for load bearing.

Soil-bearing capacity
The load that a soil can support without excessive settlement; usually expressed in pounds per square foot or tons per square foot.

Soil-testing laboratory
A laboratory especially equipped to test soil samples, such as the compressive strength of the soil, or the tendency of the sample soil to absorb moisture.

Solar access
A legal right to have access to sunlight; an outgrowth of the energy crisis, which led many communities to pass laws to restrict development of structures that might obstruct such access.

Solar collector
A heat exchanger that collects solar radiation and converts it to energy; consisting either of a flat panel with a series of photovoltaic cells, or one composed of air or water circulating over a black surface and covered with a transparent material. It uses the heat absorbed from the sun to warm fluids such as potable water for a building's hot water system, and stores them in an insulated storage tank for household use.

Solar collector

Solar degradation
The characteristic of a material to be deteriorated by the ultraviolet rays in sunlight.

Solar heat exchanger
A method of transferring the heat gained from solar collectors that is kept in storage to the area to be heated.

Solar heating, passive
A solar heating system that relies on the natural flow of heat by using a building's site orientation, design, and construction to collect, store, and distribute heat with a minimal use of fans or pumps.

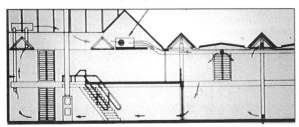

Solar house
A house designed internally, and oriented on the site to take maximum advantage of the sun's rays to produce solar energy for heating the house; generates more than half of its annual heat by using active, passive, or a hybrid system of collection and storage of solar energy.

Solar orientation
The placing of a building in relation to the sun to maximize the amount of heat gained during the coldest months and minimize the amount of heat gained during the warmest months.

Solar orientation

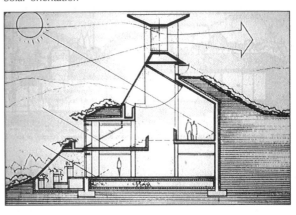

Solar radiation
The energy radiated from the sun, particularly in the infrared range which is received as heat. The types of radiation include direct, the most intense; diffused, as sunlight passes through other substances, such as clouds and haze; and reflected radiation that is bounced off the ground or other objects.

Solar resistance
The ability of a material to resist the damaging properties of solar radiation.

Solar storage
The storage of heat generated by solar energy.

Solar water heater
Water heated by solar energy is stored in an insulated tank for use when needed; includes a pump to circulate the water, a drain valve to empty the solar panels in cold weather, insulated piping, and sensors to monitor and control the system operations.

Solder
A metallic alloy which is melted with a soldering gun to join metals; used in plumbing work and for splicing lead cables.

Solder joint
A joint in copper tubing whereby the pipe fits into a fitting; the assembly is heated and solder is drawn into the joint.

Soldering gun
A tool with a pistol grip and a small electrically heated bit to melt solder to join parts together.

Solderless connector
An insulated wire nut which is screwed onto the ends of wires to make a connection. A cone-shaped spiral spring inside the nut presses the skinned wires together, replacing the need for solder.

Sole proprietorship
A business that is run by a single individual, who may or may not have employees.

Soleplate
The horizontal member which rests on the rough floor, and to which the vertical studs are nailed.

Solid bridging
A form of lateral stiffening between timber joists used to prevent them from twisting and to provide a fire stop. Short lengths of wood similar in depth are fixed between each adjacent pair of joists.

Solid-core door
A wood flush door having a solid core of lumber or particleboard or some mineral composition.

Solid-web joist
A conventional joist with a solid web formed by a plate or rolled section, as opposed to an open-web joist.

Solvent
(1) A liquid chemical compound used for cleaning, dissolving, and thinning a compatible substance. (2) The financial condition of a person or business that is capable of paying current bills, and one with no debt against it.

Solvent weld
The joining of plastic pipe by using a solvent to dissolve the interface of the parts being joined, so they can fuse together and consolidate when dried.

Sound barrier
Any solid obstacle that is relatively opaque to sound that blocks the line of sight between a sound source and the point of reception of the sound.

Sound insulation
Materials or methods of construction designed to resist the transmission of airborne and structure-borne sounds through walls, floors, and ceilings.

Sound lock
A vestibule or entranceway that has highly absorptive walls and ceiling and a carpeted floor; used to reduce transmission of noise into an auditorium, rehearsal room, or studio from the area outside.

Sound transmission
Sound passing from one room to another, normally through an air return plenum, or through a material, construction, or other medium.

Sound-insulating glass
Glass consisting of two lights in resilient mountings, separated by spacers and sealed so as to leave an airspace between them. The airspace contains a dessicant to assure dehydration of the trapped air.

Soundproofing
The application of sound-deadening material to walls, ceilings, and floors to prevent sound from passing through.

Space audit
A physical survey and record of the space that is occupied and its functional use.

Space heater
A small self-contained heater or hot-air furnace with a fan, either gas or electrical, used to heat a room.

Space planning
The definition of space in terms of size, type, activity, and adjacency for any particular type of space.

Space standards
Minimum dimensions needed in a building for various activities. Some are established by law, such as minimum widths for fire exits, or by social convention, experience, or design practices.

Space utilization
The ratio of the number of people using a space to its potential use capacity, multiplied by the ratio of hours of actual usage to the total available hours, which is then expressed as a percentage.

Spacer
A metal device that holds reinforcement bars at a proper height above the desired finished level, or from the proper distance from the edge of a beam; spacers are placed in wall forms to keep them apart during the placement of concrete. Also, small plastic pieces of uniform thickness placed between ceramic tiles or concrete paving tiles during installation to assure uniform joints.

Spackle
A paste to fill holes, cracks, and defects in the surfaces of various materials.

Spall
A small fragment or chip dislodged from the face of a stone or masonry unit by a blow or by the action caused by the elements, such as a freezing and thawing cycle.

Spalling
The loss of surface material from stone or concrete as the result of a buildup of stresses below the surface which fractures the material. Rusting steel-reinforcing bars and water infiltration are the two main causes.

Span
The clear open distance between any two consecutive supports of a beam, girder, or truss, or between the opening of an arch.

Span table
A chart listing the maximum allowable spans for structural members based on the size of the member, spacing, loads anticipated, and allowable stresses for that particular species of wood.

Spandrel
The triangular space that is formed between the sides of adjacent arches and the line across their tops. In a skeletal frame building, the area inside the columns and between the top of the windows and the sill above.

Spandrel glass
An opaque glass used in curtain walls to conceal spandrel beams, columns, or other internal structural construction.

Spandrel wall
A wall built on the extrados of an arch, filling the spandrels.

Spanish roof tile
A clay roofing tile, semicylindrical in shape, laid with the curved side alternating up and down.

Spar varnish
A varnish that is resistant to salt, sun, and water.

Special conditions
An entry in the contract documents that describes special or unique conditions to a particular project; separate from the general conditions and supplemental conditions.

Special hazards insurance
Protection against additional perils to property, such as water damage from sprinkler leakage, and coverage for materials in transit to the site or stored off-site; usually taken out at the request of the contractor, or the option of the owner.

Special use permit
The right to use a piece of property for uses that are otherwise not permitted in that particular area. See also *Variance*.

Specialties
A category of construction materials used in the finishing of the structure. See also *Specialty contractor*.

Specialty contractor
A contractor who typically installs certain specific items, such as windows, roofing, flooring, and tile.

Specification
A set of written requirements that accompany the drawings, which provide additional detail and description of the materials and workmanship; they also provide additional technical standards to be met during construction.

Speculation
A project built at one's own expense, without an owner in mind, in the hopes of selling or leasing it upon the project's completion.

Speculative builder
A contractor who develops a property or tract of land, then constructs a building, or series of buildings, on the speculation that they will be sold or leased in the future.

Spike
A heavy nail, usually with a rectangular cross-section.

Spindle
A turned wood architectural element, produced on a lathe, and used as banisters or ornamental spindlework on porches and other locations.

Spindlework
Wood ornament with circular cross-sections, such as balusters turned on a lathe; used on stairs, porches, and in gable ends of Victorian-style homes.

Spiral reinforcing
Continuous cylindrical reinforcing in the form of a helix; used to reinforce circular columns.

Spiral stair
A flight of stairs, circular in plan, whose treads wind around a central newel, or post. Also called *winding stair*.

Spire
A slender pointed element on top of a building; generally with a narrow octagonal pyramid set above a square tower.

Spirit level
A leveling instrument used for testing the horizontal or vertical position of any structural member.

Splash block
A small masonry block placed under the bottom end of a downspout to spread water away from the building.

Splayed jamb
Any jamb whose face is not at right angles to the wall in which it is set.

Splayed mullion
A mullion that joins two glazed units that are at an angle to each other, such as the mullion of a bay window.

Splayed window
A window whose frame is set at an angle with respect to the face of the wall.

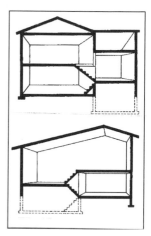

Split-face block
A concrete block with a textured roughened face that resembles stone.

Split-level house
A house with a kitchen, dining room, and living room area on the main floor, with stairs leading up to the bedrooms at a half-story higher. Other stairs may lead downward from the main floor to a family room. Other stairs may lead to a utility room or basement under the upper main level. This style was popular in the United States after 1950.

Spontaneous combustion
The instantaneous bursting into flames of a substance due to a chemical reaction of its own constituents, such as oily rags in an unventilated pile of rubbish.

Spot weld
Holding two pieces of metal together by a series of spots rather than a continuous weld. Also called a *tack weld,* which is used to hold pieces together for further continuous welding.

Spot zoning
An action taken by a municipality to change the intended use of the land in one particular area, or piece of property; usually based on a request for a zoning variance.

Spotting nails
Covering exposed nail or screw heads in gypsum board with joint compound.

Spout
A short channel or tube used to spill stormwater from gullies, balconies, or exterior galleries so that the water will fall clear of the building. Also in the shape of a *gargoyle.*

Spray gun
A mechanical device that uses compressed air to force paint or other liquid coatings through a nozzle for application by spraying, which produces a fine, even coat over the surface. The surrounding areas must be masked or protected from the spray.

Sprayed fireproof insulation
A mixture of mineral fiber with other ingredients, applied by air pressure with a spray gun; used to provide fire protection or thermal insulation.

Spraying asbestos
Spraying steel structural members with a fire-resistant coating of asbestos fibers mixed with cement and water.

Splice
The connection of two similar materials by overlapping, tying, welding, gluing, or joining by mechanical couplers.

Spline
A thin, flat piece of wood used between two pieces of heavy subflooring, taking the place of a tongue-and-groove joint; also used as a means of stiffening a miter joint.

Spline joint
A joint formed by inserting a spline of long strips of wood or metal in a slot cut into the two butting members.

Split ring connector
A metal ring used in a method of connecting members of a wood truss or built-up beam. The metal ring, often fitted with grooved teeth for driving into one member, is installed into a bored circular slot in the other piece, and then connected with a bolt drilled through the center of the metal ring.

Spraying asbestos

Asbestos was used on structures prior to 1986, then banned and removed from any structure where it presented a health risk, or when renovating a structure containing the material.

Spread footing
A footing in a foundation that is wider than the wall or column it supports. A spread footing distributes the vertical load over a wider area.

Spreadsheet
A sheet with multiple columns, used for tabulating estimates and sub-bids in the process of preparing a bid proposal. There are computer programs that provide an electronic adaptation of that same principle, yet more interactive, whereby a change in one figure automatically recalculates those that would be affected by the change.

Sprinkler head
A nozzle on a run of a sprinkler line that is activated by a heat-sensitive device to release water in the event of a fire. See also *Sprinkler system.*

Sprinkler system
A system, usually automatic, for protection against fire. When activated, it sprays water over a large area in a systematic pattern.

Spruce
A white to light brown or red-brown, straight, and even-grained wood; moderately low density and strength; relatively inexpensive; used for general utility lumber.

Spud wrench
An adjustable wrench with wide parallel jaws, used for the large locknuts on plumbing drain pipes.

Square
A quantity of materials, such as shakes, shingles, siding, or other roofing materials sufficient to cover an area of 100 square feet when applied in an appropriate manner.

Square measure
The measure of an area in square units, or one unit times itself, used in estimating construction; inches, feet, yards, and miles.

Square roof
A roof where rafters meet at the ridge in a 90-degree angle.

Squared splice
In carpentry, a type of spliced joint especially designed to resist tension; the pieces to be joined are cut to fit into each other and reinforced with a metal fish plate that holds them securely together.

Squint brick
A brick manufactured with an angular corner; commonly used in the construction of oblique corners.

Stability
The ability to remain unchanged after being acted upon by some force.

Stabilize
According to the Secretary of the Interior's standards, "to reestablish a weather resistant enclosure and the structural stability of an unsafe or deteriorated property while maintaining the essential form as it exists at the present."

Stabilized soil
Earth that has been treated with a binder such as portland cement, bitumen, resin, or a more soluble soil to reduce its movement.

Stack
A large chimney, often with a group of flues inside. Also, the vertical main of a soil, waste, or vent piping system.

Stack vent
Extension of a waste or soil stack above the highest horizontal drain that is connected to the stack.

Staff
Ornamental plastering, made in molds and reinforced with fiber, usually nailed or wired into place.

Staggered joints
End joints on boards or sheathing that are alternated so that they do not fall in line with other joints on rafters or wall framing, thus strengthening the continuity of the structure.

Staggered partition
Two rows of studs that are thinner than the top and bottom plates and are alternately offset from the surface of the plates. Each side of the wall is attached to the alternate stud. A staggered partition is used to prohibit the passage of sound through the wall.

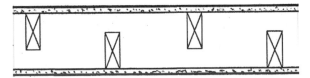

Staging
Temporary wooden or steel tubing scaffolding with wooden planks, placed in work areas on a building that allow workers to perform tasks above the ground level. Also called *scaffold.*

Stain

A coloring liquid or dye for application to any porous material, most often wood; thinner than paint and readily absorbed by the wood so that the texture and grain of the wood are enhanced; a discoloration on a piece of lumber, or any other blemish on a material.

Stained glass

Glass given a desired color in its molten state or by firing a stain into the surface of the glass after forming; used for decorative windows or transparent mosaics.

Staining

An effect on the surface of concrete in a building caused by reactions within the concrete, rust caused by the deterioration of steel reinforcing, or efflorescence caused by lime that has leached from the concrete.

Stainless steel

A high-strength, tough steel alloy; contains chromium with nickel as an additional alloying element and is highly resistant to corrosion and rust.

Stainless-steel pipe

A pipe used primarily for its resistance to corrosion in applications such as chemical, petroleum, or food-processing industries; available in various diameters and lengths, and in sizes corresponding to copper tubing.

Stair

A series of steps or flights of steps for going between two or more successive levels with connecting landings at each level, either on the exterior or in the interior.

Stair carriage

A stringer that supports the treads and risers on stairs.

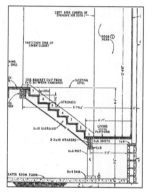

Stair riser

The vertical part of a stair step.

Stair tower

A structure containing a stair that fills it exactly; a stair enclosure that projects beyond the roof.

Stair tread
The horizontal part of a stair step that is walked upon.

Staking out
Marking off a building site for excavating using wooden stakes and string.

Standard
A grade of lumber that falls between construction grade and utility grade, and is suitable for general construction and light framing; applies to lumber 2–4 inches thick and 2–4 inches wide.

Standard forms
Preprinted contract document forms used in the construction industry; some are available from the American Institute of Architects, as well as the Association of General Contractors.

Standards of professional practice
Standards developed by professional societies as guidelines for members in conducting professional practices.

Standby lighting
A lighting system that will supply adequate illumination if the normal system should fail; usually supplied by an emergency generator.

Standby power
The power that is available within 1 minute of a power failure to operate life safety equipment and continuously operating equipment. Emergency power is the power available within 10 seconds.

Standing seam joint
In metal roofing, a type of joint between the adjacent sheets of material, made by turning up the edges of two adjacent sheets and then folding them over.

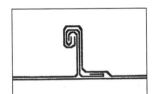

Standing seam roof
A sheet-metal roof with folded seams between adjacent sheets of metal.

Standpipe system
An arrangement of piping, valves, hose connections, and allied equipment installed in a building with the hose connections located so that water can be discharged in streams or spray patterns through attached hoses and nozzles, to extinguish a fire and protect a building, its contents, and occupants.

Staple
A U-shaped metal brad with a double point, used to fasten plastic or other sheathing to building walls or other wood framing members.

Staple gun
A mechanical device designed to drive staples into materials; either manually operated or electrically powered.

Stapler
A device for applying staples; may be mechanical or air operated, which is more capable of driving staples into hard materials at a high rate of speed.

Stapling hammer
A stapling machine similar to a hammer; the staple is inserted into the material when the head of the stapler is struck against the material being fastened.

Star drill
A steel drill with a star-shaped point, used to drill holes in masonry when struck with a heavy hammer or sledgehammer.

Static pressure
The steady pressure inside an air duct in a heating, ventilation, and air-conditioning (HVAC) system, when the unit is in operation with the fan running, and the system has reached a point of equilibrium where air flow and pressure remain at a constant value.

Statically indeterminate structure
A situation wherein the stresses in a framework of members cannot be computed using the basic laws of statics, and where more sophisticated mathematical methods are required for the structural design solution.

Statics
The principle used in structural engineering that analyzes and determines the forces acting on a body at rest. There are three basic laws of statics: the summation of all horizontal forces must equal zero; the summation of all vertical forces must equal zero; and the rotation about any point must equal zero.

Statute
A law that has become a permanent rule of procedure.

Statute of limitations
A statute specifying the period of time within which legal action must be brought for alleged damages or injury. In construction industry cases, some jurisdictions define the period as commencing with completion of the work or services performed.

Steam boiler
A boiler in which water is raised to or above saturation temperature at a desired pressure, and the resultant steam is drawn off for use in the heating system.

Steam heating
The process of heating a space by using steam created by heating water in a pressurized boiler, and circulating it through pipes to radiators in the space. The steam cools and returns back into the boiler as water, to be reheated and recirculated.

Steel
A hard and malleable metal when heated; produced by melting and refining it according to the carbon content; used for structural shapes due to its alloy of iron and carbon, which has a malleable high tensile strength.

Steel casement
A casement window made of steel sections; incorporated most often into masonry structures.

Steel erector
A specialty contractor who places, plumbs, and fastens all members in a steel structure.

Steel forms
Removable pieces of steel that hold wet concrete in the desired shapes for casting foundations, footings, and window frames on the spot. Some formwork comes with interlocking modular hardware. This type is long lasting, and it produces a clean, accurate face and is easier to set up, take down, and clean than wooden forms.

Steel forms

Steel shutters
Used in fortifications or in ordinary buildings when security is an issue, or if strong winds are a regular occurrence.

Steel square
An instrument having at least one right angle and two or more straight edges; used by carpenters for testing the accuracy of right angles and for laying out work.

Steel stud
A bent steel sheet-metal stud with holes punched out in the widest face; used as interior framing for drywall construction.

Steel tape
A flexible steel tape used for measuring. When not in use, the tape coils up in a case made for that purpose. Steel tapes are used to measure distances longer than is possible with a 6-foot folding rule, and they are available in 25-, 50-, and 100-foot lengths.

Steel troweling
A steel hand trowel, or a machine, with a series of trowels attached to a rotating ring, that creates a smooth, dense surface finish to concrete.

Steel wool
A pad of loosely woven steel fibers; used to clean metal surfaces and smooth wood surfaces to a high gloss.

Steel-framed structure

A building framed with steel members, including studs and rafters if it fits the building's use. If the steel is covered with a fire-retardant material, and gypsum wallboard is used, it will essentially be fireproof as well.

Steelworker

A craftsman skilled in erecting structural steel frameworks, or installing reinforcing steel for concrete.

Stencil

A sheet of heavy card stock with letters, numbers, or designs cut out of the sheet, which is placed on the object or surface to be marked and paint is applied over the cutouts, leaving the shapes of the cutout marked on the surface.

Stenciling

Repetitive decorative patterns applied by brushing or spraying paint onto the surface through openings cut in the stencil.

Step

A stair unit that consists of one tread, the horizontal upper surface, and one riser, the vertical face. Also called *tread*.

Step ladder

A self-supporting ladder in the form of an A-frame, with small treads on one side of the frame, and supporting legs on the other, connected by a collapsible hinge. When closed it can be easily moved from place to place.

Stepped flashing

A metal flashing used at the intersection of a wall and a sloping roof. The upper edge steps down following the inclination of the roof. The horizontal edge is inserted into a reglet.

Stepped footing

A perimeter foundation in which the footing descends in steplike sections; used in hillside construction.

Stepped voussoir

A voussoir that is squared along its upper surfaces so that it fits horizontal courses of masonry units.

Stepped windows

A series of windows, usually in a wall adjacent to a staircase, arranged in a stepped pattern that generally follows the steps' profile.

Stepped-back chimney

Any exterior brick chimney that is wide enough at the base to enclose a large fireplace in the kitchen, then decreasing in area in several steps, possibly collecting other flues from the upper floor.

Stereo photogrammetry

A process of accurately surveying property by taking two overlapping photographs from two vantage points in the survey plane, then projecting them in a stereo plotter to produce a three-dimensional image. The lines where the two photographs intersect are then plotted as the accurate contour of those points.

Stereobate

The substructure, foundation, or solid platform upon which a building is erected. In a columnar building, it includes the uppermost step or platform upon which the columns stand.

Stereogram
A drawing or photograph that can be viewed three-dimensionally.

Stereoscope
An instrument for viewing a stereoscopic pair of photographs three-dimensionally; consists of two lenses set at the correct distance apart to correspond with the separation of the stereoscopic camera lens.

Stereoscopic camera
A camera designed to produce two displaced images, called a stereoscopic pair, by means of two matched lenses and shutters, so that when viewed by a person in a stereoscope, it gives a three-dimensional view of the object.

Stick-built roof
A roof built on the site from individual members rather than from prefabricated roof trusses.

Stiffener plate
A steel plate attached to a structural member or joint to support it against a heavy local force.

Stiffness
The capacity of a member or framework to resist imposed loads without excessive deflection.

Stile
One of the upright structural members of a frame, such as at the outer edge of a door or a window sash.

Stippled
A texture imparted to plaster with the bristles of a stiff brush, applied by driving the bristles directly at the surface, rather than by using painting strokes.

Stippling brush
A brush with short stiff bristles used to give a stippled texture to plaster; can be made by cutting short the long bristles of a paint brush.

Stipulated sum agreement
An agreement wherein a fixed sum of money is allotted for the performance of the work outlined in the agreement.

Stirrup
In concrete construction, reinforcement to resist shear; normally consists of a U-shaped bar, anchored to the longitudinal side and placed perpendicular to it.

Stock
Material that is standard-size, kept on hand, and made readily available from a supplier's stock; such as precut lengths of framing lumber, door and window frames, hardware, and other standard building components.

Stock size
Material or product available in a variety of sizes readily available for purchase in the place of business, and that does not have to be specially ordered.

Stone
Native rock that has been processed by shaping, cutting, or sizing for building or landscaping use. It is fire resistant and varies according to type, from fairly porous to impregnable. There are three basic types of stone: igneous, such as granite, which is long lasting and durable; sedimentary, such as limestone, which is made up of organic remains; metamorphic rock, which is either igneous or sedimentary transformed by pressure and heat or both.

Stone house
A house constructed entirely of stone.

Stonemason
An artisan skilled in dressing and laying stone for buildings and other purposes.

Stool
The flat piece upon which a window closes, corresponding to the sill of a door.

Stoop
A platform or small porch at the entrance to a house, usually up several steps.

Stop
The molding or trim on the inside face of a door or window frame against which the door or window closes.

Stop work order
A written order from an owner or building inspector informing the contractor to cease construction, until the condition that caused the order is corrected.

Stored materials and equipment
Materials and equipment stored on the job site or in a remote location approved by the owner for future installation or use on the project. In certain instances, the contractor may bill for the materials upon delivery and storage.

Storefront
The front façade of a ground-level shop with glass display windows in minimal-sized mullions, and a recessed entrance to accommodate the outward swing of doors.

Storm cellar
An underground cellar designed to afford protection against violent windstorms, such as tornadoes. Also called *basement, substructure.*

Storm collar
A cone-shaped piece of sheet metal installed around a pipe vent that protrudes through a roof; to shed water.

Storm door
Auxiliary exterior door, installed in the same frame as the entrance door to a house, to provide added protection from inclement weather. Also called *auxiliary door.*

Storm porch
Enclosed porch that protects the entrance to a house from severe weather.

Storm sewer
A sewer designed to carry away water from storms, but not sewage. A storm sewer terminates in a river, dry lake, or natural drainage basin. Also called *sanitary sewer.*

Storm window
An auxiliary window; usually placed in the same frame with the existing window, to provide additional protection against severe weather. Also called *auxiliary window.*

Story
The space in a building between floor levels. In some codes a basement is considered a story; a cellar is not.

Straight-flight stair
A stair extending in only one direction.

Straight-line depreciation
A depreciation deduction which is calculated by subtracting any anticipated salvage value from the initial cost or value of the improvements, divided by the estimated economic life of the improvements into that figure.

Strain
The deformation caused by stress. See also *Stress.*

Strain gauge
An electrical or mechanical device used in tests to measure the strain in objects under loadings to determine their structural properties. The most common have two needles that move together while the stress is being applied. When the material fails, one needle representing the force applied returns to zero, while the other remains stationary at the highest point of rupture. This allows the operator to get an accurate reading of the test.

S-trap
A plumbing fitting shaped like the letter S on its side; installed in a drain line to prevent gases from the sewer from entering the line. See also *P-trap.*

Strap
A thin piece of metal of any required dimension used to attach, secure, or fasten an object to another. Also called *steel connector.*

Strap hanger
Metal bars with a rectangular cross-section that is bent into a channel shape and used to attach beams to purlins; also called a *stirrup.*

Strap hinge
A surface-mounted hinge with two leaves; one is fastened to the door, and the other secured to the door frame or post.

Strap pipe hanger
In plumbing work, a metal strap or band nailed or screwed to the ceiling or rafter and slung around a suspended pipe.

Straw bale house
A dwelling constructed of bales of straw, compressed and tied by wires into blocks held in place with vertical poles of wood or metal. The walls are covered with stucco or plaster. Once used on the frontiers, they are gaining popularity with ecological architects, as they are environmentally friendly, inexpensive, and very easy to construct.

Streamlined specifications
Specifications written in an abbreviated manner, yet containing all the technical information for the construction of the work.

Streetscape
A distinguishing and pictorial character of a scenario made up of buildings grouped in combination with other elements, landscaping, and street furniture, including paving, fences, benches, lampposts, mailboxes, utility poles, transit shelters, trash receptacles, street signs, and commercial signs. Other elements that contribute to a streetscape are existing building heights, proportions of façades, solids to voids, patterns of the materials on the buildings and pavement, and colors and textures. It is a smaller-scale version of a townscape or cityscape.

Strength of materials
A branch of physics dealing with stress, strain, rupture, and general behavior of materials or structural members subjected to applied loadings.

Stress
The total internal forces per unit of area, or the stress divided by the area. Types of stress include: allowable stress, the maximum permitted under the building code, which includes a factor of safety; bending stress, or that resulting from bending; combined stress, the cumulative effect of two or more loading conditions; compressive stress, or squeezing together; design stress, the stress under the design load; residual stress, or that remaining after removal of the load; tensile stress, or pulling apart; torsional stress, or twisting; ultimate stress, the maximum stress a material can take before failing; working stress, or actual stress on the member; and yield stress, where a permanent deformation occurs when the load is removed. See also *strain*.

Stress grading
The strengths of different types of woods as determined by laboratory testing, which include bending, shear, and compressive tests.

Stressed skin construction
A type of construction consisting of panels or sections having wood frames to which plywood or other sheet material is bonded with glue, so that the covering carries a large part of the load.

Stressed skin panel
A panel constructed of plywood and seasoned lumber. The simple framing and plywood skin act as a total unit to resist loads.

Stresses
Forces on a member caused by loads. Torsion is caused by twisting forces, compression by pushing forces, tension by pulling forces, and shear by cutting forces.

Stress-graded lumber
A grade applied to lumber for use in specific applications, based on the characteristics of the wood, such as the rate of growth, grain characteristics, and the number of knots, checks, and other defects.

Stretcher
A masonry unit laid horizontally with its length in the direction of the face of the wall.

Stretcher bond
In masonry, a bond which consists entirely of stretchers, with each vertical joint lying between the centers of the stretchers above and below.

Striated block
A concrete block that has a series of comblike striations on its face; usually perpendicular to the bed of the block, resulting in a vertical texture.

Striated face plywood
The patterned face of a plywood panel that has been given a striated texture of closely spaced shallow grooves, similar to the surface of Texture 1-11. See also *Texture 1-11*.

Strike clauses
Clauses that provide relief for the contractor in the event of strikes by employees or employees of companies critical to the performance of the work; includes provisions for security of the job site, and time extensions.

Striking plate
A metal plate fastened to the door jamb against which the bolt of the lock strikes, until it settles into a hole in the plate, thus closing the door.

Stringcourse
A horizontal band of masonry, extending across the façade to mark a division in a wall, may be flush or projecting, molded, or richly carved.

Stringer
A horizontal piece of timber or steel that connects the uprights in a framework and supports the floor; the inclined member that supports the treads and risers of a stair. Also called *carriage*.

Strip
To remove formwork from a concrete pour. Also, to remove old paint or lacquer with paint remover or other solvent.

Strip flooring
A long, narrow strip of wood, usually made with tongue-and-groove along its sides and sometimes along its ends as well.

Strip gutter
A continuous section of wood covered with a corrosion-resistant metal, fastened at a right angle to the pitch of the roof near the bottom of the slope to direct the flow of water along the edge of the roof.

Stripping
Removing forms from poured concrete after it has hardened.

Struck joint
A masonry joint from which excess mortar has been removed by a stroke of the trowel, leaving a flush joint. See also *Weather-struck joint*.

Struck molding
A molding cut into, rather than added to or planted onto, another member.

Structural analysis
Part of a feasibility study that includes examining the structural stability of a building, the mechanical systems, and the cost of code compliance.

Structural attachment
An attachment that is designed to carry or transfer a load; often made of metal and attached to another load-bearing structural member.

Structural clay tile
Building units molded from surface clay and molded into various shapes, some with hollow cavities.

Structural damage
Damage caused by improper design or poor construction or application of loads that the building was not supposed to carry or changes in the building environment, such as adjacent excavation for new construction undermining the foundations, placing stresses on the soil that change the way loads are carried, reverberation from traffic, or pile driving at a nearby site.

Structural design
Application of structural engineering to the design of an assembly of materials to provide a safe structure.

Structural engineering
A branch of engineering concerned with the design and construction of structures to withstand physical forces or displacements without danger of collapse or without loss of serviceability or function.

Structural failure
A rupture or other failure of a structural member to fulfill its intended function of carrying a load.

Structural frame
Consists of all members in a structure that are tied together to carry the imposed loads to the substructure, and hence to the ground.

Structural glass
Glass that is cast in the form of cubes, rectangular blocks, tile, or large rectangular plates: used widely for the surfacing of walls.

Structural glue-laminated timber
Wooden structural members that are formed by gluing smaller selected boards together.

Structural lumber
Lumber used for framing that has dimensions larger than a 2 × 4.

Structural member
Those members in a framing system that are designed to withstand imposed loads as well as their own weight.

Structural panel
A panel manufactured to performance standards for use in structural applications; composed of wood chips, plywood veneers, wafer board, or similar material.

Structural pipe
Round pipe used for structural purposes, either vertically or horizontally; due to its round cross section, it is stable as a vertical column or a horizontal brace against vertical sheet piling. See also *Caisson*.

Structural plywood
An exterior plywood composed of the highest grade; used for flooring, roofing, and siding.

Structural shape
A hot-rolled steel beam of standardized cross section, temper, size, and alloy; includes angle iron, channels, tees, I-beams, and H-sections. All are commonly used for structural purposes.

Structural shape

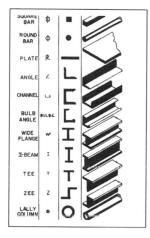

SQUARE BAR	▯	■
ROUND BAR	φ	●
PLATE	₧	
ANGLE	∠	L
CHANNEL	⊔	
BULB ANGLE	BULB∠	
WIDE FLANGE	w	
I-BEAM	I	I
TEE	T	T
ZEE	Z	
LALLY COLUMN	●	O

Structural stability
The relative structural soundness of an existing building or structure based on current and projected dead load, live load, wind, and seismic load factors.

Structural steel
Steel rolled in a variety of shapes and fabricated for use as load-bearing structural members or elements. Also called *building steel*.

Structural veneer
Facing for plywood that is composed of structural grade veneers as opposed to decorative veneers.

Structure
The load-bearing or primary structural elements of a building, individually or collectively, that support part of the weight of the building and its contents and occupants, or resist dynamic forces, such as wind or earthquake; may be divided into substructure and superstructure depending on their location within the building.

Strut
A bracing member, or any piece of a frame that resists thrusts in the direction of its own length, whether upright, horizontal, or diagonal. Also called *bridging*.

Stucco
An exterior fine plaster finish composed of portland cement, lime, and sand mixed with water, used for decorative work or moldings, and usually textured.

Stud
One of a series of upright posts or vertical structural members that acts as the supporting element in a wall or partition.

Stud driver
A device for driving fasteners into steel, concrete, and other hard material, by using a blank cartridge in a small-caliber gun. Also called a *ramset*.

Stud finder
A magnetic device that will identify the location of nail heads, and thus the studs in an existing wall. An ultrasonic device is also used to locate studs. See also *Ultrasonic stud finder*.

Stud partition
An interior partition constructed with wood stud framing and blocking.

Styrofoam
A trademark name for polystyrene plastic board, a lightweight material used for insulation.

Subbasement
One or more stories below the basement level.

Sub-bidder
One who submits a bid to a prime contractor.

Subcontractor
A specialist builder who undertakes part of a main building contract from the contractor.

Subcontractor bonds
A document supplied to the prime contractor by the subcontractor, guaranteeing performance and payment of all labor and materials in connection with that contract.

Subdivision
A tract of land divided into residential lots.

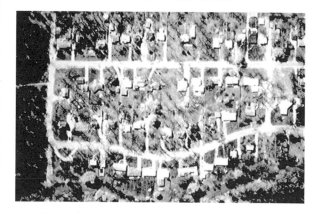

Subdivision map
A map showing dimensions and configurations of lots, or parcels of land, often including the names of the owners of the lots.

Subdivision map

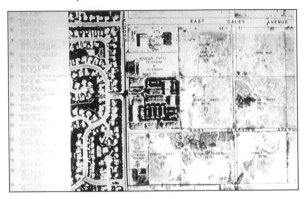

Subdivision regulations
Ordinances specifying the terms and conditions that a parcel of land can be subdivided, such as minimum lot size, water and sewer restrictions, lot coverage, and requirements as developed by local municipalities.

Subfloor
A rough floor consisting of plywood or construction-grade lumber installed over floor joists, and serving as the base for the finished floor.

Subgrade
The soil that receives the loads imposed by the foundation and supports the structure.

Submersible pump
A water pump and electric motor encased in the same housing that can be operated under water; used in deep wells in rural areas to provide water to a building.

Submittal
Providing information to gain approval for a manufacturer' shop drawing, sample, or other items requested from the contractor by the architect or owner.

Subrogate
The act of putting one thing in place of another, such as putting one party in place of another in a legal claim.

Subsidiary
A thing of secondary importance, and subordinate to another.

Subsidy
A grant of money, or sharing the cost of a project by the government or another party without direct ownership.

Substantial completion
The status of construction prior to the owner taking occupancy, where all items of work are substantially complete, and those that are not are put on a list.

Substantial performance
The performance of an obligation to a point that entitles a party to payment for a portion of the contract price.

Substitution
The offering for use of a product, material, piece of equipment, or building system that is offered in lieu of, and as being equivalent to, the specified material or process.

Substrate
The substructure or base material on which other material is placed.

Substructure
The foundation and footings, as opposed to the superstructure.

Sub-subcontractor
A person or company who provides a portion of the work at the site for a subcontractor, and whose contract is with the subcontractor.

Subsurface investigation
Soil boring and sampling for laboratory testing to determine subsurface profiles and relative strengths, compressibility, and other characteristics of the various strata within the depths likely to affect the design of the structure.

Suburb
A residential neighborhood or community away from an urban center, with primarily single-family homes, schools, and commercial development to support the area.

Successful bid
A bid that is accepted by the owner for the commencement of work; may or may not be the lowest qualified bid.

Summary judgment
A judgment awarded without a trial, relying on affidavits and legal briefings alone.

Sump
A pit or depression that holds water, or liquid waste, located below the normal grade of the disposal system; must be emptied by means of a sump pump. See also *Sump pump.*

Sump pump
A pump used to remove water from a sunken pit in the floor, usually built in a basement.

Sump stone
A long narrow concrete block with a texture that resembles adobe on the surface; used as a decorative treatment.

Sunk draft
A margin cut into a building stone that is sunk below the face of the stone to give it a raised appearance.

Superimpose
To place an item or surface on top of another one.

Superintendent
At a construction site, the contractor's representative who is responsible for continuous field supervision, coordination, completion of the work, and the prevention of accidents.

Superstructure
Any structure above the main supporting level, as opposed to the substructure or basement.

Supervision
The observation and inspection of construction work to ensure conformity to the contract documents and specifications.

Supplemental agreement
A modification to the original agreement with the approval of both parties.

Supplemental anchors
A method used to tie the elements of masonry walls together in the event of failed existing ties or anchors. Anchors are inserted into the wall and expanded to form a bond, or glued in with epoxy.

Supplemental conditions
A section of the contract documents that modifies conditions outlined in the general conditions.

Supplemental general conditions
Modifications to the original general conditions that become a part of the contract documents.

Supplemental instruction to bidders
Modifications to the instructions to bidders that become part of the final bidding requirements.

Supplemental services
Services performed by the architect that fall outside of those described in the general list of services; may include the furnishing of architectural renderings, energy studies, value analysis, promotion of the project, or expert testimony.

Supplier
One who supplies materials or equipment from off the site for inclusion in the construction of the building. See also *Vendor*.

Supply bond
A method by which a surety company can guarantee that materials will be supplied by a contractor or vendor.

Surety bond
A bond provided by an individual or bonding company that guarantees that another individual or company will perform in accordance with the terms of an agreement or contract..

Surface
To finish or make smooth by planing, such as with lumber. Also, to give a particular kind of surface to interior work by polishing, varnishing, or some other method of producing a smooth finish.

Surface coating
A method applied to brick walls to either change their appearance or to protect them against the elements; includes paints, stains, oils, and silicone paints.

Surface erosion
A condition of deterioration of masonry or concrete, caused by exposure to wind, salt, or water that exposes the aggregate beneath the surface, or if severe enough the reinforcing steel.

Surface grouting
A specialized form of repointing to fill small cracks or joints in brick walls; consists of a mortar slurry or paste rubbed into the face of mortar joints, and the excess grout removed by wiping with a damp sponge, rag, or burlap bag. After curing, the surface is washed to remove any film left by the wiping process.

Surface hinge
A hinge mounted on the surface face of a door as opposed to the edge; may be plain or ornamental.

Surfaced lumber
Wood that has been smoothed by running it through a planer.

Surplus property
According to the Surplus Real Property Act of 1972, unused or abandoned property owned by federal, state, or local governments may be transferred with minimal or no charge to another owner for rehabilitation and new use.

Surplus Real Property Act
Legislation passed in 1972 that amended the Federal Property and Administration Services Act of 1949, allowing the U.S. General Services Administration (GSA) to transfer any of its surplus property to states and municipalities, for public or revenue-producing purposes.

Survey
A boundary or topographic mapping of a job site. Also, taking measurements, conducting a use analysis or conditions assessment, reporting necessary project data, or other examinations of an existing structure, or an analysis of a building for use of the interior space.

Survey stakes
Wooden or metal stakes used to mark the boundaries established by a survey.

Surveying
Taking measurements of distances, elevations, or angles to prepare a site map.

Surveying tools
Instruments used by a surveyor to measure distances, determine angles, and elevations: such as a transit, measuring rod, and compass.

Surveyor
An engineer or person skilled in the process of surveying.

Suspended ceiling
A nonstructural ceiling suspended below the overhead structural slab or from the structural elements of a building that does not bear on the walls.

Suspended luminaire
A lighting fixture hung from the ceiling by rigid or flexible supports, leaving an airspace above the luminaire.

Suspended structure
A structure supported by tension members; usually attached to columns or poles that extend above the structure.

Suspension of work
A situation in which the contractor must stop work on a project.

Swale
A drainage channel formed where two slopes meet.

Sway brace
Any diagonal member designed to resist wind loads or other horizontal forces acting on a light structural frame.

Sweat equity
A property owner's or occupant's own labor invested in rehabilitation work in lieu of payment; applicable in programs such as homesteading.

Sweat joint
In plumbing work, a type of joint made by the union of two pieces of copper tubing that are coated with solder containing tin. The pipes are pressed together into sleeves or other joints, and heat is applied until the solder melts.

Sweating
Soldering joints in copper pipes. Also, the moisture that collects on pipes and fixtures caused by condensation. See also *Condensation*.

Sweet's Architectural Catalog
An architectural catalog file on building materials, products, systems, and engineering. A computer software version and an on-line version are also available.

Swing stage scaffold
A scaffold supported from hooks over the parapet above, using ropes and pulleys or wire cables, which permit it to be raised or lowered as needed; used on exterior work.

Swinging door
A door that turns on hinges or pivots about a vertical edge when opened.

Swinging scaffold
A swinging-type scaffold suspended from four cables attached to the top of the building or cornice. It is moved up and down by a small motor attached to two of the cables, to raise and lower the working platform to any desired level.

Swing-up garage door
An overhead garage door consisting of one piece that swing up on tracks installed on the ceiling. See also *Sectional door*.

Swirl
A finish applied to concrete during final troweling, by rotating the trowel in a circular fashion, producing a nonskid surface.

Switch
In electrical work, a device for closing, opening, or changing the connections of the circuit in which it is placed.

Switchboard
Similar to an electric panelboard, but larger in size.

Switchgear
Switching, control, and protective devices housed in a cabinet; used for the general transmission, distribution, and conversion of electric power.

Symbol schedule
A legend on a drawing that outlines and explains all the symbols used on that drawing; whether they be plumbing; electrical; heating, ventilation, and air-conditioning (HVAC); or door and window symbols.

Symbols
A graphic device used on architectural plans and elevations, to represent the name of a building component, indicated by a mark, character, letter, figure, or a combination of such characters.

System
A complete assembly of parts and components that makes up a functioning system; such as a plumbing, electrical, or heating, ventilation, and air-conditioning (HVAC) system.

T beam
An iron or steel rolled beam with a T-shaped cross-section.

T bevel
A woodworker's tool for checking the accuracy of work cut at an angle; consists of a blade that folds out from a handle, and can be locked with a turn screw at a particular angle.

Table saw
A machine with a flat bench and slot for exposing the blade of a circular saw at different elevations and angles; guides are used to pass the material past the saw blade for cutting.

Tack hammer
A small hammer with a magnetic head for holding a tack by its flat head so it is ready to drive into a surface; used on finish work and carpeting.

Tack weld
A weld designed not to carry a load but to make a nonstructural connection.

Tackle
A set of ropes and pulleys that provide a mechanical advantage in hoisting or moving heavy objects. See also *Block and tackle*.

Tail cut
The cutting of the lower end of a projecting rafter, which is often trimmed to an ornamental profile, or left in a straight cut, or plumb cut. See also *Rafter tail cut*.

Take off
A list of materials taken from the architect's plans and specifications, that identifies the kind of material, the number, size, weight, volume, or other measure, and the equipment needed to construct a project. See also *Quantity survey*.

Takeout loan
A loan issued by a permanent lender for the purposes of repaying an interim construction loan or funds advanced by the developer.

Tamp
To pound down the loose soil thrown in as loose filling around a wall.

Tamper
A hand tool for compacting the subgrade before concrete is placed; usually consists of a square iron or steel plate with a wooden handle attached perpendicularly to the flat surface.

Tape measure
A steel tape used by builders and surveyors in lengths from 25 to 100 feet. The units of measurement for surveyors and engineers is graduated in feet, tenths, and hundredths of a foot. The unit of measurement for builders is feet, inches, and fractions of an inch.

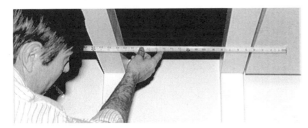

Tapestry brick
Face brick that is laid in a decorative pattern with a combination of vertical, horizontal, and diagonal elements, such as a basket-weave bond.

Tar and gravel roof
A built-up roof composed of an underlayment of felt, covered with a heavy coat of tar, followed by sand or gravel spread over the hot tar.

Tarp
Short for tarpaulin, a heavy-duty, woven fabric, used as a drop cloth, or to protect material from the weather.

Tarpaulin
A waterproofed canvas or other material used for protecting incomplete construction projects from the elements.

Task lighting
Lighting directed to a particular spot or work space, as opposed to general lighting for the area.

Tax Reform Act
Legislation passed in 1976 that created tax incentives for the rehabilitation of income-producing historic structures, penalized demolition of such structures, and established a code for determining deductions for charitable transfers of preservation easements.

Teak
A dark golden-yellow or brown wood with a greenish or black cast, moderately hard, coarse-grained, and very durable; immune to the attack of insects; used for construction, plywood, and decorative paneling.

Tee
A structural shape resembling a T in cross-section; produced by rolling steel or extruding aluminum. In pipe work, a fitting used in connecting pipe lengths, or changing the direction of a pipe run, also a fitting for connecting pipes of different sizes.

Tee beam
A precast concrete member resembling the letter T; the wide area on top takes compressive loads, the narrow stem resists tension forces with embedded reinforcing.

Tee plate
A flat, predrilled metal plate, shaped like the letter T; used for joining two pieces of wood meeting at right angles.

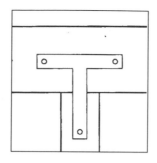

Temperature bars
Steel rods placed horizontally in concrete slabs for the prevention of cracks due to temperature changes and drying. The bars are placed parallel to the reinforcing rods. The steel rods are placed at right angles to the main reinforcing bars.

Temperature steel
Steel reinforcement used in concrete slabs and other masonry installations to reduce the possibility of cracking caused by changes in temperature, as opposed to steel required for structural reinforcement purposes.

Temperature zoning
In the design of solar-heated homes, the placement of rooms and areas according to their need for heat; those requiring the most heat being placed on the south side, and those requiring less heat, on the north side.

Tempered glass
Annealed glass reheated to just below the softening point and then rapidly cooled with water. When fractured, it breaks into relatively harmless pieces.

Tempered glass door
Application for a commercial use of tempered glass.

Template
(1) A thin piece of plastic with cutout holes, shapes, and symbols; used to transfer these shapes to paper by placing a pencil in the cutout and drawing within the outline. (2) A sheet or light frame of wood or metal, used for marking out work to be done, or as a guide for a cutting out other similar pieces.

Temporary bracing
Wooden or steel bracing installed during construction to provide support until the structure can stand on its own, at which time it is removed.

Temporary protection
Devices used to protect the public passing by a building under construction or renovation. The most common is the sidewalk bridge, or plywood barricade. Projecting elements such as cornices have nylon nets hung below them to catch any falling debris. See also *Sidewalk bridge*.

Temporary shoring
Shoring that supports a structure under construction, which is removed when construction is completed.

Tenant
The party to a lease agreement responsible for paying rent.

Tenant's improvement
Any fixed improvement on land or on a building, installed and paid for by a tenant or lessee. Such improvements become the property of the lessor unless specific agreements are previously made to the contrary.

Tenement
A building with multiple dwelling units accessed by a single stairway, with two or more apartments on each floor.

Tenon
The projecting end of a piece of wood or other material, reduced in cross-section so that it may be inserted into a corresponding mortise in another piece to form a secure joint.

245

Tensile strain
A stretching or pulling force in a longitudinal direction.

Tensile strength
The property of a material to be able to resist a tensile force.

Tensile stress
The stress or strain to which a structural member is subject when in tension.

Tension
A pulling or stretching force in line with the axis of the body; the opposite of compression, which is a pushing, crushing stress.

Tension member
A structural member in a truss or other assembly that is subjected to tensile, or pulling forces.

Tension reinforcement
Steel reinforcement in the bottom of simple concrete beams to resist the forces of bending.

Termination clause
A clause in a contract describing the conditions for termination of the contract, and means of protecting the interests of the parties.

Termination costs
The cost to terminate a professional service contract, which may include compensation earned until the termination occurred.

Termination for convenience
The right of the government to terminate a contract at will.

Termination for default
A sanction which the government may impose on a contractor for failure to perform according to the terms of the contract.

Termite
A wood-devouring insect that eats the woodwork of a structure and can ruin a building; resembles an ant in appearance and in its habit of living in colonies.

Termite barrier
A barrier to prevent termites travelling from the ground, through holes or cracks in a concrete floor slab into a building, usually consisting of a termite shield.

Termite shield
A protective shield made of noncorroding metal, placed in or on a foundation mass of masonry or around pipes entering a building to prevent the passage of termites into the building.

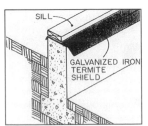
SILL
GALVANIZED IRON TERMITE SHIELD

Terne coating
A corrosion-protective coating for sheet steel used for roofing, consisting of a combination of lead and tin. See also *Terneplate.*

Terneplate
A metal protective coating applied to sheet metal, composed of a mixture of lead and zinc; used for roofing and wall cladding and decorative architectural elements.

Terrace
A flat roof or raised space or platform adjoining a building; paved or planted; most often used for leisurely enjoyment.

Terrace roof
A roof with a flat horizontal surface without a ridge.

Terra-cotta
A hard-burnt glazed or unglazed clay unit, either plain or ornamental; machine extruded or hand molded; usually larger in size than a brick or facing tile; used in building construction. Also called *baked clay.*

Terrazzo
Marble-aggregate concrete that is cast in place, or precast and ground smooth; used as a decorative surface for walls and floors.

Test
Testing buildings and components during investigation and construction; including nondestructive and destructive tests. They include soil bearing capacity, existing material testing, air infiltration tests, fire and moisture resistance tests, paint analysis, concrete slump tests, and testing of material and assemblies.

246 See also *Strain gauge*

Test cylinder
A sample cast cylinder of concrete mix, cured under job site conditions, and tested in a laboratory compressive test to determine the strength of the concrete at specific times.

Test light
A small electrical light with wires that can be plugged into an electrical outlet, to see if the circuit is live.

Test pit
An excavation of the subsurface made to examine the conditions that exist, and how they might affect the subsequent construction.

Testimony
Spoken evidence by a witness involved in a deposition, trial, or other hearing.

Testing machine
A device for applying forces or other testing conditions on construction specimens, and measuring and tabulating the results.

Texture 1-11
The American Plywood Association's name for a plywood panel with 3/8" grooves spaced at 2, 4, and 8 inches on center. The top ply has an unsanded face, providing a somewhat rustic look.

Texture paint
A paint that can be manipulated after application to give a textured finish.

Textured block
A concrete block with a raised pattern on its face to create a variety of geometrical designs when installed.

Thermal barrier
An element of low heat conductivity placed on an assembly to reduce or prevent the flow of heat between highly conductive materials; used in metal window or curtain wall designs in cold climates.

Thermal break
Any material or air space that separates two other materials, and thus reduces the thermal transfer between the two.

Thermal bridging
Any material that allows heat to be transferred through it instead of passing through the intended insulated material around it.

Thermal conduction
The process of heat transfer through a material medium in which kinetic energy is transmitted by particles of the material without displacement of the particles.

Thermal expansion
The change in length or volume that a material or body undergoes on being heated.

Thermal insulation
The reduction of the flow of heat. It is measured in units of thermal resistance.

Thermal resistance
The resistance (R value) to the passage of heat provided by the roof, wall, or floor of a building.

Thermal stress
A stress produced by thermal movement that is resisted by the building. If the thermal stresses are higher than the capacity of the materials to resist them, expansion or contraction joints are required.

Thermopane
The trade name for factory-built insulating glass window units composed of two or more glass panes in a hermetically sealed frame.

Thermoplastic
A construction material that softens when heated and rehardens when cooled.

Thermosiphoning
The process of allowing heat from solar collectors on the lower levels to rise by convection to the upper areas where it is cooled, and then to fall back into ducts that go to the collector to be reheated again.

Thermostat
An instrument, electrically operated, for automatically maintaining a constant temperature; commonly used in conjunction with heating and air-conditioning plants. Also called *automatic temperature control*.

Thimble
A protective sleeve to hold an object passing through it.

Thin shell concrete
A term for any roof structure with a thin concrete, curved surface, which depends on the arch-like shell action for its structural stability.

Thinner
Any volatile liquid that lowers the viscosity of a paint or varnish and thus makes it flow more easily. It must be compatible with the medium of the paint. The most common thinner is turpentine.

Thin-wall conduit
Steel tubing with a thinner wall than regular conduit; used where there is less likelihood of mechanical injury to the material. Also called *electric metallic tubing (EMT)*.

Threads
A series of spiral grooves cut into the end of a pipe to match grooves cut into another pipe in order to join them. See also *Male threads* and *Female threads*.

Three-prong plug
In electrical work, a plug with three contact prongs: two for the main circuit and one for the ground connection.

Three-way switch
A switch used in house wiring when a fixture is to be turned on or off from two different places. A three-way switch must be used at each place.

Threshold
A strip fastened to the floor beneath a door, to cover the joint where two types of floor materials meet or to provide weather protection. Also called *doorsill*.

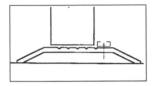 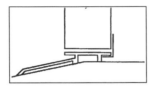

Through-wall flashing
A flashing at a parapet that extends completely through the wall.

Throw
The horizontal distance that air will travel from the outlet in a heating, ventilation, and air-conditioning system.

Tie
In building, anything used to hold two parts together, as a post, rod, or beam. In masonry veneer, a metal strip used to tie the masonry wall to the wood sheathing. In concrete formwork, devices used to tie two sides of a form together. Also called *stiffener*.

Tie beam
In roof framing, a horizontal timber connecting two opposite rafters at their lower ends to prevent them from spreading.

Tie rod
A rod in tension; used to hold parts of a structure together, usually exposed on the exterior in high-tech architecture.

Tie rod

Tie wire
In form building, a wire used to hold forms together so they will not spread when the wet concrete is poured into them. Also, the wire used to tie the intersections of reinforcing bars to hold them in place until the placing of concrete is completed.

Tile
A ceramic surfacing unit, usually thin in relation to the facial area; made from clay or a mixture of clay and other ceramic materials; has either a glazed or unglazed face.

Tile-setting adhesive
Specifically formulated glues or mastics used for setting tile. They are cleaner, waterproof, less expensive, and faster than mortar beds that are sometimes used for the same purposes.

Tilt slab wall unit
A unit cast on the ground with window and door openings in place, then tilted up into its vertical position.

Tilt-up doors
A door used for garages, consisting of a rigid panel of sheet steel, or aluminum, equipped with springs, tracks, counterbalances, and other hardware which pulls the door to an overhead position. They are often motor-operated with manual, radio, or remote driver controls.

Timber
Uncut trees that are suitable for construction or conversion to lumber.

Timber-framed building
A building having timbers as its structural elements, except for the foundation.

Time and material change orders
The time and materials method of payment applied to change orders.

Time and material contract
Work agreed to between the owner and the contractor with payment based on the contractor's cost for labor, equipment, and materials with an add-on factor to cover overhead and profit. Fee is based on material costs plus a specified amount per hour of labor that includes direct labor, overhead, and profit.

Time and materials
A contracting arrangement suitable to a project with many unknowns. Work commences knowing there will be significant changes. It is used primarily on civil engineering projects, site development, remediation work, abatement, and demolition (especially when the work is contracted separately). Also known as *cost plus fee*.

Time of completion
A specific date for the substantial completion of the construction, as stated in the construction contract.

Time-lapse photography
The study of work processes by use of a series of photographs taken at specifically timed intervals; useful for collecting video images of a construction site for posting on an intranet to monitor construction progress.

Timely completion
The completion of the specified work within the agreed-upon time limit.

Timely manner
The performance of contractual obligations on time, as well as responses in time to avoid interference to the other party's performance.

Timely payment
Payment made within the period outlined in the contract documents.

Time-with-materials-furnished contract
A contract in which the owner supplies materials and pays the contractor only for the time to install them. The savings to the owner are the markups usually added to the cost of materials; the saving to the contractor is the time and cost of obtaining bids for the material, and arranging for delivery.

Tin
A lustrous white, soft, and malleable metal having a low melting point; relatively unaffected by exposure to air; used for making alloys and solder and in coating sheet metal.

Tin ceiling
Stamped sheet-metal panels used as a finished ceiling; common from 1850 to 1920 in homes and commercial buildings.

Tin snips
A cutting instrument, similar to hand shears but with thicker jaws, used by sheet-metal workers, lathers, and plasterers.

Tinted glass
Glass that has been chemically treated with an additive in the manufacture, or covered with an adhesive film after installation, to reduce glare and to absorb a portion of the radiant heat and visible light that strikes it to filter out infrared solar energy, thereby reducing the solar heat gain.

Title block
In architectural drawing, the outlined space usually in the lower right corner, or in a vertical strip across the right side of the sheet, containing the name of the firm, project, sheet identification, sheet number, scale, date, and other similar information.

Title insurance
A guarantee of title issued by an insurance company.

Title insurance company
An insurance company that researches real estate records to make certain that there are no encumbrances or restrictions on the property before issuing a policy of title insurance.

Title report
A report issued by a title insurance company with information relative to the title of the property prior to issuing a policy of title insurance.

Title search
An investigation into the history of ownership of a property to verify the validity of the title, and to check for claims or liens against the property.

Title sheet
A cover sheet for a set of architectural drawings, usually providing the name of the architect, the construction firm, the client, the project, and an index to the drawings; often included is a perspective sketch.

To the weather
The amount of material in siding, or shingles, that is not covered by the material above, and thus exposed to the weather.

Toe space
A recessed area in the bottom of a cabinet that allows a person to stand close to the cabinet.

Toenailing
The driving of a nail or brad on a slant into the end of a piece of lumber to attach it to another piece, to avoid having the heads of the nails show above the surface.

Toggle bolt
An anchor having a machine screw and two spring-loaded collapsible wings attached to a threaded nut. The bolt is inserted into a hole in the wall, and the wings snap open and tighten against the back side of the wall as the screw is tightened.

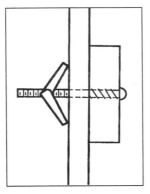

Tolerance
The measure or amount that something can vary from a specified number and be within an acceptable range.

Tongue
A projecting rib cut along the edge of a piece of timber so that it can be fitted into a groove in an adjoining piece.

Tongue and groove
A piece of milled lumber with a tongue protruding from one edge, and a groove in the other edge, that produces a locking joint when joined lengthwise.

Tooled joint
A shaped mortar joint, such as a beaded, concave, or raked joint.

Toothing
In masonry construction, the ending of a wall with projecting courses, to provide a bond with the continuation of the wall.

Top plate
The top horizontal structural member in a wood frame house, usually made up from double members the same size as the vertical studs, and attached across the tops of the studs

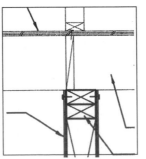

Top-hung window
A casement window hinged horizontally.

Topographic survey
A drawing that shows the contours of the site and other surface conditions.

Topographical map
A plan view of a property that shows the contour of the land and other features. The relative grade is indicated by the closeness or distance apart of the continuous lines. The map usually indicates the grade elevation of the property above sea level.

Topography
The shape of the surface of the ground.

Topping out
Raising the flag at the top of a structure when the structural frame of the top floor is completed. A long tradition, perhaps stemming from raising a tree branch at the top of the structure in earlier times.

Torque wrench
A tool used to turn nuts and bolts that includes a built-in device that measures the force applied to the nut or bolt, thereby protecting the fastener or material from damage.

Torsion
The force tending to twist an architectural member.

Total float time
In a Critical Path Method (CPM) schedule, the difference between the amount of time available to accomplish a task, and the time necessary to complete it.

Tower crane
A crane with a fixed vertical mast, topped by a rotating horizontal boom that holds a winch for raising and lowering loads. The winch is movable along the length of the boom so that it can access any of the site covered by the rotation of the boom.

Tower crane

Town
A combination of residential and related buildings in a relatively small definable area.

Town hall
A public hall or building, belonging to a town, where public offices are established, the town council meets, and the people assemble for town meetings.

Town house
An urban building, without side yards; contains one residence on one or more floors.

Town plan
A large-scale map of a town that delineates its streets, important buildings, and other urban features.

Townscape
A series of streetscapes grouped together. The silhouette of a townscape includes its skyline and other features both natural and built; church steeples, grain elevators, skyscrapers, water towers, cupolas, a capitol dome, rolling hills, craggy mountains, valleys, lakes, and woods.

Township
A political and geographic area within the boundaries of a municipal government; sometimes separate from a larger county.

Tracing paper
A semi-transparent vellum for making sketches and drawings that can be easily reproduced by a diazo or photocopy process.

Track
A U-shaped member used as a guide for a sliding door or partition; attached to a floor, ceiling, or door header.

Track lighting
A track on the ceiling that holds the internal wiring for the fixtures, including a double electrified track that holds the fixtures, which can be positioned at any location along the track.

Tract
An area of land which is often subdivided into blocks and lots for future development.

Trade
A group representing a particular occupation or craft.

Trade association
An organization formed to promote uniform standards and codes within their particular industry; consisting of manufacturers, distributors, suppliers, and service contractors.

Trade discount
A discount from a supplier to a member of a trade or profession, such as an architect, interior designer, contractor, or subcontractor.

Trade union
A combination of tradespeople organized for the purpose of promoting their common interests in regard to wages, hours of work, safety measurements, unemployment compensation, and other benefits.

Trade unions
Organizations representing workers performing similar tasks and skills. Some typical trade unions include boilermakers, bricklayers, carpenters, electrical workers, elevator constructors, hoisting trades, iron workers, laborers, lathers, painters, plasterers, plumbers, roofers, sheet metal workers, and teamsters.

Trammel
A beam compass that is used to draw circles too large for an ordinary compass; consisting of two adjustable points on a bar of wood or metal, and used by carpenters or shop workers to scribe unusually large circles.

Tranferred load
In multistory buildings, a load that is not continuous to the building foundation, but transferred through beams or girders to other members that go to the foundation.

251

Transfer of Development Rights

TDR allows a landmark to transfer lost or unused development rights to neighboring sites; first enacted in New York City in 1968. This allows the new building to be larger, while the owner retains the landmark building.

Transit

A surveyor's instrument used by builders to establish points, line up stakes, or to plumb walls; it operates in both the horizontal and vertical planes.

Transit level

A builder's level, containing a telescope and a leveling device; it can also be used to take vertical angle measurements.

Transit mixer

A truck-mounted concrete mixer; used for transporting concrete from a central batching plant to a site. The mixer slowly rotates during the journey, mixing the concrete ingredients and preventing them from settling and segregating.

Transition piece

A sheet-metal device shaped to form a transition from one shape of duct to a different shape or size of a duct.

Transmittal

A form or letter from one party to another that conveys certain actions to be taken.

Transom

A horizontal bar of wood or stone across a door or window; the crossbar separating a door from the fanlight above it; a window divided by a transom bar.

Transom bar

An intermediate horizontal member of a door frame or window frame; a horizontal member that separates a door from a window, panel, or louver above.

Transom light

A glazed light above the transom bar of a door.

Transverse loading

Loading that is perpendicular to a structural member, such as a vertical loading on a horizontal beam.

Transverse section

A cross-section of a building that is cut at right angles to its longest dimension.

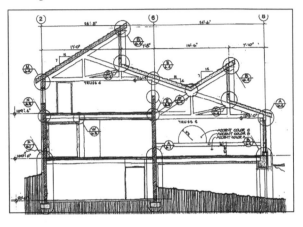

Trap

A bend in a soil drain, arranged in such a manner that it is always full of water, which provides a water seal and prevents odors from entering back through the pipes.

Trapdoor

A door that is flush with the surface; located in a floor, roof, or ceiling or on the stage of a theater. Also called *scuttle, hatchway*.

Travel time

Compensation paid for the time traveling from home to the job site; according to special clauses in the contract.

Traveling crane

A tower crane that is mounted on wheels or crawlers.

Travertine

A variety of limestone deposited by springs, usually banded, commonly coarse and cellular, often containing fossils; used as building stones, especially for interior facing or flooring.

Tread

The horizontal upper surface of a step; includes the rounded edge or nosing that extends over the riser. Also called *step*. See also *Stair tread*.

Tread width

The full width of the stair tread from the edge of the overhanging nosing to the vertical face of the riser.

Treated wood

Wood products that are treated with stains or chemicals to prevent deterioration from weathering, damage from insects, or destruction from fire.

Tree grate

A cast metal round or square grating around a tree, set level with the adjacent paving.

Triangular scale

A three-faced measuring device with six graduated edges, one containing a full-size scale, and each of the other five containing a different reduced scale. Also called an *architect's scale*.

Trim

The visible woodwork on moldings, such as baseboards, cornices, and casings around doors and windows. Also, any visible element that covers or protects joints, edges, or ends of another material. Also called *Finish work, millwork*.

Trimmer

A piece of timber in a roof, floor, or wooden partition, which supports a header, which in turn supports the ends of the joists, rafters, or studs; a small horizontal beam, into which the ends of one or more joists are framed. Also called *filler stud*.

Trimming joist

A joist supporting one end of a header at the edge of an opening in a floor or roof frame, parallel to the other common joists.

Tripartite scheme

A design scheme for a multistory commercial building, as exemplified in the work of Louis Sullivan. The building is divided into three divisions: a base consisting of the lower two to three floors, a cap of one to four stories at the top, and a shaft consisting of all the stories in between. Typically the base and cap are the most ornate with ornamentation in the spandrel panels of the shaft.

Trompe l'oeil

A phrase meaning "that which deceives the eye." It was originally used to describe precisely rendered views of earlier architectural styles, wherein painters produced a convincing illusion of reality. This has been applied to exterior and interior mural design where architectural elements and entire façades have been painted on blank expanses of buildings, indicating a particular architectural style, period, or design.

Trowel

A hand tool for working mortar or cement; the triangular trowel is used for applying mortar to masonry, and the rectangular trowel is used for finishing the surface.

Troweled joint

A mortar joint finished by striking off excess mortar with a trowel.

Troweling

Smoothing the top surface of concrete with a steel trowel.

Truck crane

A mechanical device for lifting materials loaded onto the bed of a truck.

Truss

A composite structural system composed of straight members transmitting only axial tension or compression stresses along each member, joined to form a triangular arrangement, allowing long, unsupported spans.

Truss clip
A connector used in assembling trusses or joining wood members end to end; consists of a metal plate with multiple points that were produced from slots cut into the plate and bent forward. When hammered flat, the points are driven into the wood and have the effective holding power of 20 to 60 nails.

Trussed girder
A beam, usually of timber, in the form of a truss, braced by one or more vertical posts supported by inclined rods attached to the ends of the beams.

Trussed rafter roof
A roof system composed of a series of light frame wood trusses instead of rafters.

Trustee
A person or legal entity that administers property holdings for another.

Try square
A tool used by carpenters to verify square corners in woodworking; consists of a metal straightedge with a wooden handle at right angles to the blade.

T-square
A drafting tool consisting of a straightedge with a cross piece at one end forming the letter T. It is used for drawing parallel horizontal lines, and as a place to rest triangles for drawing vertical lines. Although mostly outmoded by the more elaborate drafting machine, and by the use of computer-aided drafting, it is still useful for small jobs. See also *Adjustable triangle*.

Tubular scaffold
A scaffold for both interior and exterior work, made of tube steel. These scaffolds are lightweight, offer low wind resistance, and are easily assembled and dismantled. They are available in several lengths for varying heights and types of work.

Tubular scaffolding
A scaffold system using metal tubes for posts, beams, cross bracing, and ties, with special couplers connecting all parts. Planking or metal decking is set on each working level.

Tuck pointing
The repairing of worn or damaged mortar joints, by raking out the old mortar and replacing with a fine fresh mortar, or a fillet of putty or lime.

Tulipwood
A soft, close-textured durable wood that is yellowish in color; used for millwork and veneer.

Tumbling course
A sloping course of bricks that is set perpendicular to a gable in Dutch Colonial architecture; in imitation of a similar brick construction found in medieval houses in Flanders, The Netherlands.

Tunneling
Digging a passage under the ground, or under an object.

Turnbuckle
A coupling between the ends of two rods, one having a left-hand and the other a right-hand thread. Rotation of the buckle adjusts the tension in the rods.

Turned
Produced on a lathe, resulting in a circular cross-section, which can vary in diameter throughout the length of the piece.

Turnkey job
A project in which the contractor completes all work and furnishings of a building so that it is ready for immediate use.

Turnkey operation
Performance of all phases necessary to design and build a project by a single entity or joint venture. May not include the acquisition of land and financing.

Twist
(1) A distortion in a wood member caused by the turning of the edges of a board so that the four corners of any face are no longer in the same plane. (2) A feature with a curve or turn; specifically a curved stair railing that makes a radial turn with the change of direction.

Two-step bidding
A bidding procedure that includes one submittal for the technical part of the proposal. The proposals are evaluated, and a preselection made to allow those qualifying to submit a sealed price proposal.

Two-tiered porch
A porch whose first and second stories are similar. Each floor is supported by a separate row of columns.

Two-way switch
An electrical switch used to control a light or lights from two locations. Two two-way switches are required, one in each location.

Two-wire system
An electrical wiring system consisting of only two wires: a hot lead and a neutral lead, both of which are needed to complete a circuit in a 120-volt AC electrical system.

Tympanum
The triangular space between the horizontal and sloping cornices immediately above the opening of a doorway or a window, or the space between the lintel above a door and the arch above.

U

U.S. Green Building Council's (USGBC) LEED rating system
Since 1994 the USGBC program has accredited more than 6,500 professionals, and has produced more than 193 million square feet of green projects, enough to cover 3,000 football fields.

UBC
Abbreviation for Uniform Building Code.

U-bolt
A bolt shaped like the letter U, with both ends threaded on the straight portion of the legs; used to clamp wires together, or items to cylindrical objects such as pipes.

UCC
Abbreviation for Uniform Commercial code.

U-hanger
A metal hanger for piping. Some are threaded like a U-bolt, others are sharpened at the ends for driving into wood joists.

UL label
A certification from the Underwriter's Laboratories, Inc. that is attached to building materials, electrical wiring and components, and other devices to show that the product has been rated according to performance tests, and is consistent with comparable products that have passed fire, electrical, hazard, and other safety tests.

Ultimate load
The maximum load that a member or structure can sustain before failure occurs.

Ultimate strength
The highest load that a piece can sustain before failing.

Ultimate stress
The stress sustained by a member just before it fails.

Ultrasonic stud finder
A tool used to locate studs in an existing wall, by means of ultrasonic waves that indicate a difference in density of the wall at the location of the stud.

Umbrella liability insurance
Protection from losses not covered by employer's liability, general liability, or other liability policies.

Unbalanced bid
A contractor's bid that attempts to get payment based on increased unit costs for items in the beginning of the work, and decreased unit cost for later tasks, in order to get the maximum amount of money early.

Undercoat
A coat of paint applied on new wood or over a primer or over a previous coat of paint; improves the seal and serves as a base for the top coat, for which it provides better adhesion.

Underfloor electrical duct
A sheet metal raceway or wireway system installed in a concrete slab for pulling wires and cables, with access for fixtures through the finished floor.

Underfloor heating
Heating provided below the finished floor by electric cables or hot-water pipes; usually cast into a concrete slab.

Underfloor wiring
A system of conduits placed in the slab or other electrical chases, that allows for future changes in the location of electrical outlets for desk equipment and fixtures.

Underground service
Electrical service carried in a trench or conduit from the utility company's service line to the structure.

Underlayment
A layer of material used as a base for another finished material, such as plywood under a finished hardwood floor, or padding under a carpeted floor.

Underpin
To provide a new foundation for a wall or column in an existing building without removing the superstructure.

Underpinning
The process of transferring the loads from a foundation by inserting other members to take the loads so that the foundation can be repaired, renewed, or relocated; usually required when excessive settlement has occurred, or if the structure is to be moved, or as the result of an excavation in adjoining property that is deeper than the existing foundation.

Underwriter
A person or entity that approves the amount, the terms, and the conditions of insurance policies.

Underwriter's Laboratory (UL)
A nonprofit organization sponsored by the National Board of Fire Underwriters; classifies and produces standards and specifications, tests building materials, and inspects electric services to ensure their compliance with the National Electric Code.

Undressed stone
Not trimmed or rendered smooth.

Unearned income
Any income received as advance payment on any phase of design, preliminary drawings, production drawings, or construction job for work that is not yet completed.

Unemployment insurance
A state-operated insurance program, paid for by employers, to provide workers with compensation when they are involuntarily laid off.

UNESCO
An organization whose function it is to protect the world's landmarks, through administration of the International Council on Monuments (ICOMOS), and the World Heritage Committee.

Uniform Building Code (UBC)
A collection of standards regarding methods and materials used in construction that is the basis for all building codes in use today. First published in 1929 by the International Conference of Building Officials (ICBO), it is designed to provide uniformity of building laws and those affecting the public health and safety. This is the standard building code used throughout the United States, and upon which all state, municipal, and local codes are based.

Uniform Construction Index
The predecessor of the MasterFormat, which divided technical data, and all construction related functions into the 16 divisions now in use. It was prepared by the American Institute of Architects, Associated General Contractors, and Construction Specification Institute.

Uniform load
Load that is evenly distributed over an area.

Uniform Plumbing Code
A model plumbing code sponsored by the International Association of Plumbing and Mechanical Officials.

Uniformity
The state of being identical, homogeneous, or regular.

Union
A confederation of workers who have joined together to affect policies of their related trades.

Unit construction
A construction method that includes two or more preassembled walls, together with floor and ceiling construction, ready for shipment to the building site.

Unit price
The price per unit of known quantities of materials, equipment, and labor.

Unit price contract
A contract where payment is based on known quantities of materials, equipment, and labor.

Unknown conditions
Conditions that become apparent in the course of the job that were not known at the time of bidding, such as underground conditions, and that increase the costs or time originally proposed or bid.

Unqualified bidder
A bidder whose experience, financial capability, or past performance may indicate that they are not capable of performing the work being bid.

Unreasonable delay
A delay extending over a long period of time, which may adversely affect the outcome of the job.

Unsuitable material
Any material that is designed for one purpose and that is inadequate or inappropriate for use in a totally different application.

Unsupported wall height
A limit in the local building code to the height of an unsupported masonry wall to the thickness of the wall itself.

Urban design
The aspect of architecture and city planning that deals with the design of urban structures and space.

Urban planning
The design of urban structures and spaces.

Urban renewal
To revitalize the decaying inner city. Strategies vary and include removing the old and replacing it with a gleaming modern makeover, or restoring original buildings and public spaces.

Urbanization
The process of change from a rural area to an urban area.

Urethane varnish
A high-gloss, plastic-based varnish that dries hard and is very durable; used on wood floors subject to high wear.

Usable floor area
Space that can actually be occupied by a user.

Use
Permissible and forbidden land uses as defined in a zoning code; such as residential, commercial, industrial, and rural categories, often complemented by the intensity of development allowed within each use category.

Use district
An area designated in the zoning ordinance of a municipality within which specified types of land use are permitted, and other uses are not permitted.

Used brick
A brick that has been recycled from the demolition of old buildings; used to achieve an old, rustic, or weathered look.

Utilities
Gas, water, and electricity supplied to residences, offices, or commercial structures.

UV
Abbreviation for ultraviolet waves of the sun that are invisible to the eye, but can damage materials, such as fabric in interiors that receive sunlight.

UV inhibitor
A material that blocks ultraviolet light.

U-value
A unit of measure of heat transfer through a material. The lower the U-value, the greater the insulating value of the material.

VA loan
A government-backed home loan program which makes no-money-down loans available to veterans, and offers lower interest rates than conventional loans. The program is managed by the Veterans Administration, which only guarantees another lender against loss in the case of foreclosure.

Vacancy rate
The ratio of the currently vacant area to the total available space.

Valley
The lower trough or gutter formed by the intersection of two inclined planes of a roof.

Valley flashing
Pieces of lead, tin, or sheet metal worked in with shingles or other roofing materials along the valley of a roof.

Valley rafter
In a roof framing system, the rafter in the line of the valley; connects the ridge to the wall plate along the meeting line of two inclined sides of a roof that are perpendicular to each other.

Valley shingles
Shingles that have been cut at the proper angle so that they will fit correctly along a valley.

Valley tile
Trough-shaped building tile made for use in valleys of roofs.

Valuation
A method of estimating or appraising construction costs by comparing them to known similar types of construction, or by estimating the cost of labor and material in detail.

Value engineering
A process that studies the relative value of various construction techniques and use of materials, considering not only the cost of installation but also the estimated cost of maintenance, energy usage, life expectancy, and potential replacement cost, often resulting in the substitution of less costly materials, methods, or systems that would not seriously alter the finished product.

Valve
A mechanical device, such as a gate valve or globe valve, that closes off the flow in a pipe.

Vapor barrier
Airtight skin of polyethylene or aluminum, which prevents moisture from warm damp air in a building from passing into a colder space, causing condensation. Also called *flashing, plastic membrane, moisture barrier.*

Variable rate mortgage
A loan in which the interest rate varies with the available market rate for the lender.

Variable-speed drill
An electric hand drill operated by a trigger, which speeds up as more pressure is applied to the trigger.

Variance
The waiving of a zoning or building restriction by an authorized planning commission, building department, or architectural review board; usually based on an application by an owner for exclusion by reason of hardship.

Variegated
Said of a material or surface that is irregularly marked with different colors.

Varnish
In painting, a solution of a resin in alcohol or oil, applied to a surface to produce a hard, glossy finish to protect the underlying coat of paint.

Vault
An arched roof or ceiling or a continuous semicircular ceiling that extends in a straight line over a hall, room, or other partially enclosed space.

Vaulted
Constructed as a vault.

Vegetable glue
The most common form of this glue is wallpaper paste, and casein glue, a milk curd derivative used to glue wood.

Vehicle
The liquid portion of paint that carries the coloring pigment and produces a hard coating when dried.

Vellum
A heavyweight tracing paper with excellent transparency and durability.

Vendor
A company or individual that supplies materials or equipment for a construction project.

Veneer
A thin sheet of wood that has been sliced, rotary cut, or sawn from a log; used as one of several plies in plywood to add strength or act as a facing on less attractive wood.

Veneer plywood
Plywood made of several layers of veneer glued together, with an outer layer of a higher-quality wood, such as walnut, oak, or mahogany.

Veneered construction
A method of construction in which a thin layer of facing material is applied to the external surface of a steel, concrete, concrete block or wooden frame.

Veneered walls
A wall with a masonry facing that is not bonded but is attached to a wall so as to form an integral part of the wall.

Vent
An opening, pipe, or duct, which permits the circulation of air or the escape of gases into the atmosphere. Also called *duct, opening*.

Vent pipe
A flue or pipe connecting any interior space in a building with the outer air for purposes of ventilation; any small pipe extending from any of the various plumbing fixtures in a structure to the vent stack and roof.

Vent stack
A vertical pipe connected with all vent pipes carrying off gases from a building. It extends through the roof and provides an outlet for gases and contaminated air and also aids in maintaining a water seal in the trap.

Ventilating duct
General ductwork involved with the process of supplying or removing air by natural or mechanical means, to or from any space.

Ventilating eyebrow
A low dormer in a roof covered by a wavy line, sometimes used for ventilating attics.

Ventilation
The supply of clean outdoor air to a space for the purpose of cooling; a process of changing the air in a room by either natural or artificial means. Also, any provision for removing contaminated air or gases from a room and replacing it with fresh air. Also called *aeration*.

Ventilator
In a room or building, any device or contrivance used to provide fresh air or expel stale air.

Veranda
Similar to a balcony but located on the ground level; can extend around one, two, or all sides of a building.

Verde antique
A dark green serpentine rock marked with white veins of calcite, which takes a high polish; used for decorative purposes since ancient times; sometimes classified as a marble.

Verdigris
The greenish-blue copper carbonate formed on copper roofs and statues that are exposed to the atmosphere. The patina it produces can be carefully controlled.

Verge
The trim edge of a sloping roof that overhangs a gable wall.

Vergeboard
An ornamental board hanging from a projecting roof; a bargeboard.

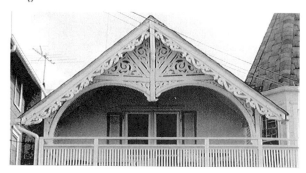

Vermiculated masonry
A form of masonry surface incised with discontinuous wandering grooves resembling worm tracks; a type of ornamental winding frets or knots on mosaic pavements, resembling the tracks of worms.

Vermiculite
A generic name for treated minerals that are used for insulation and fire protection, and often as an aggregate in plaster or concrete.

Vernacular architecture

Buildings that make use of common regional forms and materials at a particular place and time; usually modest and unpretentious, and often a mixture of traditional and modern styles, or a hybrid of several styles.

Vertical

Pertaining to anything, such as a structural member, that is upright in position, perpendicular to a horizontal member, and exactly plumb.

Vertical application

The installation of gypsum wallboard with the long dimension parallel to the studs. See also *Horizontal application.*

Vertical clearance

The unobstructed vertical height between objects in any given space.

Vertical shore

A pair of vertical struts used to provide temporary support to a wall.

Vertical siding

A type of siding consisting of matched boards that are 10 and 12 inches wide, or of random widths. The joints may have a V-cut or be covered with battens.

Vertical sliding window

A window having one or more sashes that move only in the vertical direction; they are held in various open positions by means of friction or a rachet device instead of being supported by a counterweight.

Vertically pivoted window

A window having a sash that pivots about a vertical axis at or near its center. When opened, the outside glass surface is conveniently accessible for cleaning.

Vibrator

In concrete work, a special tool for compacting and consolidating freshly placed concrete in the forms.

Video capture boards

An electronic device that allows individual frames from a videotape to be transferred to a computer for analysis, printed out, and incorporated into a progress report.

View

An object shown from a particular vantage point, such as an elevation or side view, or a plan or top view.

Village

A small group of dwellings in a rural area, usually ranking in size between a hamlet and a town; an unincorporated community smaller in population than a town.

Vinyl

Any of various tough, flexible plastics made from polyvinyl resin.

Vinyl flooring

An economical and durable floor covering made from polyvinyl chloride; available in sheets and square tiles.

Vinyl siding

A durable exterior siding made from vinyl, which needs very little maintenance.

Vinyl tile

A floor tile composed principally of polyvinyl chloride and other plasticizers; does not require waxing; usually set in mastic over a wood or concrete subfloor.

Vise

A mechanical clamp for holding a piece of material steady while it is being worked; usually consisting of two jaws, one fixed and one adjustable, which is operated by a screw which tightens the grip.

Vision-proof glass

Glass that has been given a pattern during its manufacture so that it is not transparent.

Visor roof

A relatively small section of roof that projects on brackets from a flat wall surface. Sometimes it appears below a parapet, as in the Mission style.

Visqueen

A trade name for a popular plastic sheathing.

Visual inspection

An examination of the building by physically viewing it from different vantage points to determine patterns of wear, fractures, patterns of water penetration, water discoloration, level or plumbness, cracks, dirt, efflorescence, spalling, or exfoliation of the stone or brick. Includes the skin of the building, and such ornamental features as portals, stringcourses, lintels, windows, door heads, and cornices. See also *Close-up inspection*.

Vitrified clay tile
Pipes and fittings made of clay that are baked hard and then glazed so that the parts are impervious to water; used especially for underground drainage.

Volcanic stone
A low-density, high-porosity rock composed of volcanic particles, ranging from ash size to small pebble size. The particles are compacted or cemented together. Volcanic stone is used as a building stone or as a thermal insulation material.

Voltage drop
A decrease in electrical current caused primarily by wires that are not adequate for the loads they are carrying.

Volume method of estimating
A method of estimating cost, based on the cost per unit of volume multiplied by the volume of the building.

Voussoir
A wedge-shaped block whose converging sides radiate from a center forming an element of an arch or vaulted ceiling.

V-shaped joint
A horizontal V-shaped mortar joint made with a steel jointing tool; very effective in resisting the penetration of rain.

W

Waferboard
A sheet formed with randomly placed wood wafers that are compressed and bound together with phenolic resin, and used for walls, roofs, and subfloors.

Waffle slab
A two-way ribbed slab.

Wainscot
A protective or decorative facing applied to the lower portion of an interior partition or wall, such as wood paneling or other facing material.

Waiver of lien
A document by which a person relinquishes his or her right to place a lien on a property.

Waler
A horizontal timber tied to the outside of a concrete form, used to brace the form while wet cement is poured in.

Walkup apartment house
Apartment without an elevator; usually five or fewer stories.

Walkway
A passage or lane designated for pedestrian traffic.

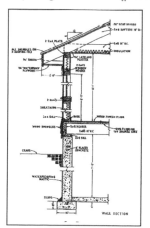

Wall
A structure that encloses a space with a continuous surface, except where fenestration or other openings occur. May be below or above grade. Floors are supported from the wall sill plates, and ceiling and roof rafters are supported from the top plates.

Wall anchor
A type of anchor used to tie the walls to the floors and hold them firmly in place.

Wall chase
A square or rectangular recess in a wall to accommodate pipes, heating ducts, and similar equipment.

Wall dormer
A dormer and window as a continuation of the main building wall below.

Wall gable
A portion of a wall in the form of a gable that projects above the roof line behind it.

Wall hanger
A support of steel or cast iron, partially built into a wall for carrying the end of a structural timber, when the timber itself is not to be built into the wall.

Wall mural
A large painting using a wall for a canvass.

Wall panel
A nonbearing wall built between the columns or piers and supported at each floor by girders or beams of a skeleton frame.

Wall plate
A horizontal piece of timber, laid flat along the top of the wall at the level of the eaves, which carries the rafters.

Wall tie
A device formed of steel wire that is used to bind the tiers of a masonry wall together. Also, a metal strip used to attach or secure a brick veneer wall to a frame building.

Wall tile
Thin tile used as a wall finish. It is glued to the wall with mastic; then the joints are grouted. Types include glazed ceramic, terra-cotta, glass, mosaic, or plastic; the tile may be square, rectangular, or any other geometric shape.

Wallboard
Large rigid sheets, made of gypsum or wood chips or other filler material, that are fastened to the frame of a building to provide a surface finish. Also called *dry wall, insulation board, gypsum board, Sheetrock.*

Wallpaper
A decorative printed pattern, in sheets or rolls, glued to the surface of walls and ceilings.

Warehouse
A place in which goods and merchandise are stored; a storehouse was usually built of masonry, which meant that there was little need for windows.

Warm air heating system
A system in which warm air is circulated through ducts.

Warm color
Red, orange, and yellow; optically they tend to advance.

Warm roof
A roof constructed with its insulating layer above the roof space rather than a cold roof, which is at the ceiling level.

Warp
Distortion in the shape of a plane timber surface, due to the movement of moisture; may be caused by improper seasoning.

Warpage
The change in the flatness of a material caused by differences in the temperature or humidity on the opposite surfaces of the materials.

Warped
Any piece of timber that has been twisted out of shape and permanently distorted during the process of seasoning.

Warranty
An assurance that what is stated in the contract is correct.

Warren truss
A truss having parallel upper and lower chords, with connecting members that are inclined, forming a series of approximately equilateral triangles.

Waste pipe
The pipe that discharges liquid waste into the soil drain.

Waste stack
A vertical pipe in a plumbing system that carries the discharge from any fixture.

Waste traps
In plumbing, a device for use in waste pipes from sinks and lavatories to prevent the escape of sewer gas from the waste pipe.

Water blaster
A device used for cleaning cracked and peeling paint from wood and masonry; powered by a pump that shoots water out of a nozzle at 50 to 100 times higher than the normal water pressure. Hazardous rain gear and protective eyewear must be worn by workers using the device.

Water closet
A plumbing fixture to receive human waste and discharge it to the sewer line.

Water level
Using water as a method of checking the level in a building.

Water stain
Discoloration on converted timber, caused by water.

Water supply system
Consists of the building supply main, the distribution pipes and connecting pipes, fittings, and control valves necessary to supply water throughout a structure.

Water table
The natural level of ground water on a site; also, a device on a wall to throw rainwater clear of the building.

Water tower
An elevated structure located above the roof of a building to create sufficient pressure to supply the fixtures within the building.

Water washing
A cleaning method that includes spraying and misting with water, pressure washing, and steam cleaning. Scrubbing is often used to remove loosened material while washing.

Water-based paint
Any paint that can be thinned with water. Includes oil-bound or emulsion paints, whose binder is insoluble in water but which can be thinned with water.

Waterblasting
The use of a high-velocity stream of water to remove paint, rust, or dirt from surfaces.

Waterproof adhesive
An adhesive that forms a bond that will withstand full exposure to the weather and is unaffected by microorganisms.

Waterproofing
A coating of asphalt or tar, or layer of synthetic membrane used to make a surface impervious to water.

Water-repellent preservative
A liquid designed to penetrate wood and repel water and provide moderate preservative protection. It is used for millwork, such as sashes and frames, and it is usually applied by dipping.

Water-resistant adhesive
An adhesive that will retain practically all of its strength when subjected to thorough wetting and drying.

Watertight
An enclosure or barrier that does not permit the passage of moisture.

Wattle and daub
A common form of primitive construction, consisting of a coarse basket weave of twigs placed between upright poles, then plastered with mud.

Weather
On roofing or siding, the measure of material exposed to the weather.

Weatherboard
Wood siding commonly used as an exterior covering on a frame building consisting of boards with a rabbeted upper edge that fits under an overlapping board above.

Weathered
Descriptive of the deterioration of a material or the surface if exposed to the elements for a long time.

Weatherhead
A watertight fitting for the service entrance pipe; used when electrical power is brought into a building with an overhead line.

Weathering
An inclination given to the surface of horizontal joints in masonry construction to prevent water from collecting in them.

Weatherproof
A general term indicating the ability to withstand natural elements.

Weatherproof switch
An electrical switch which has a cover to seal it against moisture; allowing it to be used outdoors.

Weatherstrip
A strip of wood, metal, plastic foam, rubber, neoprene, or other material applied to an exterior door or window to seal the joint with the sill, casing, or threshold.

Weather-struck joint
A horizontal masonry joint in which the mortar is sloped outward from the upper edge of the lower brick, so as to shed water readily; formed by pressing the mortar inward at the upper edge of the joint.

Weathervane
A metal form, fixed on a rotating spindle that turns to indicate the direction of the wind, usually located on top of a spire, pinnacle, or other elevated position on a building.

Weep hole
A small opening in a wall or window member, through which accumulated condensation or water may drain to the building exterior. Also called *drainage hole*.

Weld
To fuse metals together by melting a filler at the place where they will be joined together.

Weld joint preparation
The edges or surfaces to be welded are finished by cutting, grinding, or machining to prepare them for welding.

Welded joints
The connecting surfaces where metal has been fused together by welds; the five basic welded joints are the butt joint, corner joint, edge joint, lap joint, and T-joint.

Weld rod
A rod composed of the weld filler material, held at the joint of the weld and melted to provide the weld.

Welded reinforcement
Steel reinforcing bars that are joined by welding, thereby increasing their continuity and strength over simple lapped or tied splices; used most often in columns to extend the vertical bars.

Welded-wire fabric
A network of wire of various gauges, welded together at every intersection, and used as reinforcement in concrete slabs.

Welder certification
Documentation showing that a welder has the experience and ability to make welds at the standard level of acceptance.

Welding helmet
A protective hood for welders that covers the entire face and has a dark tinted eye portal.

Welding procedure qualifications
Qualification rules adopted by the American Society of Mechanical Engineers, or the American Welding Society, for the proper procedure and application of welds.

Welding symbol
A symbol on the structural or shop drawings indicating the type of weld to be made at a particular point. The industry-recognized symbol is placed along the reference line of an arrow pointing to the location of the weld. A rectangle symbolizes a plug weld, a circle for a spot weld, a V for a V-groove weld, as well as other symbols for different types of welds.

Well opening
A floor opening for a stairway.

Welt
A seam in flat metal roof coverings where the edges are folded and dressed down; also called single and double welts, depending on the number of folds.

Western Wood Products Association
An organization that oversees the production, grading, and inspection of lumber produced in western mills and used throughout the United States.

Wet rot
A fungus that feeds on wood and destroys wet timber; most often found in cellars, neglected external joinery, and rafter ends. Causes timber to soften, darken, and develop cracks along the grain and lose strength.

Wet sprinkler system
A sprinkler system that is filled with water for immediate release upon being activated by the presence of a fire.

Wheelbarrow
A load-moving device operated by hand, with a container mounted on a triangular metal frame, with a single wheel at the apex, and legs and handles on the other. Once loaded with material, it can be moved by lifting on the handles and rolled on the wheel to where the material is deposited.

White cement
A pure white portland cement. Since the gray color of portland cement comes from impurities, the white cement requires raw materials of low iron content. It is used for decorative surface finishes, and it is more expensive than ordinary cement.

White lead
An opaque white pigment, used extensively as an undercoat for exterior paint. Because it is poisonous, it is now rarely used.

White oak
A hard, heavy, durable wood, gray to reddish-brown in color; used for flooring, paneling, and trim.

White pine
A soft, light wood that works easily; does not split when nailed; does not swell or warp appreciably; is widely used in building construction.

Whiteprint
A reproduction of a drawing made by the diazo process, producing a black line on a white background. See also *Blueprint*.

Wide-flange section
A structural section whose cross-section resembles the letter H rather than the letter I; used for columns due to its capacity to avoid rotation or buckling.

Wide-flange section

Winch
A hoist consisting of a cable wound around a drum which is operated by a motor, found on the tops of many cranes. As the drum turns, the cable is raised or lowered, lifting the load.

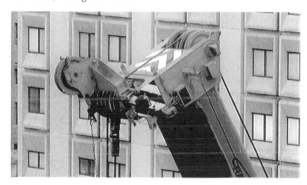

Wind brace
Any brace, such as a strut, that strengthens a structure or framework against the wind; a diagonal brace that ties rafters of a roof together to prevent racking.

Wind drift
A horizontal deflection of a frame caused by wind forces acting against it.

Wind load
The positive or negative force of the wind acting on a structure. Wind applies a positive pressure on the windward side of buildings and a negative suction to the leeward side.

Wind uplift
The aerodynamic lift caused by negative pressure on the leeward side of a roof or object.

Winders
Treads of steps used in a winding staircase or when stairs are carried around curves or angles.

Winding stair

Any stair constructed chiefly or entirely of winders. Also called *spiral stair*.

Windlass

A device for hoisting materials; consists usually of a horizontal cylinder turned by a lever or crank. A cable attached to the material winds around the cylinder as the crank is turned, raising or lowering the load.

Window

An assembly consisting of a window frame, its glazing, and any operating hardware, which fits in an opening in a wall that admits light and, if operable, outside air. The main types of windows include: awning window that is hinged at the top and opens out; bay window, made up of three units, two at an angle and one parallel to the wall; bow window, a series of slightly angled units making up a curved profile; box bay window, where the two side windows are at right angles to the wall; casement window, with hinges on the top and bottom of one side, allowing it to swing out; combination window, with one or more fixed sashes, and one or more that open; double-hung window, with two sashes that travel vertically past one another; fixed window, with glass permanently fixed in place; hopper window, hinged at the bottom and swings in; insulated window, with double panes of glass and a sealed air space between them; jalousie window, with a series of small glass slats that overlap, held in a movable metal frame; pivot window, with a central pivot at the top and bottom center, allowing it to swing around in its frame; sliding window, with one fixed sash, and one or more movable sashes that slide horizontally in a track.

Window detail

In carpentry, the framing and finishing of a window; includes the jamb, sill, and head details. Also a section in an architectural drawing showing the details of a window in relation to the wall in which it is located.

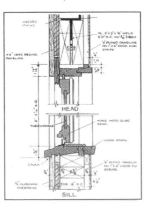

Window frame

The framework that holds the sash in place regardless of how it is hinged. *Also called casing.*

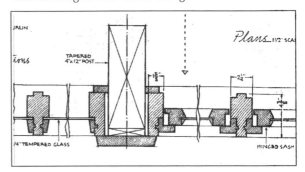

Window head

The top elements in a window installation.

Window header

A structural member at the head of a window to span the opening, and support the load above.

Window jamb

The side elements in a window installation.

Window light

A pane of glass installed in a window frame.

Window lock

A device that locks a window in a closed position.

Window mullion

A vertical member between the lights of a window.

Window muntin

A rabbeted member for holding the edges of window-panes within a sash.

Window opening

An open space in a wall where a window will be placed.

Window schedule

A table, usually located on the elevation drawings, which gives the symbol for each type of window. This code symbol is placed on the drawing by each particular window. The quantity, type of rough opening, sash size, number of lights, manufacturer's number, and type of sash and frame are also placed in the schedule. A remarks column gives information on the specific type of glass that goes in the sash.

Window seat

A seat built into the inside bottom of a window.

Window sill

The bottom elements in a window installation.

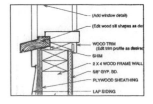

Window stool
In a window trim, the nosing directly above the apron; the horizontal member of the window finish that forms a stool for the side casings and conceals the window sill.

Window symbols
Standardized symbols used by architects and builders to designate the location and types of windows to be installed in a building.

Window unit
A complete window, with sashes or casements, ready for shipment or installation in a building.

Window valance
A spring that counterbalances the weight of a vertically sliding window.

Window wall
An outside wall consisting largely of glass.

Windowpane
One of the divisions of a window or door, consisting of a single unit of glass set in a frame.

Windward
On the side exposed to the wind; the opposite of leeward.

Wing
Projection on the side of a building that is smaller than the main mass; often one of a symmetrical pair.

Winter garden
A large greenhouse, such as a courtyard with a glazed roof, for the permanent display of plants; often includes paved paths, fountains, and sculpture.

Wire connector
In electrical wiring, a device used to join two wires; also called a *wire nut*.

Wire fasteners
A fastener secured to a structure from which hanger wires for a suspended ceiling are attached.

Wire gage
A unit of measurement for the diameter of wire, or the thickness of sheet metal; usually consists of a notched metal plate having a series of gauged slots of various widths along the edge, which are numbered according to the size of the material being measured.

Wire glass
Flat or patterned glass having a square or a diamond wire mesh embedded within the two faces to prevent shattering in the event of breakage or excessive heat. Wire glass is considered a safety glazing material.

Wire mold
A metal molding that acts as a conduit for electrical wiring, installed on the exterior surface of walls.

Wire nut
A plastic device with a coil of wire and insulation inside; it is twisted over the two wires to be spliced, and electrician's tape is applied over the entire connection.

Wire stripper
A tool for cutting wire and removing the insulation off the end so that a connection can be made.

Wire-cut brick
Bricks shaped by extrusion and then cut to length by a set of wires.

Wireway
A raceway with a removable side which allows wire to be placed in it after it has been mounted on a wall.

Wiring
The material in an electrical circuit that carries the current. Also called *cable*.

Wiring diagram
A drawing showing the location of all outlets, switches, and fixtures.

Withholding payment
The process of upholding the terms of the contract by delaying or withholding payments otherwise due, for lack of performance, failure to pay subcontractors or suppliers, or otherwise creating lien liabilities for the owner.

Wood
The hard, fibrous substance that composes the trunk and branches of a tree, lying between the pitch and the bark.

Wood brick
A wooden block, the size and shape of a brick; built into brickwork to provide a hold for nailing finish materials.

Wood door
Either solid core or hollow core with veneer. Exterior doors are coated with waterproof adhesives.

Wood fire retardant
The impregnation of wood products with fire-retardant solutions or chemicals.

Wood float
A float made of wood that is sometimes used in place of a flat steel trowel to smooth irregularities in a mortar bed.

Wood gutter
A gutter formed from a solid piece of wood, or built up from boards, and used under the eaves to carry off rainwater from the roof.

Wood joiner
A small metal plate with sharp spiked legs at right angles to the plate, for driving into wood that meets in butt or miter joints.

Wood joint
A joint formed by two boards or sheets of wood that are held together by nails, fasteners, pegs, or glue.

Wood lath
Narrow strips of wood, nailed to studs in walls or rafters in ceilings, that serve as a base for plaster.

Wood mallet
A hammer with a large cylindrical wooden head, used with a wood chisel for shaping wood.

Wood moldings
Trim members consisting of moldings which are entirely made of wood.

Wood preservative
A chemical used to prevent or retard the decay of wood, especially by fungus or insects, including pitch, tar, and creosote.

Wood screws
Wood fasteners of various types and sizes, with threads extending approximately 70 percent of the length, beginning at the pointed end. Screw heads are made in oval, round, and flat-headed types.

Wood shingle
A thin roofing unit of wood, either split along the grain or cut to stock lengths, widths, and thicknesses; used as an exterior covering on sloping roofs and on walls; applied in an overlapping manner.

Wood siding
Wall cladding for frame buildings, consisting of wooden boards; also called *clapboard siding*.

Wood veneer
A thin layer of wood of uniform thickness; used as a facing material; used to cover less attractive pieces of timber or plywood.

Wood-frame construction
Construction in which exterior walls, bearing walls and partitions, floor and roof constructions, and their supports are of wood or other combustible material, when it does not qualify as heavy-timber construction.

Woodwork
Work produced by the carpenter's and joiner's art; applied to parts or objects in wood rather than to the complete structure.

Work
The term used in contract documents that refers to the supply of all labor and materials required by the contract to complete a project.

Work capacity
The maximum number of projects that a contractor can undertake without significantly increasing overhead costs.

Work light
A lamp in a protective cage, used for temporary lighting of a work area, or under a sidewalk bridge.

Workability
The property of freshly placed concrete or mortar that determines how easily it can be worked, moved, and finished.

Worked lumber
A piece of lumber that has been matched, shiplapped, or patterned for use as siding.

Workers' compensation
An insurance system under which employers are responsible for the injury, sickness, disease, or death of workers while on the job, even if the employer is not at fault.

Workers' compensation insurance
Protection against liability from an employee's sickness, disease, or death, arising from their employment.

Working capital
The amount of cash over and above current liabilities.

Working conditions
Specific conditions on the job site; such as safety, congestion, accessibility, and the availability of lifts and hoists for materials.

Working drawing

A drawing intended for use by a contractor, subcontractor, or fabricator, which is part of the contract documents, that shows in accurate pictorial form, the design, location, dimensions, and relationships of the elements of a project. Also called *contract drawing*, *contract document*, and *construction drawing*.

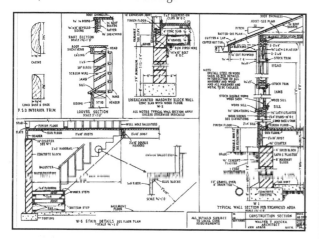

Working load

The normal dead, live, wind, and earthquake load that a structure is required to support in service. Also called the *service load*.

Working stress

The maximum stress used in the calculation to determine the size and properties of a structural member.

Work-in-progress

An inventory of all ongoing work in various stages of completion at any given time.

Workmen's Compensation

A law that stipulates that if a worker suffers an industrial injury or illness on the job, he or she is entitled to compensation payments to partially offset the loss of wages.

Workmanship

The quality of work that is executed by a craftsperson or a contractor.

Works made for hire

A rule that deems all works produced while in the employ of another, belong to the employer, not the employee.

Wrap-around mortgage

A mortgage for secondary financing where the payments to the primary lender are large enough to cover both the primary and secondary financing.

Wrecking

The process of methodically demolishing a structure.

Wrecking ball

A heavy concrete ball averaging several tons, suspended from the boom of a crane and swung against the walls of a structure or dropped on the roof to demolish it.

Wrecking bar
A steel bar used for prying and pulling nails; one end is slightly bent with a chisel-shaped tip, and the other end is U-shaped with a claw tip for pulling nails. Also call a *pinchbar*.

Wrecking strip
In concrete formwork, small pieces of panels fitted into the assembly in such a way that they can be easily removed ahead of the main panels or forms, making it easier to strip those major form components.

Wrench
A hand tool used to turn a bolt, nut, pipe, or fitting; often with jaws that can be adjusted to fit the specific size of the object.

Wrought iron
A commercially pure iron of fibrous nature, valued for its corrosion resistance and ductility; used for water pipes, water tank plates, rivets, and other ornamental forged work.

Wrought-iron work
Iron that is hammered or forged into shape, either when hot or cold; usually as decorative pieces for fences, grilles, and door hardware.

W-type roof truss
A type of truss used for roofs, bridges, and other structures in which the web members form the letter W. The members in wood roof trusses are strengthened at the joints with plywood gusset plates. Also called a *fink truss*.

Wythe
A single continuous vertical wall of bricks, one masonry unit in thickness.

X

X brace
A truss panel, or similar structure, with a pair of diagonal braces from corner to corner that form a crossed shape; used as either struts in compression or tie rods in tension.

x-mark
A mark made by a worker to indicate where certain structural members are to be placed; also used to indicate the face side of a structural member.

X-O
A standard nomenclature for a sliding window as shown on the drawings as viewed from the outside of the building. The X represents an operable sash, and the O represents a fixed sash.

X-ray examination
An investigative technique for detecting flaws or defects in welds, or in welded piping installations.

Y

Y fitting
In pipe work, a short specialized section, one end of which branches or divides, usually at an angle of 45 degrees, resembling the letter Y and forming two separate openings.

Yankee screwdriver
A ratchet-type screwdriver that drives a screw into the material as the handle is pushed downward, then returns back when released.

Yard
An area of uncultivated ground adjacent to a dwelling; in urban sites, often paved with brick, stone, or tile.

Yard lumber
Lumber that is less than 5 inches thick and is intended for general building purposes.

Yardage
A term applied to cubic yards of earth that are excavated or installed.

Yarning iron
An iron tool for packing oakum into a cast-iron pipe joint that is later sealed with molten lead.

Yellow pine
A hard resinous wood of the longleaf pine tree, having dark bands of summerwood alternating with lighter-colored springwood; used as flooring and in general construction.

Yield point
The point at which a given material begins to permanently deform under stress. Also called the *elastic limit*.

Yoke
A clamp or arrangement of members used in formwork that encircles beams or column forms to secure them together and prevent movement during pouring of fresh concrete.

Z

Z bar
A narrow sheet metal flashing with a cross-section similar to the letter Z; used to waterproof the horizontal joint where panels meet. Also, short wire shaped in the form of the letter Z that is used to tie the interior and exterior walls of a masonry cavity wall together.

Z-channel
Flashing placed at the top of exterior panels to provide waterproofing of the joint.

Zenith
In surveying, a point directly overhead; the vertical extension of a plumb line.

Zinc
A hard bluish-white metal, brittle at normal temperatures, very malleable and ductile when heated; not subject to corrosion; used for galvanizing sheet steel and iron.

Zip strip
A vinyl strip placed in a concrete expansion joint immediately after finishing. The top strip is pulled off exposing the concealed joint.

Zone
(1) A number of floors that are adjacent, that are served by the same elevators. Also applies to spaces that have different requirements for heating or cooling. (2) A portion of a city, town, or community set apart for specific purposes. Zones may be set up as business, commercial, industrial, residential, or rural. Different restrictions are placed on each area.

Zone controls
A control system that uses two or more thermostats.

Zoning laws
Rules and regulations established by local governments regarding what can be built and where; including restrictions placed on the structure, such as lot coverage, building height, setbacks, and similar conditions. See also *Variance*.

INDEX

Gypsum bloc 119k
Gypsum board 119
Gypsum board nail 119
Gypsum plaster 119
Gypsum roof deck 119
Gypsum wallboard 119
H section 119
Hack 119
Hacksaw 119
Hairpin 119
Half baluster 119
Half bat 119
Half round 119
Half section 119
Half-glass door 119
Half-landing 119
Half lap dovetail joint 119
Half-lap joint 119
Half-pitched roof 119
Half-round file 120
Half-round molding 120
Half-space landing 120
Half-timbered wall 120
Halved joint 120
Hammer 120
Hammer beam 120
Hammer brace 120
Hammer-beam roof 120
Hammerhead key 120
Hand 120
Hand brace 120
Hand drill 120
Hand file 120
Hand lever punch 120
Hand sawn 120
Hand screw 120
Hand tools 120
Hand-hewn 120
Handicap door opening
    system 120
Handicapped access 120
Handrail 120
Handsaw 121
Hanger 121
Hanger bolt 121
Hanging gable 121
Hanging gutter 121
Hanging scaffold 121
Hanging stile 121
Hard costs 121
Hard hat 121
Hardboard 121
Hardener 121
Hardness 121
Hardpan 121
Hardware 121
Hardwired 121
Hardwood 121
Hardwood floor 121
Hasp assembly 121
Hatch 121
Hatchet 121

Haul 121
Haunched beam 121
Hazardous area 121
Hazardous material 122
Hazardous waste 122
H-clip 122
Head casing 122
Head joint 122
Head lap 122
Header 122
Header bond 122
Header course 122
Headroom 122
Hearing 122
Hearth 122
Hearthstone 122
Heartwood 122
Heat balancing 122
Heat exchanger 122
Heat gain 122
Heat loss 122
Heat pump 122
Heat recovery 122
Heat resistance 122
Heat storage 122
Heat transfer 122
Heat-absorbing glass 122
Heat-actuated fire door 122
Heater 122
Heating 122
Heating load 122
Heating plant 123
Heating, ventilation, and
    air-conditioning
    (HVAC) 123
Heat-reflective glass 123
Heavy timber 123
Heavy-timber
    construction 123
Heel 123
Heel joint 123
Helical stair 123
Hemlock 123
Herculite 123
Heritage 123
Herringbone-matched 123
Hex head 123
Hex nut 123
Hickey 123
Hickory 123
Hidden line 123
Hide glue 123
Hiding power 123
High chairs 123
High gloss 123
Highbay lighting 123
High-early strength
    cement 124
High-limit control 124
Hinge 124
Hinge strap 124
Hip 124

Hip rafter 124
Hip roll 124
Hip tile 124
Hip-and-valley roof 124
Hipped dormer 124
Hipped end 124
Hipped gable 124
Hod 124
Hoist 124
Hold harmless clause 124
Hollow block masonry 124
Hollow masonry unit 125
Hollow metal door 125
Hollow tile 125
Hollow-core door 125
Hollow-tile floor 125
Homogeneous beam 125
Honeycomb brickwork 125
Honeycombed
    concrete 125
Hood 125
Hoodmold 125
Hook 125
Hook knife 125
Hooked bar 125
Hoop reinforcement 125
Hopper window 125
Horizontal 125
Horizontal application 125
Horizontal cornice 125
Horizontal roof area 125
Horizontal sliding
    window 125
Horizontal wood siding 125
Horsepower 125
Hose bibb 125
Hot mop 125
Hot water boiler 126
Hot wire 126
Hot-air furnace 126
Hot-water heating 126
House drain 126
House museum 126
House sewer 126
House trap 126
Housed joint 126
Housing code 126
Housing tract 126
Howe truss 126
Hub 126
Human scale 126
Humidifier 126
Humidistat 126
Hung ceiling 126
Hung sash 126
HVAC 126
Hydraulic cement 126
Hydraulic elevator 126
Hydraulic jack 126
Hydrochloric acid 126
Hydrostatic test 126
Hypalon 126

Hypalon roofing 126
I beam 127
IAPMO 127
ICBO 127
Ice dam 127
Icon 127
Icynene foam 127
Imitation 127
Impact damage 127
Impact load 127
Impact resistance 127
Impact wrench 127
Impedance 127
Impermeable 127
Impervious 127
Implied contract 127
Import fill 127
Imposed load 127
Impregnation 127
Impregnation of timber 127
Improved land 127
Improvement 127
Improvements on land 127
In situ 128
In situ pile 128
In the clear 128
Inadequate 128
Incandescent light 128
Incentive 128
Incentive clause 128
Inching 128
Incombustible 128
Income property 128
Income statement 128
Indemnification clause 128
Indemnify 128
Indemnity 128
Indemnity bond 128
Indented 128
Indented bar 128
Indented bolt 128
Independent contractor 128
Indirect expense 128
Indirect gain system 128
Indirect lighting 128
Indirect luminaire 128
Indirect system 128
Industrial archeology 128
Industrial hygienist 129
Industrial park 129
Industrial waste 129
Industrial wood floor 129
Industry specification 129
Industry standard 129
Inert material 129
Infilling 129
Infiltration 129
Infrared spectography 129
Infrastructure 129
Inhibitor 129
Injection molding 129
Inorganic fiberboard 129

About The Author

Ernest Burden is an architect, writer, and principal of Burden Associates, a New York-based media and marketing consulting firm. He is the author of many acclaimed books on architecture and preservation, including the *Illustrated Dictionary of Architecture, Second Edition; Illustrated Dictionary of Architectural Preservation*, and *Entourage: A Tracing File for Architectural and Interior Design Drawing*.

Mr. Burden is a frequent speaker at conventions of the American Institute of Architects, the Restoration and Renovation Conference, Build Boston, and the Society for Marketing Professional Services. He has also conducted workshops on marketing and presentation techniques for chapters of the American Institute of Architects and the Association of General Contractors.